A Sisterhood of
Suffering and Service

Edited by Sarah Glassford and Amy Shaw

A SISTERHOOD OF SUFFERING AND SERVICE

Women and Girls of Canada and Newfoundland during the First World War

UBCPress · Vancouver · Toronto

© UBC Press 2012

All rights reserved. No part of this publication may be reproduced, stored in a retrieval system, or transmitted, in any form or by any means, without prior written permission of the publisher, or, in Canada, in the case of photocopying or other reprographic copying, a licence from Access Copyright, www.accesscopyright.ca.

20 19 18 17 16 15 14 13 12   5 4 3 2 1

Printed in Canada on FSC-certified ancient-forest-free paper
(100% post-consumer recycled) that is processed chlorine- and acid-free.

Library and Archives Canada Cataloguing in Publication

A sisterhood of suffering and service: women and girls of Canada and Newfoundland during the First World War / edited by Sarah Glassford and Amy Shaw.

Includes bibliographical references and index.
Issued also in electronic formats.
ISBN 978-0-7748-2256-5 (bound); ISBN 978-0-7748-2257-2 (pbk.)

1. World War, 1914-1918 – Women – Canada. 2. World War, 1914-1918 – Children – Canada. 3. World War, 1914-1918 – Women – Newfoundland and Labrador. 4. World War, 1914-1918 – Children – Newfoundland and Labrador. 5. World War, 1914-1918 – Canada – Literature and the war. 6. World War, 1914-1918 – Newfoundland and Labrador – Literature and the war. I. Shaw, Amy J. (Amy Jeannette). Glassford, Sarah Carlene.

D639.W7S58 2012   940.3082'0971   C2012-900582-7

Canada

UBC Press gratefully acknowledges the financial support for our publishing program of the Government of Canada (through the Canada Book Fund), the Canada Council for the Arts, and the British Columbia Arts Council.

This book has been published with the help of a grant from the Canadian Federation for the Humanities and Social Sciences, through the Aid to Scholarly Publications Program, using funds provided by the Social Sciences and Humanities Research Council of Canada.

UBC Press
The University of British Columbia
2029 West Mall
Vancouver, BC V6T 1Z2
www.ubcpress.ca

Contents

Acknowledgments / vii

Introduction: Transformation in a Time of War? / 1
Sarah Glassford and Amy Shaw

Part 1: Mobilizing Women / 25

1 "In Defense of the Empire": The Six Nations of the Grand River and the Great War / 29
Alison Norman

2 The Unquiet Knitters of Newfoundland: From Mothers of the Regiment to Mothers of the Nation / 51
Margot I. Duley

3 Freshettes, Farmerettes, and Feminine Fortitude at the University of Toronto during the First World War / 75
Terry Wilde

Part 2: Women's Work / 99

4 Gendering Patriotism: Canadian Volunteer Nurses as the Female "Soldiers" of the Great War / 103
Linda J. Quiney

5 "Such Sights One Will Never Forget": Newfoundland Women and Overseas Nursing in the First World War / 126
Terry Bishop Stirling

6 Patriotic, Not Permanent: Attitudes about Women's Making Bombs and Being Bankers / 148
Kori Street

Part 3: Family Matters / 171

7 An Honour and a Burden: Canadian Girls and the Great War / 173
Kristine Alexander

8 Supporting Soldiers' Wives and Families in the Great War: What Was Transformed? / 195
Desmond Morton

9 Marks of Grief: Black Attire, Medals, and Service Flags / 219
Suzanne Evans

Part 4: Creative Responses / 241

10 Verses in the Darkness: A Newfoundland Poet Responds to the First World War / 245
Vicki S. Hallett

11 "'Twas You, Mother, Made Me a Man": The Motherhood Motif in the Poetry of the First World War / 270
Lynn Kennedy

12 "Mother, Lover, Nurse": The Reassertion of Conventional Gender Norms in Fictional Representations of Disability in Canadian Novels of the First World War / 293
Amy Tector

Conclusion: A "Sisterhood of Suffering and Service" / 315
Sarah Glassford and Amy Shaw

Selected Bibliography / 323

Contributors / 330

Index / 333

Acknowledgments

Once upon a time, beside a table full of muffins at the Canadian Historical Association (CHA) conference in Saskatoon, Sarah Glassford introduced herself to Amy Shaw, saying, "Claire Campbell suggested I should talk to you about this idea I have." Two muffins, one call for papers, twelve contributors, hundreds of e-mails, dozens of drafts, and four CHA conferences later, the result of that fateful meeting is the volume you are reading now. Our initial thanks, therefore, must go to Claire Campbell for her excellent social networking skills!

The original idea for a book about Canadian and Newfoundland women and the First World War arose during Sarah's doctoral years as she wished for such a thing to help her in her own research on the Canadian Red Cross. The courage to attempt the project came from Amy's immediate enthusiasm for the idea, and the eventual content came from scholars in various disciplines scattered across North America. Jonathan Vance, Suzanne Evans, Cynthia Toman, and Desmond Morton provided early encouragement for the undertaking, and we are immensely grateful to have found a cozy home for it at UBC Press. Early on we learned that our editor Emily Andrew entirely deserved her stellar reputation for efficiency, helpfulness, and good humour.

Many thanks to our colleagues at the University of Lethbridge history department and the University of Ottawa's AMS Nursing History Research Unit for providing moral support at various points. Thanks also to our twelve contributors for being such a great group to work with. It's been a long road and a lot of work, but they've made it a pleasure. We are collectively indebted to the peer reviewers who sharpened our insights and brought a greater cohesiveness to the sum of our research, and we thank the many librarians, archivists, and anonymous packrats without whom this foray into the past would have been utterly impossible.

Sarah would like to thank her family and friends for their love, laughter, and interest in this project; but, most of all, she thanks Amy for sharing this experience, for being a delight to work with, and for helping make this dream a reality. Amy is grateful to Sarah for her inspiration, passion, humour, and hard work, and to friends and family for their patience and encouragement.

And finally, we thank all the First World War-era women and girls of Canada and Newfoundland who suffered, sacrificed, and served in such diverse ways, leaving behind a wealth of stories for us to uncover.

A Sisterhood of Suffering and Service

Introduction
Transformation in a Time of War?

SARAH GLASSFORD AND AMY SHAW

On 24 April 1915, Helen Fowlds wrote to her mother from France, exclaiming:

> I am afraid you will think me very careless about writing the last couple of weeks – but at last I can offer a very good excuse – namely work – and lots of it ... since things began in earnest up at the front we have been full to overflowing. I think perhaps of all the nurses we are the most fortunate in many ways. We are attached to a stationary hospital which contrary to its name, moves up with the army. We are under canvas, which makes it really seem like active service – and we are the nearest Canadian nurses to the front ... and we are near Boulogne which is the main British base and therefore a very busy place. And last of all we have the most splendid lot of girls.[1]

Back in Canada, on 18 May 1918, Lois Allen joined a group of about one hundred other women, who, "filled with enthusiasm for the cause," hulled strawberries in E.D. Smith and Son's jam factory in Winona, Ontario. As Allen explained in her diary:

> These girls all came from good homes and all were anxious to do their "bit." They came from all parts of Ontario, and two even came from Montreal. The girls lived in a camp under Y.W.[C.A.] supervision, having the choice of either a room in the barracks where we ate, or a tent. Alice Goodwin and I chose a

tent. In the factory we worked for ten and sometimes twelve hours a day, enlivening the monotony of the work by "making up" parodies to popular songs and telling stories to one another. Twelve of us at the first table christened ourselves the "family," and became the liveliest group in the camp, and also some of the best workers.[2]

For two members of the large body of non-combatant wartime citizens whom author Nellie McClung called "those who wait and wonder," Canadians Helen Fowlds and Lois Allen seem to have spent the war years doing a lot more than waiting. If anything, they seem to have been having the time of their lives: eating, sleeping and working with "splendid" young women, enlivening their work with music and storytelling, and making a hands-on contribution to the war effort. From the distance of nearly a century, it reads like a grand adventure and, compared with most women's prewar experiences and expectations, perhaps even a life-changing time.

Contemporary Canadian and Newfoundland society placed certain parameters around the type of involvement acceptable for the female halves of their populations during wartime. Fighting was out of the question. For many, factory work was frowned upon. But within these bounds, the girls and women of North America's two British dominions contributed to – or in some cases spoke against – the war effort in whatever ways they could. Their access to full citizenship may have been constrained by their gender, but when their two countries and their mutual Empire went to war, women responded as quickly as men. The aim of this collection is to bring together major elements of women's wartime experience as a step towards meaningfully (re)inserting the female half of the population into the historical narratives of Canada and Newfoundland at war, from 1914 to 1918. Women were not bystanders in the Great War, quietly knitting for the duration: in a multitude of ways they were actively engaged in wartime society and deeply affected by the vagaries of war.

The First World War has been accorded enormous significance in both Canadian and Newfoundland history as a result of the scope and scale of suffering it produced as well as its political and economic impacts on each dominion. A further long-term impact is the way the war has woven itself – in a process that continues today, through memory and commemoration – into the two dominions' national myths. The decimation of the Newfoundland Regiment at Beaumont-Hamel on 1 July 1916, and the triumph of the Canadian forces at Vimy Ridge between 9 and 12 April 1917, became, in different ways, iconic moments for their respective countries. For Newfoundlanders it was a shared grief, for Canadians a shared victory. In both cases, contemporary observers and subsequent historians viewed these battles, and the entire war experience, as turning points. Classic interpreters of Canadian history have portrayed the Great War as the defining event that transformed Canada from a political coalition into a truly united country. Arthur Lower contends that Canada entered the First World War as a colony of Britain and emerged from it as something close to an independent state. C.P. Stacey sees the capture of Vimy Ridge as a milestone "on the road to national maturity." Desmond Morton and J.L. Granatstein refer to the First World War as Canada's "war of independence."[3] These interpretations have been complicated and challenged by subsequent histories that highlight rifts and divisions sparked or exacerbated by the war, but the narrative of a unifying nationalism persists. Newfoundlanders have seen the First World War in similar terms. The Newfoundland and Labrador Heritage website's extensive online digital collection relating to the Great War describes it as "a watershed in the country's history." Kevin Major calls Beaumont-Hamel Memorial Park in France "Newfoundland's most sacred soil," and he argues that the Great War "affirmed Newfoundland's view of itself as a separate nation, if but a minor one still under the considerable influence of Britain."[4] In national memory, Canadians and Newfoundlanders were transformed by the experience of the First World War.

This being the case, how do women fit into this narrative of war-leading-to-national-maturity? Does this transformation theme encompass them? Or is it more clearly a masculine story, with a focus on the exploits of the soldiers overseas? Many Canadian women received the franchise during the First World War; some women in both Canada and Newfoundland challenged gender expectations by engaging in non-traditional occupations. Did women as a whole therefore experience their own separate transformation – as women – during the First World War? If so, what was transformed, how, and why? The idea of transformation often implies notions of progress – movement towards something better. How do we measure such a transformation when the war affected women differently according to age, race, ethnicity, class, and a range of less easily categorized factors such as their personal connections to the men fighting overseas? What have contemporaries and historians had to say on the subject?

Introduction

The idea for *A Sisterhood of Suffering and Service* sprang from a sense of the remarkable absence of women and their activities from Newfoundland's and Canada's memories of the First World War. The same is true to an even greater extent when it comes to the experiences of girls (and children more broadly, although boys are not dealt with here). As the scholarly literature on the First World War continues to grow yearly, women's experiences of this period remain largely obscure. In particular, women are glaringly absent from Newfoundland's Great War history. *Pursuing Equality: Historical Perspectives on Women in Newfoundland and Labrador* (edited by Linda Kealey) addresses many silences surrounding women's political and legal experiences in the history of Newfoundland and Labrador, and Margot I. Duley's chapter in that volume reveals the international network in which Newfoundland women operated. Yet those who search for a few good books or articles on Newfoundland women and the First World War will still turn up precious little.

The main bibliographic source for available scholarly material on Canada's military history, O.A. Cooke, *The Canadian Military Experience, 1867-1995: A Bibliography*, does not include a single entry for women in the First World War. While women may have no place in the story of battlefield tactics and military strategizing in this period, a robust Canadian military history ought to recognize that women are implicated in the waging of war even when they are not engaged in planning or physically fighting it. Happily, studies of the Canadian home front in the First World War have made a valuable start: Robert Rutherdale's *Hometown Horizons: Local Responses to Canada's Great War* and Ian Hugh Maclean Miller's *Our Glory and Our Grief: Torontonians and the Great War* contain chapters detailing women's local war work, while women are integral to nearly all of Jonathan Vance's cultural analysis in *Death So Noble: Memory, Meaning, and the First World War*, which argues that Canadians interpreted the war in very traditional ways rather than adopting a cynical modernist view.[5] Rutherdale's chapter, "Gendered Fields," provides a particularly useful assessment of how "gender and class combined and encoded the specific practices and fields of activity [women and men] pursued" during the war – an assessment upheld by the chapters in this volume.[6] But the need for greater attention is not limited to histories of the war. There are important monographs on women's history that take a longitudinal approach, including the years 1914-18, but which do not pay more than passing attention to the First World War. Examples include Joy Parr's *The Gender of Breadwinners: Women, Men, and Change in Two Industrial Towns, 1880-1950*; and Mariana Valverde's *The Age of Light, Soap and*

Water: Moral Reform in English Canada, 1885-1925. *Quebec Women: A History* contains only a single page on the First World War, which discusses changes in women's paid employment. An important exception to this general neglect is Linda Kealey's *Enlisting Women for the Cause: Women, Labour, and the Left in Canada, 1890-1920*, which examines the subject of women workers and labour activists, and situates their wartime experiences within a longer history of women, work, socialism, and struggle.[7]

Similarly, Alison Prentice et al.'s *Canadian Women: A History* makes somewhat fuller reference to women's wartime experiences. Women's paid labour during the Great War is integrated into a chapter on women's work, while wartime activities (with a focus on suffrage victories) are discussed in the chapter "Marching into the Twentieth Century." In both cases, women's activities, challenges, and advances are placed within a wider context of change and continuity throughout the late nineteenth and early twentieth centuries. This is an important perspective as it inserts women's wartime experiences into a broader sweep of history than most studies can provide. Prentice and her co-authors highlight the many divisions among women that were sparked by the war – between Liberals and Conservatives, French- and English-speakers, labour and the middle class, pacifists and war supporters – that are often overlooked or underplayed in existing literature. Unfortunately, in covering so much ground in only a handful of pages, space limitations keep the authors from delving deeply into broader or more idiosyncratic responses to the war. A further strength of this synthesis is its linking of women's wartime work (paid or otherwise) to an expanded public role. By providing further examples of women's increased public presence due to wartime activities, the chapters in *A Sisterhood of Suffering and Service* not only bolster the connection made by Prentice et al. but also analyze the rhetoric and imagery of traditional femininity, which, when applied to specific activities (such as Red Cross work or women's non-traditional paid labour), kept this increased movement into the public sphere from sparking a more fundamental transformation of Canadian gender relations.

Another worthwhile but necessarily limited look at Canadian women's experiences of the Great War is the engaging documentary film *And We Knew How to Dance: Women in WWI*, which uses women's oral histories to argue that the First World War was a watershed moment for women workers.[8] While the research undertaken by Kori Street in *A Sisterhood of Suffering and Service* as well as elsewhere casts doubt on this conclusion as it applies to gender relations within Canadian society as a whole, the film leaves no doubt that, for many women, the experience of non-traditional paid labour during the Great War was transformative on a personal level.

Another notable contribution to the literature on Canadian women and the First World War is Joan Sangster's chapter on the wartime mobilization of women, which may be found in David Mackenzie's edited collection entitled *Canada and the First World War*.[9] Sangster focuses primarily on women's paid labour and morality, foregrounding issues of class in terms of Canadian women's First World War experiences. By emphasizing these two areas, Sangster passes lightly over elements such as women's voluntary work, their emotional responses to the war, and the war's effects on domestic and familial relations. Yet the chapter's focus, and its use of non-traditional, literary sources, makes it a welcome and important contribution to the literature, while also providing a fruitful direction for new research. Her argument that the war brought about an increased level of surveillance for women is supported in *A Sisterhood of Suffering and Service* by Terry Wilde's study of young women at the University of Toronto and Desmond Morton's examination of the Canadian Patriotic Fund's interactions with soldiers' wives.

In the course of preparing this volume, it became increasingly evident that, although there is a clear need for a comprehensive and authoritative scholarly monograph that draws together and interprets the varied strands of female experience, the historical forgetfulness surrounding women and the First World War is more apparent than real. There is a genuine lack of research into Newfoundland women's Great War experiences, but there is a surprising amount of literature that deals with aspects of Canadian women's experiences between 1914 and 1918. This includes such work as Barbara Roberts' biography of Gertrude Richardson and her *"Why Do Women Do Nothing to End the War?": Canadian Feminist-Pacifists and the Great War*, which reveal the activities of Canadian women who stood by their prewar pacifism and braved public scorn and hostility by protesting against the war.[10] Roberts makes it clear that, although for such women the war was a different experience than it was for their pro-war sisters, it was no less harrowing. Suffrage, nursing, and literature are among other areas that have received a certain amount of scholarly attention.[11]

The literature on Canadian and Newfoundland women exists within a rich context of international scholarship on women and the First World War. Among English-speaking countries, there has been an interesting tendency to focus on certain thematic areas. American historians have often emphasized women's pacifism and war resistance; British scholars have produced many of the more definitive works on the relationship of women's suffrage to the war; and several Australian and New Zealand scholars have focused on nursing. However, while some women's wartime experiences have held a particular interest or significance for certain countries, others appear nearly universal. Voluntary work, new fields of paid labour, and emotional turmoil, for example, seem to have been common wartime experiences for women of all the English-speaking Allied countries.

The chapters in *A Sisterhood of Suffering and Service*, which examine the First World War through the eyes of the girls and women of Newfoundland and Canada, is a place to start, not a place to end. As a result of the kind of research presently being undertaken, there is more here on Canada than on Newfoundland, more on women than on girls, more on central Canada than on the east or the west, and, regrettably, very little on Quebec. Boys deserve study as well but are not included here. Similarly, the women depicted here tend to be those who supported the war and were in society's mainstream: pacifists, enemy aliens, visible minorities, and women in leftist and labour movements are among those underrepresented or unrepresented. Poets receive more attention than novelists, although the place of L.M. Montgomery's *Rilla of Ingleside* in shaping late twentieth- and early twenty-first-century popular memory of women and the war makes it a much-cited reference throughout the volume. Artists and musicians are not included here. While these weaknesses are genuinely regrettable, an imperfect beginning is better than no beginning at all. By establishing a clearer sense of the parameters of mainstream female experience in these two dominions during the First World War, *A Sisterhood of Suffering and Service* may spur other scholars to fill in the gaps that remain. In the meantime, the chapters presented here, each comprehensive and solidly-researched, help fill a major void in Canadian and Newfoundland history.

Since *A Sisterhood of Suffering and Service* aims to encourage further research in the field, it includes a selected bibliography that lists key sources on Canadian and Newfoundland women and the First World War. Surely one way to foster future research is simply to make others aware of what is already available. There *is* a modest body of literature about Canadian and Newfoundland women and the First World War. It just does not seem, thus far, to be making its presence felt.

So why Canada *and* Newfoundland (the latter a separate country until 1949)? Why women *and* girls? Newfoundland is included in this volume not merely because the island subsequently became part of Canada but also, and more important, because there is much to be learned from comparing and contrasting the two countries' wartime experiences. Though the two British dominions were very different economically, politically, and socially, they shared a sense of affectionate duty towards their mutual motherland, a common view of women's appropriate roles in wartime, and a vast geographic distance between themselves and the battlefields.[12] This is not to say that Canadian and Newfoundland women's Great War experiences were the same. However, while respecting their unique national contexts and their divergences from one another, they deserve to be considered in tandem. Similarly, *A Sisterhood of Suffering and Service* specifically includes young girls as well as adult women because age can be a very fruitful category of analysis. Historians of the family and of childhood, as well as cultural historians, have shown that, despite generally functioning from positions of powerlessness, children do make history. They are both contributors to, and powerfully shaped by, prevailing cultural norms and social conditions. They are mobilized as powerful symbols, and concerns for their safety and development frequently provoke policy decisions and action by adults.[13] An examination of the ways in which age mediated girls' experiences, and how representations of girls were used and read in wartime, adds depth and complexity to our understandings of women's and military history. If adult women's wartime roles were limited by their gender, young women's and girls' roles were additionally limited by their youth. It is also worth noting that the term "girl" itself was used loosely at the time – denoting anything from small children to adolescents to grown women in positions of lower status. Being mindful of such nuances can only enrich our understanding of this period.[14]

One important factor in the relative historical neglect of Canadian and Newfoundland women and girls in the First World War may be a very practical one. Debbie Marshall's *Give Your Other Vote to the Sister: A Woman's Journey into the Great War* and Susan Mann's *Margaret Macdonald: Imperial Daughter* both point to the frequent paucity of records as a major hindrance to the study of women and girls in wartime. Their subjects are two of the more visible and publicly active women in Canada – the matron-in-chief of the Canadian Army Nursing Corps during the Great War and the first woman elected to the Alberta Legislature – but both authors faced the problem of an absence of records.[15]

As a result, Marshall's study of Roberta MacAdams is as much a story of Marshall's own search for evidence as it is a narrative of her subject's experiences. Where information was unavailable she took educated leaps into the dark, imagining what MacAdams' responses to certain situations may have been, and combining what records were available with secondary material about surrounding people, places, and events, to reconstruct some semblance of MacAdams' otherwise obscure life. To a much lesser degree, Susan Mann similarly places herself within Margaret Macdonald's story in order to address gaps and silences.

Mann and Marshall were forced to take an unconventional approach not only by the absence of external records but also, and more significantly, by the reluctance of their subjects to put forward their own narratives of their experiences in the war. Like many Canadian and Newfoundland women and girls, Margaret Macdonald and Roberta MacAdams (despite their public prominence and professional achievements) wrote no memoirs about their experiences in the war and preserved few letters, diaries, or other documents. A widespread public desire to return society to "normal" after the war may have contributed to this neglect.

Susan Mann raises this point when she discusses the absence of an official history of the Canadian women's military nursing service after the First World War. As matron-in-chief, Margaret Macdonald was asked to write a history of women in the war, but the task proved beyond her – possibly beyond any satisfactory telling. Macdonald, perhaps in an effort at collaboration, solicited reminiscences from former matrons and nursing sisters, but almost no one responded. Mann suggests an explanation:

> Her letter seemed to request the soldiers' stories rather than the nurses' and she had qualified it with the phrase "of historical value." What woman in the 1920's would have used that phrase to describe any experience of her own? ... Besides, as nurses they had been enjoined to silence since the very beginning of their nursing training.[16]

The question of how to tell women's stories within the male narrative of war was a hindrance to would-be women memoirists at the time, just as it continues to hinder our ability to integrate women's wartime experiences into wider wartime narratives of tactics and technologies, taxes and trade.

The chapters presented here make creative use of a diverse array of sources in their respective attempts to uncover the parts played by girls and women in the global drama of the First World War. In so doing, they demonstrate that diligent digging and a willingness to read deeply into what evidence has survived reap rich rewards. In the tradition of women's history of all periods, reading "against the grain" and "between the lines" pays off. Letters and photos carefully preserved by her family give Suzanne Evans' chapter a touchingly personal quality; Terry Bishop Stirling extrapolates from limited surviving correspondence to illuminate a broader Newfoundland nursing experience. Terry Wilde relies heavily upon that historical standby the period newspaper (indeed, most of the authors draw useful material from newspapers and periodicals of the time). Kristine Alexander, Linda Quiney, Alison Norman, and Suzanne Evans make use of material culture artefacts, including postcards, flags, medals, teddy bears, sheet music, and uniforms, to gain insight into the lives of girls and women. Many of the authors analyze the visual statements found in wartime propaganda posters. Institutional and governmental records and correspondence provide a solid base for the work of Desmond Morton, Alison Norman, Kori Street, and Margot Duley. Kori Street and Desmond Morton notably integrate quantitative data (in Street's case, from databases she herself painstakingly compiled) with more qualitative sources. Lynn Kennedy and Amy Tector unpack the imagery and ideologies present in literary works, while Vicki Hallett uses biography to complement a close reading of poetry. In short, the same kinds of sources historians draw upon for all sorts of social and cultural history topics are available for writing the wartime history of women and girls. They may be few and far between, but much can be made of them.

Another reason for the relative invisibility of female Great War history may lie in the fact that our collective memory of the First World War is often overshadowed by its successor. When we think about women and war, it is the Second World War that comes most quickly to mind, borne jauntily along by the iconic American image of Rosie the Riveter flexing her muscles and assuring viewers that "We Can Do It!" The historical scholarship on Canadian women and the Second World War is far from comprehensive, yet it has made a strong impression on the wider scholarship on Canada and the Second World War. This is primarily the result of Ruth Roach Pierson's pathbreaking *"They're Still Women After All": The Second World War and Canadian Womanhood*, which contends that the Second World War did not produce a conscious and long-term expansion of women's opportunities or fundamentally change prevailing gender norms. In his survey of the Canadian home front, Jeffrey Keshen argues that Pierson "sets the bar too high in identifying what needed to be changed or be dismantled to constitute 'real progress.'" Some restrictions remained and some hopes went unfulfilled, Keshen suggests, but nonetheless there was change – primarily in women's views of themselves and their abilities. Cynthia Toman's

An Officer and a Lady: Canadian Military Nursing and the Second World War also explores the question of transformation. Toman asserts that traditional notions of femininity constrained what nurses could and could not do within the masculine military sphere, but she also finds nurses contesting these expectations in a variety of ways. Ultimately, while technological developments aided the Nursing Sisters in reshaping their workplace relationships with male doctors and surgeons, Toman's evidence suggests that these changes did not translate into a transformation of postwar and non-military nursing settings.[17]

What we might call the "transformation thesis" – a desire to establish whether or not the popular image of the Second World War as a liberating experience for women is an accurate one – echoes through the literature on women and war in many nations. As the work of Pierson, Keshen, and Toman suggests, the answer is far from clear in the Canadian case. Applying the same question to the First World War produces even muddier results.

At the outset of the conflict, many women responded to the prospect of war with the same enthusiasm as did men. Writing for the *Canadian Magazine* in early 1917, Mabel Durham proudly asserted that, "while the men have been quick to answer the call[,] the women have not been behind them in manifesting a patriotic spirit."[18] Imperial and nationalist sentiments ran high, and the war seemed to offer an opportunity both to serve the British Empire and to display to the world the bravery, steadfastness, and pluck of Canadians and Newfoundlanders. Some Newfoundlanders and Canadians alike envisioned the war as the event that would transform their respectively far-flung and under-appreciated colonies into full members of the British Empire.[19] Many women also saw an opportunity for their sex to prove itself. Women's suffrage advocates had been agitating unsuccessfully for decades in an attempt to gain a political voice for women at the ballot box. Where words had failed, perhaps deeds in a time of crisis might succeed in transforming anti-suffragists into allies of women's cause? Emerging stories of German atrocities contributed further to existing patriotic wartime rhetoric, leading many women to support the war effort with an almost religious sense of urgency. Support for the war, in their view, was necessary to save (or avenge) the women and children of Belgium and the rest of Europe from the inhuman depredations of "the Hun." Neighbours of certain ethnic backgrounds were transformed in the public mind from fellow citizens into enemy aliens. For most, supporting the war meant aiding the individual men fighting it, upholding the collective body of soldiers overseas, or justifying the deaths of those already fallen by winning the war.

As the war on the Western Front settled into a muddy, bloody stalemate, for many of the girls and women in North America's two British dominions the underlying mood of the war years became what one author calls "this terrible strain of waiting."[20] Worry, fear, and uncertainty quickly took their toll, and any form of tangible work could become a source of much needed distraction. As a result, church groups, war charities, and voluntary organizations were flooded with female volunteers looking to do something concrete for the war effort. Many of the projects undertaken by these groups fell into the traditional categories of women's work – what the Newfoundland Women's Patriotic Association christened "distaff work" – in particular, the seemingly unending tasks of sewing and knitting comforts and hospital supplies, or bandage-rolling, undertaken individually or in groups. The knitting woman, especially the knitting mother, exemplified a societally approved means of fulfilling a female citizen's wartime obligations. By linking the comfort of a familiarly humble domestic activity to broader wartime goals, the knitting woman became a powerful and enduring icon of an engaged home front.[21] Such a connection in the minds of ordinary women had the potential to transform their views of themselves and the humble tasks they undertook. Distaff work was war work, and war work was work of national – nay, imperial – significance.

Despite its ubiquity in wartime society, knitting was by no means the only activity undertaken by girls and women in wartime Newfoundland and Canada. They also raised millions of dollars by the war's end for the Red Cross, Belgian Relief, the Women's Patriotic Association of Newfoundland, the Canadian Patriotic Fund, and a host of other causes by organizing concerts, tag days, teas, card parties, bake sales, lectures, and bazaars. Church groups and secular voluntary organizations played fundamental roles in the functioning of Canadian and Newfoundland society in the early twentieth century, so not only did women instinctively turn to these organizations as an outlet for their "desire to serve and save,"[22] but the governments of both Newfoundland and Canada relied heavily upon these voluntary organizations to assume wartime duties that later generations would deem to be state responsibilities. Given this reality, women's participation in the voluntary aspect of the war takes on an even wider significance within the broader war efforts of Canada and Newfoundland.

The work undertaken by various war charities and women's groups also held transformative potential for the organizations themselves. In its fiftieth-anniversary history, the Imperial Order Daughters of the Empire (IODE) called the years 1914 to 1918 "a turning point in the history of the Order," which diverted the IODE from child welfare work into "an efficient organization by which prompt and united action may be taken by the women and children of the Empire" – a sort of imperial women's emergency response team. Similarly, the Canadian Red Cross was transformed from a sleepy group of retired military medical men in Toronto into Canada's leading humanitarian organization, with a nationwide membership fuelled by women's labour.[23]

Throughout the war women also played active roles in recruiting men to enlist. Women and girls were an important audience and motivation for men's heroism, so women's efforts to recruit soldiers became a central element of wartime discourse and, subsequently, of the collective memory of the First World War. A significant amount of recruiting propaganda was actually aimed at women. Jeffrey Keshen notes, for example, the twenty thousand booklets distributed in Montreal by the Citizens' Recruiting League that pleaded with "mothers, wives and sweethearts ... [to] think of [their] country by letting [their] sons go and fight."[24] One poster, addressed "To the Women of Canada," directly linked the threat of German invasion, masculine pride, and women's role in the enlistment process, concluding with the appeal: "Won't you help and send a man to enlist to-day?" (see Figure 1). Newfoundland's Julia Horwood, a member of the Women's Patriotic Association, noted in 1916: "Recruiting is largely affected by the attitude of the women." She went on to claim that the bulk of Newfoundland's soldiers came "from homes where the women ha[d] put selfishness aside and not placed obstacles in the way of the men, doing their public duty conscientiously."[25] Wives, mothers, sisters, and daughters were expected to persuade their male relations to enlist, and their willingness to sacrifice loved ones for the cause of the empire at war was constructed in public discourse as an important part of female war service. A woman's decision to encourage – or not to hinder – a man's enlistment had the potential to transform the man in question from ordinary citizen into citizen-soldier. The consequences for the woman might include fear, a measure of pride, temporary elevation to head of the household, and, further down the road, the grief of loss – any one of which could transform a woman's daily life in dramatic yet intimate ways.

To ease increasing wartime labour shortages and provide material for the battle front, unmarried women entered the workforce in large numbers during the First World War, as did some married women. On farms, in factories, and in offices, women filled positions previously occupied by men. In the summertime, the YWCA recruited hundreds of female volunteers like Lois Allen from towns and cities to help on farms. Thousands of women stepped into these

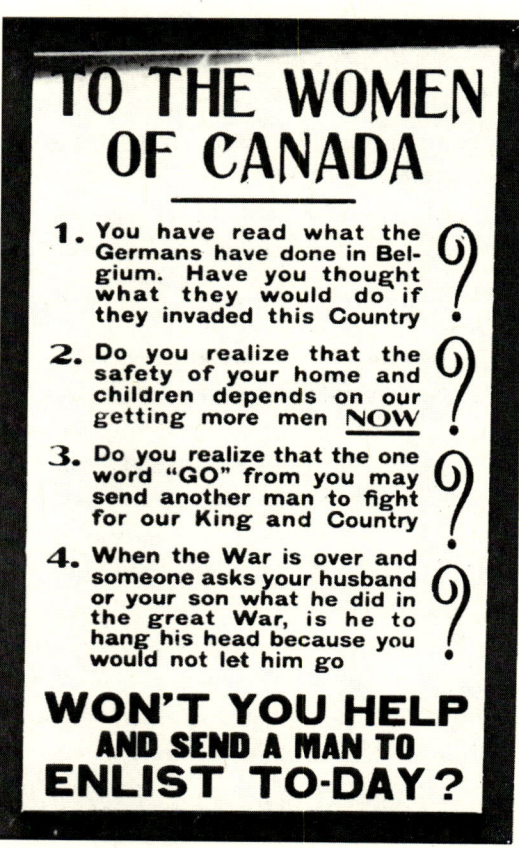

FIGURE 1 Recruiting poster. Military recruiters believed women were essential agents in the task of recruiting men. [World War I Poster Slides, Queen's University Archives, V043]

unaccustomed roles and, to some degree, were lauded for doing so, but the gender discrimination that predated the war remained the norm. Women still earned lower wages than did men for the same work, often lacked union support, and did not have access to day care facilities adequate to meet the needs of married women who went to work. Thousands of women filled jobs previously closed to them, altering the visual landscape of even such male-dominated industries as railways and steel production, yet this unprecedented change did not produce a complete transformation of either Canadian workplaces or the gender dynamics therein.

A small proportion of women came relatively close to the battlefields. Over two thousand women enlisted as Nursing Sisters in the Canadian Expeditionary Force during the First World War, while an unknown number of Newfoundlanders nursed with various British and Canadian nursing corps. Their overseas work at stationary hospitals and casualty clearing stations, on hospital ships, and on ambulance trains was often grueling and sometimes downright dangerous. An overseas posting temporarily transformed a young nurse's existence, bringing her into contact with foreign lands and peoples, and testing both her professional skills and her personal resilience under trying conditions. For a time, the Nursing Sister's life was turned upside down. Whether war service had a longer-term transformative impact, however, is more difficult to determine. Many nurses seem to have settled into a quiet, unexceptional postwar life back in Canada or Newfoundland – but does that mean the war had no transformative effect upon them at all?

Although the wartime courage and caring demonstrated by nurses from Canada and Newfoundland earned them praise and gratitude back home, there were definite limits to the ways in which Canadians and Newfoundlanders would allow their womenfolk to be involved in the war effort. A small group of Toronto women, for example, formed what they called the "Women's Home Guard." They wore uniforms, practised drill in public, and honed their rifle skills. These women wished to free up men in the official Home Guard for overseas service and take on the role of protecting Canada's home front themselves. Neither the citizens of Toronto nor the Canadian military, however, were prepared to accept this degree of deviance from conventional views of women's appropriate roles, and the Women's Home Guard experiment came to an end.[26] If members had hoped the war emergency heralded a transformation of Canadian society's views regarding women and military or paramilitary service, they were sorely disappointed.

Women's wartime service, as the preceding discussion demonstrates, was visible and tangible; their suffering and sacrifice less so. Both elements came, in time, to be linked to female suffrage at the national level. In Canada, Prime Minister Robert Borden's administration enfranchised a large number of women in 1917 through two measures. With regard to any general election held during the war, the Military Voters Act quietly included Nursing Sisters in its general enfranchisement of all British subjects, regardless of age, who had participated actively in any branch of the Canadian military. More controversially, the Wartime Elections Act granted the federal franchise to the wives, widows, mothers, and sisters of serving soldiers, provided they were British subjects and over twenty-one years of age.[27] This move has generally been understood (both at the time and subsequently) as a blatant political manoeuvre meant to ensure Borden's pro-conscription Union Party would win the upcoming election, based upon the assumption that female relatives of soldiers would champion conscription for overseas military service as a way to support the men already serving.[28] However, the gesture also seemed to offer a tacit recognition that women's contributions to the war effort had demonstrated the type of responsible citizenship deemed necessary in a voter. The Women's War Conference called by the federal government in 1918, and the passage of a dedicated women's franchise measure in the same year, seemed to reinforce this acknowledgment.[29]

However, the Wartime Elections Act was not an unmixed blessing. While it saw somewhere between 500,000 and 1,000,000 women go to the polls in the 1917 federal election, it also deliberately disenfranchised other Canadians: individual conscientious objectors, male and female members of pacifist religious groups like the Mennonites and Doukhobors, and all men and women born in enemy countries (not just ethnic Germans and Austrians but also Czechs, Slovaks, Ruthenians, and Poles) who had been naturalized after 1902. The latter was intended, in part, to exclude many immigrant women who had been naturalized by marrying British subjects. Respective provincial franchise qualifications relating to age, race, residence, and property-holding, which had hitherto applied to men, were extended to the new prospective women voters at the federal level. Aboriginal and Asian women and men were notable among those thus excluded.[30] Many suffragists, such as those in the Victoria and Regina local councils of women, opposed the Wartime Elections Act because of its discriminatory elements, believing that only universal female suffrage would achieve real social change. In Montreal, the Wartime Elections Act was so divisive among local women activists that it led to a dramatic impeachment trial for Dr. Grace Ritchie-England, long-time president of the Montreal Council of Women.[31] The Wartime Elections Act must therefore be considered, at best, as a partial transformation of women's political rights in Canada and as a divisive, rather than as a unifying, development.

The link between women's war service and the granting of the vote in Newfoundland is less direct than the Canadian example, but it is nonetheless present. In *A Sisterhood of Suffering and Service*, and in her previous work, Margot I. Duley shows that leaders of Newfoundland's women's movement considered the country's Great War nurses and Voluntary Aid Detachment personnel (VADs) as models of female citizenship, while members of the wartime Women's Patriotic Association made a smooth transition from patriotic charitable work to suffrage agitation after 1918. Their persistent efforts resulted in attaining the franchise for Newfoundland women in 1925.[32] In the Newfoundland case, then, the war did not immediately transform male Newfoundlanders' attitudes towards the idea of women's voting, but it appears to have at least contributed to transforming some female Newfoundlanders into activists for the cause of women's suffrage and hardened the resolve of others.

The chapters presented in this volume reveal a portion of the diverse range of activities in which Canadian and Newfoundland women and girls engaged during the war. All of the authors argue that women and girls made significant contributions to the war effort (often in overlooked ways), but they differ, depending upon the particular group or activity they examine, in their assessments of whether these female contributions challenged or conformed to prevailing gender norms. Some see transformation taking place as barriers crumbled and minds were changed; others see established views holding fast and identify women's efforts as arising out of older gendered traditions. This ambivalence speaks to the incredible vastness of the geographical areas in question and to the broad range of ages, classes, religions, racial and ethnic backgrounds, occupations, ideologies, political persuasions, and experiences being studied. A resounding universal "yes" or "no" to the question of transformation would be extremely surprising. Just as a serviceman's experience varied, depending upon the branch of the service in which he found himself and the arena of war in which he fought, so what women experienced between 1914 and 1918 was not one Great War but many unique individual wars – local and personal. The war's transformative impact – or lack thereof – is therefore more a question of millions of potential transformations. The chapters presented here tackle small subsets of this enormous body of experience and attempt to measure the war's impact within those particular confines.

But *A Sisterhood of Suffering and Service* also shows that there were ways in which women's experience of the war was distinctive and unifying. One munitions worker in Daphne Read's oral history *The Great War and Canadian Society* remembers:

> In meeting these people that we had never had any opportunity to meet before, and finding they were just the same as we were, but they just hadn't had the chances that we'd had for education and that kind of thing, we began to realize

that we were all sisters under the skins. Wars do bring every class together and I think we need to do a little bit more of that without war if we can.[33]

The experience of women of different classes working together – whether in industrial workplaces or volunteer sewing circles – broadened women's experience of their similarities across traditional social divides. The idea of the war's producing a certain form of "sisterhood" – in this case a sisterhood of service and suffering – is dealt with more fully in the conclusion to this collection.

Part 1, "Mobilizing Women," examines the wartime responses of three regionally, ethnically, and socially disparate groups. In the process, it not only reveals certain commonalities that suggest how we might broadly characterize the experience of women during the First World War but also examines idiosyncrasies that remind us that factors such as race, class, and region can shape historical experience as much as gender. Alison Norman traces the ways in which Six Nations Aboriginal women's voluntary knitting, sewing, and fundraising simultaneously demonstrated the acculturation of their community to an Anglo-Canadian way of life and upheld a distinctive Six Nations warrior tradition that predated both Canada and the British Empire. Margot I. Duley's examination of the Newfoundland Women's Patriotic Association reveals how the war brought a lustre of patriotic service to traditional tasks and gender roles that fed into a successful postwar suffrage movement and a general increase in public leadership roles for women at the community level. Terry Wilde's analysis of young women at the University of Toronto suggests that, although the years 1914 to 1918 dramatically altered co-eds' self-perceptions and the expectations placed upon them by their school, community, and government, the change was in some ways as restrictive as it was liberating and, in the end, proved transitory. Together these three chapters combine to enrich our knowledge of what it meant for women in Canada and Newfoundland to live, work, and learn as women in a society at war.

With this broad context for women's wartime experiences established, Part 2, "Women's Work?" moves on to consider women's participation in wartime nursing and non-traditional forms of paid labour. Linda J. Quiney demonstrates how familiar maternalist ideology and a corresponding ethic of service were mobilized by the Canadian St. John Ambulance Association with unconventional results: the portrayal of female VAD personnel as female soldiers. In her complementary examination of Newfoundland's overseas VADs and Nursing Sisters, Terry Bishop Stirling finds that, while these women shared common challenges in their overseas service, their responses to them were highly individual. Driven less by gender than by factors such as class, education, and personality, these women's unique responses make generalization about any kind of war-induced transformation difficult. In her detailed look at responses to women's moving into banking and munitions work during the war, Kori Street concludes that, although the war infused prewar gender norms with a certain flexibility, insufficient numbers of women entered the workforce to fundamentally transform prevailing views. Collectively, these three chapters demonstrate that the women of Canada and Newfoundland tackled concrete, hands-on roles during the Great War, some of which upheld contemporary gender norms, others of which had the potential to challenge long-held views about what was and was not "women's work."

Women not only took on unaccustomed activities during the war but also had to shoulder significant emotional, psychological, and economic burdens. Part 3, "Family Matters," is concerned with the significant repercussions of loneliness, privation, worry, and grief that attended the absence of fathers, husbands, brothers, and friends. Kristine Alexander surveys Canadian girls' wartime experiences on discursive, emotional, and practical levels, and she concludes that these impressionable youngsters were drawn into the conflict in ways that often proved transformative. Desmond Morton outlines the Canadian Patriotic Fund's successful but intrusive role providing financial support to soldiers' dependents, suggesting it was made obsolete by the time of the Second World War as a result of both women's experiences with it in the First World War and broader changes that had transformed Canadians' views of state and charitable responsibilities. Suzanne Evans details the material manifestations of mourning assumed by women who lost loved ones in the war, finding that the Great War altered older Victorian mourning customs but that women's bodies and homes remained primary physical sites of visible mourning. Together, these studies remind us that loss (whether temporary or permanent) was both a unique, intimate experience and a collective, public experience that irrevocably altered entire communities, regions, and nations. In time-honoured tradition, women bore the emotional and financial impacts of warfare without taking part in the fighting.

Part 4, "Creative Responses," addresses both literary representations of women and women's own efforts at writing about the war. Vicki S. Hallett's examination of Newfoundland poet Phebe Florence Miller's war poetry reveals a reliance on traditional gendered images of women as supportive, domestic figures defined by their relationships to men – images that contributed to a male-dominated Newfoundland cultural memory of the war. In her examination of the growing sense of nationhood evident in Canadian poetry, Lynn Kennedy finds a constant motif of motherhood but notes that, as the war progressed, a nurturing Mother Britain or Canadian landscape was increasingly replaced by the sacrifices of real Canadian mothers. Amy Tector's study of Canadian novels sheds light on Canadians' discomfort with the way masculine disability transformed gender roles, and it highlights novelists' efforts to reassure readers that disabled veterans could reclaim positions of patriarchal dominance. All three chapters exemplify how, through the written word, women played an important role – as authors or as symbols – in preserving and transforming Canadians' and Newfoundlanders' lived experiences of the war for future generations. That process is continued, nearly a century later, by *A Sisterhood of Suffering and Service.*

What, if anything, does this brief overview of some of the main lines of female experience in the First World War suggest about the transformative effect of the war? It indicates that, when it came to women, much-vaunted developments in labour and politics did not immediately transform either sphere. The changes were partial at best, and their real significance lies in being part of a larger, longer process of slow, incremental change, which took much of the twentieth century to transform women's lives and society's view of appropriate gender roles – a process many would argue remains incomplete. It goes almost without saying, however, that the Great War had a major impact on both Canada and Newfoundland. Women experienced that impact as much as men, participating in both celebration and mourning as national myths were being constructed; taking pride in their own contributions; suffering disappointments, losses, and unfulfilled hopes; and, in many cases, experiencing transformation on a personal, emotional level. It is perhaps most appropriate, then, to speak of the Great War not as a time of total transformation for Canadian and Newfoundland women but, rather, as a time of shifts and repositionings – as a milepost rather than as a finish line in the great transformation that was the twentieth century.

Notes

1 Helen Fowlds to her mother, 24 April 1915, "Transcripts of Helen Fowlds' World War One Letters," Letter 15, Trent University Archives, available at http://www.trentu.ca/.

2 Lois Allen, personal diary 1918, R 1792-0-2-E, Library and Archives Canada, available at http://www.collectionscanada.gc.ca/.
3 As testament to the influence and popularity of this interpretation, Arthur Lower's *Colony to Nation* (Don Mills: Longmans, Green and Company, 1946) has gone through five editions and several reprints. See also C.P. Stacey, "Nationality: The Experience of Canada," *Canadian Historical Association Historical Papers* (1967): 11; Desmond Morton and J.L. Granatstein, *Marching to Armageddon: Canadians and the Great War, 1914-1919* (Toronto: Lester and Orpen Dennys, 1989), 1.
4 Newfoundland and Labrador Heritage, "Introduction and Overview," Newfoundland and the Great War, available at http://www.heritage.nf.ca/.
5 Robert Rutherdale, *Hometown Horizons: Local Responses to Canada's Great War* (Vancouver: UBC Press, 2004), chap. 6; Ian Hugh Maclean Miller, *Our Glory and Our Grief: Torontonians and the Great War* (Toronto: University of Toronto Press, 2002), chap. 4; Jonathan Vance, *Death So Noble: Memory, Meaning, and the First World War* (Vancouver: UBC Press, 1997).
6 Rutherdale, *Hometown Horizons*, 223.
7 Linda Kealey, *Enlisting Women for the Cause: Women, Labour, and the Left in Canada, 1890-1920* (Toronto: University of Toronto Press, 1998).
8 O.A. Cooke, *The Canadian Military Experience, 1867-1995: A Bibliography*, 3rd ed. (Ottawa: Directorate of History and Heritage, Department of National Defence, 1997); Joy Parr, *The Gender of Breadwinners: Women, Men, and Change in Two Industrial Towns, 1880-1950* (Toronto: University of Toronto Press, 1990); Mariana Valverde, *The Age of Light, Soap and Water: Moral Reform in English Canada, 1885-1925* (Toronto: McClelland and Stewart, 1991); Clio Collective (Micheline Dumont, Jennifer Stoddart, Michèle Jean), *Quebec Women: A History* (Toronto: Women's Press, 1987); Alison Prentice, Paula Bourne, Gail Cuthbert Brandt, Beth Light, *Canadian Women: A History*, 2nd ed. (Toronto: Harcourt Brace Canada, 1996), 144-46, 230-35; *And We Knew How to Dance: Women in WWI*, produced by Silva Basmajian, National Film Board of Canada, 1993.
9 Joan Sangster, "Mobilizing Women for War," in *Canada and the First World War: Essays in Honour of Robert Craig Brown*, ed. David MacKenzie, 157-93 (Toronto: University of Toronto Press, 2005).
10 Barbara Roberts, *"Why Do Women Do Nothing to End the War?" Canadian Feminist-Pacifists and the Great War* (Ottawa: Canadian Research Institute for the Advancement of Women, 1985); Barbara Roberts, *A Reconstructed World: A Feminist Biography of Gertrude Richardson* (Montreal: McGill-Queen's University Press, 1996).
11 Please see "Selected Bibliography" for specific examples.
12 For a concise introduction to Canadian and Newfoundland participation in the Great War, see David Mackenzie, ed., *Canada and the First World War: Essays in Honour of Robert Craig Brown* (Toronto: University of Toronto Press, 2005).
13 Mary Jo Maynes, "Age as a Category of Historical Analysis: History, Agency, and Narratives of Childhood," *Journal of the History of Childhood and Youth* 1, 1 (208): 115-16. The entire inaugural issue of the journal helpfully frames the challenges and rewards of children's history.

Introduction

14 The history of childhood is a burgeoning field. The *Journal of the History of Childhood and Youth* was inaugurated in 2001, and works such as Paula S. Fass, ed., *Encyclopedia of Children and Childhood: In History and Society* (New York: Macmillan Reference, 2004), show that the field increasingly spans nations and cultures. Examples of Canadian histories that examine aspects of girlhood and girls' lives include: Tamara Myers, *Caught: Montreal's Modern Girls and the Law, 1869-1945* (Toronto: University of Toronto Press, 2006); Cynthia Comacchio, *The Dominion of Youth: Adolescence and the Making of a Modern Canada, 1920-1950* (Waterloo, ON: Wilfrid Laurier University Press, 2006); and Neil Sutherland, *Growing Up: Childhood in English Canada from the Great War to the Age of Television* (Toronto: University of Toronto Press, 1997).

15 Debbie Marshall, *Give Your Other Vote to the Sister: A Woman's Journey into the Great War* (Calgary: University of Calgary Press, 2007); Susan Mann, *Margaret Macdonald: Imperial Daughter* (Montreal: McGill-Queen's University Press, 2005).

16 Mann, *Margaret Macdonald*, 167.

17 Carrie Brown's *Rosie's Mom: Forgotten Women Workers of the First World War* (Boston: Northeastern University Press, 2002), alludes to this obscuring of the First World War. On the Second World War, see Ruth Roach Pierson, *"They're Still Women After All": The Second World War and Canadian Womanhood* (Toronto: McClelland and Stewart, 1986); Jeffrey A. Keshen, *Saints, Sinners and Soldiers: Canada's Second World War* (Vancouver: UBC Press, 2004), 177; Cynthia Toman, *An Officer and a Lady: Canadian Military Nursing and the Second World War* (Vancouver: UBC Press, 2007).

18 Mabel Durham, "British Columbia's Patriotic Women," *Canadian Magazine* 49, 1 (1917): 93.

19 Lady Davidson explicitly expresses this hope for Newfoundland in Lady Davidson, "Comradeship," *The Distaff* (1916): 2.

20 Durham, "British Columbia's Patriotic Women," 93.

21 For poetic examples from Canada and Newfoundland, respectively, see: Louise C. Glasgow, "Knitting," *Canadian Magazine* 44, 6 (1914): 546; Phebe Florence Miller, "The Knitting Mariana," *The Distaff* (1916): 10.

22 Adelaide Plumptre, "Canada's Love-Gifts," in *Canada in the Great World War: An Authentic Account of the Military History of Canada from the Earliest Days to the Close of the War of the Nations,* vol. 2, *Days of Preparation* (Toronto: United Publishers of Canada, 1917), 198.

23 Imperial Order Daughters of the Empire, *The Imperial Order Daughters of the Empire Golden Jubilee, 1900-1950* (Toronto: T.H. Best, 1950), 25; Sarah Glassford, "Marching as to War: The Canadian Red Cross Society, 1885-1939" (PhD diss., York University, 2007), chap. 3.

24 Secretary of the Montreal Citizens' Recruiting League to O.C. of M.D. no. 4, n.d., Department of National Defence, vol. 4479, file 25-1-20, cited in Jeffrey Keshen, *Propaganda and Censorship during Canada's Great War* (Edmonton: University of Alberta Press, 1996). Suzanne Evans discusses the propaganda aimed at women, especially at mothers, during the Great War in *Mothers of Heroes, Mothers of Martyrs: World War I*

and the Politics of Grief (Montreal and Kingston: McGill-Queen's University Press, 2007). Images of Canadian propaganda posters of the First World War are available at http://www.museedelaguerre.ca/.

25 Julia Horwood, "W.P.A. Visiting Committee," *The Distaff* (1916): 1.
26 Kori Street, "'Toronto's Amazons': Militarised Femininity and Gender Construction in the Great War" (MA thesis, University of Toronto, 1991).
27 Catherine Cleverdon, *The Woman Suffrage Movement in Canada* [1950] (Toronto: University of Toronto Press, 1978), 122-25.
28 See, for example, Robert Craig Brown and Ramsay Cook's classic *Canada 1896-1921: A Nation Transformed* (Toronto: McClelland and Stewart, 1974), 271.
29 For example, the argument that women were given the vote as a reward for their war service is put forward by one woman interviewed in the documentary *And We Knew How to Dance*.
30 Cleverdon, *Woman Suffrage*, 125-31.
31 Prentice et al., *Canadian Women*, 234-35; Tarah Brookfield, "Divided by the Ballot Box: The Montreal Council of Women and the 1917 Election," *Canadian Historical Review* 89, 4 (2008): 473-501.
32 Margot I. Duley, *Where Once Our Mothers Stood We Stand: Women's Suffrage in Newfoundland* (Charlottetown: Gynergy Books, 1993).
33 Mrs. Elaine Nelson [pseudonym], quoted in Daphne Read, ed., *The Great War and Canadian Society: An Oral History* (Toronto: New Hogtown Press, 1978), 157.

PART 1:
Mobilizing Women

> The nimble fingers of the knitting women are transforming balls of wool into socks and comforters, but even a greater change is being wrought in their own hearts.[1]
>
> – Nellie McClung, 1915

When war broke out in August 1914, a surge of patriotic propaganda and recruiting appeals quickly followed. Though this material was largely directed at their male friends and relatives, the appeal to do one's duty by King and Empire hit home with vast numbers of girls and women as well. Moreover, many women felt the call to care for soldiers and support the war effort for the sake of relatives and friends in uniform as strongly, or perhaps more strongly, than they felt the call to work for the nation and empire at war.

Women whose hearts and minds were not immediately stirred by a sense of duty or a desire to care for absent loved ones did not escape the home-front mobilization of girls and women. There were no white feather campaigns against reluctant women, such as those that strove to shame able-bodied men into enlisting in the army, but women were equally pressured and shamed into participating in volunteer war work. Newspapers printed lists of volunteers' and donors' contributions; classrooms, volunteer groups, and communities competed to raise the most money or produce the most comforts; and the wagging tongues of observant friends and neighbours worked to provide an informal network of community surveillance. Citizens were exhorted by their peers to "fight or pay" or "fight or knit," and the implication was clear: those not in uniform had better be making a contribution to the war effort in some other way.

These non-combatant, voluntary, charitable, stay-at-home roles comprised the bulk of Canadian and Newfoundland women's contributions to their respective dominions' war efforts between 1914 and 1918. Celebrated at the time as a glowing testament to the worth and splendid patriotism of the women and girls who performed them, the humble tasks of knitting, bandage-rolling, and fundraising have not fared well in our cultural memory of the war and have been largely overlooked in subsequent historiography. Sarah Glassford, Linda Quiney, Natalie Riegler, Robert Rutherdale, and, in the Australian and British contexts, Bruce Scates and Peter Grant, are among the relatively few scholars who have given serious consideration to women's First World War voluntary labour.[2] Compared to the more hands-on work of military nurses, British women's non-traditional factory work, or the dramatic Second World War-era entry of large numbers of women into the armed forces, women's humble Great War efforts with knitting needles and collection boxes seem, to modern eyes, boring and possibly frivolous.

Seen in their proper context, however, they are anything but. In 1914 women throughout the English-speaking world were fighting (with little success) for the right to vote and facing uphill battles as they tried to enter traditionally male professions, while a woman's place was still seen as being firmly within the domestic sphere. In this restricted context, the women of Newfoundland and Canada found ways to contribute to the war effort that showed them to be not only patriotic daughters of their dominions and their Empire but also capable organizers and workers. These efforts arose out of a long tradition of women's supportive work behind the lines during times of war and generally conformed to established conventions of what was "appropriate" work for women. They nonetheless played a significant role – perhaps because of their very conventionality – in convincing many observers that women were fit for the privileges and responsibilities of full citizenship.

In this section, Alison Norman surveys the war work of a group whose citizenship was considered doubly suspect at the outbreak of war: the Aboriginal women of the Six Nations reserve on the Grand River in southern Ontario. Margot Duley details the work of Newfoundland's über-war charity, the Women's Patriotic Association, which not only mobilized in aid of Newfoundland soldiers but also went on to become a key element in Newfoundland women's postwar fight for suffrage. Terry Wilde takes us inside the collegiate world of the University of Toronto as he considers the role of the Great War in altering women students' place in the then overwhelmingly male culture of the university. In each case, we see that, although the vast majority of women remained outside the realms of the army and the factory, they nevertheless comprised a massive army of voluntary labour, which they directed towards the cause of the British Empire at war. When Britannia called up her sons in August 1914, her daughters responded as well.

Notes

1. Nellie McClung, *In Times Like These* (Toronto: McLeod and Allen, 1915), 28.
2. Sarah Glassford, "'The Greatest Mother in the World': Carework and the Discourse of Mothering in the Canadian Red Cross Society during the First World War," *Journal of the Association for Research on Mothering* 10, 1 (2008): 219-32; Linda J. Quiney, "Bravely and Loyally They Answered the Call," *History of Intellectual Culture* 5, 1 (2005): 1-19; Natalie Riegler, "Sphagnum Moss in World War I: The Making of Surgical Dressings by Volunteers in Toronto, Canada, 1917-1918," *Canadian Bulletin of Medical History* 6 (1989): 27-43; Robert Rutherdale, *Hometown Horizons: Local Responses to Canada's Great War* (Vancouver: UBC Press, 2004), chap. 6; Bruce Scates, "The Unknown Sock Knitter: Voluntary Work, Emotional Labour, Bereavement and the Great War," *Labour History* (Australia) 81 (2001): 29-49; Peter Grant, "'An Infinity of Personal Sacrifice': The Scale and Nature of Charitable Work in Britain during the First World War," *War and Society* 27, 2 (2008): 67-88.

"In Defense of the Empire"
The Six Nations of the Grand River and the Great War

ALISON NORMAN

On Sunday, 5 November 1914, three months after Britain declared war on Germany, bringing Canada into the Great War, two women from Brantford, Ontario, visited the Six Nations Grand River Reserve, southeast of the city, to "found a Women's League to provide for their soldiers who are enlisting." Margaret Brown was an author and historian involved in civic affairs in the city, and Augusta Gilkison was the daughter of an Indian agent and a local historian as well.[1] Brown explained "we are doing this because we have taken a great interest for some time in the Six Nation Indians and this is an opportune time for the women to uphold the tradition of their Nation."[2] The two women went door to door and found that the women of Six Nations had been knitting socks for their enlisted men. Brown and Gilkison helped the women organize their war work into the Six Nations Women's Patriotic League, which continued its efforts throughout the war, and maintained a tradition of loyalty to the British Crown.

This chapter focuses on the various patriotic efforts of the Six Nations women from the Grand River Reserve in southern Ontario. The long Iroquois tradition of loyalty to Britain and the supportive role that Iroquois women had played during wartime in the past made patriotic work a likely response for Six Nations women in 1914. The patriotic work conducted by Six Nations women on the home front involved both traditional Iroquois women's work (helping to outfit their men for war while taking care of families at home) and very closely resembled what non-Native women in Brantford (and across the country) were doing – knitting socks, making food to send overseas, and raising money. Women's wartime work on the reserve had evolved, and their motivations had changed from seventeenth- and eighteenth-century efforts to support their own community to attempts to support their men in an overseas world war. They worked to raise money and make goods that would benefit soldiers other than their own as well as those affected by the war in Belgium. Much of this work was similar to the work women across Canada were conducting, and this suggests that, by 1914, much of the Six Nations community was acculturated to an Anglo-Canadian way of life.

The wartime contributions made by Native men during the Great War have long been ignored, but recent work has attempted to rectify this situation.[3] Women's war work has also been long overlooked, so it is not surprising that Native women are almost entirely absent from the historiography of the Great War.[4] However, Native women, and Six Nations women in particular, played an important role in work on the home front during the war. Not only did they support soldiers from their community but they also, despite the Six Nations Council's lack of support for the First World War, maintained a tradition of allegiance and loyalty to the British Crown.

The Six Nations have a long history of allegiance to the British Empire, beginning in the seventeenth century. Prior to the arrival of Europeans in North America, the Iroquois nations had established what is known as the Iroquois Confederacy, a political alliance originally made up of five nations: the Cayuga, Mohawk, Onondaga, Oneida, and Seneca (later joined by the Tuscarora). After centuries of fighting among themselves, they established what is known as the Great Peace. The subsequent period between European arrival and the Six Nations' 1784 migration from present-day upstate New York to the Grand River Valley was, as Six Nations community historian Keith Jamieson explains, "a time of alliance and conflict, of compromise and transition, extending over 300 years."[5] The colonial war that had the greatest impact on the Six Nations was the American Revolution, which divided them between those who stayed neutral, those who sided with the American rebels, and those (the majority) who fought for the British. When the British lost the war, they treated the Six Nations as loyal allies, and, to compensate them for the lost Iroquois land in upstate New York, they gave them a large territory in Upper Canada called the Haldimand Tract. Thousands of people moved to this land after the war, which became the present-day Grand River Reserve.[6] Soon after, the Six Nations fought for the British in the War of 1812 and were an integral part of the defence of

Upper Canada.[7] As the twentieth century opened, the Six Nations continued to value their alliance with Britain, and many chose to ignore the government of the relatively new country of Canada in which their lands now lay. When the British Empire went to war in 1914, wrote local historian F.D. Reville, "the Six Nations stood by their ancient treaties with the British Crown and proved their loyalty by the shedding of blood on the battlefields of Europe."

Despite how their loyalty to Britain aligned the Six Nations with non-Native Canadian society, there were important cultural differences that shaped Iroquois women's experiences. The Iroquois are a matrilineal society in which ancestral descent follows the female line: traditionally, husbands moved into their wives' homes, and lineage and clan membership were determined through female ancestors. Women held a wide range of political and economic responsibilities, playing roles very different from those of women in European or Euro-North American cultures. Iroquois clan mothers, for example, were "responsible for selecting hereditary chiefs and participated in decisions regarding the activities of warriors and fate of captives."[8] Traditionally, women had the right to select and depose chiefs of the Six Nations Council in the warlike Iroquois society. Although historians and ethnologists debate how much political power Iroquois women possessed,[9] it is clear that clan mothers were influential.

Iroquois women held wide-ranging powers. In precontact Iroquois society, and for many centuries after, there was a gendered division of labour in which women were responsible for the agricultural production and men hunted and waged war. This gave women control over much of the economic output of the household and community and, thus, power.[10] Although wives did sometimes accompany their husbands on the war party, they generally stayed home and cared for the fields and the children.[11] Their absence from battle did not, however, preclude an important contribution to the military life of the community. It was women's responsibility to outfit men for war – to make clothing, moccasins, and food as well as to clean and repair weapons and equipment.[12] Furthermore, Iroquois women had the power to initiate war, specifically to secure prisoners for adoption (to replace killed brothers, sons, husbands)[13] and, at times, to prevent wars or end them.[14] When warriors prepared for war against the wishes of the hereditary council, the chiefs would appeal to the women to prevent them. Because women controlled the crops, they could prevent war by refusing to provision the warriors.[15]

Traditional Iroquois women's political and economic power changed over time as a result of increased Euro-American contact, colonization efforts, and missionary work so that, by the twentieth century, much of the Iroquois society on the Grand River Reserve had become acculturated. The people were largely Christian, patriarchal, and culturally similar to their non-Native neighbours. However, some members of the community still upheld the Longhouse faith – a belief system made up of both Christian values and traditional Iroquois spirituality and based on the Code of Handsome Lake, an early nineteenth-century Seneca religious leader. The reserve continued to be governed by the traditional hereditary council, which consisted of about fifty chiefs who were nominated by the clan matrons. This system had been in existence prior to contact with Europeans and is a model of early representative government.

The Grand River Reserve lies southeast of the City of Brantford, covering about 185 square kilometres. At the outbreak of the First World War, the community consisted of about forty-seven hundred people.[16] Most men worked as farmers or labourers. The reserve was home to a number of day schools and some children attended a nearby residential school (the Mohawk Institute) or non-Native high schools in nearby towns. Children received a somewhat militarized education that emphasized the historical connections to Britain and imperial history. Children at the Mohawk Institute participated in the Cadets and the Girl Guides and almost one hundred graduates enlisted in the Canadian Expeditionary Force.[17] Numerous churches were established on the reserve, including Methodist, Baptist, and Anglican congregations. About three-quarters of the population were Christian, while one-quarter adhered to the Longhouse faith.[18] Men and women belonged to a wide range of voluntary associations and organizations, including temperance unions, Orange Order lodges, Women's Institutes, and the Six Nations Agricultural Society. People worked through these organizations to improve the community, and involvement in them led to leadership roles in the community.

The community was governed by the traditional hereditary council, which was composed of about fifty chiefs, although, in the decade leading up to the Great War, there was considerable dissent, especially among the Dehorners. This group of men wanted to "dehorn" the hereditary leadership (i.e., remove the deer horns worn as a symbol of leadership) and replace the hereditary council with an elected council. The Dehorners had argued for an elected government for many years.[19] In general, Longhouse followers supported the hereditary council, while Christians tended to support the Dehorners and a new elective system. This division over-simplifies the complicated problem of identity on the Grand River Reserve, where community members held varying beliefs over time, depending on the issue, and where family members could be divided in their opinions. However, in general it is fair to say that, when war broke out in 1914, people who followed the Longhouse belief system and who supported the hereditary council took an anti-war stance, while Christians (especially Anglicans), who were also supporters of the idea of an elected council, took a pro-war stance.

Members of the Six Nations Council considered themselves leaders of a sovereign Aboriginal nation, and, when war broke out, they wanted a formal request for their military help from Britain's King George V, as tradition dictated. The Six Nations were and are distinct from other Native communities and nations in Canada because, before the creation of Canada in 1867, the British Crown gave them the Haldimand Tract. They did not make treaties with the Canadian government, as did other First Nations, and so see themselves as unique. The desired request for military help never came, so the council took no official role in supporting the war through statements, recruiting, or other patriotic work.[20]

Despite the council's refusal to help with recruitment, about three hundred men (and one woman) from the reserve enlisted in the armed forces. In total, about thirty-five hundred Native men enlisted in the Canadian army during the First World War.[21] It is likely that they enlisted for a variety of reasons, including the Six Nations' historic alliance with Britain, the need for a paycheque, and/or a desire for adventure and travel. Some, like Lieutenant Cameron Dee Brant, the first Brant County and first Six Nations man to die in the war, enlisted because they had grown up with the military, through school and training in the Cadets and service in the militia. Brant also attended military college at Wolseley Barracks in London.[22] Historian Mark Moss suggests that, for Anglo-Canadian men, "the strong ties that bound the citizens of Ontario to Britain made it relatively easy for them to view conflicts overseas as 'domestic' and relevant to their own lives."[23] This was likely true for many Six Nations men as well.

First Nations people were not conscripted; the government decided that, although they were British subjects, they were wards of the Canadian state and had no right to the franchise or other privileges of citizenship. As such, they "should not be expected to assume responsibilities equal to those of enfranchised persons."[24] Official policy in the first year of the war was not to enlist First Nations as there were fears that "Germans might refuse to extend to them the privileges of civilized warfare."[25] Although some First Nations men were turned away from recruitment centres, many were able to enlist after trying different locales. James Walker suggests: "to some extent this persistence must have been prompted by young men's sense of adventure and patriotism, but they were moved as well by a consciousness that a contribution to the war effort could help them overcome the disadvantages faced by their communities."[26] Despite difficulties, they enlisted in high numbers, and, after the war, Scott wrote: "the splendid record of the Indians in the Great War must be attributed to the personal loyalty, initiative, and high spirit of the young braves who flocked to the colours."[27] Scott was a strong proponent of the enlistment of First Nations men, and he believed that veterans had proven their manhood and loyalty to Canada. For this reason, veterans were given the right to vote but were not automatically "enfranchised."[28]

Many Six Nations men enlisted in the first year of war. By the fall of 1915, the all-Native 114th Battalion was raised out of the local militia unit, the 37th Haldimand Rifles. Lieutenant Colonel Andrew Thompson (a non-Native honorary chief with familial and historical ties to the Six Nations) commanded the battalion, and 292 men were recruited from the reserve.[29] The battalion's nickname, the Brock Rangers, and its crest, consisting of two crossed tomahawks, paid tribute to the ancestors of many of the men who fought for the British under Sir Isaac Brock in the War of 1812's Battle of Queenston Heights. The battalion was broken up upon arrival in England, its men transferred to combat units, forestry units, a group that toured the United Kingdom for patriotic and recruitment purposes, and, in a few cases, to the Royal Air Force. In many cases, Native soldiers, like African-Canadian soldiers and men from certain other ethnic minorities, were not given the "privilege" of actually engaging in combat.[30] The military authorities frequently segregated these soldiers into separate units and assigned them to manual labour jobs. These Six Nations soldiers, who were willing to give their lives to fight for Britain and Canada, suffered from varying degrees of racism; some, though, were able to transcend this treatment and attain considerable military achievements. Encountering this type of discrimination was a common experience for minority colonials who served in the Great War.[31]

The first and only woman from the Six Nations to enlist in the military during the Great War was Edith Anderson Monture, who served overseas as a Nursing Sister. Monture, a Mohawk, was the youngest of the eight children of John Anderson and Mary Thomas Anderson. She attended day school on the reserve and at the Brantford Collegiate Institute.[32] She applied to several nursing programs in Ontario but was not accepted, and she believed that this was due to her race. Native women were generally not accepted into nursing programs in Canada at that time, and many crossed the Canada-US border to get their training.[33] Monture completed her training at the New Rochelle Nursing School in New York, became a registered nurse in 1914, and was hired as a nurse at a private school in New Rochelle. In 1917, when the United States joined the war effort, Monture joined the Westchester County Unit B, American Expeditionary Force. This unit had twenty nurses, fifteen of whom were Canadians.[34] After three months of further training in New York, Monture left for France in February 1918. She nursed overseas for more than a year, treating soldiers who had been engaged in trench warfare and had suffered gas attacks.

Monture's diary of her time as a nurse, kept even though it was strictly against the policy of the Army Nurse Corps and later published by her family, reveals that her experiences paralleled those of non-Native Canadian nurses in the war.[35] Just over three thousand Canadian women enlisted in the war, the vast majority in the Canadian Army Medical Corps.[36] All were single and most had a high school education, which was unusual at the time. When asked why she became a nurse, Monture replied: "It was something to do." And when asked how she had the courage to venture so far from home, she replied: "I had nothing to do."[37] Clearly, she had much nerve and determination to leave her home for training, work, and wartime service, but she downplayed these qualities. Monture did not report having suffered from discrimination. However, given that discrimination was a common experience for minority nurses in Canada,[38] there is a strong possibility that she experienced it as well. Barriers to Aboriginal nurses during this period included difficulties in acquiring enough high school education, the assumptions of hospital officials that they suffered from ill-health, and the cost and difficulty of relocating to a city with a nursing school that would accept them.[39] Monture seems to have been able to overcome these obstacles and to have been determined not to let her race or anything else stand in the way of her becoming a nurse.

Upon her return from France, Monture moved back to the Six Nations reserve and married Claybran Monture. She had four children and, for several decades, continued to work as a nurse at the Lady Willingdon Hospital in Brantford. She also worked as a midwife in the community. In 1939, she was elected honorary president of the Ohsweken Red Cross and was involved in patriotic work on the home front.[40] Monture was likely a role model for other young women on the reserve who wanted to go to into nursing, which, after the Great War, became an increasingly popular career for Six Nations women.

Because of her war service, for several decades Monture was the only woman on the reserve who could vote as, under the Military Service Act, 1917, nurses were given this right. Other Native women were not enfranchised until 1960.[41] Monture's son remembers that other veterans encouraged her to vote in federal elections with them. After her death in 1996 at the age of 106, her granddaughter, Terri Monture, stated: "Ours is a history of warriors, and Edith's story proves that our women, too, could have followed this path throughout the ages."[42] Monture's war service is part of the Six Nations' cultural memory of the Great War, and she is remembered and honoured by the community. In 2008, she was honoured at a commemoration of Six Nations women veterans held at Veterans' Park on the Grand River Reserve.[43] There is a street named Edith Monture Avenue in one of Brantford's new subdivisions, and a park named after her in the same area. While her name is not on any official plaque on the reserve, she remains well known within the community, owing to the collective memory of her large family and her several decades of work as a nurse and midwife: "she was well-known to pretty much everyone."[44] There is also a display featuring Edith Anderson Monture in the First Peoples Hall at the Canadian Museum of Civilization, Ottawa.

Edith Anderson Monture's war story was extraordinary. A far more typical role for Six Nations women involved patriotic work on the home front. The Six Nations Women's Patriotic League (SNWPL) was the first Native women's organization to be formed in Canada after the start of the war, in early November 1914.[45] This is significant as the Six Nations reserve possessed the largest population of any reserve in Canada, and the Department of Indian Affairs (DIA) considered its inhabitants to be the most "progressive," or "assimilated," Native people in the country. Indeed, the reserve was a DIA "showpiece."[46] That Six Nations women formed a patriotic league to support their men in the Great War suggests that they were comfortable using the traditions of Anglo-Canadian women's organizations. In this way, they were like non-Native women across Canada who, upon the outbreak of war, volunteered for local branches of organizations such as the Canadian Red Cross, the Imperial Order Daughters of the Empire (IODE), and various women's institutes.[47]

Once the SNWPL was founded in November 1914, Margaret Brown and Augusta Gilkison lent their support and experience to organizing the efforts of the women on the reserve. Soon after the founding of the SNWPL, Evelyn Davis, wife to reserve doctor Walter Davis, also began to work with the league. On behalf of the women of Six Nations, Brown wrote several times to Duncan Campbell Scott, the superintendent general of Indian affairs in Ottawa, asking for support for their work.[48] It is likely that these three non-Native women encouraged Six Nations women to support their enlisted men in this new way – by knitting socks and sending home-made goods overseas. These women were part of a small but growing number of non-Native allies of the Six Nations who helped them in their dealings with the Canadian and British governments.[49]

Brown and Gilkison met with women on the reserve that first month, and they quickly named Six Nations women officers of the SNWPL. Helen Hill became president, and Amelia Garlow became secretary treasurer. Hill was a widow and an active member of the Ohsweken Baptist Church; Garlow was the only child of Chief Josiah Hill, an active supporter of the war.[50] The resident missionaries' wives from some of the churches also participated. The women church members were often already involved in either a ladies aid group, a women's institute, or some other women's organization that was concerned with bettering the community. However, it is important to note that Longhouse women were involved in this wartime work too: it was not just the Christian women, despite the fact that very few Longhouse men enlisted. However, there were four longhouses on the reserve at the time, and only one, the Sour Springs Longhouse, participated in the SNWPL. It is unclear how many Six Nations women were members of, or participated in, the league as no records are extant. However, there were twenty-seven members of the executive from the fourteen churches and the Longhouse faith, so it is likely that at least a hundred, if not more, Six Nations women participated by knitting socks and raising money. While it is clear that Six Nations women were knitting before the visit of Brown and Gilkison in early November, it is unclear what form the SNWPL would have taken without the involvement of the non-Native women.

The main intention of the SNWPL was to provide their own enlisted men with comforts, including clothing and food. In December of 1914, the SNWPL sent a shipment of goods to England, consisting of socks, wristlets, mitts, caps, helmets, silk handkerchiefs, chocolate, gum, nuts, candies, individual fruitcakes, Christmas puddings, tobacco, and writing paper. A similar shipment was sent to Six Nations soldiers who were training in Toronto at Exhibition Camp.[51] After the first large shipment was sent overseas, knitting socks seems to have become the main preoccupation of the SNWPL. Socks were extremely important during the Great War: trench foot was a serious concern for soldiers who spent days and weeks in the cold, wet trenches. If their feet remained damp and cold, they could get sores and blisters, which, if infected, could lead to gangrene and amputation. Wearing clean, dry socks was an important way to combat the condition. Margaret Brown had personally donated a large amount of wool, but, because they could not afford to buy much themselves, the women of the SNWPL requested funding from the Six Nations Council to buy more wool to knit socks. Dr. Walter Davis and Reverend Edmunds (a Methodist missionary) approached the council with the request but were turned down. The council explained that the request had not come from the Six Nations women themselves. It is unclear why Davis and Edmunds were appointed; however, as the council was made up of men, perhaps the women of the SNWPL believed it would be better to send two non-Native men with some status in the community to request the funding. However, Amelia Garlow then approached the council directly, and the SNWPL was granted fifty dollars with which to buy more wool. After that difficulty, Brown attempted to bypass the council and to get funding directly from the DIA, even though the SNWPL felt that "there [was] prejudice [in the Council] against working through the white people."[52] However, the DIA refused to donate money, and, although the council continued to sporadically support the SNWPL's work, it did not do so without making things difficult. The council did not actively support the war and was therefore hesitant to provide financial support to the SNWPL. The women's efforts to get funding from both the Six Nations Council and the DIA were politically charged, but they were also simply efforts to support Six Nations men.

The SNWPL also sewed and knit for Belgian Relief, sending knit articles and handmade quilts as well as home-made jelly.[53] Neutral Belgium had been invaded and occupied by the German army in the fall of 1914, and, as the British were blockading the small import-dependent country, mass civilian starvation was a serious concern. Efforts were under way to provide relief to Belgian refugees as well as to the small enclave that managed to withstand the German invasion. Many in Canada were collecting goods to send, so, clearly, the Six Nations women were taking part in a wider, international relief effort. That they were affected by the suffering of others in a country across the ocean, and were so interested in helping, suggests that they were aware of international affairs, not just those affecting their own community. In other words, they did not see themselves as an isolated community.

The work of the SNWPL was reported in the Canadian media. In November 1914, the *Brantford Expositor* reported:

What the Indian women do, they do well, and it may be said to their credit that no finer knitted socks could be sent to the soldiers than those sent by the Six Nations women. A century ago the grandparents of those women who are now working were refugees in the wilds of Canada, driven from their home in the Mohawk Valley, as the Belgians are in England today, and their children will show in a practical way their sympathy for the Belgians. The women will continue their work during the war.[54]

A Toronto-based newspaper, the *Globe and Mail*, also reported on their efforts. In an article entitled "Canadian Indians Are Doing Their Share," the author reported that "down on the reserve of the Six Nations, at Brantford, the women are knitting for the soldiers who are going to the front – knitting assiduously under the direction of a local committee appointed among themselves – and there can be no doubt that their good wishes for the prospective wearers of articles go with them."[55] Six Nations women's work was widely reported and applauded by the non-Native community. Robert Rutherdale suggests that "journalism often enhanced stereotypes of war relief campaign enthusiasm and ethnic difference" and that fundraising drives "valorized this consensus-based, multicultural image of inclusive contributing."[56] It is likely that the reportage of the SNWPL's work was encouraging for league members.

While the Grand River Reserve community was divided during the war, it is clear that some members took great pride in the Six Nations' patriotic response to the war. SNWPL president Helen Hill apparently knit 225 pairs of socks herself, a feat so impressive that it was reported in her obituary when she died in 1921.[57] Helen's son Asa Hill, secretary of the Six Nations Council during the war, wrote: "In the awful scenes on Flanders fields, the Six Nations showed their interest. They gave themselves as they had done before for the cause, they gave their money, they contributed to Patriotic Funds."[58] An article published during the Second World War praised all of the work they did: "The women of the Six Nations ... have shown outstanding loyalty, courage and devotion to Canada by faithfully supporting the Patriotic League of the last Great War and the Red Cross Work of the present war."[59] This type of rhetoric was similar to what non-Native journalists had written earlier. The DIA noted the work of the SNWPL in its Annual Reports during the war years, but whether the league was an inspiration to women in other Native communities is unknown.

Knitting, sewing, quilt-making, and embroidery were skills in which Six Nations women had been proficient for generations, with mothers teaching daughters.[60] It is likely that Iroquois women originally learned knitting and quilt-making from Quaker women or missionaries' wives in the eighteenth century.[61] By 1872, quilt-making had become one of the judged categories at the Six Nations Agricultural Fair, where women from the community were able to show their handiwork.[62] More recently, these types of skills were taught at the Mohawk Institute, the residential school near the reserve that many Six Nations children attended in the late nineteenth and early twentieth centuries. European needlework skills were certainly different from traditional Iroquois women's handiwork, but they were not new in 1914. Six Nations women had been knitting, sewing, and doing "fancy-work" for many decades. Although little historical research has been conducted on the evolution of Iroquois women's crafts, it is clear that changes did occur with colonization.[63]

Aside from knitting and fundraising, the SNWPL made and embroidered a large flag for the 114th Battalion. According to Scott, they "worked a unique and singularly beautiful regimental flag for the [Brock's] Rangers that elicited not a little comment and admiration."[64] The flag (see Figure 2) consisted of embroidered images and symbols on a red woollen cloth background. The images include a wolf, an eagle, a heron, and a bear, which represent four Iroquois clans, with a turtle at the bottom, which references the earth as Turtle Island. At the top of the flag are a lion and a dragon for the British Crown. There are six arrows in the centre to symbolize the Six Nations as well as a white hare, representing the Ojibwa men who also served in the 114th. The battalion had to request special permission to carry the flag in addition to the King's colours and the regular regimental colours. It was a clear, self-conscious expression of their Aboriginal identity, painstakingly created by Aboriginal women and proudly flown by Aboriginal men for all to see. This flag was specially cared for and returned to the community, where it is now on display at the Woodland Cultural Centre Museum in Brantford.

In February 1916, after the Brock's Rangers (114th Battalion) were organized, some Six Nations women formed another patriotic league on the reserve. The Brock's Rangers Benefit Society (BRBS) was intended to minister to the needs of the 114th Battalion by providing food and clothing for it.[65] Mary Sophia Smith Styres was president and Henrietta Porter Hill was secretary-treasurer.[66] Both women were also involved in the Ohsweken Women's Institute and the Indian Moral Association, so their patriotic work was part of a tradition of serving the community and resulted in elite status for them within the community. During the course of the war, the BRBS raised about $350 through garden parties and

FIGURE 2   The pride and skill of Six Nations women are evident in the symbolically rich flag they embroidered for the 114th Battalion. [Photograph by the WCCM. Image used by permission of the Woodland Cultural Centre Museum, Brantford.]

tag sales.[67] When the war was over it had $200 on hand, which it used as the beginnings of a fund to build a memorial to Six Nations soldiers who died in France. Since no organization records exist, it is unclear whether the BRBS's funds were used to build a temporary war memorial in Victoria Park, Brantford, in 1919. A permanent memorial was built at Veterans Park in Ohsweken in 1933.[68]

In a clear case of racial discrimination, during an outbreak of the deadly smallpox virus on the Grand River Reserve in February and March of 1915, the Canadian military refused to transport overseas the socks knit by the SNWPL. Officials claimed Six Nations socks were infected, but they continued to accept socks from the City of Brantford, where there were more cases of smallpox than

"In Defense of the Empire"

there were on the reserve. There was a history of such discrimination in the area. In 1901, during an outbreak of smallpox on the reserve, the Six Nations Council, the local Board of Health, and area doctors all acted to protect the community and the surrounding areas by closing off a small section of the reserve and using mounted patrolmen to enforce the limited quarantine. In spite of these measures, the cities of Brantford and Hamilton responded in fear, banning any Aboriginal people from entering their cities and trying to quarantine the entire reserve.[69] A Methodist minister from Brantford went so far as to suggest that "the deplorable condition of the reserve, both morally and sanitarily," had led to the outbreak.[70] A few weeks later, the superintendent of Indian affairs replied in the local paper that, since the epidemic now included Brantford, the minister would have reason to level the same charges against the non-Aboriginal inhabitants of that city. Given this history, when smallpox broke out on the reserve in 1915, it was not surprising that the SNWPL felt discriminated against. In March 1915, Evelyn Davis, a non-Aboriginal member of the league and the wife of the reserve doctor, wrote to Margaret Brown: "Nearly a hundred pairs of socks have been on hand for some time and the Indians feel that they are being unfairly discriminated against since supplies for the soldiers are being accepted from other small-pox infected districts – Brantford, for instance – and not from the reserve, where there are now only six cases."[71] Brown wrote to Scott, insisting that "the socks [were] safe," but he told her to make sure the Brantford medical officer of health approved sending on the socks. By May, the SNWPL still did not have permission to send them. Amelia Garlow wrote to Scott: "As now that it is all passed away and no outbreak has developed in our homes where the knitted goods are stored away[,] I write to ask if we could now send them to our boys of the Six Nations [who] are still on the battlefield providing we take the necessary precautions of having all the goods fumigated." She continued, making reference to previous battles in which the Six Nations were allied with Britain: "It gives me some degree of pride and satisfaction to know that there are some Six Nations blood being shed again."[72] Scott again replied that the women needed to take the advice of the doctor. He added: "I am proud to know that the Six Nations are well-represented at the front, and I am sure that the boys will uphold the tradition of their race, and give a good account of themselves in defense of the Empire. I hope that the comforts your League has thoughtfully provided will reach them safely."[73] Finally, the socks were sent. White colonial societies commonly display an irrational fear of disease in racialized minorities.[74] No amount of patriotic work could remove the stigma of race from the efforts of the SNWPL, regardless of how much praise it otherwise earned from white Canadians.

In the fall of 1916, the SNWPL faced even more problems. The council refused to continue to support the league by providing funding for wool, in part because there had been crop failures and it was concerned about having to provide relief to members of the community in the winter. Another reason it refused support was that it believed that "the Six Nations were a sovereign nation and had not declared war on Germany, therefore, their boys were wearing foreign uniforms and were not representatives of the Six Nations."[75] Amelia Garlow again applied to Scott at the DIA, explaining: "we the mothers, sisters, wives, etc, want to knit for our boys, but unless funds are provided for, we shall be obliged to discontinue our work." While Scott approved of their work, he was unable to release any of the Six Nations money to the SNWPL. After the league submitted a report on its work to the Six Nations Council in November 1916, the council rescinded its earlier decision and again agreed to provide funds for yarn, but it wanted to make sure that the socks were going to Six Nations men in the 114th Battalion. The women continued to apply for, and receive, sporadic funding throughout 1917 and 1918. However, it might have been difficulties with the council that led to at least one vice-president's leaving the SNWPL to found the BRBS. Henrietta Porter Hill had been the vice-president (representing Ohsweken Baptist Church) of the SNWPL but became secretary-treasurer of the new BRBS in 1916.

Not only was the SNWPL only given grudging support by the Six Nations Council during the war, but the council's lack of support for the soldiers and their families back home was a major point of contention between those who supported it and those who favoured a new elected council.[76] The soldiers were so angered by the council's lack of support that, in 1917, they circulated a petition and sent it to the Canadian government. It was written by Lieutenant Oliver M. Martin, Lieutenant James D. Moses, Major C. Smith, and Sergeant William F. Powless. It stated: "circumstances have made it so that we can no longer look on our present Council with respect or confidence, and we therefore sign this as an agreement, to do all in our power to rid our nation of the said Council, and in its place to establish a government representative of the people, whereby we as Six Nations Indians in general, may be intelligently represented, and that our public affairs and national spirit may be properly looked after."[77] They received no response, but, when they returned home, they wrote another petition. It specifically commented on the lack of support their family members had received during the war: "During the whole of the time that we were overseas the Council did not do one single thing for us or our dependants. Instead of helping to make the lot of our families and ourselves easy to bear, they tried to make us suffer."[78] The petition then explains how the Haldimand County Patriotic Society (HCPS) provided financial support for the dependants, in the same way that the Canadian Patriotic Society worked to support soldiers' families (see Desmond Morton, this volume). In 1917, when the HCPS's funds ran low, it asked the Six Nations Council for support, given that it was supporting Six Nations people. The council emphatically refused. The HCPS threatened to cut off all support unless the council pitched in, but again it refused. A missionary on the reserve intervened, and the HCPS continued to provide support, but it had difficulty doing so without the council's support. This battle between the veterans and the hereditary council later evolved into a much larger argument and resulted in the creation of a new elected council in 1924.[79]

The patriotic work of the Six Nations women, alongside the enlistment of Six Nations men (and one woman), counteracted the Six Nations Council's refusal to support the war. With regard to those left in the community during the war, it was the SNWPL, not the Six Nations Council, that worked with the DIA to support Six Nations enlisted men. The SNWPL upheld the tradition of loyalty to and alliance with the British Crown during a time of war. It preserved the historic support of the British Empire despite the council's decision not to support the war or to consistently fund the league's war work at home.[80]

Gender played an important role in the Six Nations' patriotic responses to the war. The women's patriotic work combined aspects of traditional Iroquois women's work during wartime with aspects of white women's home-front work. However, this was the first time that Six Nations women worked with the Canadian government to give their men military support. The military shipped the women's goods to soldiers at the front, and the women worked through established military systems rather than through traditional ones. Six Nations women also circumnavigated their hereditary council and communicated with the DIA to try to get funding for their efforts. It was also the first time that Six Nations women worked with non-Aboriginal women and non-Aboriginal women's organizations, including the Red Cross and the Women's Patriotic League. Previously, they had not worked through churches, petitioned the council and the DIA for money, or even formally named their efforts, as they did with the SNWPL. After the war, women's organizations at Grand River were revitalized and women's participation in voluntary work increased. This was also likely the first time that Six Nations women had knit socks on such a large scale. While, as in the past, they still provided their men with clothing and food, the specific items were different and drew upon different types of skills. They no longer stitched moccasins or made corn bread for their warriors. And, possibly most important, the experiences that they gained in organizing, campaigning, letter-writing, and fundraising were put to further use during the next few decades, when women became increasingly involved in social reform, voluntary associations, and community improvement.[81]

Acknowledgments

This chapter has benefited from the thoughtful advice of several readers, including Cecilia Morgan, Denis McKim, Susana Miranda, Nathan Smith, and Cara Spittal. I am also grateful for comments from the presentation of this work at the Canadian Historical Association's 88th Annual Conference, Carleton University, Ottawa, 25-27 May 2009.

Notes

1 Margaret A. Brown, *My Lady of the Snows* (Toronto: William Briggs, 1908); John Moss, "Margaret A. Brown," in *A Reader's Guide to the Canadian Novel* (Toronto: McClelland and Stewart, 1981). Gilkison was daughter to the Indian agent at Six Nations. She had been adopted by the Cayuga into the Bear Clan in 1913 and was a prominent member of the Brant Historical Society. See Cecilia Morgan, "History, Nation, and Empire: Gender and Southern Ontario Historical Societies, 1890-1920s," *Canadian Historical Review* 82, 3 (2001): 491-528.

2 Mrs. M.A. Brown to Duncan Campbell Scott, 5 November 1914, "War 1914-1918 – Correspondence regarding funds awarded to the Six Nations Women's Patriotic League for knitting done for Indians overseas, 1914-1918," LAC, RG 10, vol. 1, file 452-5, pt. 1.

3 L. James Dempsey, *Warriors of the King: Prairie Indians in World War I* (Regina: Canadian Plains Research Centre, University of Regina, 1999); Fred Gaffen, *Forgotten Soldiers* (Penticton, BC: Theytus Books, 1985); Susan Applegate Krouse and Joseph Kossuth Dixon, *North American Indians in the Great War* (Lincoln, NB: University of Nebraska Press, 2007); P. Whitney Lackenbauer, R. Scott Sheffield, and Craig Leslie Mantle, eds., *Aboriginal Peoples and Military Participation: Canadian and International Perspectives* (Kingston: Canadian Defence Academy, 2007); P. Whitney Lackenbauer and Craig Leslie Mantle, eds., *Aboriginal Peoples and the Canadian Military: Historical Perspectives*. (Kingston: Canadian Defence Academy Press, 2007); John Moses, *A Sketch Account of Aboriginal Peoples in the Canadian Military* (Ottawa: Department of National Defence, 2004).

4 Katie Pickles, *Female Imperialism and National Identity: The Imperial Order Daughters of the Empire* (Manchester: Manchester University Press, 2002); Robert Rutherdale, "Gendered Fields," in *Hometown Horizons: Local Responses to Canada's Great War*, 192-223 (Vancouver: UBC Press, 2004); Joan Sangster, "Mobilizing Women for War," in

Canada and the First World War: Essays in Honour of Robert Craig Brown, ed. David Mackenzie, 157-93 (Toronto: University of Toronto Press, 2005); Pat Staton, *It Was Their War Too: Canadian Women and World War I* (Toronto: Green Dragon Press, 2006).

5 Keith Jamieson, *History of Six Nations Education* (Brantford: The Woodland Indian Cultural Educational Centre, 1987), 3.

6 Alan Taylor, "The Divided Ground: Upper Canada, New York, and the Iroquois Six Nations, 1783-1815," *Journal of the Early Republic* 22, 1 (2002): 555-75.

7 See Carl Benn, *The Iroquois in the War of 1812* (Toronto: University of Toronto Press, 1998).

8 Gail D. Danvers, "Gendered Encounters: Warriors, Women, and William Johnson," *Journal of American Studies* 35, 2 (2001): 196-97.

9 W.M. Beauchamp, "Iroquois Women," *Journal of American Folklore* 13, 49 (1900): 81-91; Judith K. Brown, "Economic Organization and the Position of Women among the Iroquois," *Ethnohistory* 17, 3 (1970): 151-67; Nancy Shoemaker, "The Rise or Fall of Iroquois Women," *Journal of Women's History* 2, 3 (1991): 39-57; Elizabeth Tooker, "Women in Iroquois Society," in *Extending the Rafters: Interdisciplinary Approaches to Iroquoian Studies*, ed. Jack Campisi, 109-23 (Albany: State University of New York Press, 1984).

10 Brown, "Economic Organization."

11 Beauchamp, "Iroquois Women," 82.

12 Benn, *Iroquois in the War of 1812*, 58.

13 J.N.B. Hewitt, "Status of Women in Iroquois Polity before 1784," in *Iroquois Women: An Anthology*, ed. W.G. Spittal, 53-70 (Ohsweken, Ontario: Iroqrafts, 1933); Ann Eastlack Shafer, "The Status of Iroquois Women," in *Iroquois Women: An Anthology*, ed. W.G. Spittal (Ohsweken, Ontario: Iroqrafts, 1941), 93.

14 Beauchamp, "Iroquois Women," 86.

15 Danvers, "Gendered Encounters," 197.

16 Government of Canada, *Annual Report of the Department of Indian Affairs for the Year Ended March 31 1915* (Ottawa: King's Printer, 1915), 32.

17 Alison Norman, "Race, Gender and Colonialism: Public Life among the Six Nations of Grand River, 1899-1939" (PhD diss., Ontario Institute for Studies in Education, University of Toronto, 2010).

18 Sally M. Weaver, "The Iroquois: The Grand River Reserve in the Late Nineteenth and Early Twentieth Centuries, 1875-1945," in *Aboriginal Ontario: Historical Perspectives on the First Nations*, ed. Edward S. Rogers and Donald B. Smith (Toronto: Dundurn Press, 1994), 219.

19 James E. Benincasa, "Cultural Divisions and the Politics of Control: The Canadian Removal of the Six Nations' Hereditary Council in 1924" (MA thesis, University of Western Ontario, 1994); John Moses, "History Debates the Issues: Political Change at the Grand River Reserve, 1917-1924," *CHA Bulletin* 32, 3 (2006): 11-14; S.R. Trevithick, "Conflicting Outlooks: The Background to the 1924 Deposing of the Six Nations Hereditary Council" (MA thesis, University of Calgary, 1998).

20 Duncan Campbell Scott, "The Canadian Indians and the Great World War," in *Canada and the Great World War* (Toronto: United Publishers of Canada, 1919), 301.

21 Ibid., 288.
22 Donald B. Smith, "Cameron Dee Brant," in *The Dictionary of Canadian Biography, 1911-1920*, Vol. 14 (Toronto: University of Toronto Press, 2000).
23 Mark Moss, *Manliness and Militarism: Educating Young Boys in Ontario for War* (Toronto: Oxford University Press, 2001), 3.
24 Scott, "Canadian Indians," 290.
25 James St. G. Walker, "Race and Recruitment in World War I: Enlistment of Visible Minorities in the Canadian Expeditionary Force," *Canadian Historical Review* 70, 1 (1989): 189.
26 Ibid. See also Duncan to Scott, 19 November 1915, "Enlistment of Indians for Overseas Service, WWI, 1914-1921," LAC, RG-24-C-1-a, vol. 1221, file HQ-593-1-7, pt. 1. Walker notes that a group of men from Cape Croker tried to enlist at four different recruitment centres but were turned down at all of them. See Walker, "Race and Recruitment."
27 Scott, "Canadian Indians," 302.
28 Brian E. Titley, *A Narrow Vision: Duncan Campbell Scott and the Administration of Indian Affairs in Canada* (Vancouver: UBC Press, 1986), 39, 44. See also Robin Brownlie, "Work Hard and Be Grateful: Native Soldier Settlers in Ontario after the First World War," in *On the Case: Explorations in Social History*, ed. Franca Iacovetta and Wendy Mitchinson, 181-203 (Toronto: University of Toronto Press, 1998).
29 "The Honor Roll," in Reville, *History of the County of Brant*, 618-20.
30 Walker, "Race and Recruitment."
31 J. Cowan, *The Maoris in the Great War: A History of the New Zealand Native Contingent and Pioneer Battalion, Gallipoli, 1915, France and Flanders, 1916-1918* (London: Naval and Military Press, 2004); David Huggonson, "Aborigines and the Aftermath of the Great War," *Australian Aboriginal Studies* 1 (1993): 2-9; Philippa Levine, "Battle Colors: Race, Sex, and Colonial Soldiery in World War I," *Journal of Women's History* 9 (1998): 104-31; Cecilia Morgan, "'A Wigwam to Westminster': Performing Mohawk Identity in Imperial Britain, 1890s-1990s," *Gender and History* 15, 2 (2003): 319-41; Richard Smith, *Jamaican Volunteers in the First World War: Race, Masculinity and the Development of National Consciousness* (Manchester: Manchester University Press, 2004); Angela Woollacott, "'Khaki Fever' and Its Control: Gender, Class, Age and Sexual Morality on the British Homefront in World War I," *Journal of Contemporary History* 29 (1994): 325-47; Angela Woollacott, *Gender and Empire* (New York: Palgrave Macmillan, 2006), 77; S.R. Worthy, "A Martial Race? Maori and Pakeha New Zealand Soldiers of the Great War in Imperial Context," paper presented at the British World Conference II, Calgary, 10-12 July 2003.
32 University Women's Club, "Edith Monture: Army Nurse, World War I" in *Significant Lives: Profiles of Brant County Women* (Brantford, ON: University Women's Club of Brantford, 1997), 87.
33 Aboriginal Nurses Association of Canada, *Twice as Good: A History of Aboriginal Nurses* (Ottawa: Aboriginal Nurses Association of Canada, 2007), 14.
34 Terri L. Monture Wicks, ed., *Charlotte Edith Anderson Monture: Diary of a War Nurse* (Ohsweken: privately printed, 1996), 31.
35 Ibid.

36 Andrew MacPhail, *Official History of the Canadian Forces in the Great War, 1914-19* (Ottawa: King's Printer, 1925), 228.
37 University Women's Club, "Edith Monture," 89; Karen C. Flynn, "Race, Class, and Gender: Black Nurses in Ontario, 1950-1980" (PhD diss., York University, 2003).
38 Aboriginal Nurses Association of Canada, *Twice as Good*.
39 Ibid., 19.
40 Florence Smith Hill, "Patriotic Work of the Six Nations in World Wars I and II," in *75th Anniversary of the Six Nations Agricultural Society* (Brantford, ON: n.p., 1943), 53.
41 The wives and other female family members of Native soldiers were not given the right to vote.
42 Wicks, *Diary of a War Nurse*, 4.
43 Erin Tully, "Women Veterans Honoured on the Territory," *Tekawennake*, 24 September 2008, 1-2.
44 Personal communication, John Moses, Canadian Museum of Civilization, 22 May 2009.
45 Scott, "Canadian Indians," 325.
46 Weaver, "The Iroquois," 182.
47 Pickles, *Female Imperialism*; Rutherdale, "Gendered Fields"; Sangster, "Mobilizing Women."
48 Mrs. M.A. Brown to Duncan Campbell Scott, 5 and 23 November 1914, "War 1914-1918 – Correspondence regarding funds awarded to the Six Nations Women's Patriotic League for knitting done for Indians overseas, 1914-1918," LAC, RG 10, vol. 6763, file 452-5, pt. 1.
49 See Celia Haig-Brown and David A. Nock, *With Good Intentions: Euro-Canadian and Aboriginal Relations in Colonial Canada* (Vancouver: UBC Press, 2006).
50 Hill was for enlistment and recruitment, and he supported Merritt's offer. See Amelia Garlow to Duncan Campbell Scott, 15 May 1915, "Knitting done for Indians overseas," LAC, RG 10, vol. 6763, file 452-5, pt. 1.
51 Hill, "Patriotic Work," 52-53.
52 Brown to Scott, 23 November, 1914, "Knitting Done for Indians Overseas" LAC, RG 10, vol. 6763, file 452-5, pt. 1.
53 Hill, "Patriotic Work."
54 Undated newspaper article [November 1914], "Knitting Done for Indians Overseas," LAC, RG 10, vol. 6763, file 452-5, pt. 1.
55 "Canadian Indians Are Doing Their Share: Giving Money and Knitting Warm Wear – Ready Even to Take the Field," *Globe and Mail*, 29 January 1915.
56 Rutherdale, *Hometown Horizons*, 107.
57 *Brantford Weekly Expositor*, 10 October 1921.
58 Asa R. Hill, "The Historical Position of the Six Nations," *Ontario Historical Society Papers and Records* 19 (1922): 103-09.
59 Hill, "Patriotic Work."
60 Sioux Indian Museum and Crafts Center, *Traditional Iroquois Clothing* (Rapid City, SD: Sioux Indian Museum and Crafts Center, 1987); Lee Friedlander, Daniel Newman, and New York State Historical Association, *Iroquois Crafts Sampler* (Coopertown, NY: New

York State Historical Association, 1970), slide; Carrie A. Lyford, *Iroquois Crafts*, Indian Handcrafts series (Lawrence, KA: Hakell Institute, 1945).

61 Woodland Indian Cultural and Educational Centre, *Patches: The Art of Quilt-Making on the Six Nations and New Credit Indian Reserves* (Brantford: Woodland Indian Cultural and Educational Centre, 1983), iv.

62 Ibid.

63 See Ruth B. Phillips, *Trading Identities: The Souvenir in Native North American Art from the Northeast, 1700-1900* (Montreal and Kingston: McGill-Queen's University Press, 1998); Ruth B. Phillips, "Nuns, Ladies, and the 'Queen of the Huron': Appropriating the Savage in Nineteenth-Century Huron Tourist Art," in *Unpacking Culture: Art and Commodity in Colonial and Postcolonial Worlds*, ed. Ruth B. Phillips and Christopher B. Steiner, 33-50 (Berkeley: University of California Press, 1999); Sherry Farrell Racette, "Beads, Silk and Quills: The Clothing and Decorative Arts of the Métis" in *Métis Legacy*, ed. Lawrence Barkwell, Leah Dorion, and Darren Prefontaine, 181-88 (Winnipeg: Pemmican Press and Gabriel Dumont Institute, 2001)

64 Scott, "Canadian Indians," 299.

65 Ibid., 325.

66 Reville, *History of the County of Brant*, 616.

67 Ibid.

68 John Clabran Moses, "The Return of the Native (Veteran): Six Nations Troops and Political Change at the Grand River Reserve, 1917-1924" (MA thesis, Carleton University, 2008), 87.

69 S.M. Weaver, "Smallpox or Chickenpox: An Iroquoian Community's Reaction to Crisis, 1901-1902," *Ethnohistory* 18, 4 (1971): 361-79.

70 Ibid.

71 Evelyn Davis to Mrs. Brown, 29 March 1915, "Knitting Done for Indians Overseas," LAC, RG 10, vol. 6763, file 452-5, pt. 1.

72 Amelia Garlow to Duncan Campbell Scott, 15 May 1915, "Knitting Done for Indians Overseas," LAC, RG 10, vol. 6763, file 452-5, pt. 1.

73 Duncan Campbell Scott to Amelia Garlow, 22 May 1915, "Knitting Done for Indians Overseas," LAC, RG 10, vol. 6763, file 525-5, pt. 1.

74 See also Maureen K. Lux, *Medicine That Walks: Disease, Medicine and Canadian Plains Native People, 1880-1940* (Toronto: University of Toronto Press, 2001).

75 Elliott Moses, "The Six Nations Dehorners Association, Finally Called the Six Nations Rights Association," 1973, p. 6, in Canadian Museum of Civilization, Sally Weaver Collection.

76 Moses, "Return of the Native." As the hereditary council never received a request for military help from the British Crown, it was determined to maintain a neutral position on the war. Despite this stance, hundreds of men enlisted. Moses and others argue that this stance further angered young men who believed the hereditary council did not represent them and, in part, led to the establishment of the new elected council in 1924, which included several veterans as councillors.

77 Copy of Original Petition, France, 8 August 1917, "Petitions 1862-1919 from Six Nations to the Federal Government – Political Reports," Canadian Museum of Civilization, Sally Weaver Collection, file 1, box 468, acc. 89/55.
78 1919 Petition, LAC, Six Nations Agency Archives, file 21; "Petitions 1862-1919 from Six Nations to the Federal Government – Political Reports," Canadian Museum of Civilization, Sally Weaver Collection, file 1, box 468, acc. 89/55.
79 Moses, "History Debates the Issues."
80 Government of Canada, *Dominion of Canada Annual Report of the Department of Indian Affairs for the Year Ended March 31 1916* (Ottawa: King's Printer, 1916); Government of Canada, *"The War": Annual Report of the Department of Indian Affairs for the Year Ended March 31 1917* (Ottawa: King's Printer, 1917).
81 Norman, "Race."

The Unquiet Knitters of Newfoundland
From Mothers of the Regiment to Mothers of the Nation

Margot I. Duley

The Great War, the first conflict to mobilize civilians on a mass scale, profoundly altered Newfoundland society. Among Newfoundland women, the war set in motion a heightened sense of the importance of their traditional roles, leading to a successful suffrage movement and a general postwar upsurge of women's leadership and activism in community organizations. Newfoundland women began as hard-working supporters of their menfolk at war; many ended by asserting expanded roles for themselves in community and public life, including full citizenship. New women's organizations proliferated in the 1920s, becoming a significant part of Newfoundland's civil society. The war also highlighted the economic value of women's craft work. However, the primarily maternalist ideology of the activists set limits on the ultimate degree of change in women's roles. The economic challenges of the Great Depression of the 1930s and the suspension of democracy under the Commission of Government also acted as a brake on radical change. Nonetheless, the First World War altered Newfoundland society in a multitude of ways, including through the emergence of gendered activism.

Few communities remained untouched by the war. Thirty-six percent of the men of Newfoundland and Labrador between the ages of nineteen and thirty-five served in some way, roughly half (6,241) with the Royal Newfoundland Regiment.[1] Many Newfoundland women thus had an intense personal interest in the conflict, and this helps to explain the degree to which the Women's Patriotic Association (WPA), formed to support the war effort, permeated

Newfoundland society organizationally. WPA leaders were to be key to the postwar proliferation of women's civic organizations, including the suffrage movement.

The total casualty rate for all sides in the Great War was enormous, standing to this day as a rebuke to nationalist folly and military miscalculation. Some 8,300,000 combatants and another 8,000,000 civilians died, not counting related deaths from influenza. A further 19,536,000 combatants suffered wounds; 36 percent were maimed for life.[2] The carnage that was to come was not obvious at the beginning.

At the optimistic outset, worried but proud women waved eager recruits goodbye from wharves and train stations in support of the proclaimed mission of saving civilization from the "barbarous Hun" and serving King, Country, God, and Empire. As part of "Britain's Oldest Colony" many Newfoundlanders felt impelled to do their part. Soon families anxiously read the weekly Casualty Reports printed in newspapers or, fearing the worst, rushed to post office windows or the chalk boards of telegraph offices to scan the latest lists of dead, wounded, or missing. It was increasingly clear that the war would not be "over in a year" as the British war planners had predicted. In 1917, the Newfoundland Regiment received the designation "Royal" in recognition of its numbing casualty rate as well as its persistent heroism in key engagements. To follow the path of the regiment is to follow the progress of the war itself in Gallipoli, the Somme, Flanders, and the Final Offensive. It was the only regiment to earn the title "Royal" while the war was in progress.[3] The tragedies and bravery of the regiment influenced Newfoundland's sense of itself on an international stage and contributed to an atmosphere of mingled mourning and national pride in the postwar period.[4]

The many dead and wounded included a generation of young Newfoundland men. The casualty rate of the all-citizen Newfoundland Regiment was among the highest of any country, with 37 percent wounded and another 21 percent killed. The regiment's death rate was over twice that of the Canadian Expeditionary Force or the British Empire as a whole, and it exceeded that of France, Germany, the Russian Empire, Austria-Hungary, and the Ottoman Empire.[5] Newfoundlanders were also killed or injured in the dispersed service of the Royal Navy, the mercantile marine, and other allied forces. There was an incalculable loss of Newfoundland leadership and a calculable loss of finances. As Newfoundland entered the Great Depression, $38 million of its entire debt of $50 million stemmed from its contributions to the war effort. Some argue that these losses set the stage for bankruptcy, the imposition of the appointed Commission of Government in 1934, and, ultimately, the confederation of the small Dominion with Canada in 1949.[6]

The intensity and depth of Newfoundland's involvement in the Great War, compared with some other areas of Canada, such as the Six Nations Grand River Reserve (see Norman, this volume), helps to explain the very different outcomes for women in two culturally and historically distinct settings, though in both cases women formed patriotic associations.

While the First World War stimulated a change in Newfoundland women's conceptions of the public importance of their work, it remained almost entirely "traditional." Overwhelmingly, women in the outports were employed, as they had been for decades, as shore workers, drying fish in the household-based fishing industry, working in domestic agriculture, and preserving family income by spinning, knitting, sewing, and food preservation. In towns, middle- and upper middle-class married women continued running their households. Their unmarried daughters, if employed at all, had modest opportunities available in teaching, nursing, offices, and shops.

The great wartime exception to traditional women's work was the overseas service of graduate nurses and Voluntary Aid Detachment (VAD) workers. Terry Bishop Stirling (this volume) estimates that at least eighteen Newfoundland nurses and forty-two VADs went overseas.[7] While women in Great Britain entered new fields of industrial, agricultural, and office employment during the First World War, this was only very modestly the case in Newfoundland and was restricted primarily to St. John's. Here there were small increases in female employment as women became munitions and textile factory workers as well as telegraph and office workers.[8] Most women remained homemakers and continued their long-standing community fundraising for a host of causes. Now, with the onset of war, this included support for the Newfoundland Regiment and allied patriotic causes.[9]

One important strand of the argument for enhanced equality for women that emerged in Great Britain and North America during the war was that they had "proven themselves" as capable as men in the male sphere.[10] While Newfoundland suffragists lauded the stamina and courage shown by the nurses and VADs, these inspiring examples did not usually transmit into equal rights arguments. Leaders were aware of more radical developments elsewhere, and they sometimes cited literature provided by international contacts from more urbanized settings.[11] However, the argument that the postwar women's movement found most effective was that the traditional work of homemakers – the "distaff work" that predominated during the war – was as valuable as the work of men and deserved to be affirmed and extended into the public sphere. The WPA named its official publication *The Distaff*, literally a staff around which flax or wool is wound in spinning but the broader meaning of which is the female branch of a family, or women's work, authority, or domain.[12] It was a telling choice of title.

To understand the nature and influence of the Great War on Newfoundland women, it is first necessary to examine the nascent women's movement before the war and then to explore the work of the WPA as well as the interconnected wartime prohibition and national health campaigns directed at women.[13] In this way, it is possible to assess both continuity and change.

In Newfoundland, as elsewhere in Western society, works of Christian charity had traditionally been considered an appropriate form of women's community involvement, resonating well with ideas of nurturance appropriate to women's sphere. Ladies auxiliaries were a common feature of churches, charities, and fraternal organizations. Almost without exception, these auxiliaries functioned under the aegis of overall male leadership. Women's work in church and charity rarely received much recognition. An exasperated Armine Gosling, who became a leader of the WPA and subsequently the Women's Franchise League, questioned the status of women who loyally supported institutions that relegated them to "outer darkness" in the formulation of policy: "But isn't this always the way with the Powers that be, both mundane and ecclesiastical, where women are concerned?"[14]

Two prewar women's organizations stand out as exceptions for their autonomy and assertiveness, namely, the Woman's Christian Temperance Union (WCTU) and the Ladies Reading Room. In 1891, WCTU members marched through the streets of St. John's demanding that women be included in votes for prohibition. Their campaign failed, with opponents arguing that votes for women would upset the divine order of male leadership and that women would neglect their homes. Unable to counteract these prejudices or to forge strong links across Protestant-Catholic divides, the WCTU then directed its energy towards more conventional good works. The locus of advanced views shifted to the "Ladies Reading Room," established in 1909, when a male debating club banned some women after they expressed their opinions.[15] Both the WCTU and the Ladies Reading Room activists provided leadership to the WPA.

Three other pre-existing organizations – the Cowan Mission, the Alexandra Workers, and the Imperial Order Daughters of the Empire (IODE) – also contributed leadership. All combined patriotism with medical interests and joined the WPA with public policy and organizational expertise in the medical arena. The Cowan Mission celebrated Queen Victoria's Diamond Jubilee (1897) by sponsoring the construction of a new wing of the General Hospital; the Alexandra Workers used the occasion of Edward VII's accession to the throne (1902) to advance the cause of a home for the aged; and the IODE, formed in 1910, lobbied for better municipal sanitation and tuberculosis treatment.[16]

In short, there were pre-existing women's groups, centred in St. John's, that had a growing body of organizational experience and varying degrees of gendered self-consciousness. The work of the WPA and a revival of the temperance movement during the war proved to have a galvanizing effect. The war stimulated a heightened awareness of the importance of women's roles and their exclusion from the body politic, leading to demands for an expanded sphere of influence.

Walter Davidson, governor of Newfoundland, and his spouse Margaret did not have a gendered social movement in mind when they launched the WPA as an affiliate of the Queen Mary's Needlework Guild (QMNG). Within hours of Prime Minister Asquith's war address to the British House of Commons on 7 August 1914, the governor received a copy of Asquith's speech via urgent cable. Davidson had his marching orders as Asquith had pledged that "all the resources of the Empire should be thrown into the scale" to win the war.[17] The first war of civilian mass mobilization had begun.

Less than a week after the formal declaration of hostilities, Queen Mary issued an appeal to the "Women of the Empire," announcing the formation of the QMNG. She urged all patriotic women to do their part to win the war.[18] In the words of British novelist John Galsworthy, the guild's publicist, it would be a "sisterhood of service" uniting "women of all ranks and ages" in the Mother Country and the Empire.[19] The Queen took the lead as patroness and exemplar, receiving daily reports of work done and regularly visiting the London headquarters without court ceremony but with maximum publicity.[20] The Newfoundland WPA was to function under similar, well-publicized vice-regal patronage.

The rapidity with which the QMNG was announced, and its immediate integration into the imperial war machine, suggests a high degree of advance calculation and planning. The composition of the Governing Council ensured coordination with the Cabinet and included, among others, Viscountess (Mary) Harcourt (wife of the secretary of state for the colonies), as well as Margot Asquith (wife of the British prime minister). Baroness (Mary) Northcliffe provided friendly press access to the *Daily Mail*, which was owned by her husband.

Governor Davidson seized upon the idea for a women's war auxiliary, seeing it as a solution to some of his many mobilization problems. With support from Prime Minister Edward Morris, he had already created the all-male Patriotic Association and, with it, a commitment for a volunteer regiment. However, it became obvious that, because equipment and ordinance stores in England had nothing to spare,[21] supplying it with uniforms and other items of clothing was going to be a major problem. Furthermore, Davidson realized that war costs would go far beyond salaries, uniforms, and equipment to include auxiliary medical and social services and a "dozen kindred subjects." He had wanted to broach these issues at a meeting of the Patriotic Association on 20 August 1914 but the "atmosphere of depression partly from news of war in Belgium and partly owing to financial depression both of the Government and Water Street" was so great he remained silent.[22] A women's patriotic association could provide essential assistance.

One week later, Lady Davidson held a preliminary meeting of women to "organize and coordinate work for men at the front."[23] The plan was publicly launched on 31 August at an enthusiastic meeting of seven hundred women at the British Hall in St. John's. The object of the WPA was to use "all means in [its] power to help [its] men in the defense of the British Empire."[24] Its mission was a broad one, and, though the provision of comforts was a major focus, it was by no means its only goal. The men's association proved unable to forge the same breadth of island-wide networks as the women's, leading the government to rely on the WPA to help disseminate information, raise money, produce clothing and medical supplies, and establish and operate certain medical facilities at home.[25]

Following the organizational plan of the QMNG, Lady Davidson headed the WPA's executive. She was more than a figurehead. Though Margaret Davidson took pains to stress her traditional housewifely accomplishments, such as knitting her two young daughters' dresses and trimming their hats, she was also an apt and effective public orator and a skilled organizer and motivator. She was born and bred to assume a supportive and complementary role to a male member of the British ruling elite. Her father, General Sir Percy Feilding, had served in the Crimean War; her mother, Lady Louisa, was the daughter of the Marquis of Bath; and her great aunt (Louisa Jane), the Duchess of Buccleuch, had been an intimate of Queen Victoria.[26] Lady Davidson had her own connections to the QMNG and the Victoria League, another pro-imperial women's society in London, and received information about women's patriotic work in advance of her husband's official channels.[27]

Walter Davidson was fortunate in having Margaret Feilding as his wife. Before arriving in Newfoundland, he had been governor of the Seychelles, a remote colony in the Indian Ocean. Newfoundland was a step up the imperial service ladder, and an ambitious Davidson was determined to deliver. A practical, no-nonsense administrator, Davidson was part of the "muscular Christianity" school of colonial rule. His handicaps included gruffness, poor public speaking skills, and social awkwardness.[28] Margaret Davidson remedied all these deficiencies, playing an important role in his success as governor. She would later be awarded the title Dame of the British Empire, and he became lieutenant-governor of New South Wales. Margaret Davidson was also a woman of personal charm who had sympathy for the less fortunate. Upon realizing that the Government House gardener was terminally ill with consumption, she took over the gardening herself so that he could continue on full pension.[29] This sort of personal involvement endeared her as the leader of the WPA.

Under Lady Davidson's influence, Government House was thrown open to WPA volunteers (see Figure 3). It became St. John's most elegant sweatshop. Each weekday afternoon, some 250 women occupied the Ballroom and Drawing Room in "Work Parties," cutting, sewing, and knitting; the basement became a supply depot, dispensing supplies to city and outport branches; and the Cutting Committee commandeered the Billiard Room to produce pieces for complicated items of clothing. Other rooms were occupied by an examining committee that exercised quality control; an alterations committee that rectified mistakes; and a packing and shipping committee that dispatched finished products to London. Lady Davidson was in constant attendance, encouraging the workers, and she used the new medium of political propaganda – photography – to great effect. Pictures of women patriots hard at work at Government House, under the benign patronage of the Queen's representative, were widely reproduced in contemporary publications. Upon the arrival of Governor Harris in 1917, WPA headquarters moved to a private residence, Sutherland Place, and Government House reverted to its usual social exclusivity.[30]

FIGURE 3   By 1915, WPA workers had turned the Billiard Room at Government House into a cutting room for clothing. [The Rooms Provincial Archives Division, A 51-110]

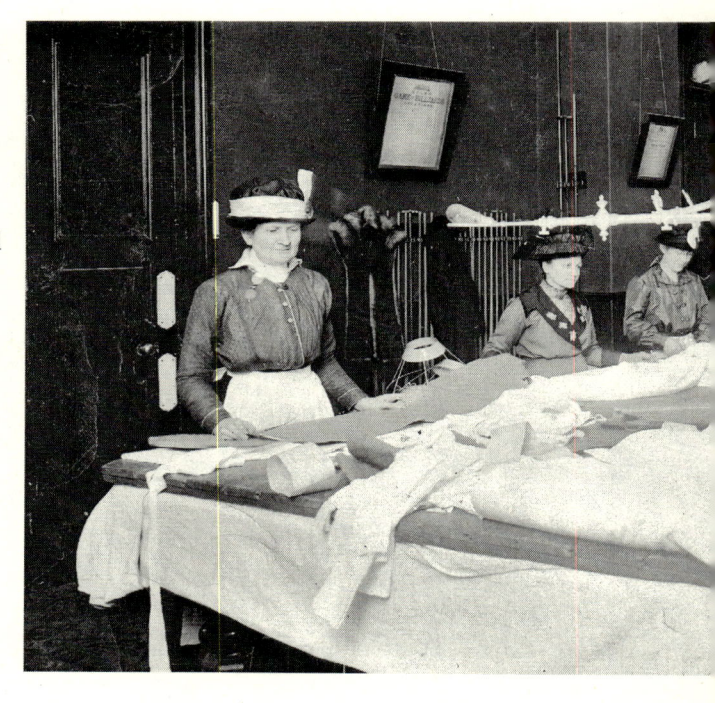

As was the case with the QMNG, the WPA Executive consisted of wives of Newfoundland's political elite, including Lady Isabella Morris, wife of the prime minister. Executive membership was carefully balanced to reflect Newfoundland's fractious religious constituencies, and it included Julia Horwood, wife of the chief justice and long active in Church of England women's organizations; Gertrude Cashin, wife of Michael Cashin, a prominent Roman Catholic politician and minister of finance; and Eleanora Macpherson, a Methodist who was a trained nurse and the wife of Dr. Cluny Macpherson, the chief medical officer of the Newfoundland Regiment and the inventor of the gas mask. As in London, much of the day-to-day administration fell to an honorary secretary. Armine Gosling, wife of the St. John's mayor, held that position for the last two years of the war. Gosling and other women with advanced views were in touch with the British Dominions Woman Suffrage Union and followed its advice to use women's war work as an argument for suffrage. Gosling published a lengthy article with this theme in *The Distaff*.[31] Subsequently, she drew upon her widespread outport WPA contacts when, in 1920, she headed the newly formed Newfoundland Women's Franchise League.

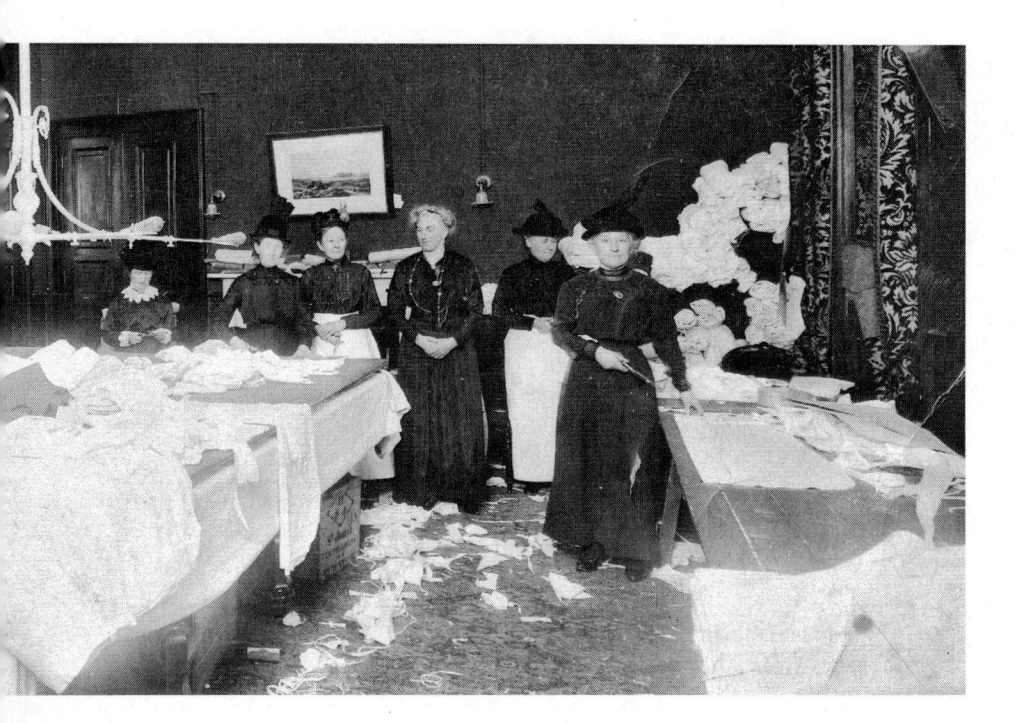

Larger outport branches of the WPA formed structures similar to those in St. John's, with women of social prominence, usually the wife of a merchant or minister or sometimes a female teacher, serving as president. The initial organizing circular, sent under Lady Davidson's signature, went to magistrates and justices of the peace asking them to convene a meeting of "prominent ladies."[32] However, the WPA attracted women of all social classes into its ranks as workers.

The name "Queen Mary's Needlework Guild" evokes images of church bazaars and gentle ladies bountiful. It conceals as much as it reveals. The term "comforts," reverberating with echoes of womanly care and used to describe the work of the QMNG, merits closer scrutiny. Poetry and prose written at the time in Newfoundland certainly evoked a patriotic, domestic, supportive image.[33] Consider, for example, the gendered sentimentality of Eunice Holbrook Ruell's "The Queen Mary's Needlework Guild":

> The Queen has need of the women
> Her arms are opened wide,

The Unquiet Knitters of Newfoundland   59

> To shelter and clothe the homeless,
> And bind up the wounded side.

It continues:

> Let us sew it, weave it, knit it,
> In stitches of silken sheen –
> Our love for Mary of England
> Wife and Mother and Queen.

The women's craftwork valorized by Ruell included the legendary knitted socks for which the Newfoundland WPA received accolades. It was claimed, likely with hyperbole, that these socks set the Empire standard.[34] Yet the "comforts" produced in Newfoundland, as elsewhere, went far beyond socks.

The QMNG in London received supplies from branches all over the globe, variously specializing in over twenty-seven items made to exacting military specifications, including belts, hats, sweaters, shirts, mittens, gloves, underwear, and, more ominously as the war raged on, operation gowns, surgeons' coats, surgical dressings of many types, blankets, sheets, pillows and pillowcases, bed jackets, pajamas, and shrouds. At the onset of gas warfare, before mechanized production could be set up, English QMNG members cut 100,000 eye pieces for gas masks by hand in one day. When submarine warfare interrupted the European supply route for troops in Mesopotamia, East Africa, and Palestine, supply lines were switched from London to QMNG branches in India, Ceylon, and Japan.[35] Within Great Britain itself, the output of the 430 QMNG branches raised fears of creating industrial unemployment among women factory workers.

The QMNG functioned as a dispersed, worldwide assembly line that augmented manufacturing output to a significant degree. The QMNG had about 680 branches, including those in the self-governing dominions, India, Ceylon, Jamaica, the African Gold Coast, British Guinea, and most other colonies. A US affiliate, the British American War Relief Fund, operated for two years before the United States entered the conflict. An early example of the importance of Newfoundland's place in this network may be seen in October 1914, when the War Office issued an appeal to "the women of the Empire" to supply 300,000 pairs of socks. Grand Falls and Bay Roberts won the Newfoundland prizes for the immediacy and size of their response.[36]

In comparative terms, Newfoundland women's supportive patriotic work in providing comforts greatly exceeded Empire-wide norms, and this degree of mobilization was important in the upsurge of postwar activism. The WPA had an island-wide reach, and it extended into Labrador. A 1916 report cited 208 branches and fifteen thousand members.[37] The WPA's supply ledgers suggest that the eventual branch total was closer to 250.[38] The number of affected communities was even larger because smaller outports affiliated with neighbouring ones. For example, Flat Island, Bonavista Bay, had members in the even smaller Coward's Island. The WPA encompassed not only the capital of St. John's, with its seventeen branches and three Red Cross affiliates, but also virtually all of the larger outports (like Burin, Twillingate, and Carbonear), the newer industrial and mining towns (like Grand Falls and Wabana), and many isolated outports, like Oderin, Placentia Bay, Pinchard's Island, Bonavista Bay, and Pools Cove, Fortune Bay) as well as the mission station at Battle Harbour, Labrador. The QMNG in Great Britain, with its far easier modes of internal communication and transportation, and vastly greater population (by a ratio of 186:1), had 430 branches. By way of further comparison, the men's Patriotic Association in Newfoundland never exceeded sixty branches.[39] The extent of Newfoundland women's war work was remarkable.

Women focused their organizational and homemaking skills in an outburst of fundraising and comfort production. This required more than a commitment of time with needles, wool, and thread. It also required persistent and varied fundraising to purchase supplies. This included staging concerts, plays, teas, bazaars, and raffles as well as selling patriotic calendars, souvenir regimental badges, and soon, sadly, artificial forget-me-nots. Activities ranged from the humble raffle of potatoes in White Rock, Trinity Bay, to grand performances of the Ladies Orchestra in St. John's. Comfort production could involve financial sacrifice. In many outport households, sheep's wool was normally sheared, spun, and knitted into family clothing or sold to the Newfoundland Knitting Mills in St. John's for much needed income.[40]

Though the grey Newfoundland sock became emblematic of women's war efforts, as was the case elsewhere the range of items the Newfoundland WPA and its medical affiliates supplied was far more extensive, including mitts, scarves, mufflers, and shirts as well as medical necessities such as pajamas, pillows, cases, bandages, and sphagnum moss (used to dress wounds).[41] Red Cross branches specialized in the production of sterilized surgical dressings, sending

115,000 to the QMNG alone. As for socks, the WPA sent at least thirty thousand pairs to the QMNG.

The sock was more than a "comfort": it was a military necessity. The War Office's Field Service Regulations included instructions on care of the feet.[42] Soldiers were incapacitated by frostbitten feet and by trench, or immersion, foot. While frostbite is caused by prolonged exposure to low temperatures, trench foot can occur in waterlogged and unsanitary conditions at temperatures as high as sixteen degrees Celsius. Blistered or sore feet from ill-fitting boots and socks were especially vulnerable. "Trench feet" could swell to several times their normal size and become gangrenous. Dry socks were essential. In wet conditions, the army recommended applying Vaseline or another grease, such as whale oil; however, in the absence of sterile conditions, this likely led to increased infection. The ill-fated attempt of the British Expeditionary Force to land on the beaches at Gallipoli to open up a Turkish front exposed the Newfoundland Regiment to conditions in which frostbite and trench foot were inevitable.

The sacrifices of Australian and New Zealand troops in the Gallipoli theatre of war are well known. Less remembered is the fact that the Newfoundland Regiment served in the same theatre from September 1915 until January 1916 and was among the last to be evacuated. The soldiers faced terrible conditions. Sent into battle clothed only in light summer kit, they had to contend with a ferocious winter that burst upon them in November. Three weeks of gales were accompanied first by torrential rains and electrical storms and then by sleet and ice. Trenches washed away, and freezing men without dry boots and socks resorted to standing in sandbags filled with straw. Over 150 were evacuated with frostbite and trench foot, and forty-three died of disease or wounds.[43] A worse fate was to await the Newfoundland Regiment on the Western Front from 1916 to 1918 in the rain-soaked, freezing, and muddy trenches of the Somme, where rats gorged on the dead.

An unusually candid letter from Private Frank "Mayo" Lind slipped by the censors and described the grim conditions of "rotten cold dampness for days and days" at Gallipoli. His distraught father sent the letter to the newspapers:

> I hope I am not complaining but I am sure I voice the sentiments of every man in the regiment when I tell you that we feel disgusted on looking through the St. John's papers and read about so many thousand pairs of socks, thousands of underclothing, etc., being knitted for our boys at the front. The question

somebody asks each day is: "Where does it all go to?" for men in the Regiment are cold and wretched standing sentry at nights with perhaps one thin shirt under their tunic.[44]

A storm of controversy ensued, some of it directed at the WPA. There were angry demands to know where the comforts had gone and dire suspicions that Newfoundland's own were being neglected in favour of others. Letters from grateful soldiers from other regiments unwittingly reinforced these fears. For example, a young corporal, Reni Boiteux of the Third Division of the Belgian army, wrote a surprised Miss Ploughman of Port Rexton, who had tucked a note into a sock: "Your socks came at a good time as I really needed them. They have already made the acquaintance of the Germans for I am in a little place 30 metres from them. I put them on tonight and they fit me very well."[45]

The most stringent criticisms came from the *Mail and Advocate*, aligned with the Fishermen's Protective Union (FPU) headed by William Coaker, and, for a time, the WPA risked splitting along class lines. The FPU had formed in 1908 to break the grip that merchant houses had on the Newfoundland fish trade. The terms on which fishers sold their catch and, in turn, received necessities were widely perceived as unfair. The WPA leadership contained members of the same merchant families whose economic power was being contested by the FPU. The *Mail and Advocate* asked: "Why are our Noble Boys left to suffer cold?" It accused the WPA of inexperience, hinted at deception in the WPA's disbursement of public funds and in-kind contributions, and printed a letter that assumed that the "well connected" committee in St. John's simply sent supplies wherever it wanted. Adeline Browning, head of the "Vigornia" Red Cross Branch, made matters worse by writing an angry, defensive rejoinder that regimental supplies were fine and that Private Lind's letter was "peevish, jealous [and] unmanly."[46] Other members were not so sure that the allegations of missing clothing could be so easily dismissed, and the governor requested that an inquiry be conducted by the colonial secretary. It was indeed true that the Gallipoli landing had fatal organizational flaws, including insufficient supply lines, but these originated at the Cabinet level and could scarcely be attributed to the WPA.[47]

The Newfoundland Regiment subsequently redeployed to the Western Front, and the supply controversy subsided as soldiers' letters began to testify that it was now well equipped with clothing. Private Lind confirmed the change: in April 1916 he wrote from "somewhere in France" that "the Newfoundland sock is the best in the world and is prized by every soldier" and that other regiments offered Newfoundland soldiers money to acquire them. Tragically, on 1 July 1916, Frank Lind was to die with many of his fellow soldiers at the Battle of Beaumont-Hamel.[48] In the wake of this catastrophe, Lieutenant Joseph Snow, home on leave, addressed a public meeting and put logistical issues in context. He "hoped that none of [the] good ladies would cease their endeavours" because some of the supplies they sent were used by other regiments. He explained that supplies went to ordinance and that: "when our boys are short they draw upon Ordinance and when the goods arrive from Newfoundland they are put back to replace that which has been given to our men."[49]

Tryphena Duley, a WPA activist with two enlisted sons, one of whom was to be killed within weeks of the Armistice, also refocused the supply controversy by using it as the inspiration for a WPA romance, *A Pair of Grey Socks,* issued in pamphlet form. The staunchly Congregationalist, upper middle-class author tellingly chose a Roman Catholic outport girl as the heroine. Mary of Sweet Apple Cove tucks an inscribed photograph of herself into a sock:

> I've knitted these socks for you, just you,
> And I've prayed that God might keep you true,
> And make you brave right through and through
> In danger's hour.

The socks find their way to Bob, an Irish soldier, who is inspired by the message to endure the hardship that surrounds him. After the war, he immigrates to Newfoundland and marries Mary. The story attempts to turn fears about comforts going elsewhere into a marital advantage.[50] This WPA counter-narrative, patriotic poetry by women, and, especially, grateful letters from Newfoundland soldiers when the comforts eventually arrived helped to turn the tide of opinion.

WPA members kept working. By the end of the war, Newfoundland's overall contributions to the QMNG Depot far exceeded its proportion of the population of the Empire. Specifically, existing QMNG records credit the Newfoundland WPA with over 159,000 items. Newfoundland's contributions were at least three times greater than its share of the population. One thousand four hundred and twenty-two Newfoundlanders, including some children, qualified for the QMNG Badge, which was given to the most productive workers.[51]

The pre-existing interest in medical issues and facilities among IODE, Cowan Mission, and Alexandra workers intensified during the war. As Terry Bishop Stirling notes, the Red Cross Branch of the WPA recruited VADs. The provision of medical facilities in Newfoundland for discharged servicemen became another major project of female activists who were horrified that the cash-strapped Newfoundland government had discharged soldiers and sailors with unhealed wounds to fend for themselves. The outcry led to the foundation of the Navy and Military Convalescent Hospital at Waterford Hall. A sixteen-member board of control, consisting of nine men and seven women representing the WPA and the Alexandra Workers, oversaw the thirty-six-bed facility, housed in a residence donated by Sir Edgar Bowring.[52] However, when postwar normalcy returned, the women were edged out of policy making and told that they should form a ladies visiting committee.[53] This simply deepened their determination to enter public spheres of influence. A similar power struggle occurred in the tuberculosis treatment centre established by Adeline Browning.

Soldiers had also returned with active tuberculosis. To raise funds, Adeline Browning arranged for a lecture tour by Private Philip Jensen, the first Newfoundland military volunteer. The result was the "Jensen Camp," a TB treatment centre that functioned from 1916 to 1921.[54] Here too, when the war ended, there was a determined effort on the part of the Military Hospitals Commission to end the influence of the female founder, who was accused of not "falling into Line."[55] Browning was to become a founding member of the Franchise League of Newfoundland, and she became its London representative to the International Woman Suffrage Alliance.

WPA members also raised considerable sums of money for special medical causes, including hospital cots overseas, the education and retraining of those blinded in battle, the Khaki Guild for disabled soldiers and sailors, the Edith Cavell Homes for exhausted and sick nurses, and the Blue Cross fund for sick and wounded animals at the front. At home, members also entertained troops at the Soldiers and Sailors Club at the George V Institute in St. John's as well as in the Caribou Hut, a canteen at regimental headquarters. In all, the WPA probably raised close to $500,000 in cash, supplies, and auxiliary services.[56]

Despite the flurry of criticism that the WPA endured in 1916, its work remained broadly popular. During the contentious conscription debates of 1917-18 Governor Harris and the pro-imperial *Daily News* directed special appeals to women to urge men to enlist, but these were unpopular, especially in outports.[57]

There is no record that the WPA as an entity issued enlistment appeals. By then, many members of the WPA had lost loved ones in the bloodied ground of Gallipoli and the Somme. Hopes of a rapid and glorious victory had evaporated, and the extraordinarily high Newfoundland casualty rate had brought mourning to many families and serious disabilities to others.[58]

The reach of the WPA reflects the intense personal stake that so many members had in the well-being of the Newfoundland Regiment. War planners saw the WPA as an auxiliary production unit and propaganda tool. Women saw themselves differently. They were mothers, wives, fiancées, sisters, aunts, cousins, and friends of the soldiers and sailors at risk. With few alternate means of support, the personal and economic stakes of the war were especially high for dependent women. Thirty-four percent of the officers of the Royal Newfoundland Regiment listed mothers or spouses as next of kin, and this was likely true of privates and non-commissioned officers as well.[59]

The work and sacrifices of the women of the war generation received widespread public praise. Thirty-eight WPA members, including outport women, received imperial honours – namely, Commander of the British Empire, Order of the British Empire, or Member of the British Empire – from the hands of Governor Harris at public ceremonies during an island-wide tour. The traditional "thanks to the ladies" had never been quite so elaborate.[60] Women's long-standing domestic labour and community voluntarism, now turned to a national and patriotic cause, received widespread public recognition in the press and in political speeches.

Though the WPA was the chief vehicle of female involvement in the war effort, there was also an upsurge of temperance and health education activism that contributed to a heightened self-awareness among women of the importance of their maternal roles and their claims to full citizenship. The temperance movement of the 1890s, which included votes for women, had failed.[61] Now the patriotism of the era helped to popularize both temperance and an associated health education movement.

Recruitment drives revealed that substantial numbers of men were medically unfit. This highlighted the long-neglected issue of rural and working-class health, framed in public discourse as the need for physically stronger bodies for a militarily stronger nation. Prohibitionists presented their case as a wartime public health measure, saying alcohol undermined military efficiency, and they attempted to mobilize women by stressing that it was their patriotic duty to rear robust, abstaining citizens. One WCTU officer asserted that alcohol was so addictive that "khaki-clad figures" faced dangers in the tavern to equal those on the front. Patriotic arguments were fused with the traditional gendered appeal that alcohol led to male unemployment, poverty, domestic violence, and the ruin of families, with women especially vulnerable to its negative effects.[62] In this heated atmosphere, prohibition arguments began to gain ascendancy.

On 23 April 1915, for the second time in Newfoundland history, women marched in St. John's in support of prohibition. A reinvigorated WCTU turned out one thousand women. Anna Pippy, evangelistic superintendent of the Newfoundland branch, subsequently embarked upon a six-week tour of major settlements, together with Mrs. Howland,[63] an organizer sent from Boston by the World WCTU. The focus of their campaign was to gain a favourable vote on a forthcoming plebiscite to prohibit the importation, manufacture, and sale of alcohol.

Early autumn saw a second organizing drive in over twenty communities led by Dr. Carolyn Geisel, a medical graduate of the University of Michigan, a World WCTU lecturer, and, reportedly, the highest-paid speaker on the Chautauqua lecture circuit in the United States.[64] Her chief sponsors were a public-minded industrialist, Harry Crowe; a group of St. John's women closely associated with the WPA; and the Newfoundland WCTU. Newspapers described her lectures as spellbinding.[65] Mixing humour and homespun tales, Geisel presented preventative health, good diets, and temperance as a quasi-religious, military crusade, arguing the body was the temple of the Holy Spirit and that a nation of weaklings could not win a war.[66] Geisel's organizing included forming women's health clubs. Her message was: "the Betterment of the Race devolved upon women and it was up to them to raise better children, great sturdy strong men and women not weaklings."[67] Though she delivered a conservative message that reinforced traditional sex roles, she nonetheless stressed the importance of women's domestic sphere, arguing that it deserved a higher status.

The wartime temperance campaign radicalized women frustrated by the indignity of having to plead with men to vote for prohibition. Activism was not restricted to St. John's. Alice Barbour electrified a temperance rally in Newtown, Bonavista Bay, where her husband was a merchant, by a recitation of her own composition entitled "Why We Should Vote."[68] The prohibition plebiscite passed narrowly with an all-male voters list. When the war was over, WCTU activists remembered anew their exclusion from suffrage.

The decade following the Great War saw an explosion of women's activism both in local and island-wide organizations. Some of it involved an intensification of work in familiar venues: new church and school auxiliaries formed, such as the Roman Catholic Knights of Columbus Ladies Association, established in 1921.[69] By 1930, thirty branches of the Ladies Orange Benevolent Association had spread across the island, their names bearing the unmistakable imprint of the Great War (such as Davidson, Edith Cavell, and Victory).[70] Women also began to assume leadership on boards in "mixed" organizations for the first time: work for the blind, the Playground Association, and the Society for the Prevention of Cruelty to Animals. Characteristic of the postwar period, however, were new organizations with gendered purposes, founded and dominated by women. These associations became an influential part of Newfoundland's civil society. These included the Child Welfare Association (1921), the Girl Guides (established island-wide in 1923), and the Newfoundland Outport Nursing Industrial Association (1920).[71] WPA leaders and activists played leadership roles in all of these groups.

A new-found recognition of the commercial value of women's traditional work was evident, especially in the Newfoundland Outport and Nursing Industrial Association, where outport women's crafts – chiefly knitting and weaving, marketed in St. John's, London, Boston, New York, and Toronto – were originally intended to support the salaries of district nurses. This evolved over time into an important source of household income.[72] This same recognition underpinned the formation of the Service League (1930) and its successor the Jubilee Guilds (1935).[73] The Great War stimulated this recognition of the economic value of "distaff work."

There were other intersecting ideological threads running through these organizations that can be traced directly to ideas prevalent during the war. For example, the preventative health movement helped to set the stage for the new Child Welfare Association. Notions of patriotism to the Crown and Empire, coupled with a wider citizenship for women, were intrinsically part of the ideology of the non-denominational Girl Guides (as well as the intensely Protestant Loyal Orange Benevolent Association). Virtually all of the Girl Guide executives were former WPA leaders, and they saw "Guiding" and women's suffrage as interdependent.[74]

At the vanguard of this generalized movement was the Newfoundland Women's Franchise League, whose support crossed class and religious lines, as had the WPA's. While its leadership was drawn primarily from Anglican, Roman

Catholic, Presbyterian, Congregationalist, and Methodist middle-class and elite women in St. John's, it is notable that the petition campaign launched in 1920 on behalf of women's suffrage eventually gained support from all over Newfoundland. At the end of the league's short but successful five-year campaign, it had gathered twenty thousand signatures, and by 1925 it had pressured the legislature into unanimous action, enfranchising women aged twenty-five or over. This was the largest petition campaign in Newfoundland's history up to that time. It was mounted against the backdrop of an economic downturn and challenging environmental conditions, including the seasonal isolation of many population centres as well as an antagonistic Liberal government headed by Sir Richard Squires. Significantly, the Great War Veterans' Association supported the demand for women's suffrage. Most of the prominent activists of the suffrage movement, among them Armine Gosling, Fannie McNeil, Adeline Browning, May Kennedy Goodridge, Margaret Burke, Helen Baird, and Mary Southcott, had been WPA leaders.

Suffragists demanded the vote because, in the opening words of their petition, they were "partners in the responsible business of Homekeeping which is so vital to the best interests of the Dominion." They had also earned it because: "The women of Newfoundland rose to every call made upon them during the Great War, and showed energy and executive ability in the organization of relief and other work, and many of them served overseas as Nurses, VAD's and Ambulance Drivers."[75] As "Homekeeper" expressed it, because of the war, "Women will never be the same again – they have awakened to a sense of their responsibilities, and will not rest until they have the right to assume them."[76]

A strong sense of postwar nationalism motivated the suffragists, coupled with a dedication to social uplift. They shared these feelings with a broader public trying to come to terms with so much loss of life. Women played important roles in fundraising for the National War Memorial in St. John's as well as for monuments to the fallen in France, Belgium, and local communities. However, honouring Newfoundland's war dead went beyond marble and stone, and focused on improving social conditions in the nation for which the dead had given their all.[77] Suffragists wanted not only to address gender-based grievances such as unequal pay and laws but also to improve the country. Gwendolyn Cooper, WPA and suffrage activist from Grand Falls, urged her audience to sign the suffrage petition and to "strive to raise [Newfoundland] to a place of honour among the nations of the world" by using their vote in favour of a variety of reforms.[78] Increasingly, the suffragists talked of Newfoundland not as "Britain's

Oldest Colony" but as "our little Dominion" or "the country," asserting, in a further phrase from their petition, that women's work was essential "to the best interests of the Dominion."[79] These newly minted phrases represented a significant rhetorical shift from mothers and sisters in service to the Newfoundland Regiment and the Empire (though imperial loyalty was not diminished) to the notion of an army of homemakers uplifting their small nation, which had suffered so much wartime loss.

Finally, and perhaps most psychologically powerful of all to a generation of women who had lost so many men on the battlefield and at sea, the vote was presented as a peace issue: "Women pay the first cost of life. They are the bearers of the race ... In the long run this instinct will make itself felt, and it will undoubtedly react against war with its hideous destruction of life." So stated the Newfoundland Women's Franchise League, whose leaders had spent four years working on behalf of the WPA.[80] Newfoundland's uplift, votes for women, community service, and the hope for peace were the results of the suffragists' effort to come to terms with the meaning and memory of the cataclysmic losses of the Great War.

The impact of the war on a significant segment of Newfoundland women was both paradoxical and profound. Mobilized by war planners in conventional terms as mothers and sisters of the regiment in service to the Empire, and valorized for their traditional homemaking skills through medals and editorials, women emerged with a new-found sense that their traditional skills and community work had public and economic value, and they demanded full citizenship in the form of the vote, thus moving into the male sphere of politics. However, there were constraints that became evident in subsequent decades: the primarily maternalist ideology of the movement was self-limiting. These were not the demands of "new women" so much as those of women who felt devalued in their traditional roles. The Depression, Newfoundland's subsequent bankruptcy, and the appointed Commission of Government in 1934 also slowed further change. What ultimately resulted was evolutionary rather than radical change. Nonetheless, this activist generation had not knitted quietly.

Notes

1 Christopher A. Sharpe, "The 'Race of Honour': An Analysis of Enlistments in the Armed Forces of Newfoundland, 1914-18," *Newfoundland Studies* 4, 1 (1988): 27-55; "Newfoundland and the Great War," available at http://www.heritage.nf.ca/.

2. Michael E. Hanlon, "The Great War in Numbers," available at http://www.worldwar1.com/sfnum.htm.
3. G.W.L. Nicholson, *The Fighting Newfoundlander: A History of the Royal Newfoundland Regiment* (St. John's, Newfoundland: Government of Newfoundland, 1964), 423-24.
4. Robert J. Harding, "Glorious Tragedy: Newfoundland's Cultural Memory of the Attack at Beaumont Hamel, 1916-1925," *Newfoundland and Labrador Quarterly* 21, 1 (2006): 3-40.
5. Nicholson, "The Fighting Newfoundlander," 508-09; Geoffrey Barraclough, ed., *The Times Concise Atlas of World History*, rev. ed. (Maplewood, NJ: Hammond, 1982), 118.
6. John Fitzgerald, "Dying beyond Its Means: Newfoundland's War Debts, Its Loss of Self-Government and Confederation," paper delivered at Newfoundland and the Great War Conference, Memorial University, 12 November 1998.
7. Margot I. Duley, *Where Once Our Mothers Stood We Stand: Women's Suffrage in Newfoundland, 1890-1925* (Charlottetown, PE: Gynergy Books, 1993), 68-72. See also Terry Bishop Stirling, "Such Sights One Will Never Forget": Newfoundland Women and Overseas Nursing in the First World War" (this volume).
8. Nancy M. Forestell, "Women's Unpaid Labour In St. John's between the Two World Wars" (MA thesis, Memorial University, 1987), 20-22.
9. Hilda Chaulk Murray, *More Than 50%* (St. John's: Breakwater Books, 1979); and Margot I. Duley, "Let Me Farm off Cape St. Mary's," paper delivered to Newfoundland Historical Society, February 2001.
10. See, for example, Helen Fraser, *Women and War Work* (New York: G. Arnold Shaw, 1918), chap. 1.
11. For international contacts, see Duley, *Where Once Our Mothers*, 77-78.
12. *Concise Oxford Dictionary* (Oxford at the Clarendon Press, 1991); *Webster's Collegiate Dictionary* (Springfield, MA: G.C. Merriam, 1960).
13. For an extended treatment of the suffrage movement, see Duley, *Where Once Our Mothers*. See also Margot Iris Duley, "The Radius of Her Influence for Good," in *Pursuing Equality: Historical Perspectives on Women in Newfoundland and Labrador*, ed. Linda Kealey, 14-65 (St. John's: Institute of Social and Economic Research, Memorial University of Newfoundland, 1993).
14. Armine Nutting Gosling, *William Gilbert Gosling: A Tribute* (New York: The Guild Press, 1935), 47.
15. Ibid., 41-52.
16. Cowan Association Minutes, Provincial Archives of Newfoundland and Labrador (hereafter PANL), vol. 1, 1897, P8/A/33. Merritt to Williams, 1910, PANL, GN1/3/A, file 49 (151/b), IODE.
17. Viscount Harcourt to Governor Davidson, 7 August 1914, PANL, GN7/10.
18. *Times* (London), 10 August 1914 (reprinted 8 October 1915).
19. Foreword, *Queen Mary's Needlework Guild: Its Work during the Great War, St. James' Palace, 1914-1919*, Imperial War Museum, London (hereafter IWM), First World War Women's Work Collection (hereafter WWC), pt. 1, reel 13/B.O.2/2.
20. Claudine Cleave, "Women and the War," pamphlet in IWM, WWC, pt. 1, reel 13/B.0.2/2.

21 Director of Equipment and Ordinance Stores, Code Telegram, 22 August 1914, PANL, Davidson Papers, G7/10/1914.
22 Typescript, Davidson journal, 20 August 1914, PANL, G7/10/1914. Water Street was St. John's main shopping district and the site of its leading merchant houses.
23 Typescript, Davidson journal, 28 August 1914, PANL, G7/10/1914.
24 Minutes of the inaugural meeting of the WPA, in PANL, Women's Patriotic Association Collection, P8/B/13/, file 2, box 6.
25 Patricia R. O'Brien, "The Newfoundland Patriotic Association: The Administration of the War Effort, 1914-1918" (MA thesis, Memorial University, 1982). See also Mike O'Brien, "Out of a Clear Sky: The Mobilization of the Newfoundland Regiment, 1914-1915," *Newfoundland and Labrador Studies* 22, 2 (2007): 401-27.
26 *Sydney Evening News*, 21 April 1921 (reprinted *Daily News* (NL), 11 June 1921; *Daily News*, 21 February 1913; *New York Times*, 18 March 1912.
27 Davidson to Morris, 15 November 1914, PANL, G7/10/1914.
28 "Royal Birthday Honors," *Newfoundland Quarterly* 14 (1914): 9-10; and Alex A. Parsons, "Governors I Have Known," *Newfoundland Quarterly* 21 (1992): 1-8.
29 Davidson journal, 22 August 1914, PANL, G7/10/1914.
30 Owned by Mary Pitts, the recently widowed wife of James S. Pitts, a former president of the Chamber of Commerce.
31 Duley, *Where Once Our Mothers*, 55-57.
32 Minute Book of the Women's Patriotic Association, 1 September 1914, PANL, WPA/P8/B/13.
33 Eunice Holbrook Ruel, "The Queen Mary's Needlework Guild," *Newfoundland Quarterly* 15, 1 (1915): 6. See also Vicki S. Hallett, "Verses in the Darkness" (this volume).
34 Lady Davidson, *Daily News*, 29 March 1915; *Daily News*, 8 July 1916; *Daily News*, 10 June 1916.
35 *Queen Mary's Needlework Guild: Its Work during the Great War*, IWM, WWC, pt. 1, reel 13/B.0.2/2.
36 *Guardian* (Bay Roberts, NL), 16 October 1914.
37 Eleanor Macpherson, Honorary Secretary, WPA, *Daily News*, 17 December 1916.
38 Women's Patriotic Association, branch ledger, September 1915-December 1918, PANL, [Report] Patriotic Association of the Women of Newfoundland, affiliated with Queen Mary's Needlework Guild and the St. John Ambulance Association, St. John's, January 1917. Copy in Provincial Reference Library, NR/Vault 369.2718 P27, St. John's, Newfoundland.
39 Patricia O'Brien, "Their Benign and Patriotic Influences: The Newfoundland Patriotic Association and the Administration of the War Effort, 1914-1917," paper delivered at Newfoundland and the Great War Conference, Memorial University, 12 November 1998.
40 See "wanted ads" from the Newfoundland Knitting Mills, *Fisherman's Advocate* (NL), November 1913.
41 For the importance of sphagnum moss, see Natalie Riegler, "Sphagnum Moss in World War I: The Making of Surgical Dressings by Volunteers in Toronto, Canada, 1917-1918, *Canadian Bulletin of Medical History* 6 (1989): 27-43.

42 *Field Service Pocket Book* (London: General Staff, War Office, 1916), 34-35.
43 Nicholson, *Fighting Newfoundlander*, 169-92.
44 *Mail and Advocate*, 4 and 11 December 1915.
45 Ibid., 3 July 1915.
46 Ibid., 4 and 24 December 1915.
47 For a Canadian parallel regarding allegations of comfort mismanagement, see Sarah Glassford, "Marching as to War: The Canadian Red Cross Society, 1885-1939" (PhD diss., York University, 2007), 245-49.
48 Francis T. Lind, with an introduction by J. Alex Robinson, *The Letters of Mayo Lind* (St. John's, Newfoundland: Robinson and Company, 1919), 135.
49 *Mail and Advocate*, 19 August 1916.
50 Mrs. T.J. [Tryphena] Duley, with verses by Margaret Duley, *A Pair of Grey Socks, Facts and Fancies* (St. John's: n.p., ca. 1916). (Her sons at the Front were Captain Cyril C. Duley, MBE, my father, and 2nd Lieutenant Lionel Duley, who was killed in the Final offensive at Keiberg Ridge, Ypres, 29 September 1918.)
51 These statistics undercount Newfoundland's total comfort production, for QMNG records apparently exclude items shipped directly to the Newfoundland Regiment from 1914 to July 1916 via Queen Alexandra's Field Force. In addition, medical supplies sent to the St. John Ambulance, of which the WPA was also an affiliate, are not included. See QMNG statistics in IWM, WWC, QMNG branches, reel 13/B.O.2/2 (Benevolent Organizations: QMNG/Introduction and Newfoundland report); population statistics derived from B.R. Mitchell, *British Historical Statistics* (Cambridge: Cambridge University Press, 1988); and B.R. Mitchell, *International Historical Statistics: The Americas and Australasia* (Detroit, MI: Gale Research, 1982).
52 PANL, WPA, P8/B/13-1/, file: Misc. Correspondence re Convalescent Hospital.
53 Ibid.
54 Edgar House, *Light at Last: Triumph over Tuberculosis, 1900-1975, Newfoundland and Labrador* (St. John's: Jesperson Press, 1981), 30-33.
55 Minister of Militia J.R. Bennett to Prime Minister W.F. Lloyd, 24 April 1919, PANL, Roche 107/2/10, Civil Re-establishment Committee.
56 Duley, *Where Once Our Mothers*, 67-68.
57 *Daily News*, 3 November 1917; *Plaindealer*, 27 April 1918; Harris to Long, 14 May 1918, PANL, secret despatch, GN/1/1/7.
58 Harris to Long, 14 May 1918, secret despatch, PANL, GN/1/17; Harris to Colonial Office, 28 September 1918, secret despatch, PANL, GN/1/1/7; *Plaindealer*, 27 April 1918.
59 Based on an analysis of service records of 270 regular and reserve officers, excluding attached officers, microfilm copy, PANL, Royal Newfoundland Regiment, Regimental Roll. Next-of-kin designations were: father (153) 60.7 percent; mother (47) 18.7 percent; wife (39) 15.5 percent; sister (8) 3.2 percent; uncle, brother, or son (3) 1.2 percent; both parents (2) 0.8; and unknown (18), which are also excluded from these calculations.
60 Duley, *Where Once Our Mothers*, app. D.
61 Ibid., chap. 1.

62 Harris to Long, 14 May 1918, secret despatch, PANL, GN/1/1/7; *Daily News*, 4 November 1915; A. Watson, WCTU Secretary, *Daily News*, ca. 10 December 1915. See also Tim Cook, "Wet Canteens and Worrying Mothers: Alcohol, Soldiers and Temperance Groups in the Great War," *Histoire sociale/Social History* 35, 70 (2002): 311-30.

63 Newspapers referred to Howland as married but gave no biographical details, making identification difficult. One possibility is Emily Howland (1827-1929) of Boston, a temperance and peace activist associated with the WCTU, though she was single.

64 Judy Jenkins, "Dr. Geisel's Story," *Preserving the Past* 4 (Tekonsha Michigan Historical Society): 2-16. I am indebted to Judy Jenkins and Becky Devenney, Tekonsha Historical Society, for generously sharing their archives and personal knowledge of Dr. Geisel.

65 *Daily News*, 1 October 1915; *Mail and Advocate*, 16 October 1915.

66 *Mail and Advocate*, 16 October 1915.

67 *Daily News*, 2 October 1915; *Guardian*, 15 October 1915.

68 *Daily News*, 26 October 1915. Alice Templeman Barbour (1874-1969), wife of merchant Samuel Barbour.

69 *Daily News*, 19 April 1921.

70 *Fisherman's Advocate* (Port Union), 22 August 1930.

71 Girl Guiding in Newfoundland, *Fifth Annual Report* (St. John's, NF; n.p., 1927), 16; Margaret Gibbons, "The Child Welfare Association, 1919-1939" (honours diss., Memorial University, 1966), 11-25

72 Edgar House, *The Way Out: The Story of NONIA, 1920-1990* (St. John's: Creative Publishers, 1990); NONIA, *First Annual Report*, 30 June 1925, 6-10. Centre for Newfoundland Studies, Memorial University.

73 Agnes M. Richard, *Threads of Gold: The History of the Jubilee Guilds and Women's Institutes in Newfoundland* (St. John's: Creative Publishers, 1989), chaps. 1-2.

74 "Suffragist," *Daily News*, 19 May 1923.

75 Legislative Council Proceedings, Legislative Library, House of Assembly, Government of Newfoundland and Labrador, 9 May 1921, 82.

76 "The Women's Petition," *Daily News*, 25 May 1920.

77 Harding, "Glorious Tragedy," 13.

78 *Daily News*, 6 July 1920.

79 Ibid., 19 May 1923; 21 May 1920; and 8 June 1920.

80 Ibid., 8 May 1925.

3

Freshettes, Farmerettes, and Feminine Fortitude at the University of Toronto during the First World War

TERRY WILDE

In her book *Men, Militarism and UN Peacekeeping: A Gendered Analysis,* Sandra Whitworth argues that "the creation of soldiers involves rituals and myths ... about masculinity, about manliness, about race, and about belonging."[1] If the fighting of wars has traditionally been framed as masculine, what becomes of civilian women during wartime? Are their roles and femininity redefined or transformed? Do the changes last? The First World War provides an opportunity to examine these questions because, as Canada's first foray into total war, it affected civilian women as much as it did military men. Between 1914 and 1918, both materials and human lives were consumed at a never-before-imagined pace. No matter how tangentially they were related to combat, each citizen was expected to contribute to the nation's cause – including women. At the University of Toronto (U of T), female students, female faculty, and faculty wives experienced dramatic changes in what was expected of them by their school and by the federal government as well as in their own self-perceptions. However, not all of these changes were sustained.[2] *The Varsity,* the university's undergraduate newspaper, allows us to compare these women's prewar, wartime, and postwar activities from their own perspectives. This source is not the final word on how U of T women participated in the Great War, but it does situate their voices within the broader war effort. The newspaper also illuminates students' feelings about, and responses to, the war, while directing our attention away from President Robert Falconer's administration and more towards students' understandings of their own participation. I argue that it took a war to get varsity women involved beyond the curriculum and that meaningful, transformative gains were neither widespread, nor consistent, nor sustained. The status quo resumed shortly after peace was established. The first section of the chapter examines the roles of women on campus before the war, the second section looks at wartime changes, and the third section considers these changes in the postwar years. Women at the U of T were, on the whole, a much younger group than Margot Duley's Newfoundland knitters and Alison Norman's Six Nations women (both this volume). The majority were from privileged backgrounds. Few were married or had children. They knew neither poverty nor the limitations of life on a First Nations reserve. The transformations they experienced therefore seemed more dramatic than did those experienced by others. Joining the war effort meant stepping away from privilege – for a time.

Female U of T Students Prior to the Great War
When, in 1827, England's George IV issued the charter for King's College (the U of T's predecessor),[3] the word "student" was tacitly understood to mean "male student." Even the term "bachelor of arts" seemed to recognize (unmarried) male exclusivity in the halls of academia. Women were not specifically excluded by the university's charter or subsequent legislation, but, because none applied or contested enrolment during the first forty years of operations, it became the practice to admit only young men to the campus. Women's acceptance into U of T was, as late as 1883, opposed by powerful university officials like President Daniel Wilson, who claimed that females were an unnecessary distraction to his (male) students.[4] By 1884, however, after several vigorous individual campaigns, women were permitted to register for lectures, labs, and seminars, and they succeeded remarkably well.[5] But the university was more than simply a site of learning: it was also a "political weapon [used] to preserve class divisions."[6] Early U of T registration rolls reflect long-established pedigrees of prestige and wealth – the elite of Upper Canadian society.[7] Over time, and through scholarship programs, the campus slowly blended Jewish, Lutheran, and Congregationalist faiths into the white Anglican population, but freshmen were "gentlemen" and, later, "freshettes" were "ladies" in the purest Victorian sense. Women in particular were expected to comport themselves as exemplars of refinement and sophistication. Yet they remained second-class citizens on campus.

University women were regarded as physically and intellectually inferior; they were grudgingly tolerated rather than openly welcomed. Some academics of the day continued to subscribe to the theory that women's monthly cycles rendered them unfit for intellectual pursuits.[8] The pages of *The Varsity* reflected a general belief that women were less capable and more vulnerable than men, unable to "rough it like a man" when away from home.[9]

From the outset, the U of T was a paternalistic institution run by older men for the benefit of younger men. For elite Torontonian males, education at the U of T became a rite of passage, a stepping-stone from youth to full adulthood. The arrival of women among their ranks had little discernible effect on the type of education offered, nor did the atmosphere of the university change appreciably. *The Varsity* rarely mentions women before the turn of the century and, when it does, it does so with a condescending tone. Female enrolment was initially so negligible, and increased so quietly, that the U of T remained a male stronghold.

By the turn of the century, women represented about 10 percent of U of T's student population. Gendering at the university followed a simple binary: women were the opposite of men. Women were vain and dainty, men were self-confident and rugged; women were gentle and nurturing, men were tough and aggressive; women were emotional and domestic, men were intellectual and political. This model was also found at other Canadian universities, as noted by A.B. McKillop in "Marching as to War"[10] and by Barry Moody in "Acadia and the Great War."[11] This black/white paradigm was rarely contested and was evident in a variety of university activities. The 1909-10 women's hockey team members, for instance, played their games wearing bonnets, skirts, blouses, and sweaters from their personal wardrobes – apparel that reinforced their femininity – while members of the men's hockey team sported varsity uniforms supplied by the school and better suited to the sport.[12]

Gender differences operated in other ways as well. *The Varsity* prefaced women's names with the appellation "Miss," whereas men were called by first and last names alone.[13] Registration rolls were prepared with the expectation that all students were males unless the name was preceded by this titular recognition. In formal debates gentlemen debated politics and world issues, ladies debated domestic issues.[14] Women could be invited to join an extracurricular group, but it was invariably a privilege (not a right), conferred by men.

Such differences were typical of the period and reflected the gendered practices and assumptions of the larger society. A joke of the time scoffed that men went to U of T to gain letters after their names but that women went to gain the letters MRS before their names. Within this context, the pages of *The*

Varsity suggest that the immediate prewar years were playful and innocent. Much was made of football matches against rivals among the federated colleges as they competed against one another good-naturedly. Women attended and cheered their home squads.

Since gaining admission to U of T, women had identified and claimed a careful middle ground somewhere between studying too hard and being considered masculine, on the one hand, and studying too little and being considered frivolous, on the other. By 1908-09, women could participate in many pastimes, including literary societies, debating clubs, choirs, basketball, swimming, hockey, volleyball, tennis, skating, dances, foreign language clubs, glee clubs,* instrumental and mixed musical groups,* acting and theatre companies,* public recitals,* public speaking competitions, social clubs that discussed travel experiences,* and the YWCA and various other Christian organizations (the asterisks indicate activities that were usually co-educational). Yet many women's clubs and teams were weakly supported, their activities frequently unreported. A February 1914 editorial laments: "at University College, we defy anyone, however ingenious her persuasive powers, to coax out more than a handful of women to any [athletic] match, be it of the last importance to the athletic reputation of the college."[15] One of the few extracurricular areas that women did dominate was drama, through the Dramatis Personae and the Women's Dramatic Club of University College. Their plays were always anticipated and very popular.[16]

In the 1909-10 academic year there were a total of 4,112 students enrolled at the U of T; less than 20 percent of them were women. Most were concentrated in the Faculty of Arts and Science. In 1911, for example, women comprised about one-third (653) of the faculty's student population of 1,895. Pictorial representations of these women in *The Varsity* depict feminine daintiness – hour-glass figures coupled with a delicate sense of high fashion. A front-page cartoon from 1909 shows two fashionable co-eds cooing, "Oh, Isn't He a Dream!" as they demurely observe a barrel-chested varsity footballer striding past.[17] The women are standing still; the athlete is in full-step. From this cartoon it is possible to extrapolate wider attitudes: men were action-oriented and physical, women were passive observers. Initiation activities illustrated the same theme: freshmen chased and grappled greased pigs or ran three-legged races, while freshettes took Autumn Tea and sang college songs.[18]

Nothing has yet been said about female faculty members, and this is simply because there were so few of them. Professors were tacitly understood to be male in the same way that students were. While some skilled and well-credentialed women did hold teaching positions, they were not hired in large numbers. They were always subordinate to their male counterparts and were too few and scattered to be a recognized force or a unified body. Administratively, women also remained in the shadow of men. Not until 1911, twenty-seven years after women started attending classes regularly, were the first two women elected to the university Senate, the school's governing body.

It was unusual for undergraduate women to stir controversy or to voice dissent about government or political issues. An October 1912 meeting of Trinity College's Literary Society that demanded "equality between the sexes in all questions" and "the uplift of women all through the world"[19] was therefore noteworthy, garnering the front-page *Varsity* headline "CANADIAN WOMEN! GO TO BORDEN FOR FRANCHISE." More common were quips about the vain, superficial female disposition, such as:

Ada: I wonder why she wears such tight gloves?
Lucy: That's the only way she can get her hand squeezed.[20]

Some female students began objecting to these sophomoric observations, saying that such jokes "offend[ed] the taste of women students." The editor's tongue-in-cheek apology concluded by earnestly welcoming women's participation on the paper.[21] Few women responded to the opportunity to become reporters, editors, or faculty representatives. Although some did join the paper as reporters, it was not until the fighting started in September 1914 that women were pushed, or perhaps pulled, into concerted and consistent action across the campus. Without the external impetus of war, campus co-eds appeared unwilling to find new ways of acting publicly.

Yet there were outside interests on the campus that were agitating for women to exert themselves. "Pankhurstism" – a term encompassing ideas and practices relating to women and the vote or the female equality movement – was increasingly afoot in campus debates. Maternal feminists in the wider Canadian society lobbied for women to bring their "natural" qualities of moral guardianship to the political arenas of the country, and the *Toronto Star* began chastising young U of T women in articles, editorials, and cartoons for declining seats offered to them on the public transit system (see Figure 4). "If a man offers a woman a seat in a [public] car she should never refuse, not even though she be a suffragette" was the response of one reader who wanted women to continue exhibiting normative, obeisant behaviours.[22]

> **IS THERE CONSPIRACY AMONG WOMEN STUDENTS TO REFUSE SEATS IN CITY STREET CARS?**
>
> (*How a "Star" artist viewed a recent street car occurrence referred to below*)

FIGURE 4 The behaviour of female University of Toronto students was being closely observed even before the war. [*The Varsity*, 9 March 1914]

In the years leading up to the First World War, women's roles at the U of T were socially prescribed and, for the most part, passive and traditional. While some co-eds were from families of modest means, a significant portion continued to represent the Ontario elite, and they were therefore expected to uphold the prevailing norms of upper-class femininity. Little was expected of these

Terry Wilde

women beyond the classroom; consequently, little was delivered. The outbreak of fighting would quickly change that.

Women at the U of T during the First World War

When the fighting in Europe began in 1914, male students at the U of T immediately began conducting loud, highly visible, two-hour long military drills on the field in front of University College. Their high-profile example was meant to inspire others to join the ranks of Canada's fighting forces. It was understood to be the responsibility, indeed the obligation, of men to enlist and hurry to the support of Great Britain. The federated colleges vied with one another to see which could enlist the most men, and, by May 1915, almost 1,300 from U of T had joined the fight: 500 undergraduates, 70 faculty members, and over 700 alumni.[23]

Freshmen were required to undergo physical examinations to determine their fitness for fighting, and the consequence of neglecting the physical exam meant exclusion from lectures and university life in general.[24] Unlike some of the Newfoundland recruits that Margot Duley discusses in this volume, most of the U of T's young men were in good health and met the standards easily.

The newly created University of Toronto Overseas Training Battalion – an infantry unit – promoted loyalty to school, country, and Empire. For men to ignore this clarion call was for them to become pariahs within the university community. The role of a male U of T student was redefined to mean a man willing to fight in the university's own regiment for a cause that the university faculty and administration had identified as necessary.[25] U of T became, in effect, a recruiting ground for soldiers; and, for this, President Robert Falconer was knighted in 1917.[26] By then more than four thousand men had gone to the Western Front from the university, and military training became a compulsory requirement for incoming male students. Thanks to administrative and peer pressures, registration at U of T ostensibly came to mean a willingness to serve in the Canadian forces.

Female students were also drawn into the hurly-burly of war activities. On 6 November 1914, President Falconer issued a blanket appeal to all women (students, faculty, and faculty wives) at U of T to meet at Convocation Hall to determine what roles they would play while the country was at war.[27] The president's wife, Sophie Falconer, subsequently took responsibility for marshalling women's time, talents, and donations across campus. All academic activities

Freshettes, Farmerettes, and Feminine Fortitude

ceased sharply at 4:00 PM every day to allow the men time to assemble and drill and to encourage the women to knit stockings, sew grey flannel shirts, provide kit bags, launder cheesecloth, or to collect scarves and hats – the same work undertaken by the Newfoundland and Six Nations women discussed in this volume by Duley and Norman, respectively. Women of the different colleges at U of T soon put aside their rivalries and met as a single group to knit or sew together while listening to public speakers who related news of the war. A few of the old rivalries were kept alive to spur playful competition and thereby achieve greater results for the university as a whole, but this common effort helped initiate a sense of unity transcending traditional college boundaries.

Eight weeks after war was declared, *The Varsity* published an editorial entitled "Women and the War," which asked: "What part may Canadian women take in bearing the burdens of the war?"[28] The first response was nursing and nursing-related activities (discussed by Linda Quiney and Terry Bishop Stirling in this volume) and the most traditional roles for young women. The number of U of T undergraduate women who immediately offered their services at the Red Cross office outstripped demand as well as the agency's ability to handle them. Women were as enthusiastic about volunteering as were men. In the end, it was not the Red Cross but the Canadian Army Medical Corps that coordinated Canadian nurses. More broadly, the Red Cross and the Salvation Army were understood to be among the principal sites at which campus women acted in support of the war effort.[29]

Knitting scarves, caps, wristlets, and leggings for the Canadian Red Cross and other voluntary aid organizations was what *The Varsity* recommended to women not engaged in nursing. By January 1915, *The Varsity* reported that women were doing "Good Work," and it enumerated the list of supplies generated by female students at University College alone: "450 bandages, 32 pairs of bed socks, six pairs of hand-knit socks, half a dozen Balaclava caps and a dozen scarves."[30] Some of these items would ultimately find their way through the international agency to wounded and injured men at the front.[31] Under the auspices of the Red Cross, U of T women also raised funds to support hospitals overseas.

Ever more was being demanded of women, and new, transformative ideas and opportunities were put forward. Sophie Falconer, who carried great influence among the co-eds, addressed the women of the Literary Society at their Autumn Tea with these words:

> [Women] cannot go on as if there were no war; we must feel our responsibilities. Let us have our pleasures as before but let them be of a simpler nature, not that we may have more money in our pockets at the end of the year but that we may render more assistance to the relief work.[32]

The president's wife then established a new campus organization called the League of Patriotic Service of Women Students of the University of Toronto (LPSWSUT). Each member had to solemnly pledge the following oath of patriotic service:

1. To do the work of my course faithfully regarding this as my first and chief means of serving the State;
2. To strive through study and observation to learn the meaning and responsibility of my citizenship;
3. To give a definite portion of my time to Red Cross work or other work for the war;
4. To practice economy in personal matters to devote the money thus saved to war or relief purposes; and
5. To adopt such habits of life as will make me physically fit for service.[33]

Like patriotic organizations on the Grand River Reserve (Norman, this volume) and across Newfoundland (Duley, this volume), the LPSWSUT also looked for new ways to serve. As a long-standing undergraduate favourite, dances became a popular new venue for supporting the war. Offering a light-hearted pursuit under the banner of a noble cause, dances amounted to sacrifice with a smile. All the proceeds were donated to specific branches of the war, medicine and hospitals being the most common.

The thrift that was advocated in Article 4 of the LPSWSUT oath was widely recommended but personally interpreted. Most women gave their time collectively, usually on behalf of a sorority, and some also made financial contributions. The nature of personal economy was left to the discretion and circumstances of each woman, but *The Varsity* printed the names of donating organizations and individuals as well as anonymous donations to a "Self-Denial Box."[34] In other words, women's contributions were monitored and publicly recorded.

Sophie Falconer (known as Lady Falconer after her husband's knighthood in 1917) set the example for faculty wives to follow, always encouraging women to make greater contributions. Other wives became tireless advocates in matters related to the University Hospital Association. The University of Toronto Base Hospital provided 1,040 beds for sick and wounded soldiers.[35] In addition to doctors and administrators, each "base" also needed eighty-four nursing sisters and 284 non-commissioned officers. Women like Mrs. F.N.G. Starr, Mrs. Hodgson Ellis, and Mrs. G.M. Wrong (wives of prominent faculty members) assumed responsibility for securing these personnel and the requisite supplies. Faculty wives also volunteered with their churches, schools, colleges, and various women's organizations.

To bring more women into the war effort, the Undergraduate Women's Association limited the number of offices a female student could hold at one time. Prior to the war some unusually industrious and enthusiastic women held up to six or seven different offices in diverse organizations.[36] Once the war started, this was not seen as a fair or efficacious use of women's time and talents. Everyone had to do their "bit," so restricting the involvement of the individual to one or two key positions meant that more women had to get involved.[37] The numbers of women active in agency offices doubled in short order and continued to build for the next three years.

Motivational speakers were brought to the U of T to promote student participation in the war. Kate Booth-Clibborn, an internationally respected Christian missionary known as the *Maréchale*,[38] packed Convocation Hall on 7 February 1915. She called on students, particularly women, to rise up as Christians and face the dire circumstances in Europe by finding new ways of helping. The *Maréchale* was openly admired by *The Varsity* for intrepidly going wherever she was needed and using her talents and abilities as she saw fit. Her example helped transform the traditional model of a female student into one that was active, involved, and vocal.

As enrolment numbers at the university began to decline (in 1915 the Faculty of Arts registered only about fourteen hundred students, which was down by a third from just over twenty-one hundred in the previous year), demands upon its women increased. Even examinations were postponed in favour of more war initiatives and activities. Anglican archdeacon Cody called for "self-sacrifice" from the male students.[39] Prime Minister Robert Borden had made a "sacred promise" to Great Britain that Canada would provide fifty thousand soldiers to the cause;[40] and, for their voluntary enlistment in the armed forces through the U of T, undergraduate males were academically rewarded. As early as February 1915, the Senate decided that fourth-year men who volunteered to serve overseas would be granted their "year in full" and therefore their degrees.[41] Men in other years would receive varying levels of credit for dedicated service to the country and the Empire.[42] Female students pursued their war work without reward or compensatory recognition on the assumption that, for women, virtue and self-sacrifice were both patriotic duties and their own rewards. Academic benefits for the much-admired student soldiers did not extend to the women who struggled to meet ever-increasing demands on their time, energy, and pocketbooks. Such contributions were neither acknowledged nor commemorated with badges or public honours as they were in other places.

To encourage women's contributions to the cause, *The Varsity* regularly printed articles on the efforts of European women, often referring to them as "sisters" of Canadian women. For example, one young female English VAD in France was heralded for "trimming between two hundred and three hundred lamps every day ... in a cold, dark cellar." According to *The Varsity*: "the thing that keeps her steadily and cheerfully at work is the fact that every lamp will be needed at night in the hospital to which the cellar belongs."[43] Thus, despite the isolation and the tedium of a repetitive task like trimming a lamp, even a lone woman could make a difference at a hospital in France. The image of a woman lighting the way was not lost on female students in Toronto as just such an illustration was used on the cover of *The Varsity*'s special annual supplement on the war. Further emotional appeals to universal sisterhood included guilt-inducing admonitions to U of T's women: "Can we afford to wear fifteen dollar shoes while the feet of the women in Europe bleed with work in behalf of our cause?"; "The women of the University [of Toronto] must surely feel that the National sacrifice is being laid upon each of us individually. Our shoulders must broaden out to share the State's burdens, as well as our own."[44] Women's roles were being transformed.

In 1915, *The Varsity* reassessed "The Value of a College Education for Women." The "Mrs. degree" was no longer snidely hinted at, and, instead, according to the editor: "[A woman is] first a human being, and as such [she is] entitled to the heritage of knowledge bequeathed her by the human beings of all other generations. And in proportion ... she is a better educated human being; is she not thereby a better woman?"[45] This new attitude was a far cry from what had been generally understood only fourteen months earlier. The editorial concluded by suggesting that "future generations [would] profit by an increased number of homes where the mothers have been educated on broad cultured lines."[46] While the editor still saw motherhood as a woman's ultimate goal, there was a sense of equality, even deservedness, in women's access to postsecondary education. This recognition sprang at least partly from the diligence they had demonstrated in maintaining the security of the British Empire.

As the war moved into its second year, *The Varsity* occasionally printed sharp rebukes on its front page, reminders that there was no room for shirking. The headline "RED CROSS – College Women Not Doing Full Share" was followed up with an article entitled, "College Women Lag in Organized Work for Red Cross." These accusations embarrassed the women, who were told that "every undergraduate women [sic] should give at least four hours a week to Red Cross working."[47] Poems employing military language and thinly veiled battle references were published to keep interest and participation high. Consider "The Charge of the Knitting Brigade," which opened with: "Half a stitch, half a stitch / Half a stitch onward, / In the Assembly Hall / Toiled the One Hundred."[48] Tennyson's acclaimed "Charge of the Light Brigade" was the model for this tongue-in-cheek attempt to get women to knit by drawing a parallel between women's patriotic needlework and male military service. No matter the number of other challenging opportunities available, women's "natural" predisposition to tasks like knitting and sewing could not be discarded, and any new work that came along was always considered to be in addition to, not in place of, what they were already doing.

On campus, more and more physical spaces and fixed resources were donated to the war. Wycliffe College was completely taken over by the army, while cafeterias, parade grounds, buildings, and rooms were reserved for exclusive use by various branches of the Canadian Army. On 1 March 1915, the Undergraduate Women's Association of the University of Toronto petitioned President Falconer for a room of its own. The administration had already commandeered its reading room at the library for the manufacture of hospital supplies and the co-eds had begrudgingly been permitted access to the men's "reading sanctorum." But the women wanted more than a table marked "Reserved for Women Students": they wanted their own space for social purposes (tea and lunches) and to encourage the single women on campus to congregate in a common area.[49] The women were clearly sensitive to the needs of the war effort. Indeed, this is evident in their appeal as they had already done some research and found an alternative space that would cost nothing. Anxious for some autonomy over how to spend their spare time, the petitioners noted "a great need for a place of meeting for lonely women students on Sunday afternoons."[50] The exigencies of the war were becoming oppressive, and women students sought a place where they could stand down from service and be in the company of others. Their request was quickly granted.

The proportion of women enrolled in studies at U of T increased to about 30 percent of all students during the Great War, thanks to an overall enrolment decline and a sharp drop in male enrolments in particular.[51] In some faculties women comprised well over half of all registrants, and, by 1917, only fourteen of the 288 teacher candidates at the Toronto Normal School were male, well down from the 15 or 20 percent they had comprised only a couple of years before. Women increased their domination of the teaching profession during the Great War and for a long time afterward.

The summer hiatus – from early April to late August each year – provided one of the most dramatic and well-documented transformations in how female students participated in the Great War. Summer vacations from 1916 to 1918 ceased being a time for personal relaxation and became a time for national service. Although no precise numbers are available, it is estimated that between three and four hundred U of T "College Maidens" signed up to work on Ontario farms. Dressed in dark bloomers and khaki blouses, the majority of the volunteers toiled in the fruit belt of the Niagara Peninsula.[52] Wages varied from one to four dollars per day on the piecework system, and the hours were long. The "girls" paid for their board (arranged through the YWCA), and, on average, they cleared between six and seven dollars per week while bringing in the Canadian fruit harvest, which would be processed into jam for soldiers. U of T's women were quickly dubbed "farmerettes" as they left their comparatively comfortable urban homes and moved into very modest circumstances in Quonset huts or musty tents on fruit and dairy farms. Some farmers were initially skeptical about using women on large-scale agricultural projects in roles that were historically occupied by men,[53] but, by the end of the season, the women's work ethic and accomplishments were reported to be exemplary. Other women from the university were also lauded for staying in the city and working in loud, dirty, and sometimes dangerous munitions factories.

As farming work blurred gender boundaries, the vocabularies that described women in new roles changed as well. When these women were on campus they were described as "fair freshies" and "lively maids" who possessed "gay" spirits. Yet when the same women performed war work on farms they were understood to be diligent, brave, and patriotic – their war work described as "thrilling adventures" that they "delighted in" – and the workers themselves described as "Women Warriors."[54] This celebration of the benefits of women's industrial and

Freshettes, Farmerettes, and Feminine Fortitude

agricultural productivity (rather than domestic reproductivity) was due, in part, to their youth. On the farms and in factories they were not "women" in the sense of being mothers or wives who had sons or husbands in active service. They were daughters and sisters, and so they were described as "girls" off campus. Yet they were not allowed to completely cast off traditional domestic associations. Romanticized newspaper reports claimed the women spent their evenings around campfires knitting and recounting their workdays.

In *The Varsity*'s "War Supplement" for 1916-17, author Mary Roberts Rinehart provides a general look at the work of the Red Cross at the front:

> I have found cultured women of every nation performing the most menial tasks. I have found an army where all are equal – priests, surgeons, scholars ... women of the stage, young girls ... all enrolled under the red badge of mercy.[55]

Her observations released women from staid ideals of femininity. "Cultured women" could embrace the menial but necessary work of war, as the social roles of all women expanded. From picking apples to trimming lamp wicks, no job was too small, and ideas about the gendering of work needed to be interrogated.

The auxiliary nursing services of the Voluntary Aid Detachment (VAD) offered a new arena for women's voluntary service during the First World War.[56] Historian Linda Quiney argues that, "without this essential female support system, the Great War would have been far costlier to the state in both financial and human terms."[57] In October 1917, *The Varsity* recognized U of T alumna "Miss Norine Butler, BA, VAD ... a popular young lady in social circles" for her daring foray into ambulance-driving in France. While reinforcing her femininity by situating her in "social circles" in Toronto, *The Varsity* lauded her "proud distinction of being the first woman from this part of Ontario to drive a motor ambulance in France."[58] Butler transcended her traditional background during the war, and her efforts were commended as examples of women's potential.

The article implicitly dared university women back in Toronto to compete for positions alongside men. Butler's first-class honours in courses on motor driving and mechanics tacitly challenged U of T women to succeed at non-traditional work. By 1917, prominent business leaders like Sir Joseph Flavelle were advocating in favour of women's asserting themselves in the workforce. Flavelle urged women "to get to work, and to prove to men in public positions that there is a real service which can be performed by women."[59] With the war in its third year, the needs of the Dominion outweighed traditional gender roles. But nowhere was transformation more evident than in the political sphere, as some women gained the franchise.

In September 1917, the federal government granted conditional voting rights to limited numbers of women. This step was celebrated at the U of T despite its providing far less than universal female suffrage and affecting only federal elections. The new law proclaimed that "all women (British subjects) over twenty-one years of age, claiming the relationship of mother, wife, widow, sister or daughter, to a British or Canadian soldier, who has served outside of Canada or to a British or Canadian sailor, may vote."[60] Clearly this was an attenuated victory for women because voting remained contingent upon a woman's relationship to a man. The wording was specific and restrictive, excluding those whose male relatives were serving in Canada or those whose sisters were nursing in Europe. It was widely understood to be a political ploy by Prime Minister Robert Borden's Union government to win the 1917 federal election; nonetheless, women across the country embraced the step as an important achievement.

At the U of T women were welcomed into the political arena and their votes courted as they participated in war debates and discussions. With rights came responsibilities. Adelaide Plumptre, vice-president of the Ontario branch of the National Council of Women, suggested that the U of T was the place where courses ought to be established to help women come to terms with social and political issues that they would be called upon to deal with as voters.[61] The university did not act on the idea; however, in the postwar years, more women began voluntarily enrolling in political economy.[62]

In 1917 *The Varsity* itself changed. Beatrice Corrigan became the first women's editor for the paper, holding creative dominion over a minimum of three columns per issue, including space on the front page.[63] Miss M.H. McCoy became the co-managing editor, and at least six other women worked as reporters, usually on topics related to women's activities and interests. During her first term on the paper, Corrigan wrote editorials that urged women to henceforth think for themselves and to assert their own interests. The war had facilitated many gains for Canadian women, but Corrigan insisted they needed to be exercised in order to be maintained.

U of T women responded generously when, as the 1917 Christmas vacation approached, a devastating explosion rocked Halifax Harbour, killing hundreds.

Freshettes, Farmerettes, and Feminine Fortitude

More than one hundred women immediately came together on the St. George campus to sew articles of children's clothing, which could be made quickly. Within forty-eight hours they delivered a large consignment to the local Red Cross detachment, which forwarded it to Halifax the next day.[64] The Anglican Club took up a separate collection for toys and gifts for the young victims of the explosion.[65] As the war entered its fourth year, women students at U of T no longer needed to be prodded and reminded of what was needed. They had taken control of their own work and were confidently finding new ways to contribute to Canada's war effort.

The first issue of *The Varsity* for 1918, released on 11 January, featured an editorial entitled "College Women and the Fourth Year of War." It began by acknowledging women's palpable fatigue with war work; it sensed monotony in the discharge of responsibilities at a time when more enthusiasm than ever was needed:

> The fourth year of war means increased physical demands on women for manual labour, agricultural work etc. Does the fourth year of war mean a higher physical standard to meet that need? If College women are undermining their energies through "movies," late hours, lack of exercise and unwholesome diet the need of the future cannot be met. Every woman must be physically fit.[66]

Sarah Glassford's work on the Canadian Red Cross Society reveals that charity fatigue was a broad-based phenomenon that affected many quarters of the nation, not just the U of T. She suggests that, because so many permanently damaged soldiers were being repatriated, "many women [had to] channel the greater part of their time and energy into caring for their loved ones at home, rather than into voluntary work for the CRCS. At the same time the increased demand for women in paid employment ... also removed some women from the voluntary sector."[67] The combination of these factors, coupled with a general sense of war weariness, brought about a decline in women's contributions both on campus and off. *The Varsity*, however, was vigilant in its efforts to motivate U of T students.

As the war entered its final year, women were called upon to find and fulfill more and more non-traditional roles, and it was anticipated that women at the U of T would move on to positions in government, industry, agriculture, and community leadership. By this time young women faced intense pressure to do and be more than what was traditional. And, just as men were urged to enlist, so women were subjected to propaganda that shamed "slackers" and "shirkers" for not doing enough.

Changed Roles of Women after the Great War
The Great War officially ended on 11 November 1918, but the U of T maintained a war posture until the end of the term in March 1919. There was still a demand for bandages, socks, and financial support. Only three days before the Armistice, President Falconer exhorted students, on the front page of *The Varsity*, to subscribe to the "limit of [their] ability" to the national Victory Loan campaign.[68] The 11 November 1918 issue of *The Varsity* did not feature banner headlines proclaiming peace; rather, it read: "Buy Bonds! and Help Foch to Bang the Boche."[69] This type of fundraising continued for the next five months, although in a more relaxed context.

Women across Canada soon began vacating some of the non-traditional jobs they had filled during the fighting; they left the manual work to the lionized veterans who were returning from Europe. The "warrior" roles women had occupied were largely abandoned, and the Armistice seems to have brought about a desire to return to the social zeitgeist of 1914. Postwar Canadians wanted to recapture the familiar and the traditional more than they wanted to venture into new territories or to establish new identities in untested fields. Deferring to returning soldiers who had sacrificed so much became a moral imperative, and welcome-home parades, dinners, speeches, and myriad other recognitions were showered upon the returning "old boys," many of whom were horribly disfigured or physically disabled (see Tector, this volume). At the U of T, Soldiers' Tower was quickly commissioned as an addition to Hart House, memorializing the hundreds of people from the U of T community who had died in the war. The high public praise conferred on women from the WPA in Newfoundland and the great transformations that resulted there were not evident for women on the insular U of T campus. Instead, a reversion to the prewar status quo seemed to be the desired way forward.

Just days before the fighting in Europe ended, *The Varsity* began touting the urgency of "reconstruction" at home. One of the key elements it considered was women's resuming traditional domestic roles:

> There are many reforms ... for which women are plainly responsible. No one has a better right than women to take full charge of every form of legislation

affecting children. Baby welfare as a national requirement ... is a form of reconstruction that leads straight to the doors of women at home today.[70]

There is no mistaking the tenor of this item: it rehabilitates women's "natural" roles as mothers and homemakers. It continued: "The establishment of a national Board of Health ... rests naturally on the mothers of the land."[71] The unnatural state of war had ended, and so women should return to the social roles for which nature had intended them.

In January 1919 the university was alive with questions by and about women students' participation in campus life. Because the men paid a mandatory fee to support *The Varsity*, it was felt that women should do so as well. A quid pro quo was being argued for with respect to physical examinations and military drills as well.[72] Meanwhile, as the War Memorial Campaign got under way in October 1919, co-eds were urged to make a meaningful contribution.[73]

Within eighteen months, however, the university returned to a peacetime atmosphere. Sports reclaimed space on the front pages of *The Varsity*, and social calendars featured rugby, basketball, and hockey games without any mention of war or fundraising. New dance crazes, influenced by the European experiences of returning veterans, flooded the Toronto campus. By January 1919, there was talk of "special courses for men returning from overseas,"[74] and activities (such as theatre night) that had ceased during the conflict were revived.[75] The work of "women warriors" transformed back into the interests of girls.

In February 1920, a series of reports in *The Varsity* looked at "Vocational Conferences for Women Students" and advertised talks for "Women to Hear of Professions Open to College Grads."[76] These sound progressive, but attendees only heard about "secretarial work, advertising, openings in department stores and factories, public health nursing, playground and recreational work" – opportunities in keeping with women's traditional roles. There was little that was innovative or daring.[77] Journalism was the only new career opportunity discussed for women, but it came with a caveat: women journalists needed "the constitution of an ox and the skin of a rhinoceros" – qualifications that were atypical of women, especially those who graduated from the U of T. Veronica Strong-Boag argues that, in the postwar period, traditional positions like "housewives and secretaries helped nurture male creativity, authority and independence," even though women's "own talents could well be lost sight of" in the process.[78]

By 1921, Louise McKinney was railing that the "greatest enemy there is and ever has been to progress is the comfortable woman ... she accepts as her right, her sheltered, pampered position and she uses it to minister to her own comforts rather than to those of others."[79] This was an admonition not to allow personal interest to diminish the rights women had gained during the war, which seemed a distinct danger as civilian women returned to the domestic sphere. Nellie McClung was equally critical of women who did not use their recently won enfranchisement to obtain greater rights and benefits. She despaired as, all across the country, women "abandoned church duties, had smaller families, and turned to golf, bridge, and tennis rather than to politics and public engagement."[80] McClung and McKinney wanted women to demand more of themselves, especially in the postwar decade.

Returning to the prewar status quo was, nonetheless, a relief to many women at the U of T. A variety of remember-when columns featured in *The Varsity* during the postwar years suggest a longing for the innocence of "the good old days." Every woman at the U of T was encouraged to look to the business world "to find her place," but few did so.[81] Expectations of marriage and motherhood were still the two predominant destinies for the majority of young Canadian women, and modelling themselves after their upper-class mothers was easier than establishing an entirely new social and public identity. Yet so many men had died in Europe that many eligible and marriage-minded women remained single and cared for male relatives who had been severely injured. The transformations and new opportunities women experienced in the war became memories rather than elements of a new lifestyle.

At the U of T, as was the case for Canada as a whole, the honours and tributes that Canadian soldiers received quickly cast into shadow the significance of women's contributions to the war effort. The postwar years were marked by the university's admiration and respect for men who had given lives and limbs for their country and Empire. For the young university women in Toronto who had been challenged and who had responded to the call of war, there was no clamour for public recognition or recompense. Women from the university who had laboured to "do their bit" faded quietly from the limelight once the war was over. While it took a war to transform U of T undergraduate women's on-campus and off-campus roles and opportunities, the restoration of peace was all that was needed for them to relinquish many of their hard-won gains.

Acknowledgments
I would like to thank Professor R.C. (Craig) Brown for encouraging the pursuit of this research, archivist Harold Averill for recommending insightful materials, and Professor Kathryn

McPherson for offering valuable advice. Any errors are entirely my own. My heartfelt thanks also extend to my mother Muriel Wilde for her love and unflagging support.

Notes

1. Sandra Whitworth, *Men, Militarism and UN Peacekeeping: A Gendered Analysis* (London: Lynne Rienner Publishers, 2004), 152.
2. See Judith Fingard, "Dalhousie Coeds, 1881-1921," in *Youth, University and Canadian Society: Essays in the Social History of Higher Education*, ed. Paul Axelrod and John G. Reid, 26-50 (Montreal and Kingston: McGill-Queen's University Press, 1989); Margaret Randolph Higonnet and Patrice Higonnet, "The Double Helix," in *Behind the Lines: Gender and the Two World Wars*, ed. Margaret Randolph Higgonet, Jane Jenson, Sonya Michel, and Margaret Collins Weitz (New Haven: Yale University Press, 1987), 35.
3. King's College became the nondenominational and secular "University of Toronto" in 1850. The University Act, 1853, secularized the institution and reduced it to granting degrees only; the teaching was done by University College. See Martin Friedland, *The University of Toronto* (Toronto: University of Toronto Press, 2002), 3-31.
4. See Daniel Wilson's biography in *Dictionary of Canadian Biography*, available at http://www.biographi.ca/; and A.R Ford, *A Path Not Strewn with Roses: One Hundred Years of Women at the University of Toronto* (Toronto: University of Toronto Press, 1985). Wilson believed higher education for women should be accomplished through a women-only college, unaffiliated with the University of Toronto.
5. Ford, *Path Not Strewn*, 3.
6. *The Varsity*, 24 January 1977.
7. See *Fasti Academici, King's College, 1827-1849* and *Fasti Academici, University College, 1850-1867* (Toronto: Harry Rowsell, 1850), University of Toronto Archives. The students' names represent the Upper Canadian elite known as the "Family Compact" and a long lineage of British stock and affluence.
8. Ford, *Path Not Strewn*, 3.
9. Ibid., 27.
10. A.B. McKillop, "Marching as to War: Elements of Ontario Undergraduate Culture, 1880-1914," in *Youth, University and Society: Essays in the Social History of Higher Education*, ed. Paul Axelrod and John G. Reid, 75-93 (Montreal and Kingston: McGill-Queen's University Press, 1989).
11. B.M. Moody, "Acadia and the Great War," in *Youth, University and Society: Essays in the Social History of Higher Education*, ed. Paul Axelrod and John G. Reid, 143-60 (Montreal and Kingston: McGill-Queen's University Press, 1989).
12. *The Varsity*, 11 March 1910. See also the photo essay "Visualizing Play," in *Home, Work, and Play: Situating Canadian Social History, 1840-1940*, ed. James Opp and John C. Walsh, 353-61 (Toronto: Oxford University Press, 2006). On separate spheres, see Kathryn McPherson, "The Case of the Kissing Nurse: Femininity, Sexuality and Canadian Nursing 1900-1970," in Opp and Walsh, *Home, Work, and Play*, 164-92, and Annmarie Adams,

"Female Regulation of the Healthy Home," in Opp and Walsh, *Home, Work, and Play*, 3-18.

13 Men involved in non-athletic pursuits, like debating societies, were often afforded the honorific "Mr." in newspaper reports. See "Varsity Wins Final Debate," *The Varsity*, 27 January 1911.
14 The Women's Intercollegiate Debating Society addressed topics such as: prayer in the home and the classroom, the effects of immigration on family morals and values, and the need for art/music/culture in a young woman's education. See *The Varsity*, 27 January 1911.
15 *The Varsity*, 12 October 1909.
16 Ibid., 18 October 1912.
17 Ibid., 19 October 1909.
18 University of Toronto, *Dramatis Personae* (1992), 2-6, Thomas Fisher Rare Book Library, University of Toronto.
19 *The Varsity*, 18 October 1912.
20 Ibid.
21 Ibid.
22 "Is There Conspiracy among Women Students to Refuse Seats in City Street Cars?" *The Varsity*, 9 March 1914.
23 *The Varsity*, 22 May 1915.
24 Ibid., 16 October 1918. Neglecting the physical exam meant "being refused admittance to lectures and participation in University life."
25 "University of Toronto Will Do Its Share," *The Varsity*, 30 September 1914; "Military Fever Rapidly Spreads through School," *The Varsity*, 7 October 1914; "Varsity Men Win Honour for Their Alma Mater," *The Varsity*, 19 January 1916.
26 Campus recruiting was popular at other universities too. See Moody, "Acadia and the Great War," 143-60; and McKillop, "Marching as to War," 75-93.
27 *The Varsity*, 6 November 1914.
28 Ibid.
29 For more information on the Red Cross and its role during the First World War, see Sarah Carlene Glassford, "Marching as to War: The Canadian Red Cross Society, 1885-1939" (PhD diss., York University, 2007), 107-81.
30 *The Varsity*, 13 January 1915.
31 Ibid. Red Cross items went to non-combatants (i.e., sick and wounded soldiers only), while items sent through other organizations went to men in active combat. During the war, much of women's voluntary work was generically referred to as "Red Cross work," despite its pertaining to a variety of organizations with different mandates. See Glassford, "Marching as to War," 154-55, 246-47.
32 *The Varsity*, 6 November 1914.
33 Ibid., 6 October 1915.
34 "Varsity Women Do Good Work for Red Cross," *The Varsity*, 13 January 1915.
35 McGill and Queen's universities, among others, also provided and supported base hospitals in France.

36 "A Sensible Measure," *The Varsity*, 13 November 1914.
37 Ibid.
38 Loosely translated from French, this implies a military rank akin to field marshal. See *The Varsity*, 3 February 1915.
39 Canon Henry John Cody went on to become president of the University of Toronto from 1932 to 1945. See Friedland, *University of Toronto*, 318-62.
40 C.P. Stacey, *Canada and the Age of Conflict*, vol. 1: *1867-1921* (Toronto: University of Toronto Press, 1992), 172-201. By January 1916, the number of soldiers was revised upwards to 500,000.
41 Conscripted soldiers did not receive any consideration at that time. Credits for service applied only to the men who voluntarily agreed to enlist. See "Senate Minutes," University of Toronto Archives.
42 One student who had failed his Spanish course miserably was summoned from the front, in the heat of battle, to receive a telegram from the University of Toronto advising him that he had been given a pass in the subject. Thanks to Harold Averill, University of Toronto Archivist, for providing this anecdote.
43 *The Varsity*, 16 October 1918.
44 Ibid., 19 November 1917.
45 "The Value of a College Education for Women," *The Varsity*, 8 November 1915.
46 Ibid.
47 *The Varsity*, 10 December 1915.
48 Ibid., 14 December 1917.
49 University of Toronto Archives, acc. A67-0007, box 36, 1 March 1915.
50 Ibid.
51 *The Varsity*, 19 November 1917.
52 "University Mobilizes Girls to Pick Fruit," *Toronto Star*, 16 February 1917, University of Toronto Archives, A73-0051, box 219.
53 Ibid. The article refers to a farming camp at Clarkville (location unknown).
54 *The Varsity*, 28 September 1917 and 14 December 1917.
55 *The Varsity*, magazine supplement (1916-17).
56 The VAD was jointly founded in 1909 by the Red Cross and the Order of St. John to complement existing resources. Most of the women were untrained nurses' aides assigned to mundane chores. See Quiney and Bishop Stirling, this volume.
57 Linda J. Quiney, "Bravely and Loyally They Answered the Call," *History of Intellectual Culture* 5, 1 (2005): 1-19.
58 *The Varsity*, 5 October 1917.
59 Michael Bliss, *A Canadian Millionaire* (Toronto: MacMillan of Canada, 1978), 281.
60 *The Varsity*, 23 November 1917.
61 "Opportunity for Women," *Toronto Star*, 3 March 1917. Adelaide Plumptre was an early Oxford alumna in political economy; an influential leader in the Canadian Red Cross, Ontario Girl Guides, and Canadian Patriotic Fund; and a future holder of municipal office.

62 See breakdowns of enrolments in *The President's Reports*, 1919-23 University of Toronto Archives, Fisher Library.
63 In 1914 the newspaper's masthead listed Miss Dorothy Josephine Ferrier as associate editor and three female reporters, but their by-lines did not surface during the research for this chapter, nor did I find that coverage of women's events had appreciably increased. Beatrice Corrigan later became a highly regarded academic in the classics department at University College.
64 *The Varsity*, 14 December 1917.
65 Ibid.
66 *The Varsity*, 11 January 1918.
67 Glassford, "Marching as to War," 249-50.
68 Open letter to students of the University of Toronto, *The Varsity*, 8 November 1918.
69 *The Varsity*, 11 November 1918.
70 "Reconstruction after the War," *The Varsity*, 8 November 1918.
71 Ibid.
72 "Important Meeting of WUA Thursday," *The Varsity*, 22 January 1919.
73 "The Women Students' Administrative Council," *The Varsity*, 27 October 1919.
74 "President Gives General Outline of Plan to Enable Non-Matriculated Veterans to Take up University Work," *The Varsity*, 8 January 1919.
75 *The Varsity*, 27 January 1919.
76 Ibid., 9 February 1920.
77 Ibid; "Prominent Women Outline Vocations Open to Graduates," *The Varsity*, 16 February 1920.
78 Veronica Strong-Boag, *The New Day Recalled: Lives of Girls and Women in English Canada, 1919-1939* (Toronto: Copp, Clark, Pitman, 1988), 18.
79 Quoted in Robert Sharpe and Patricia McMahon, *The Persons Case* (Toronto: University of Toronto Press, 2007), 57.
80 Sharpe and McMahon, *The Persons Case*, 57.
81 *The Varsity*, 9 January 1918.

PART 2:
WOMEN'S WORK?

> I don't know what is the work of women and what is the work of men. I don't think we'll ever be able to straighten it out again.[1]
>
> – ROBERTA MACADAMS, CA. 1917

Most Canadian and Newfoundland women and girls found a reasonably satisfying outlet for their energies in what the Newfoundland Women's Patriotic Association described as the "distaff side" of the war effort – fundraising and handicraft-focused voluntary war work not unlike the work women had traditionally done for their homes and communities through time immemorial.[2] Other women, as a result of either training or desire, directed their skills and energies elsewhere: into military nursing, Voluntary Aid Detachment nursing, and the paid labour force. In Canada, military nursing was open only to trained nurses, who served at home and overseas as Nursing Sisters with the Canadian Army Medical Corps. Women without prior hospital-nurse training could choose to enrol in the VAD program operated in Canada by the St. John Ambulance Association. Newfoundland women who wished to engage in wartime nursing could apply to become a Canadian Nursing Sister or VAD, or to become a British VAD, a British Red Cross nurse, or a Queen Alexandra's Imperial Military Nursing Service nurse. Women with no desire to nurse but for whom personal preference or economic necessity made voluntary war work untenable might find their way into the paid labour force.

For many people today and in the past, the phrase "women and war" brings to mind images either of white-veiled nurses at the bedsides of wounded soldiers or of the Second World War's iconic Rosie the Riveter flexing her muscles while proudly stating: "We can do it!" Not surprisingly, the historiography of the First World War (when it focuses on women) has most often turned to those women who worked as nurses or as factory workers. Although Newfoundland women's nursing and paid labour during the Great War largely remain to be studied, Canadian scholars have produced more literature on these two areas than any other.[3] In this respect, Canadian scholarship mirrors the historiography of women in the wider British Empire and the United States during the First World War.

The Great War raised questions about what was appropriately women's work. Nursing was traditionally seen as the natural province of women, but the emerging nursing profession (which relied on hospital training as the standard that protected it from being diluted by untrained outsiders) resisted the rush of ordinary women to its ranks. The VAD, which offered an outlet for untrained or semi-trained women to work in a nursing setting while performing the more menial tasks of the hospital, and which could be seen as another natural fit for women, framed itself in suspiciously martial terms. For their part, Canadian Nursing Sisters were unique in being actual members of the Canadian military. Was nursing women's work? Or military work? A variety of wartime women's work, including knitting, fundraising, and helping with the harvest, were also constructed in popular discourse as being women's version of fighting. Should women be "soldiers," even if they were removed from the front lines? In 1916, Helen Fraser urged her fellow Newfoundlanders to follow Canada's example and to use women to fill labour force positions at home (positions formerly held by able-bodied men) in order to stem the flood of Newfoundland women who were heading to Britain and the United States in order to take on more active wartime roles.[4] However, despite the exigencies of war, contemporaries in both dominions wondered whether it was appropriate for women to move into paid work that had previously been considered the exclusive domain of men. They worried that this might be too much change.

In this section, Linda Quiney argues that the VAD program offered Canadian women not only an active nursing role in the war but also a form of female soldiering. Terry Bishop Stirling examines nursing and VAD work from the Newfoundland perspective, offering detailed insights into the overseas experiences of two very different Newfoundland VADs. Kori Street turns to paid labour force participation, considering the context in which women were brought into the banking and munitions industries in Canada, and the range of attitudes and experiences that awaited them there. The women and girls of Canada and Newfoundland who lived through the Great War may not have experienced a transformation in society's thinking about their appropriate workplace roles on a scale equivalent to that of their daughters and granddaughters in the Second

World War, but they nonetheless encountered a wartime society that loosened its hold on some boundaries even as it clung tightly to others.

Notes

1. Quoted in Debbie Marshall, *Give Your Other Vote to the Sister: A Woman's Journey into the Great War* (Calgary: University of Calgary Press, 2007), 179.
2. Mabel W. LeMessurier, ed., editorial, *The Distaff* (1916): 1. LeMessurier points out that distaff is an old Anglo-Saxon word used to describe the part of the house in which women did their spinning and weaving.
3. On paid labour, see, for example: Ceta Ramkhalawansingh, "Women during the Great War," in *Women at Work, Ontario, 1850-1930*, ed. Janice Acton, Penny Goldsmith, and Bonnie Shepard, 261-307 (Toronto: Women's Press, 1974); Joan Sangster, "Mobilizing Women for War," in *The First World War in Canada: Essays in Honour of Robert Craig Brown*, ed. David Mackenzie, 157-93 (Toronto: University of Toronto Press, 2005); Kori Street, "Bankers and Bomb Makers: Gender Ideology and Women's Paid Work in Banking and Munitions during the First World War in Canada" (PhD diss., University of Victoria, 2001). The literature on wartime nursing includes: Geneviève Allard, "Des anges blanc sur le front: L'expérience de guerre des infirmières militaires canadiennes pendant la Première Guerre Mondiale," *Bulletin d'Histoire Politique* 8, 2-3 (2000): 119-33; Susan Mann, *Margaret Macdonald, Imperial Daughter* (Montreal and Kingston: McGill-Queen's University Press, 2005); Linda J. Quiney, "'Sharing the Halo': Social and Professional Tensions in the Work of World War One Canadian Volunteer Nurses," *Journal of the Canadian Historical Association* 9, 1 (1998): 105-24; Meryn Stuart, "Social Sisters: A Feminist Analysis of the Discourses of Canadian Military Nurse Helen Fowlds, 1915-18," in *Place and Practice in Canadian Nursing History*, ed. Jayne Elliott, Meryn Stuart, and Cynthia Toman, 25-39 (Vancouver: UBC Press, 2008); and Cynthia Toman, "'A Loyal Body of Empire Citizens': Military Nurses and Identity at Lemnos and Salonika, 1915-17," in Elliott et al., *Place and Practice*, 8-24.
4. Helen Fraser, "A War Register for Women," *The Distaff* (1916): 3. Fraser pointed out: "Over 160 [Newfoundland women] have left for the United States within the last two or three months, and many have gone to England to do war work there."

Gendering Patriotism
Canadian Volunteer Nurses as the Female
"Soldiers" of the Great War

Linda J. Quiney

In the early months of the war, as thousands of Canadian men rushed to enlist, eager to demonstrate their patriotism and be part of the adventure of a war that promised to be "over by Christmas," Canadian women found their options for patriotic service more constrained.[1] Only those women qualified for the work of a military nurse were eligible to serve in an official capacity overseas, as Nursing Sisters in the Canadian Army Medical Corps (CAMC). This distinction was further limited, as the civilian nursing leaders later complained, to the 3,141 nurses selected to hold the rank of lieutenant in the CAMC Nursing Service.[2] For the majority of Canadian women, active participation in the war was restricted to a supporting role on the home front in either non-traditional waged work or as unpaid volunteers in one of the numerous patriotic war relief organizations. Only the St. John Ambulance Association (SJAA) in Canada could offer civilian women the possibility of direct involvement in the war overseas as casually trained Voluntary Aid Detachment nurses, or VADs. Consequently, by the end of the Great War at least two thousand Canadian women had served as unpaid VAD nurses. Although the majority were assigned to local military convalescent hospitals at home, at least five hundred were posted to British military hospitals overseas.[3] Primarily unmarried, middle-class, Anglo-Protestant women in their mid- to late twenties, several of the VADs were educated women with university degrees, and many were employed in various women's occupations (such as teaching or clerical work). Many of those women who were offered the opportunity to serve overseas were known to have relinquished their regular waged employment for unpaid VAD service abroad.[4]

As VAD nursing was a unique exmaple of women's patriotic service, it is important to examine the rationale and organizational strategy behind the creation of Canada's VAD nurses of the Great War. The mechanisms that facilitated the transformation of earlier traditions of female voluntarism, to fit specific parameters for women's public war service through the gendering of patriotism, must also be addressed. The wartime reorientation of patriotic duty to conform to societal norms ultimately legitimated women's "active service" in the war, and, consequently, casually trained volunteer nurses were constructed in a way that paralleled the gendered ideology of masculine military service. Promoting its VAD nurses as well-bred, maternal patriots, St. John Ambulance created a unique role for Canadian women as wartime nursing volunteers. Although in no sense a feminist organization, SJAA nevertheless benefited from both the maternalist ideology and the service ethic espoused by the women's movement of the late nineteenth century. The role of VAD nursing was further legitimized through propaganda and the popular press as a direct service to the state, which could be equated to what "soldiering" was for men.

In 1914, however, when SJAA assumed responsibility for the VAD program, it had no intention of creating Canada's first female "soldiers." Initially, there was no plan to establish a large-scale association of volunteer nurses, only to provide a supportive subgroup of women volunteers to assist the men's ambulance detachments.[5] The original scheme for establishing VADs was devised by SJAA in early 1914, as a domestic resource only, in order to augment the military medical services in case of invasion, based on a British model established in 1909.[6] With the declaration of war, however, two developments fundamentally altered the anticipated configuration of Canada's VAD plan. First, the majority of the five hundred men in the existing St. John Ambulance Brigade Ambulance Divisions were quickly absorbed into the military medical services, while potential new volunteers were rapidly recruited into the military or war industries, such as armaments and munitions.[7] Second, Canadian women responded to the prospect of wartime volunteer nursing with unexpected zeal, and the resulting balance of membership in the VAD program was rapidly restructured from predominantly male to overwhelmingly female. The Canadian SJAA VAD plan thus quickly evolved into a women's voluntary nursing organization, echoing the experience of the British VAD organization and characterized by historian Anne Summers as a "women's movement," irrespective of its male-directed administration. Although proportionately only one-tenth the size of the British organization, Canada's VAD organization readily conforms to this designation.[8]

The ideal of feminine service was the military nurse of the CAMC, but only a select few could qualify. The majority of women nonetheless offered their services, paid or voluntary, according to their age, marital status, and class. Although women were denied direct access to the battlefield, the war reconfigured some traditional expectations of female service, channelling maternal energies away from the domestic front and towards the greater needs of "the boys" overseas. In Canada, working-class women demonstrated their patriotism through long hours in dirty and dangerous war factories, finding their value as non-traditional labourers had increased both financially and socially. They also replaced men on the farms, driving delivery vans and horse-drawn milk wagons or engaging in other traditionally masculine occupations.[9] As demand increased, working women doing "a man's job" saw their wages become more closely aligned to a man's pay as the workplace was regendered, legitimizing the much needed labour of women for any non-traditional waged employment that assisted the progress of the war effort. As Kori Street's chapter in this volume reveals, a process of ideological accommodation allowed women access to non-traditional worksites for the duration of the war without fundamentally upsetting the gender status quo. This did not signal a watershed, only a temporary realignment of the workforce until the men returned, at which time women were expected to redirect their energies to their "natural" centre in the home.[10]

The war offered women a brief opportunity to have new experiences, to prove their abilities, and to develop self-confidence in a wider world. Although women were bound to societal expectations, the maternalist ideology that fostered earlier traditions of community service, and supported prewar political activism, was now converted into patriotic productivity. Groups like the Suffrage War Auxiliary put middle- and upper-class women into banks and offices to release more men for armed service, the assumption being that the men were eager to be released.[11] Others worked in numerous unpaid relief organizations, helping to fill the gaps in state support for the war effort. Their energy and enthusiasm was rationalized and justified through their maternal capacities, prompting one commentator to declare that war "could never be waged if it were not mothered by women."[12]

Constructed as a feminine ideal of service, this characterization of women's appropriate patriotic behaviour balanced the masculine construction of patriotic duty regardless of class, providing a gendered definition of appropriate service for women and men. The soldier sacrificed his livelihood and family life for the duration of the war, ultimately risking all for the cause. Although women's patriotic service could not literally be equated to this type of heroism, their efforts were aligned with the cause through the language of militarism. Red Cross activities and fundraising were lauded as "heroic sacrifices of time and money," but only mothers who suffered the "supreme sacrifice" of losing a son were rewarded with equal "undying glory."[13] This point is further developed in this volume by Suzanne Evans, who examines such visible markers of wartime sacrifice as medals and flags.

Gender, class, maternalism, and traditions of community service thus prepared the way for the emergence of volunteer nursing as an ideal form of women's patriotic service in the Great War. The military nurse was armed with her status as a graduate, and she continued to perform her chosen career in uniform as she had as a civilian. However, VAD nurses – who were required to justify stepping out of their accustomed civilian roles as daughters, sisters, or fiancées to offer themselves for active service in the same way as male military recruits – assumed a new role that was certainly alien to their civilian persona. While the SJAA did not promise to transform the VAD into a qualified nurse with just a few weeks of training, it did promise to enhance the natural nursing abilities that, as a well-bred young woman, she was assumed to have. Through volunteering to nurse the sick and wounded combatants, a VAD became actively involved in the war, realizing "her nearest approach to being a soldier."[14] Ultimately, then, VAD nursing was related less to the work of the qualified graduate nurse than to an earlier generation of Victorian reformers and mission workers as the VADs moved outside of their accustomed and secure environment of home and community into an alien, and sometimes dangerous, new world.

Yet, unlike the many affiliates of the National Council of Women of Canada (NCWC), which had redirected their energies from the suffrage movement to patriotic activities during the war, the SJAA, as the progenitor of the VAD movement, could not be regarded as a woman's organization. As a historically military-medical, patriotic, and patriarchal brotherhood, traditionally Christian, conservative, and elitist, the modern SJAA was reconstituted in 1858, evolving out of the Victorian influences of militarism and imperialism that had grown with the expansion of the Empire and nineteenth-century wars, to achieve a new incarnation as a public service organization.[15] The SJAA was exported to Canada in 1883 as part of an Empire-wide campaign of social imperialism, to tame the colonial outposts with instruction in first aid, health, and hygiene.[16] Having gained a permanent foothold in Canada as a national organization by 1910, the SJAA initially concentrated on bringing first aid and ambulance training to the military, then, later, to men engaged in economic development in the manufacturing and resource industries. By 1913, the St. John Ambulance Brigade, as the active branch of the organization, had established twenty-four ambulance divisions across Canada, with nearly five hundred men trained to provide emergency first aid as ambulance attendants.[17] To gain a firm foothold in Canada, the SJAA also realized it needed to appeal to women by addressing family and community concerns regarding health, safety, and social welfare. For this purpose, the SJAA imported the home-nursing classes developed for women in Britain, unintentionally laying the foundation for the creation of Canada's VAD nurses during the Great War.[18]

War had been anticipated in Britain since the turn of the century, and both the SJAA and the British Red Cross had been actively promoting voluntary aid nursing programs since 1909.[19] Appealing primarily to middle-class women, the prewar organization of Brigade Nursing Divisions was far less advanced in Canada than it was in Britain, with only three nursing divisions having been established by 1913, two in Ontario and one in Manitoba. Involving just over fifty women in total, barely 10 percent of the men's enrolment, the nursing members provided support for the ambulance divisions during public emergencies.[20] More often, however, the nursing divisions assisted at community functions like fairs and sporting events, where, in hospital tents, the nursing volunteers treated minor injuries or illnesses, insect bites, sprained ankles, and heat stroke.[21] A woman's role in the Brigade was thus defined by maternalism, conforming to societal expectations of caring and nurturing and supporting a man's more vigorous role of emergency medical aid.[22]

As an extension of middle-class women's community public service, Brigade Nursing Divisions did not challenge the status quo and were therefore acceptable as an expression of women's role outside the home. The prewar Brigade nursing member was an updated version of the untrained, community volunteer worker of an earlier era, a public service provider with certified skills that ranked between those of a nurse and a social worker. Armed with the advantages of SJAA training, which was equated with the "organisational technologies and the technologies of applied science," Brigade nurses identified with both traditional women volunteer workers and the health care activists of the reform movement.[23]

With the declaration of war in August 1914, the Voluntary Medical Aid Plan was brought suddenly into focus as the primary function of the SJAA. Unlike in Britain, where VAD training and organization was shared with the British Red Cross Society, in Canada the SJAA had full responsibility for the VAD program.[24] At the outset, the disproportionate membership of men to women in the Brigade divisions was not regarded as a problem since it was expected that the men would take the larger role. The unanticipated departure of the trained ambulance men into military service was rapidly offset by the demand for women's classes in first aid and home nursing, which exceeded all expectations in the early months of the war.[25]

During the war, voluntary nursing was popularly romanticized due to the legacy of Florence Nightingale (the "Lady with the Lamp"), and it was further idealized with the enemy's execution of British nurse Edith Cavell in 1915.[26] Women were drawn to the idea of VAD nursing, which offered direct access to the war through the care of the wounded soldier but required only a few weeks of classroom training rather than the lengthy process of qualifying for military nursing. The sacrifice of salaried employment and the comforts of home seemed a small price to pay for the opportunity for service overseas – an opportunity no other form of women's voluntary patriotic service could provide. Yet, in the early months of the war, before military convalescent hospitals began to spread across the national landscape, Canadian VADs were little more than glorified cheerleaders, distributing candy and cigarettes to departing troops at railway stations and ports.[27] Early in 1915, without a clear purpose, VADs were already becoming restless, and some women took the initiative to apply directly to the British VAD organization in London, hoping for an overseas posting. Several travelled abroad without waiting for a call from Britain's Joint VAD Committee, although the SJAA and the Red Cross in Canada strongly advised against such initiative.

As the fear of invasion gradually subsided, the increasing need for suitable hospital space to care for the returning wounded signalled the next stage in the evolution of the Canadian VAD movement. Buildings, such as stately homes, colleges, and warehouses, were given over to the Militia Department and converted into military convalescent homes, where VADs could "hope to be able to serve in relays as probationers under graduate nurses."[28] Similar developments in other Canadian cities proclaimed a new, more formalized role for the VADs as they entered into service in a home-based military hospital environment. They now had immediate exposure to sick and wounded men returned from battle, and their role as nursing volunteers had moved beyond the ordinary scope of women's voluntary patriotic service, although it was still far distant from the battlefields overseas. Montreal VADs began assisting in local convalescent hospitals as early as March 1915 in the first of the Khaki Convalescent Homes established in that city. It was not without some discord that these VADs made their initial transition from anticipated to actual hospital service. Viola Henderson, a retired graduate nurse and commandant of the Montreal detachment, later conceded that "foes within and without in the form of sceptical minds tried to show many and varied reasons as to why it was unnecessary for such an organisation to exist in Canada." Nursing leaders and the military had protested that, unlike Britain, Canada had a surplus of trained nurses. The arguments mirrored those that successfully kept VADs out of the CAMC: the fear that unqualified women would undermine the gains made with regard to the recognition of nursing as a professional occupation based on science and acquired certified skills.[29] Determination won out, and, gradually, necessity triumphed over scepticism as the demand for convalescent nursing assistance continued to grow. One contemporary nursing historian, Dr. Maude Abbott, estimated that eventually twenty-five hundred Canadian VADs had enlisted for service.[30]

In the summer of 1916, a call finally came from the British VAD headquarters at Devonshire House in London, asking for Canadian VADs to augment the increasing demand for VADs in hospitals abroad. With the departure, in September, of the first group of sixty Canadian VADs who were destined for British military hospitals in England and France, the appeal of voluntary nursing markedly increased in Canada. Canadian VADs now had the chance to give direct assistance to sick or wounded men within the sound of gunfire. They saw their role as an auxiliary nursing service, serving as an extra pair of hands that could render the work of qualified military nurses more efficient.

Part of the appeal of VAD nursing was the relative ease and speed with which VAD certification could be acquired. The first step was the completion of the two required St. John Ambulance courses, in first aid and home nursing, in order to qualify as a St. John Ambulance Brigade nursing member.[31] If a woman was accepted into a nursing division, she was then expected to attend

Gendering Patriotism

regular meetings and practice sessions and to take part in various public activities and responsibilities. The financial outlay required for training and membership helped to define the social parameters of VAD service. There was a two-dollar fee charged by the SJAA for each of the two courses, and there was an annual membership fee of between three and five dollars.[32] The course fees and the annual Brigade membership fees, plus the costs of the required uniform, were a silent but effective means of determining the socio-economic boundaries of VAD applicants. The SJAA in Canada had full responsibility for VAD training and organization, and it stressed the high quality of VAD personnel, emphasizing class as a key component. Dr. Charles Copp, assistant commissioner of the St. John Ambulance Brigade in Ontario, was responsible for Canada's VAD organization. In a 1918 presentation, Dr. Copp noted that the applicants for VAD service had originated "in endless number from young women from the best homes in the country."[33] This observation was tied to the definition of the "best homes." Research demonstrates that Canada's VADs were primarily, but not exclusively, women from comfortable backgrounds. Far from Lyn Macdonald's description of British VADs as "gently nurtured girls who walked straight out of Edwardian drawing-rooms," Canada's VADs were more likely to have taken time from their work as teachers, secretaries, bank clerks, and other employment to train and volunteer for VAD service.[34] Certainly there were many like Newfoundland's Sybil Johnson, and Montreal's Dorothy MacPhail, who had never held or considered waged employment, but these were balanced by the many others whose family background afforded a good education that opened a path to a productive and paid career before marriage.[35] Copp was hoping to emphasize to an audience of qualified nurses that, whatever VADs might lack in skill, they compensated for in social credentials. By this, Copp seemed to imply that VADs, although not qualified nurses, were no relation to the pre-Nightingale era "Sarah Gamps" nurses, who had little nursing skill and were often of disreputable character. VADs were well-bred women whose class and social standing could only reflect positively on the nurses whom they assisted.[36]

The St. John Ambulance First Aid classes consisted of a five- or six-week program of weekly two-hour lecture and demonstration sessions, covering various emergency treatments (such as fractures, sprains, haemorrhages, burns, and poisoning), basic physiology, and a variety of bandaging techniques.[37] The home nursing program, for women only, was designed by Dr. James Cantlie in

Britain, who developed a model from the standardized course of study undertaken by nursing students in Britain's hospital training schools. Graduate nurses' training, in Canada as well as in Britain, generally involved three years of classroom and practical hospital work, but, for the home nursing course, Dr. Cantlie pared the details down to a basic overview. Hospital training was left to the discretion and organization of the individual nursing divisions, with the expectation that the nursing candidates would receive some practical training in local hospitals. Prior to the establishment of the military convalescent hospitals in Canada, however, VADs found little welcome in Canadian civilian hospitals. Copp later admitted that, among VADs selected for overseas service, it was not uncommon that "young women ha[d] been taken who ha[d] not had any hospital experience whatever."[38]

These remarks were presented to the July 1918 Convention of the Canadian National Association of Trained Nurses (CNATN). Dr. Copp was attempting to reassure the nurses, particularly their activist leaders, that the VADs posed no threat to the image or status of nursing as a knowledge-based skill, nor were they interested in continuing nursing as a career; rather, they only served in a temporary voluntary patriotic capacity. His closing remarks addressed these issues, particularly with regard to those VADs who had served overseas: "[They had] no previous desire in their hearts to enter the nursing profession, and have none now – it is pure patriotism on their part that has taken them – [and they] have done very capable service." He was equally concerned to dispel popular myths, declaring it "must be altogether discounted that those girls went over in order to get married."[39] Although he did not allay the CNATN's concerns about VAD nursing ambitions, the trained nurses could take some satisfaction from knowing that Canadian VADs had not been welcomed as nursing volunteers in the CAMC hospitals overseas but only in the overburdened British military hospitals.[40]

Throughout the war, the CAMC firmly resisted the use of VADs. The fear was that VADs would both hamper the efficiency of the qualified nursing personnel and, perhaps more significantly, undermine the status of commissioned CAMC nurses as professional representatives of the military medical service. The few VADs who were finally accepted in 1917 served only in a non-nursing capacity, as support personnel.[41] The SJAA was careful to emphasise that VAD training had no professional authority, although it based its claims for the competency of its VADs on the medical and nursing skills of the instructors.

Gendering Patriotism

Nevertheless, for women eager to experience a more active role in the war as a VAD nurse, the popular perception of nursing as the natural purview of women worked to their advantage. One St. John Ambulance proponent paraphrased Florence Nightingale when he promoted the VAD Home Nursing classes as designed to recognize that, although "every woman is a nurse, still every woman is not a skilled nurse."[42] This maternalist ideology, which recognized both the elements of skill and femininity that VAD nursing represented, was a useful justification for active patriotic service as a VAD nurse. Yet, in the prewar era, Brigade Nursing Divisions had held only minimal appeal for Canadian women due to their limited scope for leadership and autonomy within the male-directed administration of the SJAA. The more popular service organizations directed by women, like the International Order Daughters of the Empire or the Young Women's Christian Association, had offered their exclusively female membership a much greater opportunity to take leading roles. In the SJAA, women members followed orders and undertook to assist only when called upon by the more dominant male membership of the ambulance corps. The only significant advantage Brigade membership offered women in the prewar era was the uniform of the Nursing Division, a visible statement of their special training and abilities as volunteer nurses.

The SJAA nursing uniform signified a formal recognition of certification as a nursing volunteer, linking women's voluntarism to social welfare, public health, and the patriotic ideals of national military service. The literary historian Sharon Ouditt argues that the VAD uniform required a woman "to subjugate her appearance and behaviour." Clothed in the appropriate attire, the VAD became the representative of the institution. Although she lost her individual freedom, in Ouditt's words, the VAD gained "access to new and more glamorous freedoms: to be a nurse in wartime was a fitting occupation for a woman." Thus Ouditt believes that women, as much as men, were "eager to transform themselves into parcels of patriotism."[43] For the VAD nurse on war service, therefore, her nursing uniform was infused with the same representative power that fired the passion of the newly enlisted military recruit.

Long before the war, the uniform of the graduate nurse had come to represent both pride of association with her particular nursing school and pride in her own specialized training and skills.[44] The VADs experienced a similar pride in their newly acquired uniforms, which signified their unique role as women who were volunteering for active patriotic service.[45] Bessie Hall, a VAD from Nova Scotia, and a recent graduate of Dalhousie University, was breathless with excitement when she acquired her new uniform at a Halifax hospital:

> I have a thick grey coat (a beauty) and two hats and a lot of nursing clothes, aprons, etc. You should see my Cap! Wow! ... we wear a grey dress, white apron with bib, stiff linen collar, stiff cuffs, white belt and the cap, Mecca of my existence![46]

As the overseer of all Imperial VADs serving abroad, the Joint VAD Committee at Devonshire House in London, under the direction of Commandant-in-Chief Katherine Furse, outlined strict rules for the standard VAD uniform, whether the Red Cross or SJAA model. With only the SJAA setting the standard in Canada, the regulations conformed to the conventional British style St. John Ambulance Nursing Division uniform – a grey wool dress and white accessories. These latter, in particular, were more apt to vary with availability of materials and the preference of local organizations. Bessie Hall's headpiece was an earlier style of "Sister Dora" cap, most often worn by domestic servants, but, in older photographs, often seen worn by new nursing graduates. More favoured in Canada and Britain was the white veil, made of soft lawn cotton, which was not only comfortable and practical for keeping the hair neatly tied back but also flattering to almost every face. Sibyl Johnson, a Newfoundland VAD serving with the British Red Cross Colonial Division, was delighted with the veils, describing them as "white kerchiefs rather pretty and becoming."[47] More conscious of style and fashion, Violet Wilson from Edmonton found her veil was "the only attractive thing about the outfit," and, unlike Bessie, Violet was not charmed by the rest of the ensemble, which she found to be "unbelievably ugly." Violet's attempts to have the garments altered to a more stylish cut and fit before taking up her overseas VAD duties came up against the rigid regulations of Devonshire House, and the changes were only effected by a tailor who demanded the secrecy of a conspiracy.[48]

Commandant Katherine Furse considered the VADs to be in military uniform since their work in Britain and France was ultimately under the aegis of the British War Office. Although the uniform was designed to inhibit individuality, it signalled a new and positive identity for active patriotic service, which generated its own rewards. Bessie Hall discovered, to her delight, that beyond the hospital precincts the VAD uniform garnered the same discounts in the shops and restaurants of Halifax as did male military uniform.[49] In Britain also, Katherine Furse noted the "triumphs" of the uniform, which included free bus travel in London, making VADs "feel most warrantably superior to mere civilians in plain clothes."[50] Military nurses had earned their uniforms through long training and experience, unlike the VADs, who qualified after a few brief months of training. Whether civilian or military, the uniform of the graduate nurse was symbolic of her "professional competence and, above all, unquestionable moral character."[51] Worn by both VADs and military nurses, the becoming white veils were not accidentally styled to demonstrate their "saintly" aura, nor were the uniforms incidentally austere. Kathryn McPherson confirms that the civilian nursing uniforms were designed to neutralize sexuality, and the military model was apparently no less effective in realizing this purpose.[52]

Modelled on a standard nursing uniform of the era, the St. John Ambulance VAD nursing outfit was equally successful in projecting the asexual, maternal, modestly pious aura of Victorian femininity. Nevertheless, Sharon Ouditt argues that the VAD uniform had a stronger mystique, generating a new identity, like a "symbol of one's coming of age, of having entered a Symbolic Order."[53] Covering the upper body from neck to wrist, and being a regulation seven to eight inches from the floor (a distance actually measured by some hospital matrons), the earliest versions of the VAD uniform also sported detachable, starched white collars and cuffs, which chafed mercilessly. Earlier versions of caps and bonnets generally gave way to the more practical veil in most detachments, but the characteristic white-bibbed nurses' apron remained constant throughout the war for VADs on duty. However, it was taboo to travel beyond the hospital grounds in apron and sleeves as it was deemed important to maintain the dignity of the uniform as military dress.[54] Furthermore, all make-up, perfumes, jewellery, and ornaments were discouraged for fear of bringing "discredit on the Organisation."[55]

The British Red Cross VAD uniform, with its distinctive blue dress, boasted the most prominent VAD symbol – a red cross in the centre of the white apron bib. The rather more drab, grey colour scheme of the St. John Ambulance VAD uniform did not feature a red cross, only a plain white bib, with the eight-pointed cross of the Order of St. John displayed on an arm band. Yet, the emblematic red cross gradually evolved a particular significance as a universal symbol of the patriotic service of military nurses and VADs. Despite the incorrect association, a 1917 group photograph of the newly organized Calgary VAD Nursing Division displays prominent red crosses appliquéd on the white bibbed aprons

Calgary Nursing Central.Div. No.39.V.A.D.
(Class, 1917)

FIGURE 5   VAD work allowed women to make a hands-on contribution to the war effort. Shown here are Calgary trainees from the Class of 1917. [Glenbow Archives, NA 2267-4]

of their St. John Ambulance uniforms (see Figure 5). The irregular size and shape of these emblems betray their unofficial status as the handiwork of the VADs themselves, proclaiming their association with their sisters-in-service overseas.[56] The gesture demonstrates how powerful the symbol of the red cross had become for Canadian nursing volunteers, marking their communal patriotic service. The red cross became a favoured symbol of artists and illustrators, denoting both the pious and the maternal image of the war nurse as well as validating women's unique association with the wartime military medical services.

Gendering Patriotism

Although deeply rooted in Christian tradition dating back to the Crusades, the SJAA did not adopt the red cross as the official emblem of its uniform; however, this appears not to have discouraged the Calgary Division from assuming it. The SJAA itself drew on the iconography of a holy war, as waged by the ancient holy Order of St. John of Jerusalem during the Crusades. This rich history and imagery infused its modern, militarist service ethic, which provided emergency nursing assistance to fallen warriors through its own army of patriotic volunteers. The image of the military nurse, as a dominant symbol of patriotic womanhood, was potent. Whatever their service affiliation, all uniformed women served as a constant symbol of how reliant wartime society had become on the abilities of women, thus upsetting a social order long accustomed to masculine dominance in the public sphere.

As if to reinforce this fact, the visual propaganda of the war fully embraced the evocative symbolism of the war nurse, employing the white veil and red cross to signify piety and purity imbued with a militarist spirit. The illustration of "The Greatest Mother," designed for the American Red Cross by Alonzo Earl Foringer, was arguably among the most successful visual images of the war, and it still fuels heated debate among feminist scholars.[57] The angelic, pieta-styled central figure, draped in classical white robes adorned with a red cross, clasps a miniaturized wounded soldier to her breast. The image clearly emphasizes the importance of the healing maternal qualities of the war nurse over and above her acquired training and skills. Echoed in countless photographs and illustrations, this imagery blatantly links the concepts of religion, class, patriotism, and maternal duty.[58] Governments and war relief organizations frequently commissioned artists to promote a specific image, or idealized tableau, to promote their particular efforts. Photographs of hospital scenes were arranged in set poses to generate an aura of order, decorum, and scientific efficiency. Like the code of silence demanded of nurses and VADs regarding their work inside the hospitals, the reality of the internal workings of the hospital wards was further masked by the serenity projected in the approved photographs. One rare photograph of the interior of a St. John Ambulance hospital ward depicts neat rows of well-disciplined patients, lying in immaculate hospital cots in a large, airy room. As in other similar photographs, the men are watched over by rigidly erect, and aseptically proper, nurses and VADs, reinforcing the Victorian ideals of order, decorum, and unassailable propriety between the nurse and patient.[59]

Photographs produced for the SJAA promoting the VAD program repeatedly emphasize the innocence and femininity of the nursing volunteers. A portrait of the "Three Shining Lights of Pine Hill Military Convalescent Hospital," Miss Marion Doull, VAD; Miss Madeline Scott, VAD; and Miss Edith Pike, VAD, the first VADs permitted to serve in a Halifax military hospital, testifies to the success of the decision to allow civilian volunteer women access to the wards, despite much resistance to the idea. To fully emphasize the innocence, femininity, and Victorian demeanour of the VADs, this group was posed in the precocious style of the "three little maids" from the Gilbert and Sullivan operetta *The Mikado*.[60] Another Victorian image was evident in a popular photo-portrait of a British VAD entitled: "Reverie: A Red Cross Worker." Commissioned from a professional photographer, the pose was designed to enhance the image of the VAD and to promote recruitment. The title and pose were meant to evoke both a romantic femininity and a pious devotion to patriotic work. Photographic historians Condell and Liddiard note how the imagery is borrowed from the romantic and ethereal Pre-Raphaelite style and how the "virginal religious aura is strengthened by the Madonna lilies in the background."[61]

This style of portrait – delicate, romantic, and spiritual – was in marked contrast to the more natural images recorded by Canadian photo-journalists for the War Records Office. A Canadian VAD ambulance driver serving with the Red Cross Convoy at Étaples, Grace MacPherson, was selected to represent Canadian women's war service abroad. From Vancouver, Grace was one of the fortunate few Canadian women selected for the "glamour" posting of a VAD motor ambulance driver. Successful candidates were expected to know how to drive a car in addition to taking responsibility for all maintenance and repairs. The non-traditional nature of the work aligned these women more closely to the work of the soldier than did any other volunteer post open to them. As an inherently masculine undertaking, this was the nearest women came to carrying a gun. Although film and literature have romanticized the idea of Red Cross women ambulance drivers skirting the dangers of the battlefields to rescue the fallen, Anne Summers confirms that "the pre-war division of labour stood firm, and the work remained a male preserve." Women drivers were responsible only for ferrying men between the distant transfer points of the military hospitals, ambulance trains, and hospitals ships.[62] Nevertheless, this work was not without its hazards, especially without headlights on dark, rain-swept nights on remote, deserted French roads.

Unlike the romantic image of the Red Cross VAD, the photographs of Grace MacPherson present an energetic young woman, healthy, hard-working, and with a handsome attraction rather than someone with a fragile femininity.[63] In her plain service coverall, hair tousled and hands oily, Grace's photographs emanate a rugged elegance as she sits at the wheel of her ambulance, changes the tire, cranks the engine, or fills the radiator. All the while, Grace smiles out with a reassuring candour, although in her diary she records that the day was "an awful ordeal."[64] The photographs served to reassure Canadians half a world away that the young women on war service could retain their wholesome and healthy femininity even when their patriotic service was associated with masculine prowess.

Although neither nurses nor VAD drivers were engaged in combat, dangers from enemy action threatened all women on war service. Despite precautions, Allied nurses and VADs did lose their lives, sometimes as the result of direct bombing or the torpedoing of hospital ships but more often to disease. The six Canadian VADs known to have died on service all succumbed to illness or infection, while forty-six CAMC Nursing Sisters were lost through a combination of illness and enemy fire. When the Canadian hospital ship *Llandovery Castle* was torpedoed off the Irish coast in June 1918, fourteen CAMC nurses perished in the sea.[65] This outrage fuelled the fires of propaganda, and one well known dramatic poster depicts a martyred nurse being cradled gently above the waves by a Canadian soldier, defiantly shaking his fist at the retreating enemy. The caption reads: "Victory Bonds Will Help Stop This." Ironically, the nurse, who achieved the ultimate glory of the soldier – dying in the service of her country – was depicted in the uniform of a British Red Cross VAD rather than that of a CAMC Nursing Sister.[66]

The gendered language of war, combined with these visual images, reinforced the perceptions that equated VAD service with that of the soldier. The popular support for VAD nursing was based on its maternal qualities, which were necessary in order to legitimize the active service of women as casually trained nursing volunteers. This was not the case with military nurses, whose work was validated by their recognized qualifications. For VADs, however, patriotic maternalism provided a tenable argument with which to persuade reluctant families, who feared for a daughter's physical and moral security in hospitals overseas. Janet Watson argues that young, middle-class women, particularly those of British origin, raised and educated in the same imperialist traditions of service to King and Empire as their brothers, had an almost innate response to the call for war service. Their generation had been taught, in Watson's words, "the same language of patriotism, honour, sacrifice and empire as their brothers." Doreen Gery, a Canadian VAD, recalled the profusion of posters that bore the insistent plea: "Your King and Country Need You!" Sisters as well as brothers responded; after her own brother enlisted with fifteen of his classmates, Gery followed him to France as a VAD.[67] For those women fortunate enough to be accepted as a VAD nurse, particularly if they were posted abroad, "the hospital became their displaced trench."[68]

The concept of the "warrior-nurse" was encouraged by the SJAA, which was the progenitor of the Canadian VAD program, and it was widely reinforced through the voice of the popular press. Journalists like Moore collectively identified nurses and VADs as "sympathetic women and ... brave soldiers."[69] Watson argues that it was the VADs, rather than the qualified nurses, who, by the nature of their volunteer status, more closely conformed to the essence of soldiering. For CAMC military nurses, war service was an extension of their regular peacetime occupation, not a complete change from their former paid status as civilian nurses.[70] By comparison, the VADs, like the soldiers, had relinquished their usual peacetime occupations to undertake their war service, and some VADs had risked their job security for the opportunity to engage in patriotic service. While VADs and soldiers alike expected to return to their usual civilian pursuits at the war's end, the military nurses would return to the work of nursing in a civilian capacity, the war having altered only the location and description of their work rather than the essential content.[71]

The gendering of patriotism thus enabled the VAD to maintain her femininity. Like a CAMC military nurse, she wore a military style uniform that cloaked her sexuality in its long skirts, a starched white apron that extolled her efficiency, and a saintly veil that proclaimed her allegiance to a "holy war." She had enlisted voluntarily, much like a soldier, and, following a similarly brief training, she had relinquished her civilian status – but, unlike the qualified CAMC nurses, only for the duration of the war. Gendered as a patriotic service, VAD nursing maintained the aura of soldiering while demanding respect for the nurse's essentially feminine role. The framework of gender and class had defined the nineteenth-century traditions of women's community service and, in the early twentieth century, had rendered VAD nursing socially acceptable for civilian women volunteers during the Great War.

In Canada, the tradition of the SJAA as an elite, militarist, and Christian service organization validated its enlistment of casually trained wartime nursing volunteers and enhanced the VADs' status as well-bred, dedicated patriots. Recruited out of their private lives to undertake a brief, but essential, war service as volunteer nurses, St. John Ambulance VADs in Canada enjoyed an unprecedented opportunity to serve in the capacity of female soldiers. Anne Summers contends that the concept of VAD service evolved from its earliest inception as a form of organized camp follower supporting the work of male ambulance attendants, ultimately transforming into the framework of a "woman's movement."[72] Thus VAD service gave shape to the patriotic idealism of women in the war generation who, like Jean Sears, decided that: "England was in danger, Canadian men were going over and if Canadian women got a chance to go, they should go and help!"[73] Firmly grounded within the expectations of women's work, volunteer nursing posed little challenge to societal norms and was supported by the perception of its middle-class foundations in "the best homes."

The social discourse that valorized patriotic service as a Christian cause, and wartime nursing as the work of "angels of mercy," was promulgated through the print and visual propaganda of the war era. Like the hastily acquired combat skills of the soldier, the VAD's training had only been in following instructions, but that was enough to grant her an active part in the war effort. Speaking for the SJAA in 1921, Marie Taschereau confidently declared:

> Young women, keyed up to the same spirit of patriotism that spurred their young brothers to enlist, will never regret the training they received under the St. John Ambulance. They were by this given the opportunity to serve and bravely and loyally they answered the call.[74]

In essence, if not in fact, St. John Ambulance Voluntary Aid Detachment nurses had become Canada's first female soldiers, and the VADs could ultimately view their efforts as a small triumph in breaking down the barriers to women's active service in war.

Acknowledgments

An earlier version of this chapter was presented at the 2002 Canadian Historical Association Annual Conference in Toronto. The author gratefully acknowledges the generous support of this research by the Hannah Institute for the History of Medicine through Associated Medical Services, Inc., Toronto.

Notes

1 Desmond Morton and J.L. Granatstein, *Marching to Armageddon: Canadians and the Great War, 1914-1919* (Toronto: Lester and Orpen Dennys, 1989), 7. See also Sandra Gwyn,

Tapestry of War: A Private View of Canadians in the Great War (Toronto: Harper Collins, 1992), 49. Sandra Gwyn notes that thirty thousand Canadian men had enlisted by September 1914.

2 Representing the Canadian National Association of Trained Nurses, Jean Gunn noted that the majority of qualified women who applied were not required by the CAMC. See Jean Gunn, "The Services of Canadian Nurses and Voluntary Aids during the War," *Canadian Nurse* 15, 9 (1919): 1975; Meryn Stuart, "War and Peace: Professional Identities and Nurses' Training, 1914-1930," in *Challenging Professions: Historical and Contemporary Perspectives on Women's Professional Work,* ed. Elizabeth Smyth, Sandra Acker, Paula Bourne, and Alison Prentice, 171-93 (Toronto: University of Toronto Press, 1999).

3 See Linda J. Quiney, "Assistant Angels: Canadian Women as Voluntary Aid Detachment (VAD) Nurses during and after the Great War, 1914-1930" (PhD diss., University of Ottawa, 2002).

4 Ibid., chap. 3. At least 194 were in waged employment prior to their VAD service overseas.

5 Originally, the Voluntary Aid plan called for "Men's Detachments" of fifty-five members to act as emergency ambulance personnel. The "Women's Detachments" of twenty-three members would assist as nurses and cooks, setting up rest stations and temporary hospital shelters. See Militia Department, *The Organisation of Voluntary Medical Aid in Canada,* 3 March 1914, 53, Regulation No. 7.

6 Jeffrey A. Keshen, *Propaganda and Censorship during Canada's Great War* (Edmonton: University of Alberta Press, 1996), 6; and War Office, *Scheme for the Organisation of Voluntary Aid in England and Wales* (London: HMSO, 1909).

7 Dr. Charles Copp, "The St. John's Ambulance Brigade," *Canadian Nurse* 14, 7 (1918): 1165.

8 Anne Summers, *Angels and Citizens: British Women as Military Nurses, 1854-1914* (London/New York: Routledge and Kegan Paul, 1988), 253. The author estimates that at least twenty-three thousand British women served as VAD nurses (270).

9 Gwen Szychter, "The War Work of Women in Rural British Columbia: 1914-1919," *British Columbia Historical News* 27, 4 (1994): 8-9.

10 For a comprehensive study of women's non-traditional war work, see Ceta Ramkhalawansingh, "Women during the Great War," in *Women at Work: Ontario, 1850-1930,* ed. Janice Acton, Penny Goldsmith, and Bonnie Shepard, 261-307 (Toronto: Canadian Women's Educational Press, 1974). See also Daphne Read, ed., *The Great War and Canadian Society: An Oral History* (Toronto: New Hogtown Press, 1978); and Barbara M. Wilson, ed., *Ontario and the First World War, 1914-1918: A Collection of Documents* (Toronto: University of Toronto Press, 1977), lxxxv-xciv.

11 Wilson, *Ontario and the First World War,* lxxxvi.

12 Wealtha A. Wilson and Ethel T. Raymond, "Canadian Women in the Great War," in *Canada in the Great World War* (Toronto: United Publishers of Canada, 1921), 6:176.

13 Wilson and Raymond, "Canadian Women," 177. The authors noted of the mother's sacrifice that, "supremest of all was the giving up of their first born." The language of "heroic sacrifice" is well documented in Alan R. Young, "'We Throw the Torch': Canadian

Memorials of the Great War and the Mythology of Heroic Sacrifice," *Journal of Canadian Studies* 24, 4 (1989/90): 5-28.

14 Olive Dent, "On Home Service," in *The War Illustrated: A Pictorial Record of the Conflict of the Nations*, ed. J.A. Hammerton (London: Amalgamated Press, 1918), 9:175.

15 Summers, *Angels and Citizens*, 167; Strome Galloway, *The White Cross in Canada, 1883-1983: A History of St John Ambulance* (Ottawa: St John Priory, 1983), 17-21.

16 Galloway, *White Cross in Canada*, 25-6; G.W.L. Nicholson, *The White Cross in Canada: A History of St John Ambulance* (Montreal: Harvest House, 1967), 29.

17 Archives of Ontario, F823/MU6858, Administration Records 1909-1977; File A.K. Prentice, 1913-1955, *Annual Report for 1913 of the St John Ambulance Brigade Overseas: Within the Dominion of Canada* compl. Capt. G.R.N. Collins, 12.

18 Nicholson, *White Cross in Canada*, 37-41; Galloway, *White Cross in Canada*, 33-37.

19 Summers, *Angels and Citizens*, 170.

20 *Annual Report for 1913*, 13. St. John's, Newfoundland, had a British Red Cross Brigade Nursing Division.

21 Nicholson, *White Cross in Canada*, 37-54; Galloway, *White Cross in Canada*, 33-48.

22 *Annual Report for 1913*, 14.

23 Gale Wills, *A Marriage of Convenience: Business and Social Work in Toronto, 1918-1957* (Toronto: University of Toronto Press, 1995), 14.

24 Galloway, *White Cross in Canada*, 50. See also "St. John Ambulance Association, Central Executive Report, 1915," 9-10, Imperial War Museum (IWM), Women's Work Collection (WWC), British Red Cross Society (BRCS) 1/4.

25 "Ottawa Centre, Secretary's Report, 1915," 2, Ottawa City Archives, MG 26 D83, St. John Ambulance Association Records, Ottawa Nursing Division no. 32, 1910-27.

26 Nightingale's work in the Crimean War (1854-55), and subsequent reforms in nurses' training and practice, heralded the modern era of organized nursing. See Summers, *Angels and Citizens*, 29-68; Sue M. Goldie, ed., *"I Have Done My Duty": Florence Nightingale in the Crimean War, 1854-1856* (Iowa City: University of Iowa Press, 1987). Cavell was executed for spying in 1915. See A.E. Clark-Kennedy, *Edith Cavell: Pioneer and Patriot* (London: Faber and Faber, 1965).

27 Annmarie Adams, "Borrowed Buildings: Canada's Temporary Hospitals during World War I," *Canadian Bulletin of Medical History* 16, 1 (1999): 25-48.

28 "Report of the Commandant: Ottawa Women's Voluntary Aid Detachment," 8 November 1915, 3, Ottawa City Archives, MG 26 D83, St. John Ambulance Association Records.

29 Mrs. Viola Henderson, "VAD Work in Montreal," *Canadian Nurse* 14, 8 (1918): 1245-46. The Khaki League equipped these homes, which were generally converted buildings or large houses previously used for other purposes.

30 Maude E. Seymour Abbott, MD, "Lectures on the History of Nursing," *Canadian Nurse* 19, 3 (1923): 149. This is the only known reference to this number. My research indicates at least two thousand. The official St. John Ambulance total to the end of 1917 was 1,789. See Nova Scotia Archives and Records Management, Archibald papers, Red Cross History, MG26, Volume 321, *Report of the Chief Commissioner for Brigade Overseas: 1 October*

1915 to 31 December 1917, compl. Earl of Ranfurly, 35. The fifty-one from Newfoundland makes a combined total of 1,840 women at the close of 1917.
31 Militia Department, *Organisation of Voluntary Medical Aid,* 6.
32 *Annual Report for 1913,* 22. Costs varied by location, lecturer's fees, and the cost of materials.
33 Copp, "The St. John's Ambulance Brigade," 1165.
34 See Lyn Macdonald, *The Roses of No Man's Land* (London: Penguin, 1993); and Quiney, "Assistant Angels," 123-37.
35 See "Sybil Johnson," Centre for Newfoundland Studies, collect-201; "Sir Andrew MacPhail," LAC, MG 30 D150.
36 Charles Dickens, *Martin Chuzzlewit* (Oxford: Oxford University Press, 1992 [1844]).
37 Ibid., 23.
38 Copp, "The St. John's Ambulance Brigade," 1166.
39 Ibid.
40 Quiney, "Assistant Angels," 65.
41 Matron E.M. McCarthy, Principal Matron, France, BEF, "Report on Work in France of the Canadian Army Medical Corps," Public Records Office, Kew, no. WO222/2134, miscellaneous files, 1914-18.
42 *Leader* (Regina), 28 January 1911, 10. Nightingale is quoted as declaring that "every woman is a nurse."
43 Sharon Ouditt, *Fighting Forces, Writing Women: Identity and Ideology in the First World War* (London/New York: Routledge, 1994), 17.
44 Kathryn McPherson observes that the uniform set the trained nurse apart from untrained women, unqualified practical nurses, and midwives. See Kathryn McPherson, *Bedside Matters: The Transformation of Canadian Nursing, 1900-1990* (Toronto: Oxford University Press, 1996), 43.
45 Ibid. See also *Annual Report for 1913,* 10.
46 "Bessie Hall to Mother, 2 October 1918," Nova Scotia Archives and Records Management, McGregor-Miller Collection, MG1, vol. 661, no. 8.
47 "Letter, Christmas Day, 1916 (Tuesday a.m.)," CNS, Sybil Johnson Papers, collection-201, file 2.01.013.
48 "Violet Wilson Interview," c. 1970, *Voice of the Pioneer,* LAC, acc. 1981-0111.
49 "Bessie Hall to Mother, 2 October 1918," Nova Scotia Archives and Records Management, McGregor-Miller Collection, MG1, vol. 661, no. 8.
50 Katherine Furse, *Hearts and Pomegranates: The Story of Forty-Five Years, 1875 to 1920* (London: Peter Davies, 1940), 302.
51 Irene Schuessler Poplin, "Nursing Uniforms: Romantic Idea, Functional Attire, or Instrument of Social Change," *Nursing History Review* 2 (1994): 153.
52 McPherson, *Bedside Matters,* 37.
53 Ouditt, *Fighting Forces, Writing Women,* 18.
54 Stella Bingham, *Ministering Angels* (London: Osprey, 1979), 143. See also IWM, WWC, BRCS 10.2/12.

55 IWM, WWC, BRCS 10.2/12.
56 "Calgary Nursing Division #39, Class of 1917" [photograph], Glenbow Museum and Archives, NA 2267-4.
57 Entitled "The Greatest Mother in the World," the illustration was created for an American Red Cross fundraising campaign, circa 1918. See Joseph Darracott, ed., *The First World War in Posters* (Toronto/London: General Publishing/Constable, 1974), 1 [Plate 56]. For interpretations, see Sandra M. Gilbert, "Soldier's Heart: Literary Men, Literary Women, and the Great War," in *Behind the Lines: Gender and the Two World Wars,* ed. Margaret Randolph Higonnet, Jane Jenson, Sonya Michelle, and Margaret Collins Weitz (New Haven/London: Yale University Press, 1987), 212; Jane Marcus, "The Asylums of Antaeus: Women, War and Madness: Is there a Feminist Fetishism?" in *The Difference Within: Feminism and Critical Theory,* ed. Elizabeth Meese and Alice Parker (Amsterdam/Philadelphia: J. Benjamins, 1989), 64; and Sarah Glassford, "The Greatest Mother in the World: Carework and the Discourse of Mothering in the Canadian Red Cross Society during the First World War," *Journal of the Association for Research on Mothering* 10, 1 (2008): 219-32.
58 The visual representations of the Great War and women's part in it are examined in Diana Condell and Jean Liddiard, *Working for Victory? Images of Women in the First World War, 1914-1918* (London: Routledge and Kegan Paul, 1987). See also John F. Hutchinson, *Champions of Charity: War and the Rise of the Red Cross* (Boulder: Westview, 1996), pictorial essay, plates 1-24.
59 See Order of St. John, *St. John in Focus: A History of St. John Ambulance in Photographs* (London: Order of St. John, 1987). The Hollywood myths of romance between patient and nurse did occur, but a rigorous monitoring by supervisors curbed much of the fraternization.
60 M.S. Hunt, *Nova Scotia's Part in the Great War* (Halifax: Nova Scotia Veteran Pub. Co., 1920), 434. Victorian values were projected onto a Japanese setting in the *Mikado,* produced by W.S. Gilbert and Sir Arthur Sullivan in London, March 1885. See also Mrs. Archibald, *Nova Scotia Red Cross during the Great War: Nineteen Fourteen-Eighteen* (Halifax: Nova Scotia Provincial Branch CRCS, 1920), 57.
61 Condell and Liddiard, *Working for Victory,* 20. Photograph produced by Horace W. Nicholls, 1918.
62 Summers, *Angels and Citizens,* 269.
63 Gwyn, *Tapestry of War,* 435-38. These photos were part of an exhibition of Canadian war images held in London in July, 1917 and one was reproduced in a wartime newsletter, *The Canadian Daily Record.*
64 Grace MacPherson Diaries, "9 June 1917," Canadian War Museum, 58A1 21.12. See also, "Canadian VAD Ambulance Driver with BRCS, Étaples Motor Convoy," 8 June 1917, photograph of Grace MacPherson, LAC, PA1315.
65 G.W.L. Nicholson, *Canada's Nursing Sisters* (Toronto: Samuel Stevens, Hakkert, 1975), 94-96.
66 Maurice F.V. Doll, *The Poster War: Allied Propaganda Art of the First World War* (Edmonton: Royal Alberta Museum, 1993), 40.

67 Silva Basmajian, producer, *And We Knew How to Dance* (National Film Board, 1993). Gery's brother was among the fourteen classmates who died.
68 Janet Sledge Kobrin Watson, "Active Service: Gender, Class and British Representations of the Great War" (PhD diss., Stanford, 1996), 23.
69 Mary Macleod Moore, "Canadian Women War Workers Overseas," *Canadian Magazine* 52, 3 (1919): 738.
70 Quiney, "Assistant Angels," chap. 5. See also, Watson, "Active Service," 161-64.
71 Quiney, "Assistant Angels," chap. 7.
72 Summers, *Angels and Citizens*, 253.
73 Read, *Great War and Canadian Society*, 97. The quotation is attributed to "Mrs. Jane Walters," a pseudonym for Jean Sears Suydam, who served overseas in Britain as a VAD for a year. See also Personnel Card Indexes: Military Hospital Files/Record Cards, British Red Cross Society Museum and Archives, Barnett Hill, Guildford, Surrey; and "Jean Marita Sears (Suydam)," 23 July 1974, LAC, A1 9903-0008, The Great War and Canadian Society Project.
74 Mme. Marie Taschereau, "Home Nursing of Value to Women," *St. John Ambulance Association, First Aid Magazine* 2, 7 (1921): 3.

5

"Such Sights One Will Never Forget"
Newfoundland Women and Overseas Nursing in the First World War

Terry Bishop Stirling

> There were so many poor boys coming in all the time, that we kept going at top speed and fell into bed at night exhausted. We had to feed the blind and write letters for them. My heart used to break just to see them – but usually I was too busy rushing around and doing things for them to even think of whether I had a heart.[1]

The above quotation from a former Newfoundland Voluntary Aid Detachment worker depicts both the pain she felt when tending servicemen during the First World War and her determination to put her own feelings aside in order to "do her bit." Jeanette Coultas was typical of many young women who felt compelled to join their brothers, friends, and sweethearts in defending the Empire. Although most of the middle- and upper-class women who served as nurses and VADs lived fairly conventional and protected lives before 1914, they were also raised to have a sense of duty to their communities. These were the daughters of women who supported local churches, organized charitable efforts, and led the social and artistic life of their hometowns. Growing up in Newfoundland, they would also have imbibed the intense imperialist sentiment in Britain's "oldest colony." When the war started, Newfoundland women, like their counterparts throughout the Empire, looked for ways to support the cause. Despite witnessing horrendous suffering, few regretted their decision to join. They felt great pride in the gratitude of their patients and the praise of their superiors in the hospitals and in their hometowns. While these women shared common challenges, their reactions to these varied depending on their background, prior experience, and personality. Proximity to the front also dictated the severity of wounds and number of deaths they witnessed, and it affected their comfort, security, and access to friends, family, and other supports.

When Britain declared war in August 1914, Newfoundland automatically pledged its full support. The country was a patriotic member of the British Empire, and its contribution to the war effort was disproportionate to its small population and its modest economic means. Over the next four years, Newfoundland outfitted and paid for its own regiment and naval reserve and supplied many other men for the British and Canadian services. In all, over twelve thousand Newfoundland men served, either with the country's own regiment or naval reserve, or as part of the British or Canadian services. In the regiment, naval reserve, and merchant marine alone, over sixteen hundred men lost their lives.[2] On 1 July 1916, the tight-knit Newfoundland Regiment was devastated near the town of Beaumont Hamel on the opening day of the Battle of the Somme. Approximately eight hundred men advanced from their trenches and were mowed down by German machine guns; 233 died on the field, 477 were reported wounded or missing.[3]

While men volunteered for overseas service, women also looked for ways to contribute to the cause. In many parts of the Empire, they worked in arms factories or replaced servicemen in "male" jobs. In Newfoundland, the one arms factory created after 1914 did not last, and, while a few more clerical jobs may have opened up in the larger towns, there was no noticeable increase in non-traditional work for women.[4] As Margot Duley (this volume) discusses, thousands of Newfoundland women found comfort and fulfillment knitting socks, rolling bandages, and organizing fundraisers for the war effort. Others wanted to be closer to the action and of more immediate help to servicemen. As soon as the war began, they sought opportunities to work overseas as nurses or as members of the British Voluntary Aid Detachment, an organization founded in 1909 to provide nurses' aides in military hospitals.[5]

Both nurses and VADs were largely drawn from Newfoundland's business and professional families and many of them knew one another. Nursing students had to have the equivalent of a high school education and be from families who could manage without their wages or labour while they completed their training. As the background of VADs demonstrates, however, the middle class is a wide one. Frances (Fanny) Cluett, for example, was from a leading family of merchants, fishers, and boat builders in Belleoram on Newfoundland's south coast. She was educated at the small local school and at the time of her service she was a mature and steady thirty-three-year-old and was teaching in her hometown. From 1916 to 1920 she was a VAD in England, France, and Constantinople.[6] Born in 1887, Sybil Johnson was the daughter of a Supreme Court judge and was significantly wealthier than Cluett. Johnson attended finishing school in England and studied music in Germany for two years. When war broke out she was engaged to an up-and-coming young lawyer, Brian Dunfield, and supporting various charitable causes, often using her musical training. She and her sister Jill joined the VAD in 1916, and Sybil went on to serve for nineteen months at the 1st Western Military Hospital in Liverpool.[7] Similarly, ambulance driver Armine Gosling was the daughter of St. John's mayor; her mother was the leader of the country's prewar women's movement.[8] Others were from more modest backgrounds. At the outbreak of the war, VAD Jeanette Coultas, for example, was working as a store clerk in the capital.[9] Nurse Bertha Forsey was the daughter of a policeman.[10]

Initially, the British War Office maintained that it did not require the service of colonial nurses or VADS, reporting that there were enough eager British volunteers to meet demand. A few would-be nurses' aides simply disregarded official discouragement. By 1914, Janet Miller had already shown her determination in the face of official resistance by successfully fighting a law society ban on women law students. When the war started the twenty-two-year-old put her studies on hold and followed her fiancé Eric Ayre to Scotland, where they were married. Miller's father was a successful furniture maker and the Ayres were one of Newfoundland's most prominent and wealthy merchant families. In Scotland, Miller worked in canteens and hospital kitchens. After Eric's death at Beaumont Hamel she moved with her mother-in-law to London, where she worked as a VAD and trained as an ambulance driver. As with her law studies, her ambitions were again thwarted by the war and her sense of familial duty. After her only brother died of pneumonia while on leave in London in December 1916, both her mother and mother-in-law objected to her plan to go to the front and the dutiful Miller stayed to comfort the two grieving mothers.[11]

When British authorities rebuffed her offer to serve, Nurse Maysie Parsons used family connections to obtain a spot with one of the first contingents of Canadian overseas nurses. Her brother, Dr. W.H. Parsons, was serving with the Canadian Army Medical Corps. Through his influence Parsons was assigned to the Royal Victoria Hospital Corps, which left Montreal for Belgium in April

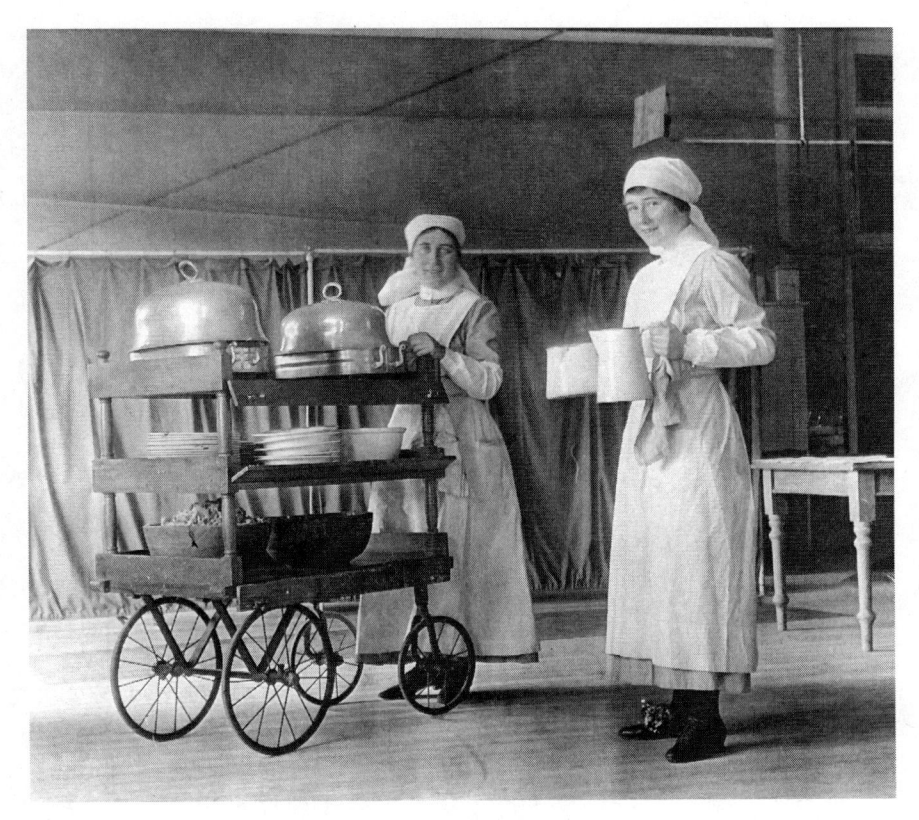

FIGURE 6 Newfoundlander Ruby Ayres (left) and fellow VAD "Georgie" bring around the noontime dinner trolley at Ascot Military Hospital in Berkshire, England, 1916. [Ruby Ayre Collection, MUN Archives and Special Collections]

1915. The government granted her leave with pay and agreed to cover her transportation costs. She went on to a long war service in Belgium, London, Lemnos, Cairo, and Salonika.[12]

As the conflict claimed more and more young men, it required more women to cook and clean and to nurse them. By the middle of 1916, British authorities were actively recruiting both nurses and VADs in their self-governing colonies. The first officially sanctioned VADs left Newfoundland fifteen months after the war started. In November 1915, responding to a British War Office request, four women left under the care of graduate nurse Frances Morey; two days later, a fifth set sail. These first five VADs included Madeline Donnelley, daughter of the finance minister, and Jean Emerson, daughter of the chief justice.[13] At least two other Newfoundland women were serving overseas by the end of 1915, but it is unclear whether they were also sent in response to requests or whether they travelled at their own expense and joined the VAD through British channels; both could have afforded this route to war work. Elsie Crowdy's father was manager of the St. John's branch of the Royal Bank.[14] Ethel Dickinson was head of a domestic science school in St. John's and was related to several wealthy families.[15] While perhaps never having the social élan of the first upper-class British VADs, early Newfoundland VADs were well educated and financially secure. The war work of these daughters of Newfoundland's elite also supports Quiney's argument in this volume that VAD service was more closely related to Victorian notions of upper-class duty than to any interest in nursing. At least eighteen trained Newfoundland nurses served overseas, mainly with Queen Alexandra's Imperial Military Nursing Service (QAIMNS). A further forty-six women joined the British VAD services, working as nurses' aides and ambulance drivers.[16] They served in the British Isles, the Dardanelles, Greece, Belgium, France, and Egypt. Several also worked on hospital ships.

Undoubtedly, both nurses and VADs included women who were looking for adventure or escape from restrictions at home, but the evidence supports the findings of historians in Britain and Canada that most were driven by a strong sense of patriotic duty. Like their counterparts elsewhere, the Newfoundland women also followed brothers, boyfriends, and friends overseas. Coultas, for example, was discouraged by her mother and her employer but saw no reason why she should not follow her fiancé overseas to help in whatever way she could.

Sybil Johnson also stressed duty as her main motivation; several times she mentioned that she could not bear to be a "slacker." She followed her brother and no fewer than fifteen cousins serving in the First World War. Johnson also maintained a sentimental attachment to soldiers and a romantic view of their service, even in the face of the great suffering she witnessed. She was annoyed throughout the war that her fiancé had not enlisted.

> You don't know how I long to hear that Brian is coming over, though I shall be scared stiff needless to say. But it is no use, a soldier is the only man who counts nowadays, among the "physically fit."[17]

While a sense of duty and a sentimental patriotism may have been Johnson's main reasons for enlisting, her letters also reveal some uncertainty and dissatisfaction with her life. In boasting of her good health in England, she wrote: "I was never really delicate, you know, and it was only ever boredom and laziness which made me slack or 'run down' at home."[18] In addition to feeling "useless" and "bored" Johnson expressed some misgivings about her engagement to Dunfield. She confessed that the two had been drifting apart before the war. Scholars have questioned earlier assumptions about the liberating effects of the First World War. Johnson's experience demonstrates the temporary nature of much of this liberation. Through most of her time in Europe her work as a VAD made her feel strong – physically, psychologically, and morally. By the spring of 1918, however, a combination of exhaustion, a new unpleasant supervisor, and pressure from home saw her resume her life much as she had left it in 1916.

For graduate nurses, caring for men on the battlefield was at the very foundation of their profession. Mary Southcott, founder and director of the School of Nursing at the General Hospital in St. John's, saw war work as a noble and appropriate path for her nurses. In a March 1915 talk she read from letters of British nurses serving in military hospitals and outlined requirements for those wishing to serve overseas.[19] Southcott trained at least thirteen of the eighteen nurses who served in the Great War. In a letter recalling her war days, nurse Bertha Forsey stated that she had signed up, "with encouragement from Miss Southcott." Like the other women mentioned, Forsey was also inspired by the example of male loved ones: her future husband and her three brothers all served overseas. On 29 July 1916, Forsey left for London, where she was accepted as a Nursing Sister in QAIMNS. She spent the next two years at military hospitals in England and France.[20]

All of the Newfoundland nurses mentioned in this chapter were graduates of a three-year nursing program at the General Hospital in St. John's or at institutions in Britain or the United States. Training for VADs, however, had to be arranged before the costly voyage overseas. The first VADs completed several weeks of St. John Ambulance training and spent time in local hospitals. The length, extent, and method of training, however, varied over the war years. These changes likely reflected demand rather than any differences in the experience or class of applicants. Following the Battle of the Somme, for example, there was a rush to get volunteers overseas. Some VADs who had been working in local hospitals for as much as a year left for England in this period.[21] Others were quickly pushed through a few weeks training in October 1916 and were on their way to England by the middle of November. In London they went to British VAD headquarters and were assigned to military hospitals somewhere in England.[22] Those who were interested could put their names down for consideration for "overseas" service. While many women were happy to stay in the relative comfort and safety of England, others, driven by romantic ideas of sharing the soldiers' hardships or by a sense of duty or adventure, wanted to get closer to the theatres of war. Quiney points out that, in Canada, nursing and military leaders successfully blocked Canadian VADs from service at the front.[23] Newfoundland women, who entered VAD service directly through British organizations, did not face this barrier and many of the known VADs served on the eastern or western fronts. Cluett signed up for work in France as soon as she arrived in England and never seemed to regret it. In an unusual move she was selected for overseas service only five months after beginning work, and she worried that more senior VADs would feel jealous.[24] Perhaps her superiors quickly recognized her strong character, or her early "promotion" to France may simply have reflected increasing urgency at the front.[25]

Others VADs chose the dangerous work of ambulance driving, which sometimes saw them working even closer to the lines of fire. While there is much debate about the long-term impact of the First World War on women, many sources cite the temporary release from some conventional restrictions as a benefit; women's own writing frequently mentions driving and wearing comfortable, functional clothing as wartime boons. Ambulance driver Armine Gosling, raised by a liberal reforming father and a feminist mother, seemed prepared for such a challenge. A photo reprinted in several contemporary sources shows her in an ankle-length leather trench-coat, gloves, and aviator cap. Staring into the camera, with her fist slightly clenched and only a hint of a smile, Gosling appears strong and fearless.[26] Like Johnson, she had followed her elementary school education in St. John's with public school in England. There, she would have had lessons in music and languages in addition to the standard subjects of a liberal education. She travelled to England on the same voyage as the Johnson sisters and participated in a concert on board. Johnson described Gosling's performance as "inaudible." It seems that she was more comfortable in her driver's uniform than demonstrating her musical accomplishments for an audience. Gosling may have looked for a post that limited the formality and authoritarianism of an English military hospital. Canadian ambulance driver Grace MacPherson also suffered under such restrictions, and when she first arrived in France she found a friend in Gosling. In this instance, temperament and shared circumstances were more important than any differences in the women's social or national backgrounds.[27]

Old and new friendships sustained both trained and untrained women as they tried to deal with the wounded and dying. Jeanette Coultas spent her whole war service at the 3rd London General Hospital at Wandsworth. Her brief reminiscence published in 1954 does not mention whether or not this was by choice. She may have been content at Wandsworth because many of Newfoundland's wounded ended up there. Additionally, at least three other Newfoundland women served at this hospital, two of them starting the same day as did Coultas. It is likely she travelled with them and may have found support with friends from home nearby. Unlike men of the Newfoundland Regiment, Newfoundland women who served did not form a distinct unit. Their national identity was subsumed in their service within Canadian, American, and, most commonly, British forces. British VAD directors, however, appear to have tried to place Newfoundland VADs together, at least in England.[28] At least twenty Newfoundland VADs served at hospitals with other women from home. Typically, several VAD recruits would make the voyage to England together, sometimes under the care of a graduate nurse. During their shared training and their sometimes dangerous trips across the Atlantic, Newfoundland women forged friendships that helped them deal with the new challenges they faced in Europe.

Trained nurses were, of course, in greater demand than VADs, and there was no similar pattern that shows that these women served together. Working within American, Belgian, French, British, and other imperial units, they shared with many colleagues a "British" and a professional identity. With very limited sources from Newfoundland nurses, it is not possible to tell whether they experienced any slurs on their colonial credentials or whether they were bothered at being identified as Canadian or British nurses.[29] Women like Parsons, who served with Canadian hospital contingents, might be sent directly to the front. Most Newfoundland nurses, however, served with the QAIMNS and were initially assigned to military hospitals in England. Rather than reflecting concern about the competence of the colonial nurses, this was more likely an attempt to ease nurses into war work before they faced the far more difficult living and working conditions closer to the front. In these "home" military hospitals, nurses gained valuable experience that they would not have attained in a civilian hospital.

Bertha Forsey, for example, spent two years at Catterick Military Hospital in Yorkshire before being sent to France. She made no mention of feeling disadvantaged because she came from one of the colonies; rather, she displayed pride in her growing professional skills. At Catterick she assisted in the operating room, treated German prisoners of war, and cared for servicemen suffering from shell shock. Her reminiscence is told in a professional matter-of-fact tone, and she clearly took pride in the skills and knowledge she gained, including further training in anesthesia. Unfortunately, the only available account of Forsey's war service is her recounting of events, written almost forty years later. Undoubtedly, letters or a diary written at the time would have revealed more of her feelings as she encountered "these young lads," broken in body and spirit.[30] In nursing school, probationers learned to control their feelings so that they could deal with patients professionally and objectively. But in a civilian hospital they would not have treated a continuous stream of maimed young patients, many of whom would not recover.

Of course, even experience in a relatively safe English military hospital could not prepare nurses for all they might face. Newfoundland nurse Elizabeth Holden was forced to prove her professional competence under harsh conditions at Salonika, where medical doctors and nurses treated the injured and ill men who had been evacuated from the disastrous campaign at Gallipoli. Holden was a St. John's native who graduated from the Long Island School of Nursing. When the war began she went overseas as one of the first eleven women to serve with the American Red Cross. But the United States was still officially neutral, and when authorities discovered Holden's British citizenship she was forced to resign. She immediately travelled to Montreal and joined the CAMC and, by the middle of 1915, had been posted to Salonika. Newfoundland men were among the soldiers involved in the Dardanelles, so Holden would not have experienced the same dissatisfaction as did Canadian nurses, some of whom resented serving in a post where they would not have the chance to treat any of their own servicemen.[31] She would, however, still have dealt with the poor supply of clean water, the temperature extremes, the insects, and the high incidences of typhoid, malaria, and other illness related to living conditions both on the battle lines and at the hospital. Holden's coping skills were tested during a hospital evacuation in the face of an enemy advance. She was left as the only medical attendant for thirty-six patients. A bomb destroyed a roadway, cutting off the personnel who were supposed to reinforce her. When they finally arrived three days later, Holden was still working and all her patients were doing fine. She was later awarded the Royal Red Cross in recognition of her distinguished service.[32]

In English military hospitals, and even more so in those in France and Eastern Europe, living and working conditions clearly varied. Depending on their backgrounds and personalities, Newfoundland's nurses and VADs coped with these challenges by leaning on friends and family and by trying to find fun and beauty around them. As Donner argues, the VADs' greatest comfort came in feeling useful and obeying the "moral imperative of sacrifice and service."[33] Nurses shared many of the same motivations, but they also saw the war as a professional duty, an extension of their roles in their home communities.

By 6 December 1916, Frances Cluett was established in her first posting, Lincoln Hospital in London. Her travelling companions from Newfoundland were still with her and she shared a room with fellow Newfoundlander Henrietta Gallishaw. The Johnson women arrived in England in December but spent Christmas with family in Devon. Sybil and Jill took up their positions at the 1st Western Hospital near Liverpool at the beginning of January 1917 and were delighted to be rooming together. They spent their time off together, shared letters, went to the movies, and shopped or had tea in town. Johnson's letters home mention spending time with other VADs in their hostel, but while Jill was with her, she remained her closest confidante. Cluett did not have a sister with her, but she cherished the continued ties with her travelling companions from home.

Jeanette Coultas recalled that, even with all the work and sadness, she managed to have fun with her fellow VADs. They saw all the sights of London and were given free admission to the theatre and other attractions: "Your uniform brought kindness from everybody. You weren't worth a glance in mufti." She was grateful for this generosity because VADs were paid so poorly. She explained that, because Newfoundlanders were part of the British VAD organization, she was paid only a shilling a day, compared to the "princely" $1.10 the Canadians and Australians paid their workers. Coultas did not find this a real financial hardship because she received everything she needed. It did, however, cause resentment in some of her colleagues. She recounted how her overtures of friendship towards a girl in her hostel were rebuffed because she assumed Coultas was better off than she was: "I found out she thought I was a Canadian, rolling in the riches of $1.10 a day to her shilling pay. We became good friends when she knew I was on the same low financial footing as herself."[34] Coultas expressed no nationalistic need to distinguish herself from the Canadians, but she did remember the economic distinction. Donner is undoubtedly correct in arguing that women did not engage in VAD work primarily for economic gain. Nevertheless, as the war continued, British authorities had to recruit nursing help beyond England's shores and below its higher classes; therefore, perhaps not all VADs could afford to be immune to financial considerations. By December 1916, the War Office announced a raise in pay for experienced VADs, with the promise of continued increases every six months to a maximum of £30 a year.[35]

The Johnson sisters had no particular money troubles, and their accommodations were among the most comfortable mentioned in surviving sources. The 1st Western Hospital was well equipped and, throughout the war, had only minor problems with food shortages. The regular gifts of money from their father helped alleviate any financial shortfalls and allowed them a few small luxuries. The Johnson sisters stayed at a clean and comfortable convent about eight miles from the hospital and were generally transported back and forth by ambulance. Even in England, however, not all the hospitals or living quarters were so pleasant. Coultas complained of mice in her room at Wandsworth and rats in the hospital. She caught the mice but continued to live in fear of the rats, which she judged the worst part of her VAD experience. Cluett was often cold in her hostel, and she complained that the food was limited and monotonous, thanks, in part, to rationing.[36]

Despite such problems, conditions in most English hospitals would have seemed luxurious to women who were serving in France or the Dardanelles. Once she began working at the 10th General Hospital in Rouen, Cluett had to sleep on a thin mattress called a "biscuit," was very cold much of the time, and regularly dealt with rodents and insects. During her subsequent posting to Constantinople she described the wind howling through one end of her tent.[37] At La Panne, Belgium, Maysie Parsons found the accommodation adequate and the food better than expected; however, she noted that they had to boil the water. For her, any physical discomfort was far outweighed by the psychological adjustment to life near the front. Writing to her father in the spring of 1915, Parsons confessed that while working within six miles of the trenches, she found it hard to deal with the sound and lights visible during big battles: "We can hear the guns and see the flashes ... and to think that every flash means so many deaths!"[38]

For VADs who had come to do domestic work and to soothe the brows of bedridden soldiers, the adjustment to the horrors of the war must have been even more difficult. They worked up to twelve-hour shifts, with a couple of hours off each day. Their experience varied: they wrote letters and shopped for the men, performed basic housekeeping chores, and helped with dressings. Francis Cluett also mentions simply, or not so simply, sitting with dying men. Both Cluett and Johnson make particular note of their first time assisting with dressings. This was perhaps the most common VAD nursing task. It was, therefore, a vote of confidence from supervising Sisters, and it marked the VAD's transition from solely domestic to nursing helper. Cluett's introduction to dressings came after only five days at Lincoln. Perhaps it was a little too early as she fainted when she saw the wound revealed.[39] This is the only time she described fainting on duty, but she admitted that she sometimes had to turn her head away from wounds.

Johnson did not help with dressings until she had been on duty for three months, and she felt that she had performed well.[40] But some dressings were harder than others. She later recounted helping with a dressing for a man with a fractured spine. The experience prompted feelings of both horror and pride: "The man had sores all down his back and it was altogether a fearful and repulsive business. I hadn't much to do but hold him steady when I helped roll him over on his side. He was a Scotchman and so game and plucky and kept talking away to me and held my arm and his hand was like a firebrand – he had a high temp. In a way I was glad to help but it was horrible."[41] The contradictory sentiments in this last sentence are common in VADs' writing: the stated need to help despite their own distress reflects their strong sense of duty.

Nurses would have been experienced in dressing wounds, but the number and severity of injuries must have overwhelmed even the best-trained women. Parsons mentioned that the wounds were terrible, but, in a letter to her former superintendent, she also displayed her professional background in judging the work interesting.[42] Similarly, Forsey's account focused on her professional growth during her war service and did not dwell on her emotions or on descriptions of injuries and illness. She worked in the operating room for a year, assisting in hundreds of operations and learning to administer anesthesia, and she was then "promoted" to night supervisor. When she was sent to a stationary hospital in France she was put in charge of a separate camp reserved for contagious disease cases; she emphasized that this assignment required "skilled nursing care." Her help consisted mainly of VADs and orderlies.[43] While nurses certainly had empathy for their patients, their training helped prepare them to maintain a certain emotional distance. The work itself left little time to brood and could even bring the satisfaction of learning new skills and the reward of being trusted with greater responsibility than they would have achieved – at least so quickly – in civilian hospitals.

Cluett did not have the professional training of Parsons or Forsey, so in Rouen she had to draw on all her personal strength to help her patients and to preserve some peace for herself. Furthermore, she worked closer to the front than did many other VADs. By the time men reached hospitals in England, their wounds had at least been cleaned and dressed. While she never pursued an active pacifist cause after the war, Cluett's reaction to suffering patients included declarations that the war was "hell upon earth."[44] On her second day in Rouen she helped with a horrendous dressing: "There was one man wounded in the thigh: there was a hole right through from side to side. It was like you cut it with an axe ... You can read about war, and the wounded, but when you are brought face to face with it, I tell you, it is heart rending."[45] In France she also saw the immediate effects of poison gas, a horrifying new method of warfare. Cluett's remarkably candid letters written from France lack both the professional distance of the trained nurses and the positive, nostalgic tone of Coultas' reminiscence.

Apart from the difficult medical tasks, nurses would also have been accustomed to performing very personal services for their patients, both male and female. The young well-bred women who made up VAD detachments would not have been exposed to such tasks, and some found this almost as hard to deal with as the wounds. Ideally, military hospitals in both England and near the front had male orderlies to help move men and to bathe them, to deal with bed pans, and to minister other personal services.[46] For Johnson, bathing the men and dealing with bed pans were the worst part of the job. While the matter-of-fact Cluett simply mentioned giving a bed bath as part of a general description of a day's work, Johnson was horrified by the task. Occasionally, all the orderlies were called up or reassigned, a practice Johnson complained about bitterly. On 1 April 1917, she explained to her mother that, since the orderlies were gone, "all sorts of appalling jobs fall on us and truly I can't face them! You know my leaning to Primness!"[47] It is interesting that in a letter to her father on the same day, she gave far fewer details about these misgivings, focusing instead on the comic antics of the patients.[48] This may reflect her fear of her father's reaction or a reticence in talking with him about the men's most personal needs. Though she claimed to adjust enough to hide her discomfort from the patients, Johnson continued to hate this part of the work. Her sheltered upper-class background did not prepare her to deal with men's naked bodies and their personal hygiene needs. When she learned in June that her ward would be getting an orderly, she announced it in a letter which opened with: "I burst with Joy!"[49]

Throughout her time as a VAD, Johnson wavered on the idea of volunteering for service in France and even on how long she should continue in England. This reflected the reality of her daily work: she had good days and bad days. During her first term she had more good experiences than bad and, by early February, was already talking about signing a new contract in August. Her sister Jill had more trouble adjusting, and Sybil's letters often expressed pity for her. Jill worked in the ward next to hers, and Sybil wrote that her younger sister had more difficult cases and less pleasant and reasonable Sisters. By June, however, Sybil believed that Jill was doing much better, and she was annoyed when her sister decided to leave: "She meets lots of nice people and has lots of fun and is doing her bit. What more does she want! ... she came over here to nurse or do war work ... the canteen idea doesn't sound to me to be up to much."[50] By the time Johnson wrote this letter, Jill had become engaged to a young soldier who had been a patient and had broken the heart of another. Perhaps her romances, strictly against regulations, contributed to Jill's own restlessness and to her problems with her superiors.

Quiney and others have written about class and professional jealousies between VADs and nurses, and the wartime *British Journal of Nursing* was filled with suspicion that VADs threatened nurses' fragile hold on at least a semi-professional status. Many nurses resented the fact that patients and much of the general public referred to VADs as nurses. Occasionally, however, trained women wrote the *British Journal of Nursing* to share their appreciation for VAD help.[51] Bertha Forsey described the VADs under her as "great girls."[52] Of the VADs studied for this chapter, only Sybil Johnson expressed resentment for nurses' authority. Even in this case, however, it was not a consistent complaint and is most obvious in her last few weeks of service. Throughout most of her time overseas she got along well with her superiors and had no problem taking orders, though she occasionally complained about arbitrary rules or about "cold" or unfair nurses, tellingly remarking that "a servant" would not stand for such treatment.

After she returned from her last leave in the spring of 1918, however, Johnson's complaints increased. The new matron forbade music on the wards.

Johnson had always enjoyed playing the piano or her "fiddle" for the men and thought this rule arbitrary and pointless. To make matters worse, she soon got on the wrong side of one of the ward Sisters. She concluded that the reprimands she received were based on class and professional jealousy.

> The Sisters most of them like to pretend that VADs are practically servants, because most of us are what they would consider "grand" in their natural sphere of life – and they really are fearfully jealous if any of us play or sing. They think that the officers are something grand and just dread their being nice to us ... Matron thinks we have all come nursing with the fixed intention of ensnaring one of these young gods.[53]

Such outbursts certainly illustrate class tensions, but it is important not to generalize about Johnson's entire nineteen months of service. By the spring of 1918 she seems to have reached the end of her rope and her letters are filled with references to counting the days and planning her new life with Brian.

Neither Coultas nor Cluett complained about unfair treatment by nurses, but the sources on these women – a nostalgic reminiscence written forty years after the fact and a small collection of a couple of dozen letters – makes comparison difficult. If we had daily letters from these women they would likely tell more complex stories that would reveal more of their own strengths, weaknesses, and doubts and paint fuller pictures of the women who served with them.

As the war dragged on, even trained doctors and nurses struggled to maintain their professionalism in the face of appalling numbers of casualties and the severity of injuries and illnesses. For VADs, who had come to hold patients' hands, change beds, and assume the domestic tasks of the trained nurses, the reality of what they saw must have been overwhelming. Many simply could not cope. Jill Johnson left the 1st Western Hospital as soon as her initial contract was up. She stayed in England, rested for awhile, worked in recreation huts for a few months, and finally enlisted again as a "General Service" VAD with less direct responsibility for soldiers' medical care.[54] In March 1918, she returned to Liverpool, much to Sybil's delight, assigned to a convalescent home where patients were already through the worst of their recovery.[55] Despite her sentimental nature and protected background, Sybil Johnson stuck with it, serving her probationary month plus three six-month contracts. Cluett signed on for the duration and stayed on to help with demobilization once the war ended. These women were not immune to the heartache they saw, and they each had moments and days when they felt unable to cope, but they found ways to escape the sadness. Although they engaged in various activities to provide a diversion from the war, their strongest coping mechanism was the work itself. They reminded themselves that they were useful to the nurses and a comfort to their patients.

VAD nursing was not all stress and sadness. Johnson reported on several ward concerts and other amusements, at Christmas and throughout the year. The men often put on humorous skits and constantly played jokes on one another and on the staff. Given her extensive training as a violinist, it is not surprising that Johnson took great comfort in music – both playing and listening. She was always pleased to play for the men and she regularly purchased new music. She also shopped for the men, using her own money or donations from family members to buy them little treats. She and Jill found a few nice tea shops in the area where they indulged in scones, sandwiches, and good tea from nice cups. One of their favourite cafes had a piano, and the Johnsons, as well as other VADs, often performed there.

As mentioned, Johnson's family was her strongest support during her VAD service. In addition to Jill, she had relatives right in Liverpool who frequently entertained the sisters on their days off. A little farther away, her uncle Henry lived in Devon, where he was a minister. Sybil, Jill, and their brother MacNess all spent leave there, and the three even managed a visit together before MacNess was shipped to India. Correspondence with family and friends back home was also a major part of Johnson's life, and she was always thrilled with a "big mail." These letters often included copies of poems, another of Johnson's passions. She also wrote poems but felt they were never good enough to share. She enjoyed receiving newspapers and magazines from home, and she often commented on local events.

While Cluett did not have any family close by, she maintained strong friendships and kept up with her family by mail. She spent her leave with close friends and joined other VADs in long walks and excursions to nearby towns for a meal or shopping. Like Johnson, Cluett helped decorate the hospital for Christmas and often enjoyed concerts put on at nearby camps. Unlike the former, however, she did not perform at these events. But Cluett also found solace in her artistic skills. She took numerous photographs and sketched and painted her surroundings, perhaps focusing on the beauty outside the hospital as an escape from the horrors she saw inside its wards. She was also a passionate gardener and enjoyed the beautiful blooms of France. She planted flowers around her hut, finding comfort in the familiar activity; she even sent home a slip from a rose tree she had planted.⁵⁶ This may have been an attempt to preserve some memories from this extraordinary time in her life.

Like their counterparts in other parts of the Empire, Newfoundland women hoped that by working overseas they would be able to see friends and loved ones serving with the allied forces. Coultas, Johnson, and Cluett all mention seeing boys from home, and the latter two comment on any news about Newfoundland servicemen. Johnson followed the fate of the Newfoundland Regiment through papers from home and expressed her sorrow when local boys were reported dead or missing. Coultas was stationed at Wandsworth, where many Newfoundland servicemen were treated. She did not smoke herself but accepted any cigarettes offered her and gave them to Newfoundlanders.⁵⁷ In 1915, VAD Ethel Dickenson was posted at Ascot Military Hospital, but one account of her war service reported that she spent much of her free time visiting Newfoundland men at Wandsworth. Given the workload of VADs, such devotion might help explain Dickenson's eventual physical exhaustion. She was sent home to rest in the summer of 1918 but by that fall was helping to combat the first wave of Spanish flu. Dickenson died fighting the epidemic, and a monument was built in her honour, making hers the only memorial to Newfoundland's war nurses or VADs.⁵⁸

Cluett had spent her whole life in her small community and identified with and sought out Newfoundlanders during her war service. She made friends among her fellow VADs in France but maintained her closest ties with women from home. In Rouen, Cluett seemed to be in regular contact with Newfoundland servicemen. Whenever she heard that there were Newfoundland men in the area she used her time off to walk miles to visit them, cheer them up, and share news from home. She felt chilled as she saw them move up the line, singing and calling out. Though she went out to wave and cheer them on, she found the ritual very poignant. Having lost her dear cousin, the fate of the Newfoundland men was always in her thoughts. Using the maternal language so ubiquitous to nurses and VADs, she worried about the fate of Newfoundland "boys."

> The NFLD regiment is getting served pretty badly: in the last attack nearly all the officers were killed. While I was talking to Sergt. Dewling, the phone rang, which told him of more deaths of our boys. He says our boys are getting cut up altogether; he cannot think how the ranks are going to be filled again; yet they are still coming; as seventy are now on their way.⁵⁹

When her cousin Vince died, Cluett asked every Newfoundland soldier she met whether they could tell her anything about him. Her concern for Newfoundland soldiers reflected her sense of her local identity and provided a continued link to her own lost loved one.

Even at their lowest times, VADs were clearly glad that they had come. During her last few unhappy weeks in Liverpool, Johnson asserted that she never could have forgiven herself if she had shirked her duty and stayed home. For Cluett, the last months of the war only increased the horror around her. In March and April German bombers struck several hospitals and casualty clearing stations, increasing the load on the rest. In addition, the physical threat to medical personnel became more real. Patients and staff were killed and several stations had to be abandoned. On 31 March 1918, Cluett reported that twenty nurses had to flee to her hospital, which became, in effect, a clearing station. Patient numbers increased dramatically and she had to adjust to the severity of the wounds of men who had come straight from the fighting, without even the initial cleaning and treatment she was used to. Cluett worried that the staff simply could not keep up: "Boys are dying for want of attention; they cannot be attended to before being sent down here; wounds lying so long of course must kill them. It is horrible mother." Despite her distress, Cluett's sense of duty prevailed. The letter closed: "Nothing would induce me to give it up mother."[60]

When war broke out, Newfoundland women responded with patriotism, empathy, and a determination to prove that they were useful. For some, nothing but overseas service could meet that need. Each woman's war service was unique, but they all had to find ways to cope with tragedy, fear, and the everyday challenges and frustrations of hospital and military life. They drew on their friends and family for support, both in person and through correspondence, and they chose paths that best suited their personalities and experience.

As Duley shows in this volume, the war service of Newfoundland women, both at home and overseas, helped the postwar suffragettes make their case that women deserved the vote. Whether the experience was transformative for the individual women involved is more difficult to assess. After the war, most Newfoundland nurses and VADs resumed their lives with little apparent change in their prewar plans. Johnson married Brian Dunfield as she had planned; they lived in St. John's, where they raised their three children. Francis Cluett upgraded her teaching qualifications and returned to assume control of the school in Belleoram. She was known as an excellent, though demanding, teacher and a force in her community. She never married but helped her widowed brother Arthur raise his son. Bertha Forsey married a decorated Newfoundland war veteran and moved to Saskatoon; she retired from nursing to raise her four children, and she became active in community affairs. In 1939, she proudly donned her uniform and was presented to the King and Queen when they visited Saskatoon. Two of her sons served in the Second World War.[61] Her daughter Grace followed in her mother's footsteps, becoming a nurse and serving overseas in the Second World War. She recalled that all this was done with her mother's encouragement.[62]

But were these women the same wives, teachers, and mothers they would have been without their wartime experience? The overseas work they undertook likely marked them deeply. As Cluett put it: "This is a wicked world mother: you cannot realize what sufferings there are: Some of the misery will ever live in my memory: it seems to me now as though I shall always have sad sights in my eyes."[63] This was a sentiment common to women who cared for servicemen in the Great War but so too was Jeanette Coultas' conclusion that it was the happiest time of her life. For most of the women mentioned in this chapter, the war was a short, extraordinary interval in their lives, and we can only speculate about how their years overseas shaped their subsequent, more traditional experiences as wives, mothers, workers, and citizens.

Notes

1 Jeanette (Coultas) Wells as told to Iris Power, "I Was a VAD," *Atlantic Guardian* 11, 5 (1954): 29.
2 Newfoundland Historical Society, *A Short History of Newfoundland and Labrador* (St. John's: Boulder Press, 2008), 105.
3 Robert J. Harding, "Glorious Tragedy: Newfoundland's Cultural Memory of the Attack at Beaumont Hamel, 1916-1925," *Newfoundland and Labrador Studies* 21, 1 (2006): 7.
4 Grayzel points out that Australia, similarly involved but distant from the action of the First World War, saw little change in work opportunities for women. See Susan Grayzel, *Women and the First World War* (London: Pearson Education, 2002), 34.
5 Anne Summers, *Angels and Citizens: British Women as Military Nurses, 1854-1914* (London and New York: Routledge and Kegan Paul, 1988), chap. 9.
6 Bill Rompkey and Bert Riggs, eds., *Your Daughter Fanny: The War Letters of Frances Cluett, VAD* (St. John's: Flanker Press, 2006).
7 Memorial University (hereafter MUN), Archives and Special Collections (hereafter ASC), Johnson Family Papers, Queen Elizabeth II Library (hereafter QEII), file 14, coll-201.
8 Margot I. Duley, *Where Once Our Mothers Stood We Stand: Women's Suffrage in Newfoundland, 1890-1925* (Charlottetown: Gynergy Books, 1993), 117.

9 Wells, "I Was a VAD," 26.
10 Bertha (Forsey) Porter to G.W.L. Nicholson, 13 January 1973, Lillian Stevenson Nursing Archives and Museum (LSAM), file 2.39.001, "Bertha Forsey." Forsey's account was a straightforward professional biography sent in response to Nicholson's enquiries related to his official history of Canada's wartime nurses.
11 Linda White, "Janet Miller Ayre Murray," *Newfoundland Quarterly* 101, 1 (2008): 3-8. British VAD Vera Brittain and many others experienced similar conflict between their desire to serve and their family's needs. After her brother's death and again when her mother became ill, Brittain had to abandon her war work. See Joyce Ann Wood, "Vera Brittain and the VAD Experience: Testing the Popular Image of the Volunteer Nurse" (PhD diss., University of South Carolina, 2000), 206.
12 Colonial Secretary to James Harris, Public Works, 31 March 1915, Public Archives of Newfoundland and Labrador, GN214.189. See also, "Maysie Parsons," *The Distaff* (1917): 9.
13 The others were Isabel LeMessurier, Cecile Windeler, and Cecily Moffat. See *Daily News*, 5 and 6 November 1915.
14 Duley, *Where Once Our Mothers*, 116.
15 "A Faithful Nurse and Heroine," *Evening Telegram* (St. John's), 17 September 1973. Dickinson completed teacher training in Chicago and a two-year domestic science course at Guelph, Ontario. Such studies in the United States and Canada indicate her strong economic status. Although I am unsure of her father's occupation, her mother's brother was James Pitts, a leading businessmen and philanthropist in Newfoundland. When Pitts died in 1914 he left Dickinson £2000, which would have helped when she decided to leave her school for the poorly paid work of a VAD. See "Will of James S. Pitts," probated 1914, Grand Banks Genealogical website, http://ngb.chebucto.org/.
16 This may be a conservative estimate. Rompkey and Riggs cite a figure of 175 but provide no source for this. My numbers include only those women I can clearly identify. With a few exceptions, they do not include Newfoundland-born women who were living outside the country in 1914 and who joined the war effort through Canada, the United States. or directly from Great Britain – a difficult number to estimate at this point.
17 Johnson, 30 December 1917, MUN, ASC, Johnson Family Papers, QEII, file 14, coll-201.
18 Johnson, 26 April 1917, MUN, ASC, Johnson Family Papers.
19 *Daily News*, 18 March 1915.
20 Porter to Nicholson, LSAM, file 2.39.001, "Bertha Forsey."
21 Henrietta Gallishaw, Edith LeMessurier, and Jennie Roper all fall into this category.
22 Rompkey and Riggs, *Fanny*, 33-38.
23 For an explanation of Canadian opposition to VADs serving at the front, see Quiney (this volume).
24 Rompkey and Riggs, *Fanny*, 70.
25 Information in wartime editions of the *British Journal of Nursing* demonstrates the military's desperate need for nurses and VADs. In December 1916 the War Office announced raises for experienced nurses and VADs who were willing to sign on for the duration. They also began to discuss giving VADs some postwar credit towards nurses

training, an idea much criticized by British nursing leaders. See, for example, *British Journal of Nursing*, 26 August 1916 and 16 December 1916, available at http://rcnarchive.rcn.org.uk/.
26 *Newfoundland Quarterly*, 17, 4 (1918): 8.
27 MacPherson was born in Vancouver in 1895. Her civil servant father died when she was a teenager, leaving her family comfortable but far less well off than Gosling. In contrast to Gosling's postsecondary education at a British public school, MacPherson was in business college before the war, preparing to earn her living. See Sandra Gwyn, *Tapestry of War: A Private View of Canadians in the Great War* (Toronto: Harper Collins, 1992), 444-45, 451. In contrast to her friendship with MacPherson, Gosling and the Johnson sisters (who would have moved in the same social circles in St. John's) did not seem to socialize even when travelling together.
28 Quiney, "Assistant Angels," table 3.3, p. 433
29 For a discussion of such feelings among Canadian nurses serving near the Eastern Front, see Cynthia Toman, "'A Loyal Body of Empire Citizens': Military Nurses and Identity at Lemnos and Salonika, 1915-17," in *Place and Practice in Canadian Nursing History*, ed. Jayne Elliot, Meryn Stuart, and Cynthia Toman, 8-24 (Vancouver: UBC Press, 2008).
30 Porter to Nicholson, LSAM, file 2.39.001, "Bertha Forsey."
31 Toman, "Loyal Body of Empire Citizens."
32 "Holden, Sarah Isabel," *Encyclopedia of Newfoundland and Labrador* (St. John's: Newfoundland Book Publishers, 1984), 2:997.
33 Henriette Donner, "Under the Cross: Why VADs Performed the Filthiest Task in the Dirtiest War – Red Cross Women Volunteers, 1914-1918," *Journal of Social History* 30, 3 (1997): 687-704.
34 Wells, "I was a VAD," 30. In 1915 a shilling was worth about twenty-five cents, so the Canadian VAD was making more than four times Coultas' pay. Cluett also commented on the "high" pay of Canadians.
35 *British Journal of Nursing*, 16 December 1916.
36 Rompkey and Riggs, *Fanny*, 65-66.
37 Ibid., 158-59.
38 Maysie Parsons to her father, 18 June 1915, published in *Daily News*, 7 July 1915.
39 Rompkey and Riggs, *Fanny*, 56.
40 Johnson, 7 March 1917, MUN, ASC, Johnson Family Papers.
41 Johnson, 25 September 1917, MUN, ASC, Johnson Family Papers.
42 Maysie Parsons to Dr. Lawrence Keegan, 26 May 1915, LSAM, file 2.51.001, "Maysie Parsons."
43 Porter to Nicholson, LSAM, file 2.39.001, "Bertha Forsey."
44 Rompkey and Riggs, *Fanny*, 146.
45 Ibid., 83.
46 Mann notes that, since Canadian overseas hospitals did not use VADs, male orderlies did these jobs. See Susan Mann, *The War Diary of Clare Gass, 1915-1918* (Montreal and Kingston: McGill-Queen's Press, 2000), xxxi.

47 Johnson, "My Dearest Mummy," 1 April 1917, MUN, ASC, Johnson Family Papers.
48 Johnson, "My Dearly Beloved Daddy," 1 April 1917, MUN, ASC, Johnson Family Papers.
49 Johnson, undated letter (written between 14 and 19 June 1917?), MUN, ASC, Johnson Family Papers.
50 Johnson, 24 June 1917, MUN, ASC, Johnson Family Papers.
51 See, for example, *British Journal of Nursing*, 24 March 1917 and 7 April 1917.
52 Porter to Nicholson, LSAM, file 2.39.001, "Bertha Forsey."
53 Johnson, 2 May 1918, MUN, ASC, Johnson Family Papers.
54 Created in 1916, General Service VADs performed clerical and domestic work that would free men and trained nurses to go overseas. See Sharon Ouditt, *Fighting Forces, Writing Women: Identity and Ideology in the First World War* (London: Routledge, 1994), 16.
55 Johnson, 3 March 1918, MUN, ASC, Johnson Family Papers.
56 Rompkey and Riggs, *Fanny*, 99. Similarly, Clare Gass sent home seeds from particularly lovely pansies growing near her hospital in France. See Mann, *War Diary*, 229.
57 Wells, "I Was a VAD," 29.
58 *Evening Telegram*, 17 September 1973.
59 Rompkey and Riggs, *Fanny*, 121.
60 Ibid., 150. Throughout March and April 1918, several hospitals and clearing stations were bombed as part of the German's spring advance. Cluett does not specify which bombings affected her workload.
61 Porter to Nicholson, LSAM, file 2.39.001, "Bertha Forsey."
62 Grace Hession to Joyce Nevitt, 24 September 1979, MUN, ASC, Joyce Nevitt Collection, QEII, file 12.02.009, coll-177.
63 Rompkey and Riggs, *Fanny*, 78.

6

Patriotic, Not Permanent
Attitudes about Women's Making Bombs and Being Bankers

Kori Street

On Dominion Day 1916, an estimated three thousand women marched through downtown Toronto in support of the Great War. An editorial in the Toronto *Globe* described the parade as an indication of women's liberation: "'The discovery of women' has been declared the greatest event of the twentieth century ... It came to many as a surprise when they realised, through higher education, professional training, experience in prominent and responsible positions and independent ventures in commerce and finance that they possessed the qualities they had been taught to regard as reserved exclusively for men." The author suggested that women's advancement was among the compensations of war.[1] Not all Canadians, however, accepted women workers with equanimity. For instance, Kingston's street railway employees were openly hostile towards female employees: "They'll never be able to climb along the sides of the car to collect the fares ... If Nickle keeps these girls in the summer, there are going to be some dead conductorettes under the sod before the snow comes round again."[2]

This chapter explores how Canadians understood women's wartime paid work in terms of gender. For some women, the war provided economic opportunities. Others were motivated by a sense of patriotism, similar to that motivating the VADs (see Quiney and Bishop-Stirling, this volume). While women's participation in paid work garnered praise in some corners of the country, it brought concern or condemnation in others. While there was some fluidity in gender-related work as a result of the war, which resulted in concerns about morality and motherhood, women's working in Canada during the war did not result in a lasting challenge to, or transformation of, gender ideology. Despite a lingering belief that large numbers of women entered the workforce during the war and were transformed as a result, Canadian women were not perceived as dangerous enough to warrant the backlash experienced elsewhere. Any challenge posed to gender was mitigated by a process of ideological accommodation that ensured that gender ideology remained fairly static during the war.

Women's participation in the paid workforce increased between 1911 and 1921 by approximately 34 percent (see Figure 7). The types of jobs open to women changed during this period as well. Defined by the cult of domesticity, which dictated the same sexual division of labour in the public sphere as in the private sphere, women had few opportunities outside of domestic work prior to the war. By 1921, however, there was a wider variety of jobs available to women.[3] The war seems to have increased women's opportunities in banking and munitions. In munitions, such opportunities only expanded for the duration of the war, and only in specific instances (largely in central Canada). Only approximately eleven thousand women were employed in munitions (previous estimates have suggested the number was as high as thirty-five thousand), and most of them were working in factories in Toronto, Hamilton, and Montreal.[4] While the overall extent of women's participation was not dramatic, evidence suggests that, for a short period of time, the gender division in a number of foundries and metal shops was significantly altered. In the case of banking, there was a significant increase in women's participation in the workforce. Women's horizons were particularly expanded in one field that, before the war, had been the preserve of men: clerking. Women gained access to positions as clerks because of the war, and they kept them after the war had ended.

Women's wartime participation varied according to their class and where they lived. Working-class women's horizons expanded in munitions shops, where middle-class women joined them. However, their experiences were not the same. Middle-class women were hired in positions of higher status than were working-class women. Similarly, rural and urban women had different experiences and opportunities. Rural women did not have access to munitions jobs, and their experiences in the banks were different from those of their urban colleagues. Age and marital status also affected women's wartime participation. More married women were hired into the munitions industry, while, during the war, the banks continued to hire only young single women.[5]

Figure 7

Women's participation in the workforce

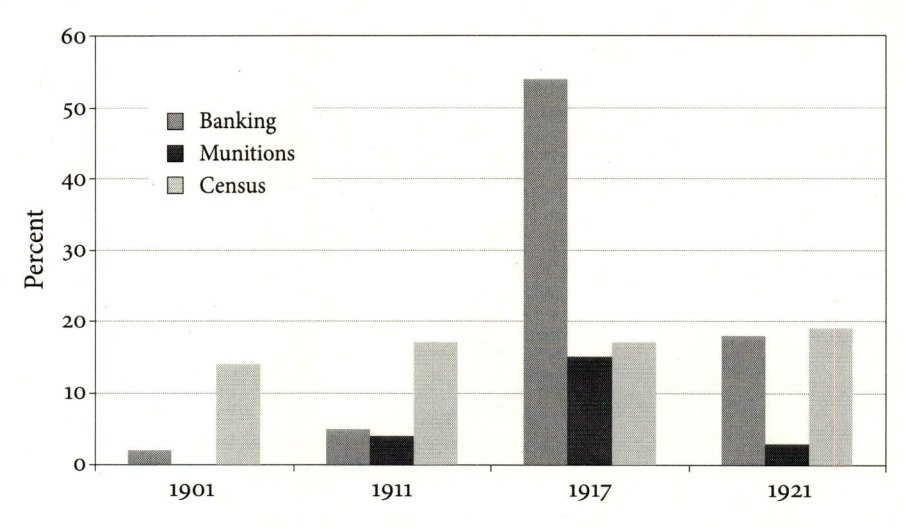

[Bar chart showing percentages for Banking, Munitions, and Census categories across years 1901, 1911, 1917, and 1921]

Source: Datasets are based on employment records from the BNS and Canadian Pacific Railway. Various qualitative sources were mined to create a dataset that captures women's work in munitions. For a lengthier explanation of methodology, see Street, "Bankers and Bomb Makers," 9-15.

The historiography of women and war is characterized by a debate regarding its liberating effect for women.[6] Some historians suggest that the wars of the twentieth century offered women expanded and liberating roles in paid employment.[7] Others take the position that the wars did little to liberate women and, instead, reinforced ideas about femininity.[8] In Canadian historiography Sandra Gwyn argues: "The Great War ... was to give many women the opportunity – in many cases the necessity – to move out of a familiar environment that, even when typing and shorthand were involved, was essentially an extension of their homes. In tens of thousands they moved into the kind of strange, intimidating workplaces to which men were accustomed, removed from their homes." Because of that participation, Gwyn concludes, a "sociological and psychic change had already taken place: the war had already liberated many women from their own hearth."[9] Several historians take this approach, including Graham Lowe, who argues that "old fashioned views about women's work were challenged and public opinion began to accept that perhaps women had a right to earn their own living, and indeed, could make vital contributions to the economy."[10] On the other side of the debate, historians argue that little substantive change for Canadian women can be attributed to wartime service. For instance, James Naylor and Linda Kealey both conclude that the war resulted in little long-term change for working women.[11]

An additional complication of the historiography of women and war in Canada is that women's participation is investigated in terms of the debate around the transformative nature of the war. "It [was] the Great War that mark[ed] the real birth of Canada," wrote Sandra Gwyn. "Thrust for the first time upon the world's stage, we performed at all times credibly and often brilliantly ... the effort of mobilising and equipping a vast army modernised us, and our blood and our accomplishments transformed us from colony into nation."[12] Jonathan Vance contends that we developed a national mythology regarding the "Great War," including a belief that, more than any other process or event, participation in the war created our national identity, and that this mythology imbricates the historical record.[13] In this context, women's wartime participation becomes part of the myth of transformation. Their work transformed them into fuller citizens. The relatively low level of hostility that met Canadian women in the workforce in the First World War should not be interpreted within traditional historiographical frameworks. Remaining wedded to such paradigms results in reductive approaches that belie not only the nuances of women's experiences and society's responses to them but also the subtleties of the shifts in gender ideologies. In order to understand what meaning wartime work had in terms of gender it is necessary to look carefully at the degree to which attitudes changed, and to read this within particular contexts.

As we have already seen, there was public support for women's employment. Two companies, Inglis and Russell Motor Car, which, in 1916, had been reluctant to even hire a woman, insisted, in 1917, on including their female employees on their floats in a patriotic parade. Indeed, when it was suggested that only one of them needed to include female employees, both of the companies wrote to the Imperial Munitions Board (IMB) saying that they would refuse to participate in the parade at all if both of them were not allowed to showcase their female employees.[14] Similarly positive attitudes towards women workers were also found in banks, an industry that initially described hiring women as a "courageous experiment." According to *Maclean's Magazine*, women appear to have been generally accepted in banks by 1916:

No sooner do we get a nice boy installed as manager or teller than the bugles come lilting down the street ... A week later you go in to deposit your little cheque, and lo, the nice boy is gone, melted out – enkhakied! And another reigns in his stead ... Yesterday I went by, glanced in for the redheaded Scotsman and found, to my surprise, a neat and precise little girl with a tailored blouse and an office manner correct to infinity, crouched on the high stool as though she'd grown there always.[15]

At the same time, however, the suggestion that women might be hired on street railway systems sparked outrage and collective action among male workers in several cities, particularly Kingston and Toronto. It also prompted an attack on women's morality. The Toronto union argued that "no self-respecting female would desire to force her way through the jam that overcrowd the cars during certain hours of the day when passengers are wedged together about as thick as herrings in a box."[16]

Although fairly unusual in Canada, the response of the street railway workers was similar to attitudes in Great Britain. There, women workers, particularly munitions workers, who dressed in male attire, worked in traditionally male occupations, and sometimes received a man's pay, regularly faced censure and hostility. According to Sylvia Pankhurst: "Alarmist morality mongers conceived most monstrous visions of girls and women, freed from the control of fathers and husbands who had hitherto compelled them to industry, chastity and sobriety, now neglecting their homes, plunging into excess and burdening the country with swarms of illegitimate infants."[17] According to British historians Angela Woollacott, Penny Summerfield, and Gail Braybon, what explains these hostile attitudes is the threat to traditional gender ideology that female workers in Britain presented. Such public censure undermined the legitimacy of women's working in non-traditional fields and reinforced traditional concepts about masculinity and femininity. While avoiding the moral panic that occurred in Britain, women workers in Canada did arouse some public concern. Investigating the varied responses towards women's work and its connection to gender identity illuminates women's First World War experiences.

Although this chapter attempts to draw conclusions about "Canadian" attitudes, there was no single attitude shared by all Canadians with regard to women's wartime work. The war was experienced as both a local and a national event, a point Bishop-Stirling makes in this volume in regard to Newfoundland's VADs, and many factors framed how people made sense of events and issues.

For instance, regional differences in attitudes towards women reflect regional differences in the nature and scope of women's participation. Several exchanges between public officials and the IMB's director of labour, Mark Irish, illustrate these. Mark Irish and Joseph Flavelle (chair of the IMB) needed to ensure that munitions factories had sufficient labour. In 1916, they both wrote to the federal minister of labour, T.W. Crowther, regarding the labour shortages in manufacturing and the urgent need to employ women. Crowther, who took six months to reply, regarded munitions as a largely central Canadian issue.[18] When he finally responded, it was to remind Irish and Flavelle that munitions production was not the only industry in the country facing pressure. He informed the two men that, while there was a shortage of male workers in some areas, a surplus existed in the western provinces and Quebec. The need to employ women was a regional issue that munitions manufacturers in Ontario and some areas of the Maritimes needed to address. Crowther did not believe that it required the attention of the Department of Labour. R.B. Bennett, a Calgary MP and chairman of the National Service Commission Board (NSCB), also believed that concern about women's working, particularly in munitions, was a regional and not a national issue. Irish lamented: "Mr. Bennett has some peculiar views on woman labour, springing largely, I feel, from the local conditions arising in the Riding which is distinguished by his representation."[19] For Bennett, the real labour crisis was on the farms in rural Canada, not in the factories in urban Ontario.

Bennett's perspective was made clear in a 1917 NSCB report that declared that there were as many women employed in munitions as possible and that women needed to look elsewhere to participate in the war effort. The "most serious problem demanding immediate solutions was that relating to the providing of sufficient labour to seed the land available and ready to crop this Spring."[20] Indeed, 375,000 acres above what had been harvested in 1916 were ready for cultivation, and the labour shortage on the farms was estimated at fifteen thousand.[21] This enraged Irish because of the potential damage that could be done to the recruitment of female munitions employees. In letters to Flavelle, Irish accused Bennett of pandering to regional agricultural concerns at the expense of munitions.[22] The discussion reveals very real differences among regions in Canada. In the west, there was very little change in attitudes regarding women's work because the labour situation did not require the same degree of mobilization as did that in Ontario. The need for women in the west was for volunteer work and farm labour.[23] As Robert Rutherdale suggests, understanding the local context of specific discourses is an important step in more fully understanding public responses.[24]

Attitudes were not only affected by different regional circumstances: the exchange between Irish and Bennett shows that class affected attitudes towards women's non-traditional wartime work. Bennett recognized that wartime participation, particularly in munitions, was, for working-class women, about working and making a living wage, and he anticipated that they might be reluctant to give up jobs that paid well. He worried that "the employment of women [would] create a female industrial army doing the work of men at a lower wage, which, when the Overseas Forces return[ed], [would] be opposed by a male army of unemployed ... Women once engaged in factory work [would] never give it up."[25] Bennett was concerned that this temporary reserve army of labour would want, inappropriately in the context of contemporary gender ideology, to become permanent and to compete directly with men in the postwar economy.

While Irish also regarded women's mobilization in terms of temporary service to the state, he expected that women would not want to remain in the factories after the war – an assumption shared by other middle-class men and women. For example, one manufacturer wrote of women working in the shell-making industry: "Much credit is due to those women who have recognised the needs of an unprecedented situation and adjusted themselves to an occupation that in normal times might be considered beneath their dignity."[26] As far as Irish was concerned, women's participation was an emergency measure in support of a grand cause.

How women from working-class backgrounds felt about their wartime experience is largely unknown because they left few accounts, and these were often viewed through a middle-class lens. In Britain, female munitions workers wrote in newsletters and shop magazines about questions that concerned them. Their voices were undiluted.[27] In contrast, the voice of the Canadian woman munitions worker is heard mostly through the mainstream media. Women working in munitions factories were occasionally quoted in newspapers' accounts of their efforts. Their stories were appropriated and packaged for a specific local audience. These quotations seem to reflect a middle-class attitude towards women's work and the war, with the women interviewed discussing their work in terms of its temporary nature and as wartime service.

One columnist for the *Globe* suggested that every woman working in one factory she visited felt that they were helping win the war. Bride Broder wrote:

"'Duty' – over and over again the visitor heard the word as she stopped to talk to the workers, some of them young war brides ... its use brought the conviction that things are not too bad with a nation whose sons fight for duty's sake abroad and whose daughters work in its strength at home." One worker admitted: "Yes, we are dead at nighttime, but it's little enough to do for the fighting men." Another said: "when I think of my poor hubby in the dirt of Camp Borden I feel that I've got an easy way of doing my duty." The article ended by quoting a woman who had four sons in the military: "Don't' ee [sic] think as we've cause to thank God greatly for giving us this chance of helping our dear men?"[28]

Oral history suggests that working- and middle-class women had differing views on being employed. The oral history project that resulted in Daphne Read's *The Great War and Canadian Society* interviewed two munitions workers. The woman from a middle-class background framed her experience entirely in terms of patriotic service: "Things were bad for the war, for us, and we felt we had to get our shoulder to the wheel and get down to business ... It was the thing to do ... Everybody wanted to be there; you were in the swim of things; everything was war, war, war." The working-class woman raised other issues. She talked about the pride she had in doing a good job in a position that was "very hard." She found her job turning shells "interesting work but very hard on your nerves." The parallel she drew between the war and her work involved her describing an instance when a machine blew up, which gave her "a little experience of what it was to be right in a war shooting up."[29] Similarly, neither of the women whom I interviewed who worked at McAvity's, a munitions and plumbing fixtures manufacturer, defined their work in terms of the war or patriotism. Certainly, they recognized that, if not for the war, there would have been no munitions work, but they did not associate their decision to work at McAvity's with patriotic service. Jennie Arbo needed to work and her uncle got her the job at the factory. Louise Poiret was interested in the opportunity to work in a factory rather than continuing with the domestic work she had been doing. These examples suggest that the attitudes of working-class women towards wartime participation may have been quite different from those found in the dominant discourse. The same holds true for working-class men.

We might expect working-class men to have had the most negative attitudes towards women workers. Generally speaking, they had the most to lose since their wages and labour processes were most threatened. Some working-class men did indeed resent women's workforce participation, regarding it as a direct threat. Others regarded women workers as sisters in a struggle against

FIGURE 8   These women munitions workers are labouring over percussion fuses in the Thread Milling Department of Toronto's Russell Motor Car factory, 1917. [LAC, PA-024638]

manufacturers. Several strikes occurred during the war, particularly between 1916 and 1918, caused by issues arising from the employment of women. Workers at the Empire Manufacturing Company struck for twenty-three days because they did not want the company to hire female operators; instead, the employees agreed to the implementation of new machinery. Similarly, Toronto Street Railway workers went on strike to protest the hiring of women. They chose to accept mechanization in the form of fare boxes, which replaced conductors on the streetcars, rather than to accept female conductors.[30] In contrast, employees at the Russell Motor Car Company struck to ensure the reinstatement of several female operators whom they felt had been unjustly fired, while the employees at Willys-Overland struck to secure equal pay for equal work.[31]

The strikes at Russell and Willys-Overland suggest that some working-class men supported women's right to work in male industries, but it is more likely that the men at Russell and Willys-Overland shared the sentiments of their colleagues at Empire Manufacturing and the Toronto Street Railway. The Russell strikers assumed, not uncommonly, that female workers were used by the manufacturers to undercut wages and deskill jobs. The Toronto District Labour Council agreed and worked towards protecting women and, in turn, male unionists from such practices.[32] Striking to ensure that women were paid the same rate as men was a pragmatic move geared less towards protecting women than it was towards protecting men's jobs. Raising women workers' wages made them less attractive as employees. By taking away that advantage, the workers at Willys-Overland protected the jobs of male unionists.

Women's wartime service both challenged and reinforced ideas about femininity. Women's successful participation in the paid workforce did little to alter some traditional beliefs about femininity, including the notion that women only work until they can marry.[33] Women themselves often reinforced this belief. During the war, one female bank employee argued that even the most successful banking woman would "cheerfully retire to her own hearthstone, preferring the love of a husband and little children to thousands a year and a seat in the council of the mighty."[34] Another wrote: "No bank or business firm can count absolutely on a woman. Experience has taught them that the majority desert for homes of their own just when they have reached the point of efficiency."[35] Such attitudes were not unique to the banks. Dr. Marjory MacMurchy, an active volunteer during the war, wrote:

> For telephone operators the average length of service is only three years. A young woman remains in stenography on an average between six and seven years. The wage or salary earning woman may leave one paid occupation to enter another, but this does not happen often. When she gives up her employment, as a rule she does so to marry ... A very large proportion, therefore, of women in Canada are first in paid employment and afterwards enter the more important occupation, socially and economically, of creating the homes of the country.[36]

Railroad shops turned over to munitions production also claimed that women would marry "just when they [had] attained the highest measure of usefulness." One article identified marriage as the fundamental detriment to hiring women:

"When a man takes a wife his anchorage is assured; but when a girl enters into matrimony she is invariably lost with all the training she has acquired. The brighter they are the greater is this danger, as I know from bitter experience. I have had ten office assistants of the gentler sex, and seven of them were lost to me through marriage. I am in mortal dread that the eighth is moving stealthily in the same direction."[37] Such attitudes not only supported views that women made unsuitable long-term employees but also relieved the banks and shops of the responsibility of training them (as they would male employee) and of restricting their promotion. The dearth of women in senior positions is evidence that this very central feature of traditional gender ideology – that women's primary role was to marry and raise children – was left unchallenged.

Another sign that traditional gender ideology remained relatively unchanged by the war is the continuity of the idea that women were, by nature, subordinate to men. The most obvious evidence of this is the serious under-representation of women in supervisory positions in both industries. Traditional gender ideology dictated that women required supervision and guidance, and their wartime work did not change that attitude. This was true at home, where the male breadwinner was the titular head of the household, and it was also true in the workplace. In munitions work, inspectors oversaw the production of the armaments, and if something was done incorrectly, it was their responsibility to bring that to the attention of the operator. Even in the Packard Fuze Company, which was almost wholly operated by female workers, men supervised the work.

When the IMB first suggested that manufactures hire female inspectors, the inspection companies protested vehemently. G. Ogilvie, vice-president of the Canadian Inspection Company, argued: "There was no question that women should not inspect work that men had done, even if that work was being inspected by educated, middle or upper class women. It was quite unimaginable that such a policy would be effective."[38] Aurelien Boyer, of the Canadian Inspection and Testing Labs, joined him in his opposition. Both men felt that women inspectors would prove "disastrous."[39] Similar attitudes were held at the Canadian Pacific Railway. No female supervisors show up in the data for the manual labour occupation groups.[40]

The belief that women were not capable of holding supervisory positions was quite widespread in the Bank of Nova Scotia (BNS) as well. Women held no management or supervisory positions, with one exception: supervision of a branch fell to senior clerks, accountants, and managers, which could theoretically include women. A comparison of advancement in the BNS branches reveals that men received promotion to accountant or assistant manager over women with equal or greater service. Although there were fewer women with long careers, and therefore fewer women with the necessary experience to advance into senior positions, a small percentage had the experience to warrant their attaining supervisory positions. Yet, of the male and female clerks with the BNS in 1916, 56 percent of the men had advanced into senior or supervisory roles (other than tellers) by 1922 compared to only 2 percent of the women.[41]

Most bank workers actively maintained that women's gender limited their suitability for a career in banking. One female bank employee wrote:

> The obstacles to promotion lie largely in the women themselves. In the first place very few of them can rise above their prejudices, which is a great handicap to success ... indecision is another fault, and always one must reckon with physical weakness – at least as compared with men.[42]

The general attitude was that women were acceptable for the short term but could not sustain the effort required for a banking career. According to Jean Graham, a bank employee, "Women are splendid at rising to an occasion and at coping with an emergency but they lack the capacity for sustained effort."[43] Middle-class conceptions of femininity regarded paid work as unfeminine, and, thus, the notion of a full-time or permanent *woman* worker was difficult to imagine.

While banking was outside that region of duties vaguely known as "woman's sphere," for the most part female clerks won a grudging respect from management. Some felt the women offered better service than some of the male clerks. One commentator suggested that the routine tasks of banking were quite suited to women. This could suggest a shift in attitude either towards equalizing gender roles or, as Graham Lowe suggests, towards feminizing banking. Arguably, it was neither. Even as commentators, both male and female, cheered women, they qualified praise with gendered references to women's inferiority. For instance, women were regarded as timid and less mathematical, which made them ill-suited for a career that required adding sums or protecting the assets of the bank. "When it came to assembling a mass of tabulation sheets and striking what are termed 'balances,'" claimed J.L. Payne, "the male clerks showed an undoubted superiority. The girls shrank from any complexity, or what might

Patriotic, Not Permanent

be broadly defined as responsibility."[44] Some members of the banking world suggested that women's work in the branch would make them better wives: "If she marries and leaves the business world altogether, she is in a position by virtue of this training to manage her share of the financial arrangements of her home much more intelligently and with a proportionately greater degree of success and consequent happiness."[45]

Throughout the war, and indeed into the 1960s, the BNS remained wedded to the idea that banking was a masculine career, suggesting that the war was not particularly transformative. Bankers may have been prepared to accept women as a part of the workforce during the war, but only in a subordinate role. By restricting women's access to the normal banking career path, the BNS maintained and reinforced traditional attitudes towards gender boundaries, effectively mitigating any challenge posed by the female workforce.[46] Working in different branches was essential to gaining the experience necessary to advance in banking. Despite evidence that female clerks were willing to move, banks held to the belief that it would not be appropriate to transfer them, so women were denied the varied experiences that opened the way to promotion. The bank's main concern in this was the necessity for female employees to secure suitable, supervised (and therefore respectable) lodging. A woman's morality could be suspect if her home was unsuitable, and this, in turn, could throw the bank's reputation into question. Because suitable lodging for single women was difficult to find, asking them to move to take a new position was not considered appropriate. By contrast, male employees could live in suspect lodgings for a short term without raising concerns about their morality.

The morality of women workers concerned Canadians during the war, though it was not a new issue. Social reformers at the end of the nineteenth century and the beginning of the twentieth century were concerned with the social and moral implications of large numbers of young, single women working in urban environments. Carolyn Strange has examined the moral dilemma caused by wage-earning women in Toronto between 1880 and 1930. Although there appears to have been little increase in concern about women's morality during the war, she suggests that anxiety increased following the war. Throughout the war women were exhorted to do their duty and to work for pay in support of the war effort. Once the war was over, women who were focused on their careers and wages were considered to be "bad girls." "Good" working girls – that is, those who did not think of themselves, have a social life, or request higher wages – would be rewarded by marriage.[47] Employers and concerned citizens were determined to protect women's morality and their health and safety. The nature and expression of these concerns further highlight the nuanced challenges to gender ideology.

Literature that justifies the hiring of women often emphasizes that banks were relatively safe environments for women. One suggests that,

> compared with farm work, school teaching or shop positions, the routine employment of a bank is less arduous – or at least less exhausting ... the element of social companionship is not to be forgotten ... many of the banks provide luncheon, and ... [i]t cannot be denied that pleasant surroundings and a sheltered scene of activity mean much.[48]

There were few dangers to the female banker, other than perhaps monotony.[49] In contrast, there was a great deal of concern about the health and safety of women munitions workers. Munitions work was much rougher, heavier, and more dangerous than bank work. The IMB and Canadian manufacturers were also aware of the damage done to female munitions workers in Great Britain. Prolonged exposure to various chemicals had turned the skin of thousands of plant workers, known as "the canary girls," yellow. There was concern that, in damaging the health of women, Britain was losing future generations, along with its current losses on the battlefield. Canadians were unwilling to jeopardize the health of their future mothers. The IMB regulated the length of women's shifts, reorganized factories to make them safer and healthier, provided canteens and restrooms, and made special arrangements to ensure that women received sufficient nourishment. The rationale for all of these measures was to protect women as mothers.[50]

In this, the IMB relied on the work of the British Ministry of Munitions' Health of Munitions Workers Committee. It was set up to address the conditions in factories that could have a negative impact on "those contributions which women alone can make to the state."[51] The IMB, employers, and, particularly, Mark Irish worked to ensure that Canadian factories met the standards established in Britain. For example, Irish tried to avoid the practice of hiring women for night work, an initiative supported by the Province of Ontario's Superintendent of Labour.[52] The IMB approached the YWCA to set up canteens in factories to ensure that the women had access to wholesome food and appropriate company.[53] In 1918, Irish also supported several factories in requesting exemptions from regulations set out by the Canada Food Board regarding restaurants. The regulations restricted the length of time restaurants could serve certain foods, which effected the canteens in the factories. Irish was concerned that munitions workers on evening or night shifts, who ate their main meal in the morning, would suffer because the restrictions said that meat could only be served as part of evening meals. Irish wrote to the Canada Food Board directing it to consider the impact such restrictions had on the welfare of munitions workers, particularly women.[54]

Closely linked to many of the concerns about the physical welfare of women workers were concerns about their moral welfare. The Ministry of Munitions committee on the health of munitions workers recommended that all factories that were employing women should hire a forewoman, a nurse, and welfare supervisors to watch over and protect them. Canadian factories followed their British counterparts and hired women in these positions. Russell Motor Car Company, Inglis, and McAvity's all had female matrons, nurses, forewomen, and supervisors. The duties of a welfare supervisor were similar to the duties of a mother. She was charged with discipline, supervising and preparing meals, ensuring that employees were dressed appropriately, monitoring and keeping a register of appropriate lodgings, giving advice, ascertaining the type of transit that workers took to work, and investigating irregular behaviour. The welfare supervisor "secur[ed] good order and protect[ed] the moral welfare of the girls under her charge."[55]

Mark Irish was also concerned about keeping any suggestion of impropriety among female munitions workers out of the press. Irish wrote to Chief Censor Ernest J. Chambers to ask that he consider censoring stories that had a negative impact on women and munitions work. Chambers responded by urging publishers to exercise "special caution" in reporting "any occurrences which might tend to discourage a reasonable extension of the system of using female labour in munitions factories such as women workers being harassed in the streets on their way to or from work."[56]

With a labour shortage by 1918, the passing of conscription legislation, and the demand for munitions growing, munitions manufacturers and the IMB were concerned about their ability to procure workers. This prompted Howard Murray, chairman of the explosives department of the IMB, to approach Flavelle regarding the use of women in the explosive plants that were being developed in Ontario. Murray appealed for the employment of women to release men for more important duties. He assumed, based on his review of the successful use of women workers in the cordite factory at Gretna Green in Britain, that women could be used successfully in the manufacture of explosives. At Murray's insistence, Flavelle urged Irish to look more seriously at the possibility.[57] Their final recommendations reveal the ambiguities surrounding gender relations in the munitions workforce as well as the interrelated concerns about women's moral and physical welfare.

Irish's opposition to the employment of women in explosives plants was unequivocal. "It is my opinion," he wrote, "that this branch of employment should constitute our last effort ... and not our first ... To do otherwise is, to my mind, economically unsound and to be deplored from the humane phases of the situation." Irish's opposition to this scheme was rooted in a chivalrous notion of protecting the mothers of future generations from unnecessary harm: "The inherent danger in an Explosives Plant, no matter how well conducted, is such that one must be loath to expose women to it except under dire necessity." Even in England, where the labour crisis was more severe, the state had delayed using women in explosives until there seemed no alternative. He cited Ministry of Munitions memoranda that discussed the debilitation, illness, and disfigurement of women workers, and he argued that it was simply inhumane to subject the women of Canada to such danger if it were not a dire necessity. He claimed that there were still men who were working in non-essential jobs that were more suited to women and that women should take on these jobs so as to free up the men for more dangerous work.

Beyond health concerns, Irish was also concerned that the explosives scheme raised moral issues for the IMB. Work in explosives plants was simply not suitable for women and would require "sustained welfare work afterward." Even in his discussion of the financial soundness of the plan, propriety was his first concern. The expenditures required to introduce women "on lines that would cause [them] no shame" were untenable (unless the British were paying). Although he had worked to increase women's opportunities in the public sphere, Irish's arguments to keep women out of explosive plants were founded on a middle-class gender ideology that idolized women's role as mother. Flavelle's final response to Murray shared Irish's recommendation to reject, or at least to delay, the employment of women in explosive factories in Nobel, Trenton, and Renfrew. Flavelle may have been prepared to employ women in non-traditional ways, but he was not willing to jeopardize the mothers of future generations, either morally or physically.

Women's non-traditional work during the First World War was couched in terms, usually of patriotic service, that served to undermine any real challenge to the status quo. As would be the case again during the Second World War, society reassured itself that women were feminine and, as such, deferential to and dependent upon men. While many contemporary observers praised women for assuming male space, attire, and behaviour, they also focused on how the activities remained within the boundaries of femininity. A discourse that reassured the public of female workers' femininity accompanied, and made possible, women's inclusion in masculine spheres of work. The process of ideological accommodation that accompanied women into the wartime workplace rendered any redefinition of gender roles unnecessary.[58]

Female bank employees recognized that their positions existed in order to support the war effort. One female bank officer wrote: "In every age our menfolk have gone forth to war while the women remained at home to plant, and reap, spin and weave, bake and brew, and do the thousand and one things needful at that time for the well-being of the nation. Once more the call is heard ... and once more women rise to the occasion, willing to do not only the things their grandmothers did, but also to go into the counting houses and market places of the world."[59] Women were simply doing what needed to be done. That the female clerks and tellers proved themselves fully capable of working in a bank did not change the attitude that women were not suited to banking. Similarly, munitions manufacturers and the IMB defined female munitions workers as a supportive, temporary measure. In a letter to Prime Minister Borden in 1917, Flavelle expressed a common understanding that women had "a general obligation to offer [themselves] for service" because it was "necessary for the good of the State."[60] Women's participation was crucial, but employing them only as wartime substitutes undermined any challenge their participation may have posed to gender ideology.

Reassurance that wartime workers remained feminine was common. Even as the women were welcomed and encouraged to transgress gender boundaries by working in the non-traditional roles and spaces of the BNS and munitions factories, they were kept in their place. Pride in female munitions workers was as common as assurances that their work did not make them less feminine. As one commentator wrote, in an article praising women munitions workers: "Not all the munitions work in the world can eradicate the Eternal Feminine, however, as soon as those girls saw that I had some photographs they were bent upon seeing their industrious young selves."[61] Another article described the work done in a factory in domestic terms: "A blue-eyed girl who looked as if she would scream at sight of a rat put a pellet into gaine [sic] and dabbed a little powder on top as calmly as if she were making sandwiches for a party."[62] In a militarized society, definitions of femininity expanded to include anything that was required to further the war effort.

The language of service, duty, and sacrifice legitimized the mobilization of women. Women workers were "volunteering" for service on the home front in order to do their bit for the war effort. This point was made clear in the *Globe*:

> Women who offer themselves for positions ordinarily occupied by men cannot be looked upon as in any way invading the territory belonging to male labour – they are simply offering their services to fill positions for which no man can be obtained. No man able to work, whether a returned soldier or one unfit for military service, need be out of employment to-day. The position of women is, therefore, identical with that taken by every patriotic section of our people – namely, they are expressing their willingness to serve the Empire in any way in which the need of the hour is greatest.[63]

Whether the author was reminding women of the nature of their role or simply identifying a common understanding, the statement reveals that women's work in non-traditional occupations was regarded as appropriate only in the militarized society. Women were not working to improve their position or to earn money and improve their day-to-day lives: they were serving the country. The latter was acceptable in a way that the former was not.

The patriotic spirit that permeated Canadian society during the war years produced endless calls for women to do their duty. For example, between 1916 and 1918, in its women's section, the *Montreal Star* ran a column entitled "What Girls May Do." It outlined "women's duty" during the war. Women were exhorted not only to do volunteer work and to be thrifty but also to work in war industries. One Toronto journalist stated: "The boys are fighting to make this a better world for ourselves and the coming generations to live in. They need help; therefore the girls and women must do all in her power to assist. Girls, you can help! Open the shutters and appear with your talents. Then you will be a soldier 'doing your bit.'"[64] In 1915, a recruiter in Nova Scotia wrote that women, like men, needed to be pressed into service if the war effort was to be sustained. David Carnegie, who had worked with the IMB, recalled: "The women managed the work, but it was the 'moral sense' that they brought to the work that is most worthy of mention." By "the moral sense" he meant that the women factory workers believed they were helping to win the war by performing an essential war service. His ideal munitions worker was one who continued to work after hearing that her son had been killed: "[she] set her face like a flint and worked harder than before, after but a short moment of shock."[65]

In Great Britain, the spectre of independent women workers caused a mild moral and social panic. As Penny Summerfield suggests:

> A woman dressed like a man was sending a lot of signals. She could be titillating men by inviting them to reveal the truth about her body and therefore her sexual identity ... Her apparent claim to be equal to a man could challenge men to prove their superior masculinity by dominating her physically and sexually ... Her manly appearances might mean that she would develop manly characteristics and male patterns of behaviour: drinking, swearing, spending her earnings, and making sexual advances.[66]

Women dressed like men, doing men's work, did not seem to worry Canadians unduly. Certainly, there were concerns about women's moral and physical health, but very few feared a postwar population of manly women. Instead, Canadians worried about whether women who worked during the war would be able to fulfill their roles as mothers. Canadians, particularly those of the middle class, also worried specifically about women workers' morality, but these concerns were not unique to the war period, nor were they significantly exacerbated by an increase in the number of female wage earners.

One explanation for the muted response towards women workers in Canada is simply that there were not sufficient numbers of paid women workers to undermine the foundations of gender ideology and thus to result in a lasting transformation. The increase in women in the paid workforce was small enough that it could be explained in the context of the war without requiring masculinity and femininity to be redefined. As Marjory MacMurchy writes: "Working for pay was no longer a dangerous departure from domesticity or a contributing factor in the social evil; in short, it had become a patriotic duty."[67]

The nature of the work women did further mitigated any potential threat to the prevailing order. Limits to advancement and rules about supervision maintained a sexual division of labour. Furthermore, women were firmly identified as temporary, unskilled workers. Their wartime work, extraordinary as it was, did not shake the foundations of society. A patriotically infused notion of femininity allowed women to remain feminine, even as they donned smocks and overalls. As commentators discussed the parallels between fuse production and baking, and how a short-term career in banking assisted in training good wives, they kept women firmly in their place ideologically, even as those same women moved out of their accustomed physical spaces and into the workplaces of men.

Notes

1 "Meaning of the Parade," *Globe* (Toronto), 4 July 1916.
2 *Kingston Daily British Whig*, 24 August 1918, in Barbara Wilson, *Ontario and the First World War, 1914-1918* (Toronto: Champlain Society, 1977), 140.
3 Census of Canada, 1901-1921 (Dominion Bureau of Statistics, 1924); F. Denton and S. Ostry, *Historical Estimates of the Canadian Labour Force*, Census of Canada, cat. no. 99-425, 1961; Bank of Nova Scotia (hereafter BNS) database. For a lengthier explanation of methodology, see Kori Street, "Bankers and Bomb Makers: Gender Ideology and Women's Paid Work in Banking and Munitions during the First World War in Canada" (PhD diss., University of Victoria, 2001), 9-15; and Marsha Courchane and Angela Reddish, "Women in the Labour Force, 1911-1986: A Historical Perspective," in *False Promises: The Failure of Conservative Economics*, ed. Robert C. Allen and Gideon Rosenbluth, 146-62 (Vancouver: New Star Books, 1992).
4 Street, "Bankers and Bomb Makers," 30.
5 Ibid., chap. 3.
6 Angela Woollacott, "Sisters and Brothers in Arms: Family, Class and Gendering in World War I Britain," in *Gendering War Talk*, ed. Miriam Cooke and Angela Woollacott, 128-47 (Princeton, NJ: Princeton University Press, 1993); and Angela Woollacott, *On Her Their Lives Depend: Munitions Workers in the Great War* (Berkeley: University of California Press, 1994).
7 Arthur Marwick, *The Deluge: British Society and the First World War* (London: Bodley Head, 1965); Arthur Marwick, *Britain in the Century of Total War: War, Peace and Social Change, 1900-1967* (London: Macmillan, 1968); Arthur Marwick, *War and Social Change in the 20th Century: A Comparative Study of Britain, France, Germany, Russia and the United States* (London: Macmillan, 1974); Arthur Marwick, *Women at War, 1914-1918* (London: Croom Helm, 1977); and Gordon Wright, *The Ordeal of Total War* (London: Oxford University Press, 1968).
8 Woollacott, *On Her Their Lives*; and Woollacott, "Sisters and Brothers." See also Gail Braybon, *Women Workers in the First World War* (London: Routledge, 1989); Deborah Thom, "Women and Work in Britain," in *The Upheaval of War*, ed. R. Hall and Jay Winter, 297-326 (London: Oxford University Press, 1988); Gail Braybon and Penny Summerfield, *Out of the Cage: Women's Experiences in Two World Wars* (London: Routledge Press, 1987); Penny Summerfield, *Women Workers in the Second World War: Production and Patriarchy in Conflict* (London: Routledge, 1984); Janet S.K. Watson, "Khaki Girls, VADs, and Tommy's Sisters: Gender and Class in First World War Britain," *International History Review* 19, 1 (1997): 32-51; Nicole Ann Dombrowski, ed., *Women and War in the Twentieth*

Century: Enlisted with or without Consent (New York: Garland, 1999); and Krisztina Robert, "Gender, Class and Patriotism: Women's Paramilitary Units in First World War Britain," *International History Review* 19, 1 (1997): 52-65.

9   Sandra Gwyn, *Tapestry of War: A Private View of Canadians in the Great War* (Toronto: HarperCollins, 1992), 438.

10 Graham S. Lowe, *Women in the Administrative Revolution: The Feminisation of Clerical Work* (London: Polity Press, 1987), 30. See also Desmond Morton and J.L. Granatstein, *Marching to Armageddon: Canadians and the Great War, 1914-1919* (Toronto: Lester and Orpen Dennys, 1989), 97; and John Herd Thompson, *Harvests of War: The Prairie West, 1914-1918* (Toronto: McClelland and Stewart, 1978), 106-7.

11 Ceta Ramakhalawansingh, "Women during the Great War," in *Women at Work: Ontario, 1859-1930*, ed. Janice Acton, Penny Goldsmith, and Bonnie Shepard, 261-308 (Toronto: Canadian Women's Educational Press, 1974), 261-308. See also Ruth Pierson, "*They're Still Women after All*": *The Second World War and Canadian Womanhood* (Toronto: McClelland and Stewart, 1986); James Naylor, *The New Democracy: Challenging the Social Order in Industrial Ontario, 1914-25* (Toronto: University of Toronto Press, 1991); Linda Kealey, *Enlisting Women for the Cause: Women, Labour, and the Left in Canada, 1890-1920* (Toronto: University of Toronto Press, 1998); Robert Rutherdale, *Hometown Horizons: Local Responses to Canada's Great War* (Vancouver: UBC Press, 2004); and Joan Sangster, "Mobilizing Women for War," in *Canada and the First World War: Essays in Honour of Robert Craig Brown*, ed. David Mackenzie, 157-93 (Toronto: University of Toronto Press, 2005).

12 Gwyn, *Tapestry of War*, xvii.

13 Jonathan Vance, *Death So Noble: Memory, Meaning, and the First World War* (Vancouver: UBC Press, 1997); Morton and Granatstein, *Marching to Armageddon*, 1.

14 Mark Irish to Joseph Flavelle, LAC, MG 30 A 16, vol. 38 Irish.

15 B.D. Thorley, "Bringing Up the Fourth Line Reserves," *Maclean's Magazine*, May 1916, 42.

16 "Will Oppose Installation of Women Conductors," *Industrial Banner*, 17 May 1918.

17 As cited in Braybon, *Women Workers*, 108.

18 Flavelle to R.L. Borden, 17 February 1916, LAC, MG 26 H, Borden Papers, vol. 51, H1(a), 108925. See also correspondence between R. Durley and Flavelle, 5 April 1916, LAC, MG 26 H, Borden Papers, vol. 51, H1(a), 118732.

19 Series of letters and reports between Bennett and Irish in spring 1917, LAC, MG 30 A16. vol. 33.

20 Ibid.

21 Minutes of the National Service Conference, 5 February 1917, LAC, MG 30 A16, vol. 38.

22 After Flavelle criticized his first draft as too personal and too angry, Irish wrote: "this letter was a model of self-restraint. I should have liked to have written in a closed room, in company with Bennett and done all the writing with my fist shut tight and my glasses off." He later wrote Bennett a more restrained letter. See draft letter to Bennett from Irish, 17 February 1917, and Flavelle's response, 21 February 1917, LAC, MG 30 A16, vol. 38.

23 Sheila McManus, "Gender, Work and Politics: Southern Alberta Farm Women, 1905-

1929" (MA thesis, University of Victoria, 1993).
24 Rutherdale, *Hometown Horizons*, xiii.
25 Bennett to Irish, attached Irish to Flavelle, October 1916, LAC, MG 30 A16, vol. 38.
26 *Canadian Machinery* 17 (26 April 1917): 426.
27 See Deborah Thom, *Nice Girls and Rude Girls: Women Workers in World War I* (London, New York: I.B. Taurus Publishers, 1998), 10-14.
28 Bride Broder, "Where Women Forge Weapons for Men's Defence," *Globe* (Toronto), 14 August 1917.
29 Daphne Read, ed., *The Great War and Canadian Society: An Oral History* (Toronto: New Hogtown Press, 1978), 156.
30 LAC, RG 27, vol. 308, file 18(67); LAC, MG 28 I44, file C-4589.
31 "100 Machinists on Strike," *Globe*, 27 June 1918; "Machinists Want Women Reinstated," *Toronto World*, 11 July 1918; "Employers State Their Side," *Mail and Empire*, 9 July 1918. See also LAC, RG 27, vol. 308, file 18 (67).
32 Toronto District Labour Council minutes, 20 May 1916, LAC, MG 28, C-4589.
33 Linda Quiney and Terry Bishop-Stirling in this volume both make similar observations about women in the Voluntary Aid Detachments and nursing.
34 E.G. Cowdry, "Woman in the Banking World," *Journal of the Canadian Bankers Association* 23, 4 (1919): 321.
35 Ibid.
36 Marjory MacMurchy, *The Woman – Bless Her* (Toronto: S.B. Gundy, 1916), 37-38.
37 J.L. Payne, "Women in the Offices of the Canadian Railways: Equal Men in Accuracy and Performance on Simple Jobs, but Are Not So Good for Complex Work," *Railway Age Gazette* 65, 15 (8 November 1918): 822.
38 Correspondence to Flavelle from G. Ogilvie, 7 June 1916, LAC, MG 26 H, Borden Papers, vol. 210, reel C-4399, 118701-02.
39 Ibid., 118727.
40 CPR database.
41 BNS database.
42 Agnes Harris Graham, "The Future of the Business Woman," *Journal of the Canadian Bankers Association* 24, 4 (1917): 317.
43 Jean Graham, "The Woman Bank Employee and the Canadian Bank," *Journal of the Canadian Bankers Association* 26, 4 (1919): 364.
44 Payne, "Women in the Offices," 821.
45 Jessie MacDonald Murray, "Woman in the Banking World," *Journal of the Canadian Bankers Association*, 23, 4 (1916) 314.
46 Graham, "Woman Bank Employee," 307.
47 Carolyn Strange, *Toronto's Girl Problem: The Perils and Pleasures of the City, 1880-1930* (Toronto: University of Toronto Press, 1995), 196-99.
48 Graham, "Woman Bank Employee," 364.
49 MacDonald Murray, "Woman in the Banking World," 316.
50 Ministry of Munitions Memorandum on the Health of Munitions Workers, AO, RG 3, box 17.

51 Ministry of Munitions Memorandum on the Health of Munitions Workers, AO, RG 3, box 17.
52 "Employment, Female, 1918-1919," AO, RG 12-0-10.
53 Letter to George Edwards from Irish, 21 June 1917, LAC, MG 30 A16, vol. 28.
54 LAC, MG 30 A16, vol. 13, file 139 – Food Regulations.
55 Ministry of Munitions, memoranda 1 and 2 of the Health of the Munitions Workers Committee, AO, RG 3.
56 Mark Irish, LAC, MG 30 A16, vol. 33.
57 Irish had looked into the issue early in 1917. He cooperated with Murray's initial examination into the situation in Trenton by sending Mrs. Fenton, whom Irish valued very highly for her work with him on dilution with the IMB, Department of Labour.
58 For a discussion of militarized gender roles, see Cynthia Enloe, *Does Khaki Become You? The Militarization of Women's Lives* (London: Pandora Press, 1983); Cynthia Enloe, "Feminists Thinking about War, Militarism and Peace," in *Analyzing Gender: A Handbook of Social Science Research*, ed. Beth B. Hess and Myra Marx Ferree, 526-41 (Beverly Hills: Sage, 1987); Micaela di Leonardo, "Morals, Mothers and Militarism," *Feminist Studies* 11, 3 (1985): 599-617; Margaret Higonnet and Patrice Higonnet, "The Double Helix," in *Behind the Lines: Gender and the Two World Wars*, ed. Margaret Higonnet, Jane Jensen, Sonya Michel, and Margaret C. Weitz, 31-47 (New Haven: Yale University Press, 1987); Woollacott, *On Her Their Lives;* Michele J. Shover, "Roles and Images of Women in World War I Propaganda," *Politics and Society* 5 (1975): 469-86. More recently, Robert Rutherdale has incorporated similar paradigms into *Hometown Horizons*. For instance, Rutherdale argues that recruiting materials "exploited the appeal to militarized masculinities," which depended in part on a "specious relegation of women's roles" (199).
59 Cowdry, "Woman in the Banking World," 320.
60 Flavelle to Borden, 17 February 1916, LAC, MG 26 H, Borden Papers, 108925.
61 *Saturday Night*, 15 July 1916.
62 Mary MacLeod Moore, "Women and Munitions," *Saturday Night*, 26 August 1916.
63 *Globe* (Toronto), 19 August 1917.
64 "A Girl's Duty in Time of War," *Globe* (Toronto), 22 September 1917.
65 David Carnegie, *The History of Munitions Supply in Canada, 1914-1918* (London: Longman's Green, 1925), 257.
66 Penny Summerfield, "Gender and War in the Twentieth Century," *International History Review* 29, 1 (1997): 7.
67 Cited in Strange, *Toronto's Girl Problem*, 195.

PART 3:
Family Matters

> I thank God that Chester is not old enough to go – and as I thank Him I shrink back in shame, the words dying on my lips. For is it not the same thing as thanking Him that some other woman's son must go in my son's place?[1]
>
> – L.M. Montgomery, 1915

The removal of tens of thousands of men from their families in Newfoundland and Canada had enormous repercussions for those they left behind. Wives, mothers, grandmothers, sisters, aunts, cousins, daughters, friends, girlfriends, and fiancées faced altered social, cultural, political, and economic landscapes in the wake of their loved ones' departures. Even the visual landscape of women's lives was drastically altered as they carried on in communities bedecked in khaki and devoid of large proportions of their usual male inhabitants. Women felt the absence of such a large number of men in a variety of ways, both tangible and intangible. New opportunities opened up, fresh challenges arose, homes seemed a little emptier, beds felt a bit colder, family dynamics changed, and so did family finances. Recent monographs by Desmond Morton and Suzanne Evans have brought to light some aspects of the war's impact on the families left behind, and Jonathan Vance's *Death So Noble* examines how Canadian society as a whole tried to make sense of the war. Yet the field remains wide open for historians of Canada and, especially, of Newfoundland.[2] The broader international literature on women and the First World War has similarly underplayed the personal, emotional side of the war, but Australian and British scholarship provides a number of useful models.[3] Only when we understand what the war meant not only for the soldiers who fought it but also for the vast number of Newfoundlanders and Canadians who stayed home will we truly have a sense of what it meant for these two British dominions to be at war.

In this section, Kristine Alexander tackles the previously unstudied subject of Canadian girls at war, considering their relationships with absent soldier-fathers, their use as symbols in wartime songs and War Bond advertising campaigns, and their own work for the war effort. Desmond Morton surveys the bureaucratic side of the war's economic impact on Canadian families through an examination of the Canadian Patriotic Fund, a national voluntary organization and war charity that provided financial support for soldiers' dependents. Suzanne Evans then turns our attention to the war's emotional toll on families left behind in Canada, made visible in mourning attire, medals, and service flags. For those left behind – the overwhelming majority of Canadian and Newfoundland girls and women – the war that was being fought so far away produced real changes in the most immediate, fundamental unit of society: the family. How they dealt with the attendant challenges and opportunities are important elements of Canadians' and Newfoundlanders' experiences of the Great War.

Notes

1 L.M. Montgomery, *The Selected Journals of L.M. Montgomery*, vol. 2: *1910-1921*, ed. Mary Rubio and Elizabeth Waterston (Toronto: Oxford University Press, 1987), 160.
2 Suzanne Evans, *Mothers of Heroes, Mothers of Martyrs: World War I and the Politics of Grief* (Montreal: McGill-Queen's University Press, 2007); Desmond Morton, *Fight or Pay: Soldiers' Families in the Great War* (Vancouver: UBC Press, 2004); Jonathan Vance, *Death So Noble: Memory, Meaning, and the First World War* (Vancouver: UBC Press, 1997).
3 Australian examples include: Joy Damousi, *The Labour of Loss: Mourning, Memory and Wartime Bereavement in Australia* (Cambridge: Cambridge University Press, 1999); Elizabeth Nelson, "Victims of War: The First World War, Returned Soldiers, and Understandings of Domestic Violence in Australia," *Journal of Women's History* 19, 4 (2007): 83-106; Catherine Speck, "Women's War Memorials and Citizenship," *Australian Feminist Studies* 11, 23 (1996): n.p. British examples include: Janis Lomas, "'So I Married Again': Letters from British Widows of the First and Second World Wars," *History Workshop Journal* 38 (1994): 218-27; Jessica Meyer, "'Not Septimus Now': Wives of Disabled Veterans and Cultural Memory of the First World War in Britain," *Women's History Review* 13, 1 (2004): 117-38; Virginia Nicholson, *Singled Out: How Two Million Women Survived without Men after the First World War* (New York: Oxford University Press, 2008).

7

An Honour and a Burden
Canadian Girls and the Great War

KRISTINE ALEXANDER

When Quebec farmer Lawrence Rogers enlisted with the 5th Canadian Mounted Rifles in 1915, his ten-year-old daughter Aileen gave him her favourite teddy bear as a keepsake. Rogers, who wrote dozens of letters to Aileen, his wife May, and son Howard throughout the war, carried the stuffed toy with him at all times – during his army training at Camp Valcartier and while tending to the wounded as a stretcher bearer on the Western Front. A tangible and poignant link to his family back in Canada, the bear was in Lieutenant Rogers' pocket when he was killed during the Battle of Passchendaele in October 1917. The well-worn little bear was sent back to Rogers' wife and children, who by that time had left their farm in the Eastern Townships and had moved to an apartment in Montreal. Newly widowed and grieving, May Rogers put the bear and her late husband's letters away in an old suitcase, where they remained virtually untouched for over eighty years. In 2003, Aileen Rogers' teddy bear and her father's correspondence received considerable public attention when they were donated to the Canadian War Museum (CWM) through an initiative organized by the Dominion Institute and the *Globe and Mail*. Lieutenant Rogers' military career and tragic death were discussed in local and national newspapers, and the bear now occupies a prominent place in the CWM's First World War gallery. These artifacts also captured the attention of academic and popular historians, and they are the subjects of an illustrated children's book by Stephanie Innes, Lawrence and May Rogers' great-granddaughter.[1]

Journalists, curators, historians, authors, and family members have all placed Aileen Rogers' bear within a narrative that focuses on her father's war experiences, his attachment to his family, and his tragic death at the age of forty. Perhaps predictably, they have shown far less interest in the ways in which Aileen herself experienced and understood the war that changed the world and took her father's life. For while no Zeppelin raids or enemy troops threatened their immediate safety, Canadian children were nonetheless implicated and involved in their country's war effort in a variety of ways. Young people played important roles in total war both discursively and practically – as symbols of national virtue and as sources of patriotic labour. Many of them were also, of course, drawn into the conflict on a personal level as the family members and neighbours of soldiers. And yet, despite the obvious importance of all civilians to this global conflict, children in general and girls in particular are conspicuously absent from the historiography of Canada and the First World War.[2] This chapter, then, begins to redress this scholarly imbalance by answering the following three questions: (1) How were Canadian girls represented in wartime propaganda and popular culture? (2) How were they affected by the enlistment of their male relatives? and (3) How were they mobilized for voluntary war service "at home"?

While feminist historians have rightly questioned the particular extent to which distant military conflicts changed the lives of Canadian girls and women, these groups were clearly affected by the Great War in a number of ways.[3] The absence of male relatives and neighbours, the material constraints caused by wartime production and inflation, and the opening of some industrial and especially clerical jobs to women changed many girls' lives. New charitable organizations like the Canadian Patriotic Fund mitigated some of the war's economic strain, but, as Desmond Morton shows in this volume, only after conducting countless intrusive investigations into applicants' home lives. Throughout the war, Canadian girls corresponded with each other and with enlisted relatives at the front and were avid consumers of news reports, propaganda, and other cultural products. They were also, through a range of voluntary organizations, mobilized in support of Canadian military efforts overseas.

It is, of course, impossible to generalize about how *all* girls across Canada and Newfoundland experienced and understood the First World War. The 7 million Canadians who remained "at home" during this conflict were characterized more by diversity than by uniformity, with experiences and outlooks influenced by a range of factors, including ethnicity, class, race, culture, religion, region, and age. The persecution and internment suffered by Canadians of Ukrainian and German descent, for example, differed markedly from the experiences and attitudes of the country's self-confident ethnically British majority. French-Canadian girls, especially in Quebec, would also have understood the war in general and conscription in particular quite differently from their anglophone counterparts. While the larger project from which this chapter draws deals with these broader issues, I concentrate largely on English-Canadian girls between the ages of five and fifteen.

The Great War was at once an honour and a burden for Canadian and Newfoundland girls, who were drawn into the conflict in often transformative ways on discursive, emotional, and practical levels.[4] Representations of these girls as innocent and dutiful daughters who were worth fighting for were central to the wartime efforts of numerous propagandists and cultural producers. Images of young white-skinned girls as daughters – domestic comfort and femininity personified – were ubiquitous throughout the war, and they were used in a variety of ways to pressure and inspire soldiers and civilians alike. These representations of the nation's girlhood as healthy, innocent, and in need of protection were also likely meant to elicit comparisons with the reported rape and mutilation of Belgian women and children by German soldiers.[5] While subsequent research has disproven the allegations contained in most of such atrocity stories, the Canadian government purchased thousands of British propaganda pamphlets during the war for distribution to newspapers, churches, and provincial departments of education across the country. John Herd Thompson argues that the effect of this atrocity propaganda, much of which focused on the alleged acts of sexual and physical violence suffered by Belgian girls, on English Canadians' view of the war "cannot be underestimated."[6] The impact of atrocity propaganda and the place of girls within those discourses are also evident in L.M. Montgomery's 1920 novel *Rilla of Ingleside* when Walter Blythe, elder brother of the novel's eponymous young heroine, explains his decision to enlist by saying: "There were girls as sweet and pure as you in Belgium and Flanders. You – even you – know what their fate was. We must make it impossible for such things to happen again while the world lasts."[7] Canadian sermons, political speeches, and newspaper articles all focused on the young victims of these alleged atrocities, as did popular "shaming" recruitment posters (which, as Desmond Morton and Jack Granatstein have noted, attracted the disapproval of Canadian military officials). One such poster, visible in public places across the nation, appealed to "The Women of Canada" by saying: "You have read what the Germans have done in Belgium. Have you thought what they would do if they invaded this Country? Do you realize that the safety of your home and children depends on our getting more men NOW?"[8]

The association of Canadian girlhood with domesticity, innocence, and the safety of "home" (ideals, it was implied, that were worth protecting at any cost) was also employed in several official Canadian propaganda campaigns. Idealized images of smiling young girls – invariably chubby, ringletted, and barely out of babyhood – were used especially prominently to sell Victory Bonds, the precursors of Canada Savings Bonds, which were used to finance the nation's war effort. Five different bonds were released for sale between 1915 and 1919, each of which was supported by a poster campaign coordinated by the Victory Loan Dominion Publicity Committee. Jeffrey Keshen notes that these poster campaigns were "sparse and unspectacular" until the fourth Victory Loan campaign in 1917, which bombarded Canadian citizens with the message that "duty, national pride and even self-interest demanded their patriotic response."[9] Bond sales more than doubled in the wake of the 1917 campaign, and in November 1918 Canadians bought bonds worth $660 million. While many Victory Bonds posters depicted Canadian soldiers as brave heroes fighting for a just cause, the extra-successful fourth and fifth campaigns also featured idealized images of young Canadian girls, which implied that investing in the war effort would both please girls in the short term and guarantee them a safe and prosperous future. These posters featured drawings of blond-haired girls (the precursors, almost, of Shirley Temple) asking their fathers to buy bonds for them. "Oh please do! Daddy, Buy Me a Victory Bond," one such poster asked, the latter phrase spelled out in alphabet blocks.[10]

Loving relationships between young daughters and their presumably enlisted fathers were portrayed in similar sentimental terms in many cultural products that were created and consumed in Canada during the war. Sheet music was an especially popular commodity in the days before radio, as families bought music to play and sing at home and listened to the same songs on gramophone and phonograph machines. Many wartime songs focused on sentimental and patriotic themes and were written by Canadian composers and published by Canadian music publishers. These songs, characterized by what Jonathan Vance calls a "mix of escapism and utility," also appeared on the programs of many war-related charity concerts across the country.[11]

The importance of the imagined relationship between enlisted fathers and their young daughters at home – a theme that characterized much of this music

– is especially evident in two Canadian songs published in 1916: "I Want to Kiss My Daddy Good Night" by Gordon V. Thompson (see Figure 9) and "I Want My Daddy" by Morris Manley. Thompson and Manley were prolific composers of sentimental and patriotic songs who clearly recognized the affective power of young children during wartime, and they used their depictions of lonely daughters to create emotional tributes to the men overseas. In Manley's "I Want My Daddy," the song's tearful narrator tells "her little story as plain as it could be / I love my dear old daddy though far across the sea / The first to join the army he loved the Union Jack / Each night I kneel and pray that God will bring my daddy back."[12] Thompson's "I Want to Kiss My Daddy Good Night" also uses a child's perspective to great effect: "Last night I had an awful dream / I saw my daddy there / Some naughty men were hurting him / They never seemed to care. / But oh! I'm glad it was not true / For somewhere far away, / He wrote my mamma he'd be back, / And when he comes he'll stay!"[13] American songs on similar themes – with titles like "Just a Baby's Letter Found in No Man's Land" and "Just a Baby's Prayer at Twilight (For Her Daddy Over There)" – were also sold and sung in Canada after the United States entered the war in 1917.[14]

The covers of these pieces of sheet music, like Canadian Victory Bond posters, also equated an idealized white girlhood with the conventionally feminine values of purity, piety, and domesticity. The cover of Gordon Thompson's "I Want to Kiss My Daddy Good Night," for example, features a photograph of a young girl descending a staircase in her nightgown, superimposed on a drawing of her mother sitting reading a letter by the fireplace, the smoke from which curls into a drawing of two Canadian soldiers firing a piece of artillery. The themes of lonely daughters, bedtime, home, and brave enlisted fathers were also featured on a number of photographic postcards produced and sold in Canada to be sent to soldiers overseas. These Canadian cards, part of what French historian Marie-Monique Huss calls the "patriotic fantasy" genre of wartime postcards, depicted a range of familial relationships between civilians at home and soldiers at the front. Like the covers of sheet music, these postcards often depicted soldier fathers and their children through the use of photomontage, a technique that, as Huss notes, made it possible to bring together in a single frame "people or concepts which would otherwise be separated."[15]

Two examples of photomontage postcards display these themes particularly clearly. One card, in tones of sepia and red, features a photograph of a young girl sitting at a desk, putting pen to paper and looking pensive. The upper left corner of the card features a soft-focus photograph of her father in uniform.

FIGURE 9   The sheet music for Thompson's 1916 wartime hit, "I Want to Kiss Daddy Goodnight," has an unintentionally creepy cover image. [Copyright Canadian War Museum, CWM 20020077-007]

178 Kristine Alexander

The words "A Message to Daddy" appear in the upper right-hand corner, and the lower left corner of the card says: "My own dear Daddy / I'm writing to you, / We send our love, / And kisses too."[16] Another card similarly connects home and battlefield by depicting a mother and her young daughter gazing into a fireplace, while their uniformed father and husband looks down on them from above. With the words "Memories Sweet" in the upper left corner, the card proclaims: "In the fire-lights glow, at eventide, / We think of you dear one, / And pray that Heaven will keep you safe, / And that Victory may be won."[17]

Drawing on the same stock of images as contemporary propagandists, composers, and photographers, Canadian educators, journalists, and charitable organizations told young people in no uncertain terms that they should be proud of their enlisted male relatives. The Canadian Patriotic Fund, for example, distributed buttons to Toronto children emblazoned with the words "My Dad is at the Front."[18] Rather than fostering feelings of national unity, however, these buttons (which featured a line drawing of a Canadian soldier holding a rifle and bayonet and were only given to the children of enlisted men) sometimes worked to emphasize differences between young people as they meant that children of German or Ukrainian descent, or those whose fathers had not enlisted, could easily be singled out or excluded.

Canadian girls – no matter who their fathers were – were avid consumers of information about the conflict overseas; rumours, atrocity stories, and growing casualty lists fuelled their fears about the safety of fathers, brothers, cousins, uncles, and neighbours as well as about the state of the world more generally. The prolonged absence of male relatives (especially fathers) also often caused considerable changes in families' earning and living arrangements. While many families undoubtedly did worry as portrayed in music and postcards, they also adapted with the help of neighbourhood networks, extended families, and grandparents. Although the reason – total war – was new to Canadians, the situation was not entirely novel. There had been many absent fathers, blended families, and female-headed households in Canada before 1914, just as there would continue to be after the Armistice.

Literacy and letter-writing were central to how many Canadian girls experienced the prolonged absences of their enlisted fathers and brothers. Popular agricultural publications like the *Family Herald and Weekly Star* (published in Montreal) and the Winnipeg-based *Free Press Prairie Farmer*, for instance, ran correspondence clubs for children and adolescents, providing opportunities for young readers from across the country to describe their experiences and to forge friendships with one another. Many Canadian girls wrote letters to these clubs discussing their enlisted family members and asked to correspond with other young people whose relatives were overseas. Fourteen-year-old Lillian Davidson, for example, wrote to the *Family Herald and Weekly Star*'s "Maple Leaf Club" from her family farm in the Okanagan in February of 1916. Stating first that she would like rural life "better if it wasn't so quiet," Davidson devoted most of her letter to a description of her older brother, who had enlisted the previous year. While asking for pen pals of a similar age, she also described visiting her brother's army training camp in Vernon, British Columbia. Echoing the high diction and language of national pride that characterized most public discussions of the war, she wrote that he and his fellow recruits were "so well drilled that they marched just as one man" and added that "Canada ought to be proud of her brave soldiers."[19] Less than a month later, the Maple Leaf Club published a letter from ten-year-old Olive Powless of Wilsonville, Ontario. "I am a little girl, ten years old," she wrote, "and I belong to the Mohawk tribe of the Six Nations Indians. My father has enlisted, and so have many others from this reserve. I would like to correspond with some other little girl of my age, whose father has enlisted."[20] Olive, whose father William Powless of the 114th Battalion of the Canadian Expeditionary Force is mentioned in Alison Norman's chapter (this volume), was proud of the Six Nations' unique contribution to the war and hoped at the same time to make connections with other young members of the Canadian national community.

Unlike their counterparts from Britain and France, Lillian Davidson's brother and Olive Powless' father were too far away to come home on leave. The average Canadian soldier spent two years away from home, but some men were gone for as many as five (from 1914 to 1919). Letters and cards, though heavily censored, were therefore a vital point of contact between Canadian girls and their fathers and brothers overseas. Aileen Rogers wrote to her father on a regular basis, but the contents of her correspondence can only be surmised based on her father's letters, which often thanked her for her drawings, letters, and valentine cards. As Martha Hanna argues, wartime letters and cards were more than mere sources of information: they were "physical artefact[s] that could cultivate intimacy by making the absent correspondent seem almost palpably present." Hanna writes of French fathers during the Great War being "moved by the sight of [their] children's handwriting," a phenomenon that seems to have been experienced by some Canadian soldiers as well.[21] On 4 April 1917, for example, Lawrence Rogers told Aileen: "the letter you sent me enclosed with

Mother's was very nice and your writing is getting much better soon you will be able to write better than I can."[22]

Young Jessie Tyrell from Ottawa also corresponded with her father George, an accountant who had joined the 58th Broad Gauge Railway Operating Company (Canadian Railway Troops) in 1916. She pasted her father's letters, postcards, and Christmas cards in a scrapbook, along with several photographs of her posing beside a favourite doll in a baby carriage. In his letters, George Tyrell thanked Jessie for her cards and notes, described his unsuccessful attempts to buy her a doll while on leave in France, and listed activities he hoped they would do together once the war was over. "Well Jess: what do you think of this old war?" he wrote in a 3 April 1918 letter from "Muddy France." He went on: "Lasting quite a while, but there is no doubt it will finish some day and then your old Dad will be home to buy candy and ICE CREAM for you, wont [sic] that be good?"[23] Margaret Ormsby (b. 1909), who would later become a pre-eminent historian of British Columbia, wrote a letter to her father George, a general merchant from the north Okanagan village of Lumby, who was serving overseas with a Canadian infantry battalion. "Dear Dadie," the letter begins, "we are going Vancuvr I wonder when you wil be back." In a few more lines of smudged cursive writing, she thanked her father for a bracelet he had sent, asked when he would be home, and ended by saying "I hope yuo [sic] wil be safe."[24] But girls' letters sometimes expressed emotions other than hope and sadness; wartime correspondence also provides occasional glimpses of the anger and frustration many girls must have felt, as demonstrated by George Tyrell's words to his daughter Jessie: "Mother says you are angry at me for not answering your letters, please excuse me, but I thought they were answered."[25]

Fathers' letters, which could prompt a bewildering range of emotions, were also sources of information about European geography and life at the front. In a November 1915 letter to Aileen from Caesar's Camp in England, Lawrence Rogers wrote: "It is very cold here and has been raining for three days till we all have the blues or as we call it the Willies and the mud is something to be seen to understand what it is like." In the same letter he added: "I will have to learn to play all over again because all I know how to do now is order a lot of men around clean horses and carry a great big heavy rifle and it gets very heavy after carrying it awhile. It weighs over nine pounds. Then we have a big pack on our backs which weighs a lot more but it is the only way to carry our clothes. It takes a strong man to carry it all. We had two men left behind because they could not carry them."[26]

An Honour and a Burden

But there was, of course, more to waging war than marching and carrying heavy packs. Soldiers' letters to their children occasionally offered small glimpses of the unspeakable realities of the battlefield, though men never discussed their own roles as killers. On 4 April 1917, Lieutenant Rogers wrote to Aileen: "The big guns are making an awful lot of noise and the ground is shaking so that the candles are jumping but we are used to that now. It is worse than the biggest thunder storm you ever heard ... our gas masks look awful funny when we have them on and smell nasty but we have to wear them or we might get killed."[27] Such statements, however, were rare. As Paul Fussell argues, the horror of wartime events and the limits of the triumphant nineteenth-century language available to describe them made it extremely difficult to convey a soldier's experiences to those back home – even before their letters reached the censors. As a result, many men tried "to fill the page by saying nothing and to offer the maximum number of clichés."[28]

Aileen Rogers' father was, in many ways, an exceptional correspondent – conscientious, articulate, and (especially after being made an officer) possessed of enough space and time to write to his wife and children individually. With fewer opportunities and resources, most Canadian soldiers communicated with their daughters and other family members in ways that were far more brief and formulaic. Many Canadian girls heard from their fathers through field service postcards – the first mass-produced form letters, on which, for example, men were to cross out inapplicable phrases to indicate if they were "quite well" or "sick/wounded."[29] Mass-produced postcards, meanwhile, offered a slightly more personal form of quick and easy correspondence. As Marie-Monique Huss argues, postcards met a "need for light relief from both the tedium and horror of war. The picture postcard, as opposed to the state subsidized military card, was a small gift for the recipient, a kind of surprise."[30] Embroidered postcards also acted as gifts and surprises for family members back home; sold to Allied soldiers by the thousands from 1914 through 1919, they featured hand-embroidered sentimental, patriotic, or regimental designs on strips of fine cotton or silk cloth. These designs were embroidered by French and Belgian women in their homes before being cut and mounted on factory-produced cards.

Pipe Major Alexander Campbell from St. John New Brunswick, who had joined the 26th Battalion of the CEF in 1914, sent his daughter Dora a number of embroidered postcards throughout the war. For Christmas 1916, for example, she received one whose cover was a sheer white silk envelope embroidered with blue flowers, green leaves, a pink garland, and the words "To my dear Daughter."

Inside the envelope was a small card with colour drawings of all the combatant nations' flags and the words "Souvenir de la guerre" and "Forget Me Not 1914-1915." To this Campbell added his own brief handwritten messages: "To Dear Dora Campbell from dada with love and Kisses. Xmas 1916"; "Be good little girl till dada comes Home – very soon I hope."[31]

Surviving wartime father-daughter correspondence contains many expressions of affection, which, as James Marten argues regarding the American Civil War, suggests "that wartime absences prompted more intense relationships between family members."[32] Postcards and the personal messages they contained also provide proof that home life and their identities as fathers continued to be important to many enlisted men. Fathers like Alexander Campbell, John Harding, and Lawrence Rogers used their correspondence to give advice, reassure loved ones, and celebrate their children's achievements – the other side of the rough homosocial soldiers' world that has been studied by Tim Cook.[33] As Jessica Meyer notes, for soldiers recruited from civilian populations, writing to their families improved their morale and allowed them to "present themselves to their families not only as soldiers, through their descriptions of war experiences, but also as domestic men through their continuing involvement with domestic concerns."[34]

In addition to letters and postcards, many Canadian girls also received war-related souvenirs through the post. Many of these were also made by French and Belgian women as part of the wartime economy. Jessie Tyrell's father, for instance, sent her a small handkerchief in April of 1917 and apologized in November of that year: "[Sorry that I could not] get anything nice for your Xmas gift but your old dad is nearly broke. Enclosed are four lace butterflys which will show you that I thought of my dear little girl."[35] Lawrence Rogers, meanwhile, sent his children a variety of war souvenirs, including a photograph of himself in uniform and, in November 1915, "three of [his] badges made into pins ... as keep sakes."[36] On 4 April 1917, he asked Aileen: "How did you like the things I sent to you from Fritzie?"[37]

While enlisted fathers' letters contained souvenirs, sanitized news, and sentimental holiday greetings, they also provide proof that some aspects of their children's lives remained relatively unchanged during the war. New pets, report cards, school holidays, medical problems, and sibling rivalries were all discussed in Lawrence Rogers' correspondence with his daughter. "Mother tells me you have had a fine time this winter, with skating, tobogganing and your dancing lessons," wrote Rogers in April 1917: "You will be able to teach me how to dance the new dances when I come home for we dont [sic] get any dancing over here. It is not very polite of the boys to throw snow-balls at the girls and I hope that Howard [Aileen's brother] does not do it."[38] On 4 May 1917, Rogers wrote to Aileen that her mother had sent him one of her school reports: "It was fine and Dad was so proud of it he showed to all the boys and Dan came and of course I had to show it to him, he was almost as pleased as I was."[39] A common childhood rite of passage was his subject on 16 June 1917: "How did you like the chicken pox hop [sic] you did not scratch your face and make it all full of little holes like some poor people have done for I surely would not like anything to happen to you like that. Write again soon for I like to hear from you your letters are so nice."[40]

But for Aileen Rogers and thousands of other Canadian girls, the daily rhythms of school, work, and play were interrupted by reminders of the war's heavy human cost. As Desmond Morton shows, advances in medical care meant that injured and unwell soldiers, many of whom would not have survived in earlier conflicts, were visible in Canadian cities and towns from at least 1915 onward.[41] One girl who signed herself only as "Lover of Khaki" wrote to the Maple Leaf Club on 17 October 1917 as follows: "I lived in the city of Winnipeg all last fall and winter, and when I was there I saw what I thought a terrible sight – over one thousand returned soldiers on parade, those that were unable to walk were riding in cars provided by the Returned Soldiers' Association of Winnipeg. I have seen them both leaving for the front and coming home maimed and disabled for life. I had a cousin who joined up in the early part of the war, but was killed about last October."[42] Another Maple Leaf, eleven-year-old Flossie Thompson, wrote in 1916 describing Governor Sir Walter Davidson's recent visit to her hometown of Bonavista, Newfoundland. Before speaking to a large crowd at the Orange Hall, the King's representative and his wife stopped to visit "all the homes of those whose sons had been killed at the front."[43] Veterans' parades, vice-regal condolence visits, and other such tangible evidence of the war's impact brought the conflict to children's doorsteps.

Sometimes the war came right into young people's homes, affecting their immediate families and forcing them to deal with loss and grief. Evelyn Price from Ewing, Alberta, whose letter also described her five siblings and pony named Babe, wrote to the Maple Leaf Club in June of 1918. "Our family has had pretty near its share of the war," she said. "My father was killed in action in the Passchendale [sic] Ridge Battle in November, and my uncle is in France now. There are six children in our family. Three boys and three girls. My baby brother was born two days before dad left for France and it is hard to believe he will never see him again."[44] Lawrence Rogers's last letter home is dated 19 October 1917; he was killed less than two weeks later and has no known grave. George Tyrell wrote his last letter to his daughter Jessie on 3 April 1918, saying that he would buy her candy and ice cream when he returned home. Tyrell proved unable to keep that promise, dying in a military hospital in Northampton, England, instead of rejoining his family in Canada. His daughter's scrapbook preserves fragments of his death's unfolding impact on her life: the telegram informing his family of his demise, an obituary clipping, his death certificate, photos of his grave, and an article from the *Ottawa Journal* about the unveiling of the Grave of the Unknown Soldier in Westminster Abbey in November 1930.

Whether they experienced such traumatic losses or not, girls from across the country also played active and direct roles in the Canadian war effort. Like many of their mothers, girls were mobilized in support of their nation's military, through school, church, and a variety of voluntary organizations.[45] The Girl Guides, a British-based and imperialist youth organization first established in Canada in 1910, was especially enthusiastic in its promotion of war work. Combining uniforms and military-style discipline with promises of domestic training and outdoor adventure, the Guide movement encouraged girls to demonstrate their loyalty to Canada and the British Empire in a variety of ways.[46] During the war, Guide meetings, badges, and fundraising activities all focused on supporting Allied military efforts. Guiding was seen as good for girls and good for the war effort, providing supervision for children whose fathers were away and whose mothers might be at work or busy with wartime voluntary efforts.

Canadian Guide leaders, public figures, and journalists often described the movement's wartime activities as patriotic endeavours of national and imperial importance. From the Canadian Guide movement's head office on Toronto's Yonge Street, Dominion Council Secretary Miss E.M. Mairs wrote in 1915, for example: "From the very beginning of the war the Girl Guides in Canada as well as in England have shown great readiness to assist in every way possible the many societies organized for relief work and in carrying out the various duties assigned to them have shown an efficiency which proges [sic – should be "proves"] the value of the Girl Guide training."[47] As of April 1917 the Guide movement in Canada boasted 281 companies, with approximately 9,400 members.[48] In May 1916, Manitoba lieutenant-governor Sir James Aikins linked Guiding's emphasis on discipline, self-sacrifice, obedience, and preparedness to the broader Allied war effort. Speaking to a group of Guides in the Prairie town of Brandon, he insisted: "Girl Guide principles will win this war." And he claimed: "if the British Navy had not been prepared at the outbreak of the war the present conflict would have been quickly over with disastrous results to the allies."[49]

Thousands of Canadian girls adhered to "Guide principles" throughout the war by making and collecting goods to be sent overseas, both to war-affected children and to Canadian and Allied troops. In 1914, for instance, Canadian Guides collected toys, books, candies, and clothing for a "Christmas Ship" that was sent overseas to provide aid to Belgian orphans. The Girl Guides' efforts in this regard received nationwide press coverage, with *Saturday Night* magazine, for example, reporting that contributions came from locations across Canada, including Herward, Saskatchewan; Olds, Alberta; Dauphin, Manitoba; Sherbrooke, Quebec; and Chatham, Ontario.[50] Canadian Guides also sent parcels to overseas troops throughout the conflict. For example, in December 1914, a Toronto newspaper claimed that the handkerchiefs, scarves, newspapers, shoelaces, gum, chocolates, and Christmas cards sent by the Guides to Canadian soldiers were proof that Canadian girls "have ... real work to do for their country and her brave defenders."[51]

Canadian Guides were also encouraged to supplement their provision of material aid by raising money or volunteering for other war-related charities. The 1914-15 Canadian Girl Guides' Dominion Council Report, for example, boasted that the Guide spirit of self-sacrifice was demonstrated by "the fact that many denied themselves their annual Summer Camp, which as every one knows is a supreme joy to all young girls, donating the funds for Red Cross supplies while most of those who did not entirely forego the pleasure spent an hour or two of each day in camp at Red Cross work."[52] Guides from across southern Ontario also took part in regular fundraising events at Casa Loma, the palatial home of Toronto financier Sir Henry Pellatt, whose wife Lady Mary Pellatt was then chief commissioner of Canadian Girl Guides. In September of 1915, for example, "a very successful rally and garden fete" was held on the grounds of the estate. Together, over five hundred Toronto Guides and one hundred girls from places like Ottawa, Niagara Falls, and Sherbrooke, Quebec, demonstrated their marching, first aid, and signalling skills, and provided an "excellent display of plain and fancy needle work, knitting and crochet work, butter, cheese and preserves, cakes and pastry, flowers and vegetables."[53] They also sold flowers, homemade cakes, candies, and ice cream at the event, donating the proceeds of $357.90 to the Red Cross.

Across the country, groups of Girl Guides gave material aid and financial support to local patriotic funds, Soldiers' Comforts, the Belgian Relief Society, the Duchess of Connaught's Prisoners of War Fund, Secours National, the Navy League, the Blue Cross, various Trafalgar Day campaigns, and, especially, the Red Cross. They were also encouraged to save their money and to invest in Victory Bonds. The movement's 1918 annual report boasted: "when the last Victory War Loan was launched an appeal was sent out to all local branches to give all possible assistance and the response was splendid, while as Companies assistance was given in the distribution of literature, in preparing floats, and taking part in parades, individual Guides everywhere invested their savings. One company (Chatham, Ont.) reports a total of $4,300 invested, another (Gananoque) $4,850, and another (Toronto) $2,000."[54] Canadian Guides also cooperated with companies from England and other parts of the British Empire to purchase and equip an ambulance and two recreation huts for Allied soldiers in France.[55] Press coverage of Guides' charitable endeavours sometimes stressed the movement's pan-imperial nature as well, as when the *Toronto Daily Star* reported on 8 March 1918 that Guides in India had raised 2,243 rupees for Allied prisoners of war in Germany.[56]

Canadian Guides were encouraged to keep track of their voluntary war work in order to earn the movement's special War Service Badge. With separate requirements for those over or under the age of fourteen, the War Service Badge required girls to produce a certain quota of comforts and hospital supplies or to provide a set number of hours of voluntary or paid work for health care institutions, war charities, or companies doing government-sanctioned war work. In addition, Guides had to fulfill the usual gendered requirements of the Cook's Badge and either the Ambulance Badge or Home Nursing Badge. Alternatively, they could replace those two badges with a five hundred-word essay on "A Girl's Duty to her country in time of war."[57] As during the Second World War, most of these activities encouraged girls to play traditional female roles, a fact that Tamara Myers and Mary Anne Poutanen argue reinforced the idea that girls' "future lives would be properly circumscribed by home and voluntary labour."[58]

Some Canadian Guides also worked in less conventionally feminine ways to alleviate the national food crisis that emerged near the end of the war, when military recruitment caused agricultural labour shortages in Ontario, Manitoba,

Saskatchewan, and Alberta. Like the National Food Controller's Office (created in June 1917), Guiding encouraged Canadian girls to use food thriftily, grow their own produce, and volunteer on farms. Starting in mid-1917, several Toronto companies "obtained permission to use a number of vacant city lots where flowers and vegetables were grown and afterwards distributed among the poor of the City." That same year, Guides from the Ontario town of Thamesville planted and sold potatoes and other vegetables, donating the proceeds to various war charities. The Thamesville Guides' venture "was so successful," the Dominion Guide Secretary reported, that the Department of Agriculture at Ottawa requested the captain to send a report of it for publication in the "Gazette."[59] The "Canadian Girl Guides" column in the *Toronto Daily Star* reported that "many guide companies are adopting the 'Greater Production' slogan for spring. The convener of the Badge Committee has sent in the names of the successful candidates for the 'Gardens' badge. Their vegetable gardens were inspected last fall at Glen Garland (Henry Pellatt's estate in the Ontario township of King) and bulbs were grown during the winter."[60]

Many Canadian Guides earned badges and volunteered to help with food production, and the movement's 1918 annual report proudly described Canadian farmers' claims that, had it not been for the efficiency and helpfulness of the Guides, "large crops of fruit would have been wasted." The 26th Toronto Guides, for example, camped near Oakville for seven weeks, during which time thirty-six girls "took part in farm work. Besides hoeing and weeding, 11,970 baskets of strawberries, raspberries and cherries were picked. The three officers superintended the camp and the girls did their own cooking and housekeeping &c. There was no outside assistance. All expenses of camp were paid out of their earnings and they had $50.00 over which they invested in a war bond for Company funds."[61]

The war ended not long after the conclusion of the 1918 harvesting season, and Canadian girls joined in the celebrations that took place across the country when the Armistice was announced. Once the festivities were over, however, many of them knew that their lives would be permanently transformed. Families of soldiers who had survived the war faced difficult adjustments as fathers and children worried about being able to recognize each other and as familial roles and responsibilities were renegotiated. Many men returned with psychological and physical scars and had trouble reintegrating into civilian society. The massive influenza epidemic and labour unrest that punctuated 1918-19 further hindered an orderly return to peacetime life. Veterans' families also faced a range of economic difficulties in the aftermath of the war. As Desmond Morton shows, the Canadian government ensured that many "disabled veterans and their families would remain poor by basing pensions on the wage rates of an unskilled labourer."[62] Others who were not disabled got fired or quit jobs because they were restless. Even the Soldier Settlement scheme – the federal government's primary effort to help veterans readjust – did not work as planned. By 1930, almost half of the 24,709 soldiers who settled on new land with hopes of farming had given up the attempt.[63] For the children of veterans, this could all mean tension at home, moving house, and poverty. These difficult experiences, combined with grief, also affected families like the Rogerses and the Tyrells, whose relatives had been killed.

The Armistice also ushered in a range of new opportunities and hopes for girls and young women. As Veronica Strong-Boag shows, the end of the First World War and the federal enfranchisement of most Canadian women led many to believe that a "New Day" was dawning for women and girls.[64] The new opportunities that opened up included political participation and some expanded educational and employment choices. Most provinces raised the school-leaving age to fifteen or sixteen in the 1920s, for example, though adolescent wages remained important for many families. Aileen Rogers graduated as a registered nurse from the Montreal General Hospital School of Nursing in the 1920s and spent her career working in health services at McGill University. Olive Powless got married and moved to Toronto, where she worked for the Canadian Pacific Railway and raised two children with her husband Thomas Badcock. Margaret Ormsby earned a BA (1929) and an MA (1931) in history from the University of British Columbia, along with a PhD (1937) from Bryn Mawr College in Pennsylvania. She taught at several Canadian universities but spent most of her career at UBC, where she produced a range of influential studies of the history of British Columbia.

The girls who had bought Victory Bonds, written misspelled letters, and belonged to the Junior Red Cross and the Girl Guides during the war also took advantage of the many new leisure and consumption possibilities that opened up in the postwar years. Many became modern girls and flappers – the first teenagers, depicted in Hollywood movies, targeted in department store advertisements, and immersed in a culture of cinema, dancing, and commercial amusements. But these changes were accompanied by continuities as postwar reformers, experts, and journalists continued – as they had during wartime – to link girls and women to maternity, domesticity, and the private sphere. Many modern young women who smoked, wore makeup, occupied public spaces, and worked for wages therefore had also to deal with increased surveillance and regulation.

Involvement in the Great War was an honour for some Canadian girls and a burden for others. Between 1914 and 1918, they viewed idealized representations of white domestic girlhood in propaganda and popular culture, lost male relatives and friends (sometimes permanently) to the Western Front, and provided voluntary labour in support of the Canadian war effort. Although few of them expressed it, some girls would likely have agreed with one member of the Maple Leaf Club who wrote, in late 1914, that the war was "a dreadful thing" because of the "innocent lives it [was] taking ... [and] the money, expense and trouble it [was] causing."[65] Perhaps this is why so many people continue to react so strongly to Aileen Rogers' teddy bear: like the wartime experiences of Canadian girls more generally, it speaks to one of the defining characteristics of modern warfare – what Paul Fussell terms "the ironic proximity of violence and disaster to safety, to meaning, and to love."[66]

Notes

1 Tim Cook and Natascha Morrison, "Longing and Loss from Canada's Great War," *Canadian Military History* 16, 1 (2007): 53-60; Stephanie Innes and Harry Endrulat, *A Bear in War* (Toronto: Key Porter Books, 2008).
2 Robert Rutherdale, *Hometown Horizons: Local Responses to Canada's Great War* (Vancouver: UBC Press, 2005); Desmond Morton, *Fight or Pay: Soldiers' Families in the Great War* (Vancouver: UBC Press, 2004); Ian Hugh MacLean Miller, *Our Glory and Our Grief: Torontonians and the Great War* (Toronto: University of Toronto Press, 2002); Jonathan Vance, *Death So Noble: Memory, Meaning, and the First World War* (Vancouver: UBC Press, 1997); Jeffrey A. Keshen, *Propaganda and Censorship during Canada's Great War* (Edmonton: University of Alberta Press, 1996).
3 Veronica Strong-Boag, *The New Day Recalled: Lives of Girls and Women in English Canada, 1919-1939* (Toronto: Copp Clark Pitman, 1993), 4.
4 James Marten, *The Children's Civil War* (Chapel Hill and London: University of North Carolina Press, 1998), 242.
5 James Morgan Read, *Atrocity Propaganda, 1914-1919* (New Haven: Yale University Press, 1941); Nicoletta Gullace, "Sexual Violence and Family Honor: British Propaganda and International Law during the First World War," *American Historical Review* 102, 3 (1997): 714-47.

6 John Herd Thompson, *The Harvests of War: The Prairie West, 1914-1919* (Toronto: McClelland and Stewart, 1978), 35.
7 L.M. Montgomery, *Rilla of Ingleside* (Toronto: Seal Books, 1996), 119. See also Owen Dudley Edwards and Jennifer H. Litster, "The End of Canadian Innocence: L.M. Montgomery and the First World War," in *L.M. Montgomery and Canadian Culture*, ed. Irene Gammel and Elizabeth Epperley, 31-46 (Toronto: University of Toronto Press, 1999); Alan R. Young, "L.M. Montgomery's *Rilla of Ingleside* (1920): Romance and the Experience of War," in *Myth and Milieu: Atlantic Literature and Culture 1918-1939*, ed. Gwendolyn Davies, 95-122 (Fredericton: Acadiensis Press, 1993).
8 Desmond Morton and J.L. Granatstein, *Marching to Armageddon: Canadians and the Great War, 1914-1919* (Toronto: Lester and Orpen Dennys, 1989), 42; Susan R. Grayzel, *Women's Identities at War: Gender, Motherhood, and Politics in Britain and France during the First World War* (Chapel Hill and London: University of North Carolina Press, 1999), 47.
9 Jeffrey A. Keshen, *Propaganda and Censorship during Canada's Great War* (Edmonton: University of Alberta Press, 1996), 54-55.
10 Canadian War Poster Collection, McGill University Library, WP1.B37.F5, "Oh Please Do, Daddy!" See also Canadian War Poster Collection, McGill University Library, WP1.B37.F5, "Do It Again Daddy Please! – Buy Me a Victory Bond."
11 Jonathan F. Vance, *A History of Canadian Culture* (Don Mills, ON: Oxford University Press, 2009), 221.
12 Morris Manley, "I Want My Daddy" (Toronto: M. Manley Publishing Co., 1916), Canadian War Museum (hereafter CWM), 20020077-006.
13 Gordon V. Thompson, "I Want to Kiss My Daddy Good Night" (Toronto: Thompson Publishing Co., 1916), CWM, 19850374-010.
14 "Just a Baby's Letter Found in No Man's Land" (New York: Joe Morris Co., 1918), CWM, 19810333-00; Sam Lewis, Joe Young, and M.K. Jerome, "Just a Baby's Prayer at Twilight (For Her Daddy Over There)" (New York: Waterson, Berlin and Snyder Co., 1918), CWM, 19801269-006.
15 Marie-Monique Huss, "Pronatalism and the Popular Ideology of the Child in Wartime France: The Evidence of the Picture Postcard," in *The Upheaval of War: Family, Work and Welfare in Europe, 1914-1918*, ed. Richard Wall and Jay Winter (Cambridge: Cambridge University Press, 2005), 337. See also John Fraser, "Propaganda on the Picture Postcard," *Oxford Art Journal* 3, 2 (1980): 39-47.
16 CWM, 19990037-004.
17 CWM, 19990037-005.
18 CWM, 20030334-006.
19 Quoted in Norah L. Lewis, ed., *"I Want to Join Your Club": Letters from Rural Children, 1900-1920* (Waterloo: Wilfrid Laurier University Press, 1996), 232.
20 Quoted in Lewis, *"I Want to Join Your Club,"* 227.
21 Martha Hanna, "A Republic of Letters: The Epistolary Tradition in France during World War I," *American Historical Review* 108, 5 (December 2003): 21.

22 Letter from L.B. Rogers to Aileen Rogers, 4 April 1917, CWM, 20040015-005, Lawrence Rogers Collection.
23 Scrapbook of the Great War, kept by Jessie Tyrell (1915-18), 3 April 1915, CWM, 20020058-003.
24 Letter from Margaret Ormsby to her father George Ormsby, CWM, 200013-001. For more on Ormsby's military career, see Tim Cook, "'My Whole Heart and Soul Is in This War': The Letters and War Service of Sergeant G.L. Ormsby," *Canadian Military History* 15, 1 (2006): 51-63.
25 Scrapbook of the Great War, kept by Jessie Tyrell (1915-18), 3 April 1918, CWM, 20020058-003.
26 Letter from L.B. Rogers to Aileen Rogers, 2 November 1915, CWM, 20040015-005, Lawrence Rogers Collection.
27 Letter from L.B. Rogers to Aileen Rogers, 4 April 1917, CWM, 20040015-005, Lawrence Rogers Collection.
28 Paul Fussell, *The Great War and Modern Memory* (Oxford: Oxford University Press, 2000), 182.
29 For more on field service postcards, see Jessica Meyer, *Men of War: Masculinity and the First World War in Britain* (London: Palgrave Macmillan, 2009), 16-17; Fussell, *Great War and Modern Memory*, 178-87.
30 Huss, "Pronatalism," 334.
31 CWM 20050177-006.
32 Marten, *Children's Civil War*, 69.
33 Tim Cook, "The Singing War: Canadian Soldiers' Songs of the Great War," *American Review of Canadian Studies* 39, 3 (2009): 224-41. Tim Cook, "Anti-heroes of the Canadian Expeditionary Force," *Journal of the Canadian Historical Association* 19, 1 (2008): 171-93.
34 Meyer, *Men of War*, 45.
35 Scrapbook of the Great War, kept by Jessie Tyrell (1915-18), 28 April 1917, CWM, 20020058-003; Scrapbook of the Great War, kept by Jessie Tyrell (1915-18), 17 November 1917, CWM, 20020058-003.
36 Letter from L.B. Rogers to Aileen Rogers, 2 November 1915, CWM, 20040015-005, Lawrence Rogers Collection.
37 Ibid., 4 April 1917, CWM, 20040015-005, Lawrence Rogers Collection.
38 Ibid.
39 Letter from L.B. Rogers to Aileen Rogers, 4 May 1917, CWM, 20040015-005, Lawrence Rogers Collection.
40 Ibid., 16 June 1917, CWM, 20040015-005, Lawrence Rogers Collection.
41 Desmond Morton, *When Your Number's Up: The Canadian Soldier in the First World War* (Toronto: Random House of Canada, 1993), 253.
42 Quoted in Lewis, *"I Want to Join Your Club,"* 226.
43 Ibid., 233.
44 Ibid., 226.
45 For more on the First World War and Canadian schooling, see Norah Lewis, "'Isn't This a Terrible War?': The Attitudes of Children to Two World Wars," *Historical Studies in*

Education/Revue d'histoire de l'éducation 7, 2 (1995): 193-215; Nancy M. Sheehan, "Philosophy, Pedagogy, and Practice: The IODE and the Schools in Canada, 1900-1945," *Historical Studies in Education/Revue d'histoire de l'éducation* 2, 2 (1990): 307-15; John Herd Thompson, *The Harvests of War: The Prairie West, 1914-1919* (Toronto: McClelland and Stewart, 1978). On the voluntary "mobilization" of Canadian women, see Linda J. Quiney, "'Bravely and Loyally They Answered the Call': St. John Ambulance, the Red Cross, and the Patriotic Service of Canadian Women during the Great War," *History of Intellectual Culture*, 5, 1 (2005): 1-19.

46 For more on Canadian Guiding, see Kristine Alexander, "The Girl Guide Movement and Imperial Internationalism in Interwar England, Canada, and India" (PhD diss., York University, 2010); Kristine Alexander, "Une pédagogie des rôles sociaux dans le guidisme canadien Anglophone," in *Toujours Prête ou toujours prêt? Le guidisme comme lieu d'éducation unisexe et coéduqué*, ed. Thierry Scaillet, Françoise Rosart, and Sophie Wittemans, 195-210 (Louvain-le-Neuve: Académia bruylant, 2007); Bonnie MacQueen, "Domesticity and Discipline: The Girl Guides in British Columbia, 1910-1943," in *Not Just Pin Money: Selected Essays On The History of Women's Work in British Columbia*, ed. Barbara K. Latham and Roberta J. Pazdro, 221-35 (Victoria: Camosun College, 1984).

47 "Canadian Girl Guides Organization Report of War Relief Work, 1914-1915," Archives of the National Council of the Girl Guides of Canada-Guides du Canada (hereafter ANCGGC) Toronto.

48 "The Canadian Girl Guides – Secretary's Report, April 1st 1917," 1, ANCGGC.

49 "Girl Guide Concert Splendid Success: Many Presentations," clipping from *Brandon Daily Sun*, 26 May 1916, ANCGGC, Scrapbook, 1912-61.

50 Clipping from *Saturday Night*, 19 December 1914, ANCGGC, Scrapbook, 1912-61.

51 "Girl Guides Send Troops Xmas Gifts," clipping from unknown Toronto newspaper, December 1914, ANCGGC, Scrapbook, 1912-61.

52 "Canadian Girl Guides Organization Report of War Relief Work, 1914-1915," ANCGGC.

53 "The Canadian Girl Guides 1915-1916 Report," 5-6, ANCGGC.

54 "Annual Report of the Canadian Girl Guides, June 1918," 6, ANCGGC.

55 Clipping from *The Toronto Daily Star*, n.d. [likely 1918], ANCGGC, Scrapbook, 1912-61.

56 Clipping from *The Toronto Daily Star*, 8 March 1918, ANCGGC, Scrapbook, 1912-61.

57 "The Canadian Girl Guides – Report, 1912-1920," 3-4, ANCGGC. Between December 1916 and December 1919, just over four hundred War Service badges were awarded in Canada. Only one out of every twenty-four Canadian Guides received the badge, a possible reflection of the badge's demanding requirements and of girls' tendency to participate only in activities that appealed to them.

58 Tamara Myers and Mary Anne Poutanen, "Cadets, Curfews, and Compulsory Schooling: Mobilizing Anglophone Children in WW II Montreal," *Histoire Sociale/Social History* 76 (2005): 385. William Tuttle similarly comments on the gendered nature of American children's war work. See William M. Tuttle, Jr., *"Daddy's Gone to War": The Second World War in the Lives of America's Children* (New York and Oxford: Oxford University Press, 1993), 146. See also Sarah Glassford, "'The Greatest Mother in the World':

Carework and the Discourse of Mothering in the Canadian Red Cross Society during the First World War," *Journal of the Association for Research on Mothering* 10, 1 (2008): 219-32.
59 "The Canadian Girl Guides – Secretary's Report, April 1st 1917," 3, ANCGGC.
60 Clipping from *The Toronto Daily Star*, n.d. [likely 1918], ANCGGC, Scrapbook, 1912-61.
61 "Annual Report of the Canadian Girl Guides, June 1918," 4, ANCGGC.
62 Morton, *When Your Number's Up*, 264.
63 Ibid., 271. See also Robin Brownlie, "Work Hard and Be Grateful: Native Soldier Settlers in Ontario after the First World War," in *On the Case: Explorations in Social History*, ed. Franca Iacovetta and Wendy Mitchinson, 181-203 (Toronto: University of Toronto Press, 1998).
64 Strong-Boag, *New Day Recalled*, 1.
65 Quoted in Lewis, *"I Want to Join Your Club,"* 112.
66 Fussell, *Great War and Modern Memory*, 269.

8

Supporting Soldiers' Wives and Families in the Great War
What Was Transformed?

DESMOND MORTON

"Many the times and often that I wish I was with you," wrote Sergeant Frank Maheux from his chilly dugout in France in December 1916:

> I'll say to myself Angeline is sleeping now. I don't know what I would give to be beside you. Instead I'll have my rifle beside me. So you see for a poor beggar no[t] used to think too much that will drive fellow crasy [sic]. I am prett[y] near but not quite yet ... Condy [their daughter] she write very well I understand every word she write. It is good.[1]

For almost a hundred thousand Canadian families at any moment in the First World War, letters were almost the only means of contact between men overseas and the women and children they had left behind. Much has been written about soldiers but very little about their families. Even our knowledge of their wartime communications is one-sided: it was easier for most families to collect a soldier's carefully censored cards and letters than for soldiers to preserve communications from home, however cherished. Since soldiers were obliged to carry all their possessions on their backs, few had space for more than a few of their most recent letters, creased with much reading and streaked by rain or perspiration.

The imbalance in evidence made it easier for war historians to remember men and forget the women and children they believed they were defending.

Even this venture into the family policies of Canada's wartime government hardly restores the balance. This chapter argues that policy led to perceptible transformation as women, the designated beneficiaries of Separation Allowance, Assigned Pay, and the Canadian Patriotic Fund (CPF), began to support the expensive proposition that their husbands and sons deserved salaries big enough to discharge their familial responsibilities. The complex, patient work of unearthing the experience of the wives, mothers, and children of soldiers can benefit from an understanding of the intentions of government officials when they accepted "the manly duty," as they viewed it, of providing for soldiers' families.

War, wrote the historian of the CPF, came "like a thunderbolt."[2] Within weeks, ten thousand British army reservists living in Canada had dutifully responded to their obligation to "return to the colours." So had several thousand French and Belgian reservists. Many of them, victims of a sharp prewar depression, left their families to subsist on meagre prewar savings and the charity of neighbours. By mid-August, the first of more than thirty-five thousand men began boarding trains for Valcartier, where the first contingent of the new Canadian Expeditionary Force (CEF) took shape through the month of September.

For many volunteers at Valcartier in the beautiful fall of 1914, a major anxiety was that the fighting and the glory would be over before they could join the war. Editors, economists, and even most generals agreed that modern wars had to be swift and decisive. Even if powerful, modern technologies failed to deliver quick victories, complex modern economies would simply collapse under the strain. The prophets, of course, were wrong. The Great War was not over by Christmas. It continued for 53 dreadful months. Instead of a few months of separation or, at most, a long and difficult year, some soldiers' families were torn apart for more than four years and tens of thousands would never be reunited.[3]

Out of a population of about 8 million Canadians in 1914, 619,586 men and women joined the CEF between 1914 and 1919, of whom 487,772 were single, 120,607 were married, and 5,794 were widowers. Of the 424,589 who went overseas, 88,347, or about one in five, left wives. Even many of the single men had been the sole support of their parents or other family members.[4] After the war, close to twenty thousand widows, mothers, and other soldiers' "dependents" received pensions designed to keep them in respectable poverty until their death or until someone else could be persuaded to provide for them.[5] The war, in short, affected many people who never wore a uniform.

When Colonel Sam Hughes, minister of militia in Sir Robert Borden's Conservative government, issued the orders to recruit Canada's contingent for the Great War, his intentions were clear enough. Unmarried men would have priority, married men without children would have second priority, husbands with children were to be discouraged. Moreover, the minister insisted, "not a married man shall go without the consent of his wife and family."[6] Apart from Hughes' feminist instincts, there were practical reasons for considering a wife's opinion before accepting her husband as a soldier. If she expected to live on his army pay, she and any children of the marriage would starve.

In peace or war, soldiers were badly paid. By 1914, a Canadian manual worker needed at least two dollars a day to support himself and a wife and children.[7] No self-respecting man expected his wife to earn wages. A Permanent Force (PF) private earned seventy cents a day. Meagre pay reflected a soldier's social status and helped explain a high rate of desertion. Even a sergeant's pay rose to only $1.25. This was higher than British rates of pay for men in the ranks; however, by the same token, Canadian officers received less pay than did their British counterparts: a lieutenant earned two dollars a day and a lieutenant colonel received five dollars.[8]

In the PF in 1914, lieutenants could marry only with the permission of the Militia Council, which needed an assurance from the officer's commanding officer that "the officer's means [were] such as [would] enable him to maintain himself and his family in a manner befitting his position as an officer." Other ranks who wanted to marry had to persuade their commanding officer "that the applicant [was] financially able to marry and that the woman [was] a desirable character." An officer's bride was presumed to be a lady and above such questions. The chief benefit of submitting to official approval was access to free married quarters or subsistence allowance "in lieu of quarters, rations, fuel, light, and medical attention." A soldier who married without permission could be compelled to live in barracks and clearly had no allowance, however meagre, to support his wife and children.[9] Those were the peacetime rules for the Canadian PF. However, by decision of a distant British government, at midnight on 4 August 1914, Canada was at war.

On 27 August 1914, Colonel Hughes announced the pay scales for the CEF. CEF privates would earn a dollar a day, with an extra ten cents a day as

Supporting Soldiers' Wives and Families 197

field allowance.[10] A sergeant like Frank Maheux would receive $1.35 a day and fifteen cents as field pay. With quarters, rations, clothing, and equipment all provided, this might seem a comfortable wage for a single man with no greater responsibility than to be an open-handed chum for his fellow soldiers.

No one pretended that it was enough to support a family. No wonder thick stacks of letters and telegrams soon buried Hughes' desk in Ottawa and at Valcartier where he spent his time choosing officers and settling policy issues. Some messages came from mothers, protesting that their sons could not face the rigours of army life, but most were from women who complained that their husbands had left them destitute or that their son was their sole support in widowhood or old age. Mrs. John Smith of Latchford, Ontario, was typical. Her husband had left Timmins with the 97th Regiment but without her knowledge or permission: "if he gone for the War he must come Back or els [sic] the Government will have to Surport [sic] me ... he might not Say he married but he is." Etta Bouller in Vancouver had three little girls, an invalid husband, and a son, Stanley, whom she wanted back: "Now, Colonel Hughes, am I asking too much?" Perhaps she was, but those sent home after protests from wives or parents were the largest category after the men released as medically unfit.

With the outbreak of war, it was apparent that the difficulties of raising a volunteer army would be compounded if soldiers' families were doomed to live in poverty. Yet the tremendous costs of waging war for a country still struggling out of a deep depression also called for frugality and restraint. Even the life struggle of the British Empire must not interfere with Canada's need to attract settlers and capital by maintaining low levels of taxation. What could be done?

Happily, even an unmilitary Canada had some wartime traditions. One of them was the Patriotic Fund. During the War of 1812, a Loyal and Patriotic Society in Upper Canada had collected funds to finance medical treatment for members of the militia and relief for their families. By January 1900, the Boer War had inspired leading citizens to gather in Ottawa to form a Canadian patriotic fund association to raise funds for widows, orphans, disabled soldiers, and for "the benefit of wives and children and dependants separated at home from those serving in South Africa."[11]

On 18 August 1914, the Governor General, the Duke of Connaught, convened a meeting of national notables to revive or replace the Boer War association. Afterwards, a smaller committee thrashed out the details of the new Canadian Patriotic Fund (CPF). The special emergency session of Parliament, called to deal with war issues, approved the new fund's charter. The task of the CPF was to:

collect, administer and distribute the fund ... for the assistance in case of need, of the wives, children and dependent relatives of officers and men, residents of Canada, who, during the present war, may be on active service with the naval and military forces of the British Empire and Great Britain's allies.[12]

Unlike its predecessors, the new CPF would leave the problems of widows, orphans, and disabled soldiers to others. On the other hand, its beneficiaries could include the families of allied reservists whose pay, even by British Army standards, was meagre indeed. The Boer War fund provided its successor with a bank balance of $76,000.

The honorary secretary of the fund and its animating spirit was Herbert Ames. Since 1904 a Conservative member of Parliament for the downtown Montreal riding of St. Antoine, American-born and Harvard-educated, Ames was as good an example of the contemporary "progressive" reformer as Canada could boast. Ames-Holden, his family's prosperous shoe factory in Montreal, left him time and wealth to pursue his enthusiasm for municipal and social reform. As a Montreal alderman, he had battled corruption at City Hall. Later, he had applied the Rowntrees' technique for studying poverty to the working-class slums of downtown Montreal. The results, published in 1897 as *The City Below the Hill*, gave Ames a national reputation and a self-confident grasp of what should be done to raise the working poor to middle-class standards of hygiene, education, and welfare.[13] With Ames in charge, the CPF would do more than collect money and merely hand it out again.

As president, the Duke of Connaught lent his prestige to a circular urging provinces, counties, and communities to create local organizations. The response was impressive. War fever had swept the Dominion; creating a patriotic fund struck local leaders as an ideal way to respond. In Saskatchewan, a meeting in Regina announced that the province would organize in a single unit. Alberta split between north and south; British Columbians decided on separate organizations for Victoria, Vancouver, and the rest of the province. Attempts to create a single organization for New Brunswick were frustrated when local committees insisted on communicating directly with Ottawa. In Ontario, most CPF organizations were based in cities and counties.

The Borden government's decision to finance its war effort with a few minor excise taxes and, later, by expanding the national debt meant that charitable giving had an open field. With posters, public meetings, and personal calls, local notables reminded stay-at-home Canadians that there was now a way to share

FIGURE 10   CPF poster. By providing for the women and children left behind, the CPF enabled more men to go overseas. [Copyright Canadian War Museum, CWM 19890086-900]

the soldiers' sacrifice. "When some women are giving their men – and when some men are giving their lives – what will you give?" ran a popular slogan. Another CPF theme was "Fight or Pay."[14] "Through the Canadian Patriotic Fund," Orillia's *Simcoe Packet* reminded its readers, "Canadians said to the soldiers: 'Go to the front and we will take care of your wives and kiddies.'"[15]

Running the CPF from Ottawa raised the usual suspicions of bloated bureaucracy and red tape. At the same time, because both prosperity and depression had spread unevenly across Canada, Ames quickly realized the need for national standards. The poorest regions had recruited the most soldiers and, in consequence, would have the most families to support. If rich and poor areas treated families differently, a sense of grievance would soon emerge.

The CPF circular in September 1914 urged local branches to form a finance committee, prepared to work in short bursts of fundraising, and a relief committee that would work through the year, disbursing funds to soldiers' dependents. Each branch was expected to raise "a reasonable amount of money according to the wealth of the community." The money was then sent to the treasurer in Ottawa who would send back whatever the community required, while providing close supervision and control. Staff in Ottawa checked that payments respected agreed benefit scales and hunted for evidence that a beneficiary might be getting help from other branches.

By early 1915, the government and CPF officials boasted that, once they received their pay, allowances, and grant from the CPF, soldiers' wives and families were better off, on average, than they would have been as civilians in the depressed prewar economy. In 1913, the *Labour Gazette*, official guide to matters statistical in Canada, insisted that an urban family needed sixty dollars per month for food, rent, fuel, and light, or forty dollars without a man. If she received Separation Allowance and a CPF grant, a woman with three children in Toronto or Montreal could count on forty-five dollars a month, not including any of the pay that her husband had assigned to her. Local committees could pay up to 20 percent less, and branch executives, usually dominated by local employers, were seldom disposed to extravagance. "To give the woman in the small village an income that would maintain a woman in the city was unwise," Morris recalled, "while to bring the city woman's income down to the level that was adequate in the country was unjust."[16]

Some beneficiaries might well agree about their relative good fortune. "You will get $25.00 a month from the Canadian patriotic fund and $20.00 from the Government," Frank Maheux assured Angeline, his "poor wife," in November

1914. Compared to the twenty-two dollars a month he would have earned for his family by working in a lumber camp, it may have seemed to Angeline a fair exchange for losing her husband to the army.[17] If Maheux forgot to mention the Assigned Pay, he was not unique among army husbands in avoiding the issue. For a logger and a South African War veteran, the manly pleasures of drink and revelry took priority over the manly but tiresome responsibility of supporting his family. Not until June, after Maheux had been sternly lectured by a Nursing Sister during a bout in hospital and his battalion had left for Halifax, was Angeline's income properly established.[18]

CPF managers certainly believed in their generosity. When Ames proposed to the November 1914 meeting of the National Executive that the CPF might publish a circular explaining its benefits, the proposal was rejected: "in view of the fact that, if widely distributed, this circular might stimulate enlistment beyond the point that is at present considered necessary."[19]

Relief committees were instructed to verify claims through proofs of marriages, of the children's ages, and that the former breadwinner had, in effect, enlisted for overseas service: "A thorough investigation into the circumstances of the family should be made with the view of ascertaining whether there are any sources of income other than the pay and allowances received from the Federal Government, and whether the family, by the manner of living, is worthy of assistance from public monies." While most of the claimants were from the lower ranks, a special subcommittee of the fund executive discreetly dealt with 19,906 claims from dependents of commissioned officers, many of them serving in a British Army that made no provision for Separation Allowance for officers and still assumed that most of them lived on private means. Officers who lived on their pay found that they could not afford to send much home to their families.

Creation of the CPF undoubtedly lightened Ottawa's responsibility for the welfare of soldiers' families; it did not, however, wholly relieve it. Prewar militia regulations allowed soldiers on active service to "assign" part of their pay to their dependents. The untrained paymasters at Valcartier discovered that arranging "assignments" was complicated and sometimes the most awkward part of an unfamiliar job. Frank Maheux was far from the only soldier to assume that he was entitled to his full pay and that other agencies were sending his wife more than she could possibly need.

On 4 September 1914, the Department of Militia announced that CEF members could apply for a Separation Allowance for their family, ranging from twenty dollars a month for a private to sixty dollars for a lieutenant colonel.[20] The Department of Militia assumed that, to qualify for Separation Allowance, a soldier would also assign part of his regular pay to his wife and family. Could it insist on a pay assignment? A legal opinion from Hughes' crony, Colonel Henry Smith, the judge advocate general, insisted that it would be quite illegal for the Department of Militia to tell a soldier how to spend his money.

It soon emerged that there were other opinions on the question, notably at the CPF. By October, the fund's national executive had agreed on a maximum monthly scale of $30 for a woman, $7.50 for a child aged ten to fifteen, $4.50 for a child of 5 to 10 years, and $3 for a child under 5. To avoid discouraging pay assignments, the CPF agreed to ignore them in assessing a family's need: "although it was recognized that under these conditions many women would be receiving considerably more than their men folk had been able to give them while in civilian life and more, perhaps, than was necessary to meet their reasonable needs." By November, CPF managers felt less generous. Surely it was wrong to let Canadian soldiers pass their manly responsibilities to a patriotic charity. A 50 percent pay assignment must be the prerequisite for granting a soldier Separation Allowance.[21]

One reason for caution was the complexity of getting all the systems of family support implemented. After barely a month at Valcartier, the first Canadian contingent had embarked for England. Paymasters, often chosen because they seemed unlikely to be effective leaders of troops, had to learn on the job. The evidence to satisfy the regulations might well be on the other side of the world in Canada. When it came to family issues, some soldiers had much to hide. Private Gerald Wharton had left his wife penniless, debt-ridden, and in Buffalo. "I think that you will agree that I am better off without him," she confessed to the Department of Militia, "but I do not think that he should go free and me be tied down to work to keep myself and his child as well as mine." She was too late: her man had already changed his name and left for England.[22]

In England, Canadian soldiers were well paid but there were many ways to spend their money. Widespread absenteeism, drunkenness, and venereal infections might have been curbed if the Canadians had had less money to spend. That was the opinion of Colonel W.R. Ward, the chief paymaster: "I may say that Lord Kitchener is quite annoyed to think that our men are getting 4/6 a day and separation allowance for their families as against the fighting 'Tommy Atkins' who is willing to serve his country in the new Army for 1/[one shilling] a day."[23] Compulsory pay assignments were Ward's answer. If a man protested, let him prove that his wife was not in need of support – or discharge him from the army.

Colonel Hughes was easily persuaded. British Army regulations and, even more, the sweeping powers of the War Measures Act dissolved any objections that Colonel Smith or the Department of Justice might have had to telling a soldier how he must spend his pay. However, families had to be patient. The CEF's paymasters were as inexperienced as was anyone else in Canada's improvised army. Background experience as a small-town merchant or an accountant was no instant preparation for handling a thousand pay accounts, a unit's financial transactions, or the Department of Militia's bulky and changeable regulations. A battalion going overseas needed as many as fifty thousand separate documents. Many of them required the cooperation of soldiers who were usually poorly educated and sometimes illiterate. Even Colonel Ward concluded that many married soldiers had declared themselves single "not ... with any idea or desire to deprive their families of support, but possibly, dictated by the desire to serve in the Contingent well knowing that it was difficult for a married man to enlist."[24]

Working in tents or in the open air with documents that might be rain-soaked or scattered by the wind, harried paymasters responded slowly to the flow of complex and changeable official directives. Haste meant errors that, if they hurt the government, must be repaid from the soldier's or the paymaster's own pocket. While the first pay assignments were mailed at the end of September 1914, others had to wait for November as officials completed their records during their Atlantic voyage or on the rain-sodden Salisbury Plain. In November, despairing of accurate records and responding to public criticism, the Department of Militia issued a flat twenty dollars as Separation Allowance, provoking another flood of complaints from those who had legitimately expected more.[25]

At all levels, pay officials struggled to find systems that would record men whose pay status had changed because they had been promoted, discharged, or simply deserted, often far from their original unit and their pay records. According to his wife's lawyer, Private John Clovis Martin of the 42nd Battalion had enlisted as a widower and assigned his pay to another woman. Mrs. Martin wanted it back.[26] Howard Ferry's mother demanded his support, but it took weeks to find the right Ferry in the 36th Battalion. Wesley Peters left his child with a woman when he joined the First Contingent, and it was Peters' mother who appealed for aid. "This man is an Indian," a scornful CPF investigator explained, "and, evidently, he did not know enough to apply for any allowance for his mother."[27]

In the debate on the incorporation of the CEF, a few critics had warned of the complications possible from an undefined word like "dependant," only to be reassured by government ministers that the best legal advice would allay their fears.[28] While wives and children were obvious dependants, soldiers often claimed to have become their mothers' sole support. Such claims had to be rigorously investigated since there might be other sons and daughters who should be supporting their mother. A widowed mother was allowed to expect that the CPF would supplement her Separation Allowance up to a combined total of thirty-five dollars a month. On the other hand, the CPF would do nothing for a soldier's mother who had a living, able-bodied husband: "Such a claim should be immediately dismissed."[29]

A year's experience taught officials that Canadian family structures were not quite as simple as they had anticipated. Defining the meaning of "wife" troubled every bureaucracy involved in family support. By November 1915, Department of Militia officials must surely have thought that they had the right definition of "wife":

> For the purpose of the provision of separation allowance, "wife" means the woman who was married to the officer or the soldier in question under the laws of the country where the marriage was solemnized and who has not been separated from her husband by a judicial decree or "separation from bed or board" or other similar decree parting her from her husband's home and children, but where a wife so separated is entitled either by the agreement or separation to regular payments from her husband, or by an order or a competent court to alimony, such wife should be entitled to the extent of such payments or alimony, to the separation allowance.[30]

It was still not enough. Eventually, the government had to acknowledge that there were cases where, even without a court order, a separated wife would be entitled to payment and might even have the benefit of the doubt "if it do [sic] not appear that the husband [had been] absolved from the obligation of maintenance."[31] Early in 1917, the CPF's national executive ruled that it had no obligation to let deserted wives know that the Department of Militia recognized alimony claims. If a man deserted his wife, she had no claim on the CPF, though the soldier-son of a deserted mother could make a claim for her as a dependant.[32]

Women whose marriages had never been solemnized might scandalize middle-class values, but, in the eyes of the soldiers who left them to defend their country, they were wives and mothers as much as were those who could present their "marriage lines." In the eyes of a tattling landlord, Sergeant Sharpe had lied when he described Alma Freed as Mrs. W.H. Sharpe on his enlistment documents, but she had borne him a son. Yet, when Sharpe formally married Freed in 1916, she learned of a CPF ban on supporting wives who had married after their soldier-husband had enlisted.[33] Other wives were unmarried because their "husbands" would have committed the serious criminal offence of bigamy. A Canadian order-in-council in September 1916 confessed: "quite a large number of cases of soldiers having two wives had come to light." Usually the first wife had been deserted in England when her husband immigrated to Canada and remarried. Would the Canadian wife be left without support and Canadian funds be redirected to the legal wife in England?[34] The British Army had ruled that Separation Allowance would go to the wife and family supported at the time of enlistment, provided there were two prior years of support, and not to any wife and relatives unsupported when a man enlisted.

Who could improve on British justice? Separation Allowance, explained a Parliamentary Reply of 2 February 1917, went to "Legal Wives," widows whose sons were their sole support, persons designated to care for a soldier's children, judicially separated wives, motherless children, and women who have been supported "on a bona fide domestic basis for two years prior to enlistment, but who have not been married to the soldier, and the children of such a union." Clergy and other civic moralists might protest, but the Canadian state had not tested would-be soldiers on their marital integrity, and neither had the Mother Country.

On some issues, the CPF and the Department of Militia drew a more cautious line. In April 1916, a regulation reminiscent of the prewar PF required a soldier to secure approval from his commanding officer and proof of a pre-enlistment engagement before claiming Separation Allowance. Major-General John Wallace Carson, the Montreal mining magnate who served as Hughes' representative in England, was horrified. "There is no doubt at all but that we are being 'soaked' with many men that are getting married," he complained. It was easy to get a CO's permission and come up with a suitable certificate: "I have no hesitation in saying that, in most cases, these certificates are not genuine." Carson expostulated: "Nevertheless their production takes the matter out of the hands of our responsible officials who simply have to acquiesce and 'pay up.'" The task of investigating the problem was given to Lieutenant Colonel H.A.C. Machin, an Ontario Conservative MPP, soon to be better known and deeply engaged as the chief enforcer of Canada's Military Service Act.[35]

Since marriage in 1914 routinely removed most women from the paid labour market, soldier-husbands expected the CPF to support even a young childless wife. Within a year, branch officials and the national executive were besieged by their own wives on the labour market issue that most preoccupied middle-class women – the supply and price of domestic labour. Were the CPF's donors rewarding idleness and exasperating their wives by supporting the class of women who normally laboured in their kitchens and laundry rooms? On the other hand, what would the general public say if the CPF was seen to be forcing soldiers' wives into the increasingly despised role of domestic service? After wrestling with the issue, the fund executive was saved by the general wartime labour shortage in Canada and the explosion of earning opportunities for women in jobs vacated by men or created by the Imperial Munitions Board – a situation explored by Kori Street in this collection. "If a wife has no children" and "is a young woman unburdened by the necessity of maintaining a home," the national executive instructed local branches of the CPF, "it is not expected that a larger allowance than $5.00 per month will be paid her."[36]

Family support had been designed for soldiers going overseas to risk their lives for King and Empire. Political pressure, however, kept a substantial force on active service in Canada throughout the war. Home service troops could assign their pay to dependants. What about Separation Allowance or the CPF? Certainly many wives or mothers of soldiers stationed at Halifax or in Kapuskasing were in need. Some CPF branches compromised by giving less to the families of home-service soldiers; however, Morris reported: "Several large subscribers objected in most emphatic terms to the money being used for the benefit of any other dependants than [overseas troops]."[37] On 13 October 1914, the executive ruled that help for home-service families would end as of 1 December. The mood did not soften. In June 1915, when Sir Sam Hughes pointed to the discrepancy between the twenty-dollar Separation Allowance for men overseas and the $6.50 a month for families of home-service troops, his cabinet colleagues were unmoved.[38]

Defenders of the CPF boasted of the flexibility of a private organization that was easily able to apply common sense while any government program was bound up in rules, red tape, and politics. They had a point. Separation Allowance, a Department of Militia program, proved extraordinarily difficult to apply. Even after the department accepted the most generous possible definition of a wife, could it really continue Separation Allowance if a soldier's wife was demonstrably unfaithful to her distant husband or if the Children's Aid Society had to rescue their children from neglect? Because public money was being spent, could a government ignore public opinion? Even more complex was the problem of determining whether other family members were genuinely dependent. Mrs. Joseph Carey had an apparently wealthy husband. Two of their three sons were overseas with the CEF. When Mr. Carey died, he proved to be penniless. Before the two sons could obtain Separation Allowance for their mother, they had to prove that their brother was an invalid. "Is it possible that the curse of red tape which seems to have settled upon your department since the beginning of this war," the family's lawyers enquired, "has so blinded those who are busy winding and unwinding the same that they are no longer able to see things in their proper light?"[39] Perhaps so, but as Major C.M. Ingalls of the Separation Allowance Branch responded, there were so many cases of improper applicants that they had to take great care.[40]

Ingalls' branch required substantial administrative machinery. During 1916, the year when most Canadian soldiers went overseas, its number of accounts grew from 85,100 to 231,518. Cheques were lost, forged, stolen, and complained about when they did not reach the family on the same day each month. The Separation Allowance Branch pleaded for staff to investigate claims of fraudulent marriages, deserted wives, and widowed mothers who had no real need for a son's support.[41] Until the summer of 1917, Assigned Pay and Separation Allowance were mailed as separate cheques. Efficiency came slowly, with time clocks to discourage absenteeism, cheque-writing machines, mechanized mailing, and, as of February 1917, a Separation Allowance Review Board under Major J.W. Margeson, with Philip Morris of the CPF as one of the members. With "visitors" from local Patriotic Fund Branches doing its field work, the Review Board "produced great savings."[42] So did second thoughts on other issues. When the new Pension Board set the payment for a soldier's orphan at a mere twelve dollars, paying twenty dollars in Separation Allowance to a motherless child suddenly seemed "needlessly high." Setting the reduced rate at fourteen dollars regardless of the father's rank generated as much protest about ignoring social differences as it did about the reduction itself.[43]

Dealing with a remote and often unresponsive bureaucracy in distant Ottawa was an uncommon experience for most Canadians. When a mother in Winnipeg lost her Separation Allowance after one of her two sons was killed, an official letter from Ingalls' branch directed her to ask her other son for help even though he was a prisoner of war in Germany. In 1916, when the Department of Militia decided to eliminate the "working pay" it had granted to soldiers with useful skills – such as carpenters, electricians, and chauffeurs – the sharp reduction in an affected soldier's income was soon reflected in reduced Assigned Pay. When dependants sought an explanation, the department informed them simply that the cuts had come "at the request of the soldier."[44] Since soldiers could direct their Separation Allowance to only one dependant, a man who married had to switch the Separation Allowance from his mother to his new wife. It hardly encouraged a warm relationship with a resentful mother-in-law. As Jeannie Hall complained to her MP, one of her sons had been "estranged through the influence of a woman."[45]

Applicants also had trouble adapting to the needs of a large bureaucracy. In 1917, Ingalls reminded a parliamentary committee of the case of a Manitoba widow who, when seeking Separation Allowance, had misidentified her son's battalion. By the time militia authorities had tracked down her son, the widow herself had disappeared, leaving no forwarding address. A local clergyman had to be persuaded to locate her. It also turned out that she had written earlier to the Department of Militia without giving her son's name, number, or battalion. The letter had been set aside as impossible to answer.[46]

Separation Allowance had been intended for women. What if men became dependent? John Grant, paralyzed since 1902, had depended on his wife, a former nurse who kept a boarding house in Sault Ste. Marie. Mrs. Grant died on 22 May 1915, leaving her husband destitute and helpless. Two sons at the front had never considered assigning pay to their mother because she had always coped. Could Mr. Grant be helped? By August, the Treasury Board had come to its conclusion: "instead of dealing with the individual case it would be preferable to have submitted for consideration a general recommendation dealing with cases of this character." "As both Mr. & Mrs. Grant have died of want since this case was submitted to the Treasury Board," noted the Department's chief accountant, J.W. Borden, in a chilling minute, "there is no need for an O/C [Order-in-council] now."[47] One was adopted, however, and in January 1916, James Stevens could gratefully write that a CPF investigator had confirmed that he was, indeed, paralyzed and that his cheque for six months of Separation Allowance had arrived.[48]

The CPF's two responsibilities were to raise funds and to spend them on soldiers' families on the basis of need. Determining need required an investigation that, "done tactfully and kindly," insisted the Montreal Branch's Relief Committee, "[did] not offend the woman with common sense." Initially, the CPF's investigations were conducted by its male committee members. As a colder spirit of charity replaced patriotic fervour, the demand for more thorough investigation grew. Errors would have been avoided, claimed the CPF's national bulletin, if men "had enlisted the services of their wives and daughters and persuaded the latter to form a ladies' auxiliary to keep in touch with the Fund's beneficiaries ... Without an auxiliary, it is practically impossible to exercise the supervision that is desirable."[49] Increasingly, the donors to the CPF insisted that recipients be "deserving." Donations must not be squandered on extravagant living. Were soldiers' families living better than they had when the male breadwinner was at home? Were wives in need because of an extravagant taste in bonnets or a susceptibility to salesmen who offered furniture on the installment plan? Surely the wives and daughters of the civic leaders who ran the local patriotic associations would be prudent and frugal supervisors of their families' generosity.

The second responsibility (spending its funds on soldiers' families in need) led some CPF branches to what Ames proudly described as "the Third Responsibility." "By force of circumstances," Morris explains in his history of the fund, the CPF "assumed everywhere a third responsibility, that of acting as counselor and business agent to soldiers' families who, deprived temporarily of their managers, found themselves faced with difficulties that singlehandedly, they could not overcome."[50] Business advice took many forms. In Saskatchewan, branch officials wrestled with the dilemma of persuading a wife to continue her husband's payments on what they regarded as a useless piece of land and running "the risk of incurring a soldier's displeasure."[51] A Montreal branch official, G.W. Elliot, boasted that it had taken him forty minutes to persuade a wife to pay her husband's life insurance premiums. The time was well spent, Elliot reported, because, seven months later, the man was killed. No doubt Elliot would have denied any patronizing tone:

> Our experiences are frequently amusing and illustrate the strange perverseness of human nature. We have argued with a woman for an hour over the relative value of a new skirt and a policy on the life of her husband, at the time actually

dodging German souvenirs in Flanders. Another woman would allow her husband's policy to lapse rather than take the premiums out of the savings Bank. Our Savings Bank pamphlet apparently overworked in this case.[52]

As chairman of the CPF, Ames was an eager proponent of the Third Responsibility. It reinforced his conviction that poverty could best be overcome by teaching thrift and self-restraint, echoing the views of the more conservative wing of the prewar social reform movement. The CPF became an instrument to prove his argument. To reinforce Ames' belief, the CPF's head office in Ottawa released a "Message to the Canadian Soldier's Wife," warning that obvious extravagance would repel donors and deprive families of a postwar nest egg. Saskatchewan's organization enforced thrift on its beneficiaries by imposing a compulsory savings plan in the summer of 1915. Half a family's CPF cheque would be banked during the summer months; these compulsory savings could be released in the event of urgent need. The policy, local organizers confessed, was controversial. But it worked.[53]

Similar plans were initiated with more or less rigour by other branches across Canada. "Let us again remind you of the advisability of STARTING A SAVINGS BANK ACCOUNT" headlined a circular distributed to CPF beneficiaries in Galt (now Cambridge), Ontario. Savings would be a help in trouble and sickness and, especially, when the soldier came home.[54] F.S. Jarvis, treasurer of the Galt branch, admitted that the wives objected to the constant references to savings but said that those who were not interested could ignore the advice: "our only interest being to help in any way possible." And who could ignore the extravagance of women who purchased three-cent stamps and fed their families imported oranges rather than locally grown apples?[55] Women who devoted their wartime income to paying off prewar debts, reducing their mortgage, and restoring fortunes damaged by hard times and perhaps by the absent husband, earned special praise in the CPF's regular bulletins to its affiliates, particularly after the conversion of savings to government bonds became the main means of financing Canada's war effort. If, as Kristine Alexander and Suzanne Evans underline in their respective chapters in this volume on girls and mourning women, frugality was presented to soldiers' wives and daughters as a war-winning strategy, then the CPF was "doing its bit." So were its beneficiaries. In 1918, the Hespeler branch, next-door to Galt, boasted that its beneficiaries had accumulated $18,000 in Canadian Victory Bonds and that thirteen of its women had paid off their mortgages.[56]

Nowhere was the Third Responsibility more in evidence than in Ames' own city of Montreal. Although, like others, the Montreal branch was managed by local businessmen, the driving force behind its auxiliary was Helen Reid, a vigorous prewar worker in Montreal's public health movement. Thanks to Reid and her allies, cheques from the Montreal branch were accompanied by circulars explaining how to report building defects and sanitary faults to landlords and to City Hall. Reid was unmarried, but her crusade against infant mortality was reflected in leaflets that advised mothers on milk, flies, adenoids, nutrition, and, a terror of the time, infantile paralysis. A visiting housekeeper was hired to instruct women how to cook, buy, manage a household, and, above all, to economize.

In 1917, inflation began to soar across Canada. Reid persuaded her branch to organize bulk purchases of coal during the summer to cut the cost of next winter's fuel. Other CPF branches followed suit. She advised local hospitals on what the CPF's families could afford to pay, and she divided CPF families by districts, appointed a visitor for each of them from her auxiliary's list of volunteers, and insisted that each visitor maintain "a businesslike record of her families," with written reports every two months. The volunteers of 1914, she reported four years later, were still working, "weary, yes. But bigger, broader, finer and braver women than when they started." Visitors and organized volunteers, Reid reported, had staffed an office where wives "on the Patriotic Fund" could bring their problems: "It is in this room," she recalled, "that our workers are for the first time brought face to face with the tragedies that war brings in its train." "Tears are the daily accompaniment of demands that sometimes cannot be considered," Reid continued:

> Unemployment, desertion, immorality, bigamy, eviction, hardhearted landlord, land lots to be forfeited, a piano to be sacrificed, furniture not paid up, a child lost, a boy drowned in a cellar, street car accidents, infantile paralysis, delay in receipt of government allowances, mother died and children to be placed, transportation needed, all these and other sad tales have to be considered and disposed of.[57]

There were even crueler duties: "not infrequently," Morris recalled in his CPF history, agents had to "separate children from an immoral mother" and place them "under the care of some society."

Whatever a committee could do to assist such a woman to regain her footing, to break away from old influences, was gladly done. Many women, especially those who had escaped the more unfortunate consequences of their indiscretion, were enabled, with the Fund's assistance, to rehabilitate themselves, while in cases where the husband had become aware of the state of affairs, the Fund has not infrequently induced him to take a tolerant view.[58]

The Hamilton branch rejoiced that a woman who had "misconducted herself" had been restored to her children when, after repeated kindly acts and interviews, she had agreed to "remove herself from the companions who had caused her so much trouble."[59]

CPF managers not only had a high opinion of themselves and their work, they also relied on "patriotism" as a weapon to challenge critics. Though Alberta Liberal MP Frank Oliver found the courage to criticize the CPF in Parliament, only a single colleague followed up his attack on the fund's paternalism and authoritarian meddling. Perhaps the worst threat to the CPF and its patriotic shield was late-war inflation and the widespread popular belief that its root cause was profiteering.

If the prewar meat-packing baron "His Lardship" Sir Joseph Flavelle, wartime chair of the Imperial Munitions Board, could add to his fortune selling bacon to the British Army, if Canadian munitions workers could stay home and earn wages unprecedented for factory workers, why must Canadian soldiers, risking their lives for King, Empire, and Canada, be denied enough income to support their families? By the last year of the war, the CPF had virtually ceased to function in British Columbia as angry labour radicals fought employers who forced workers to hand over their pay or forfeit their jobs. Ideological conflict at the western extremity of Canada had few if any echoes in Ontario, Quebec, and the Atlantic provinces, but it was evidence that the CPF could become a framework for trouble.[60]

In every war since 1812, Canadians had organized a patriotic fund to cover financial burdens no contemporary government could be expected to meet. When Canadians entered the Second World War in 1939, there would be no patriotic fund. Probably the needs were as great or even greater. Canadians who enlisted in 1939, like their fathers in 1914, sought to escape a brutal depression by finding paying jobs as soldiers, sailors, or airmen. The soldiers earned only a few cents more per day than did their fathers and uncles in 1914, but costs of living soon rose with the revival of Canada's economy under wartime pressure. Why no fund? Was this part of the "transformation" so often claimed for the earlier conflict?

For all its self-congratulation, the CPF had not made many lasting friends during its lifetime. During the ensuing Great Depression, the middle-class women Helen Reid had deployed to control the spending and curb any waste on the part of her First World War CPF clients were displaced in large measure by professional social workers, trained in the scientific ideals and techniques of social control that Ames and Reid had applied as a self-help remedy for poverty. Like many soldiers' wives, relief recipients found it galling to live under the supervision of officials who appeared to them as meddlesome and even cruel busybodies.

In the circumstances, reviving the patriotic fund for a new war struck a wartime Liberal government as more likely to deter voluntary enlistment than to encourage it. A more popular institution, the Canadian Red Cross, took on the role of meeting emergencies among soldiers' families, much as its American counterpart had done in the earlier Great War. Helping to feed Canadian prisoners of war, supply overseas hospitals, roll bandages, and provide a sense of patriotic involvement for women with a little time to spare brought the Red Cross closer to both the Second World War and to Canadians than had ever been possible or even desirable for the CPF.

The "Patriotic" was a major channel for female participation in Canada's Great War. It reflected the values and expectations of its time, and it offered women a greater role in Canada's war effort than any previous conflict had allowed. If times and institutions changed, who could regret that women had made their feelings sufficiently influential to sway governments?

Acknowledgments

The Institute for Canadian Studies at McGill University generously funded an international conference on military next-of-kin that highlighted Canada's role in this domain. The CPF's tradition of voluntary support for soldiers' families continues today through the efforts of Canadians like Diane Collier, a soldier's wife who has organized "Red Fridays" to encourage Canadians' sympathies for family members left behind when Canadian soldiers, male and female, went to Afghanistan.

Notes

1 Frank Maheux to Angeline, 19 December 1916, LAC, MG 30E 297, Frank Maheux Papers (hereafter FMP).

2 Philip Morris, *The Canadian Patriotic Fund: A Record of Its Activities from 1914 to 1919* (n.p., n.d., [1920]), 7.
3 During the Great War, 59,544 members of the CEF died, and there were 172,950 cases of wounding or injury. Disability pensions are a measure of veterans who were severely affected by wartime service: 69,204 pensions were in effect in 1920. The number fell sharply after 1920 and rose again more slowly as age and liberalized legislation restored and enlarged eligibility for disability pensions. See G.W.L. Nicholson, *Canadian Expeditionary Force, 1914-1919: Official History of the Canadian Army in the First World War* (Ottawa: Queen's Printer, 1962), 548, table 4; Desmond Morton and Glenn Wright, *Winning the Second Battle: Canadian Veterans and the Return to Civilian Life, 1915-1930* (Toronto: University of Toronto Press, 1987), 234-35; Sir Andrew MacPhail, *History of the Canadian Forces, 1914-1919: Medical Services* (Ottawa: King's Printer, 1925), 246-54.
4 Department of National Defence, Directorate of History and Heritage, GAQ files, statistics of the CEF. The numbers recorded by Colonel Duguid's clerks were smaller than estimates published elsewhere. The Honourable H.S. Beland claimed that 44.5 percent of members of the CEF were married. See H.S. Beland, "The Returned Soldier," *Annals of the American Academy of Political Science* 107 (1923): 3.
5 See *Canada Year Book 1940* (Ottawa: Statistics Canada, 1941), 1066; and Morton and Wright, *Winning the Second Battle*, 234.
6 *Montreal Gazette*, 15 August 1914.
7 Guidance on wages and living costs comes from various issues of the *Labour Gazette* (Ottawa: Labour Canada). In 1914, the average weekly family cost of living, based on food, fuel, light, and rent costs in sixty Canadian cities, was $14.31; it fell slightly in 1915 to $13.84, and then resumed a sharp inflationary trend. See *Labour Gazette* 26, 15 September 1916, 1584. On wages and costs in 1914, see *Labour Gazette* 25, 8 February 1915.
8 *Handbook of the Land Forces of British Dominions, Colonies and Protectorates Part I: The Dominion of Canada* (London: HMSO, 1911), 118-19. Additional allowances were paid to soldiers in the artillery, engineers, army service corps, and other specialized organizations. Significant allowances (working pay) were given to skilled trades – saddlers, farriers, cooks, bakers, chauffeurs, and so on, amounting to fifty cents to one dollar a day, depending on skill and length of service. See *Handbook of the Land Forces*, 120-22.
9 See *Handbook of the Land Forces*, 120; *King's Regulations and Orders for the Canadian Militia, 1910* (Ottawa: King's Printer, 1910), ss. 830-40, 139-41.
10 P.C. 2264, 2 September 1914, cited by A.F. Duguid, *Official History of the Canadian Forces in the Great War, 1914-1919*. General Series (Ottawa: King's Printer, 1938), vol. 1 app. 91, 1:61.
11 The association was incorporated on 23 May 1901 by 1 EDW VII c. 92.
12 Canadian Patriotic Fund Act, 5 Geo V, c. 8, s. 3, cited by Morris, *Canadian Patriotic Fund*, 10. See also, in slightly different words, the objects as understood by the executive committee, in minutes of the executive committee, 1914-17, LAC, MG 28 I5, vol. 1.
13 On Ames, see Henry J. Morgan, *Canadian Men and Women of the Time, 1912* (Toronto: W. Briggs, 1912), 22. See also J.T. Copp, *The Anatomy of Poverty: The Condition of the Working Class in Montreal, 1897-1929* (Toronto: McClelland and Stewart, 1974), 9-20 and

passim; Herbert B. Ames, *The City Below the Hill: A Sociological Study of a Portion of the City of Montreal, Canada* (Montreal: Bishop Engraving and Printing, 1897).

14 Cited by Margaret McCallum, "Assistance to Veterans and their Dependents: Steps on the Way to the Administrative State, 1914-1920," in *Canadian Perspectives on Law and Society: Issues in Legal History,* ed. W. Wesley Pue and Barry Wright (Ottawa: Carleton University Press, 1988), 159; see also Morton, *Fight or Pay,* poster facing page 204.

15 *Simcoe Packet,* 4 November 1915.

16 Ibid.

17 Frank Maheux to Angeline [date illegible] November 1914, LAC, MG 30 E297, FMPm file 1. See also Frank Maheux to Angeline, 14 October 1914, LAC, MG 30 E297, FMP, file 1; E.S. Green, Secretary, Wright County CPF to Pte. F. Maheux, 18 November 1914, LAC, MG 30 E297, FMP, file 1.

18 Desmond Morton, "A Canadian Soldier in the Great War: The Experiences of Frank Maheux," *Canadian Military History* 1, 1-2 (1992): 80-81; Maheux to Angeline, 22 March 1915, LAC, MG 30 E297, FMP, vol. 3.

19 CPF Executive Minutes, 11 November 1914, LAC, MG 28 I5, vol. 1.

20 The British Army did not pay a Separation Allowance to their officers, and the many CEF officers who obtained British commissions had very little money to spare for their families. See Frank Arnoldi to Sir Edward Kemp, 14 April 1913, LAC, MG 27 IID9, Albert Edward Kemp Papers, vol. 34, file 1198.

21 CPF Executive Minutes, 13 October and 11 November 1914, Executive Committee Minutes, LAC, MG 28 I5, vol. 1; Ames to Hughes, 8 November and 1 December 1914, LAC, RG 24, HQ 593-2-35, vol. 1271.

22 Mrs. Wharton to Department of Militia and Defence, 5 December 1914, LAC, RG 24, HQ 593-2-35, vol. 1271, file 2.

23 Col. W.R. Ward to Militia Headquarters [n.d.]LAC, RG 24, HQ 593-2-35, vol. 1272. See also Morton, *Fight or Pay,* 93.

24 Ward to J.W. Borden, 4 November 1914, LAC, RG 24, HQ 593-1-35, vol. 1271.

25 See memoranda, LAC, RG 24, HQ 593-3-22, vol. 1343; Duguid, *Canadian Forces,* app. 230, 163-64. Among the victims of delay were the poorly paid families of Permanent Force soldiers, left penniless when men were hurriedly summoned to Valcartier in August. See Major J.R. Forbes to Militia Headquarters, 21 November 1914, LAC, RG 24, HQ 591-1-11, vol. 1225. One Permanent Force sergeant had to refund sixty dollars in Assigned Pay because he was kept in Canada as an instructor and forfeited the higher pay and benefits his rank earned overseas with the CEF. See Militia Headquarters to Paymaster, 3rd Division, 24 November 1914, LAC, RG 24, HQ 591-1-11, vol. 1225. Some politicians encouraged complaints. John Douglas, a former MP, visited soldiers' wives in Glace Bay and sent collect telegrams to Ottawa on behalf of women who had not received their cheques. See LAC, RG 24, HQ 592-1-12, vol. 1235. His conduct was regarded in Ottawa as unpatriotic.

26 Paul Rainville to Minister of Militia, 10 July 1915, LAC, RG 24, HQ 593-1-12, vol. 1234.

27 Desmond Morton and Cheryl Smith, "Fuel for the Home Fires: Taking Care of the Women They Left Behind," *The Beaver* 75, 2 (1983): 13.

28 Canada, House of Commons, *Debates*, 28 August 1914, 91-92.
29 Instructions cited by Morris, *Canadian Patriotic Fund*, app. A, 338.
30 P.C. 2605, 28 November 1915, amending P.C. 2266, 27 August 1913. See LAC, RG 2, A-a, boxes 1122 and 1127. See also Morton and Smith, "Fuel for the Home Fires," 15.
31 P.C. 2246, 1 September 1916.
32 CPF National Executive minutes, 20 February 1917, LAC, MG 28 I5, vol. 1 (1917-22).
33 Sharpe's case was raised by Freed's landlord, L.S. Fraser, who claimed that the marriage was forced on Alma Freed by her employer, Toronto's Board of Control, "on pain of losing her city wages." See Fraser to Lt. Col. C.S. McInnis, 22 August 1916, LAC, RG 34, HQ 593-1-12, vol. 1235. Sharpe, who had been wounded overseas, returned and was commissioned in the 116th Battalion. Sharpe had never claimed Separation Allowance for Alma Freed.
34 For one such case, see Mrs. Alex S. Seeley to Militia Department, 1 January 1916, RG 24, HQ 593-1-12, vol. 1234. By the time the department succeeded in locating Mrs. Seeley's husband, he had been discharged as "medically unfit (hysteria)" and seemed unlikely to be able to support either wife.
35 Carson to Hughes, 3 June 1916, LAC, RG 9 III, 6-M-377, vol. 178; *CEF Regulations and Orders*, no. 597, 7 April 1916.
36 Morris, *Canadian Patriotic Fund*, 16, and app. A, 138.
37 Ibid., 34; CPF National Executive Minutes, 13 October 1914, LAC, MG 28 I4, vol. 1.
38 Hughes to Governor General-in-Council, 6 June 1916, LAC, RG 24, HQ 593-1-11, vol. 1229.
39 MacNeil and Beattie to Kemp, 10 March 1917, LAC, RG 24, HQ 593-1-12, vol. 1523.
40 Major C.M. Ingalls to acting A&PMG, 25 March 1917, LAC, RG 24, HQ 593-1-12, vol. 1523. For an example, see R.P. Brown to Deputy Minister, 19 December 1916, LAC, RG 24, HQ 593-1-12, vol. 1234, about a woman who purported, under several names, to be the mother to several soldiers.
41 Memorandum No. 3 on the work of the Department of Militia and Defence (1916), 56-9, LAC, MG 26 H, Robert L. Borden Papers, OC 333, 39157.
42 Ibid., no. 4 (1917), 24-5, PC 447, 16 February 1917.
43 LAC PC 1997, 28 August 1916. On the protests from those affected, see LAC, RG 24, HQ 593-1-12, vol. 1234.
44 Both criticisms were made by T.W. Ewart, a Winnipeg lawyer and frequent critic of the government. See Ewart to Borden, 19 December 1917, LAC, Borden Papers.
45 Kemp to Accountant and Paymaster-General, 16 October 1916, LAC, MG 27 IID9, Kemp Papers, vol. 34, file 1198.
46 Major Ingalls's testimony to Canada, House of Commons, *Select Committee on Returned Soldiers* (Ottawa: The King's Printer 1917), 1164.
47 JWB minute to Secretary of the Treasury Board to Fiset, 10 August 1915, LAC, RG 24, HQ 593-1-12, vol. 1234. See also A.C. Boyce, MP, to J.W. Borden, 22 May 1916, LAC, RG 24, HQ 593-1-12, vol. 1234.
48 James Stevens to Kemp, 12 January 1916, LAC, MG 27 IID9, Kemp Papers, vol. 34, file 1198.

49 CPF *Bulletin*, 4 (September 1915), LAC, MG 26 H, Borden Papers, 30065, C-4308.
50 Morris, *Canadian Patriotic Fund*, 41.
51 Ibid., 45.
52 Ibid., 41; CPF *Bulletin* (December 1916), LAC, MG 26 H, Borden Papers, 30065, C-4308. In other cases, Elliot admitted, he acted without the wife's consent.
53 On the Saskatchewan savings scheme, see CPF *Bulletin* (October 1915), LAC, MG 26 H, Borden Papers, C-4308.
54 CPF *Bulletin* (October 1915), See also *Bulletins*, July-September 1915. LAC, MG 26 H, Borden Papers, 30065, C-4308.
55 CPF *Bulletin* (March 1917), LAC, MG 26 H, Borden Papers, 30065, C-4308.
56 Morris, *Canadian Patriotic Fund*, 42.
57 Helen Reid, "Report of the Montreal Branch," cited by Morris, *Canadian Patriotic Fund*, 245.
58 Morris, *Canadian Patriotic Fund*, 37.
59 Next to Montreal, Hamilton was probably the most conscientious branch with regard to its Third Responsibility. See Morton, *Fight or Pay*, 125-26.
60 On hostility to the Patriotic Fund in British Columbia and Alberta, see Morton, *Fight or Pay*, chap. 6.

Marks of Grief
Black Attire, Medals, and Service Flags

SUZANNE EVANS

"I was to Trafford's grave today," wrote Horace Jones to his sister Netta, "and enclose a few little flowers which I picked from it."[1] With these words Private Jones began his last letter to his older sister from the impossible return address, "Somewhere in Belgium." Two months before, on 26 May 1916, he had sent her a letter describing his first visit to the cemetery where the body of their younger brother Trafford lay. Trafford Jones, lieutenant in the Royal Flying Corps, had been shot down ten days before. The grave at Reninghelst near Ypres was a fresh mound of earth, but Horace assured Netta: "It will be planted with grass and flowers soon. It is back from where the shells fall and will not be disturbed ... It was pretty lonely standing there at his grave."

Netta saved Horace's letters from the front and passed them on to her youngest sister Gwen, whom she had raised as she had her four other siblings after their mother died in childbirth. Gwen, in turn, gave the letters to her daughter Aileen. Aileen Howes, my father's cousin, gave my great-uncle Horace's letters to me, and now they are in the Toronto Public Reference Library – including the pressed flowers.

Through the nineteenth century and onward, women in Canada and elsewhere have often acted as historians, keeping alive intimate and personal memories of ordinary people. In his essay "Memory and Identity" John Gillis argues that, as gender roles became more clearly divided, women, "thought of as belonging more to the past ... came to serve in various (and usually unpaid) ways as the keepers and embodiments of memory."[2] Melissa Zielke concurs, stating that women in Victorian-era Canada were thought to be society's "memory banks."[3] Women adapted this role to suit their interests and concerns within the world that was open to them. They focused on family and friends, revolving around the sites of memory over which they had the most control, "the home and the female body itself."[4] According to Zielke, in their role they became "the nation's chief mourners."[5] The end of the Victorian era, in combination with the First World War, changed how families coped with and marked death. What did not change is that physical sites of remembrance – women's bodies and the homes that were their chief sphere of influence – continued to be used to express grief over dead soldiers.

By 1914, the long-lasting tradition of women's wearing mourning black had begun to decline. War losses called it back into use, but this time with a reframed meaning. Where formerly mourning black had held the status of class, in the war it also carried the mark of sacrifice. A woman in black became for some a symbol of appropriate female behaviour, giving to the cause that has long been expected of women in wartime. In addition to black, women had new symbols of grief to wear. Two medals were created specifically for women, the Memorial or Silver Cross[6] and the bronze medal of the International Order of Allied Mothers in Sacrifice (IOAMS). The Canadian government created the former and the Associated Kin of the Canadian Expeditionary Forces produced the latter. With these medals, which are discussed in more detail later in this chapter, the state and the Associated Kin were able to publicly acknowledge the importance of women to the war effort without questioning women's traditional wartime role of home front supporter and producer of soldiers. Finally, for the home, a new flag was created to depict both honour and grief. This Canadian service flag was modelled after an American one. The number and colour of maple leaves, rather than the stars of the American flag, indicated how many men from the family had gone to the front and how many had been killed.

With mourning black, medals, and the new flag, women were offered symbols of loss presented, with a positive turn, as sacrifice. Historian Joy Damousi says of the Australian experience: "Women giving their sons became the quintessential emblem of feminine sacrifice; it was used shamelessly for propaganda purposes by those for and against the war."[7] Jonathan Vance, in writing about Canada's memory of the First World War and the eventual national identity built upon it, refers to the status conferred on Canadian women for having a relative – alive or dead – in uniform and how this sacrifice became part of the country's founding mythology.[8]

Although many have explored the links between war and its effects on women's status, Tanja Luckins takes a step back from the political in her analysis of Australian memories of bereavement and the First World War. She believes that "loss and the Great War is best understood not as a matter of identity and 'becoming Australian,' but as a matter of shared experiences and human relationships."[9] "There is a danger" she states, "that an emphasis on the politics of identity can become a simple reflection of public political discourse."[10] While I do not believe this danger is present in what has been written about women and wartime bereavement in Canada, it is important to remember that understanding grief and the Great War includes more than politics and national myth making.

The following exploration of three tangible marks of grief melds the personal with the political. Through the manipulation of these symbols women could announce their affiliation with the cause. However, whether they were worn or, in the case of the flag, hung in that spirit or not is a question only the individual women could answer. Of these marks of grief, only the Silver Cross is still being made and awarded. The IOAMS, the flag, and the custom of wearing black for years of mourning ended either with the war or soon after. Both the Silver Cross and these now defunct but once-potent symbols are worthy of our attention because they indicate how the decoration of women's bodies and their domestic domains became part of a complex and fluid communication with the world about economic and social status, support for the war, and the growing independence of women's voices. And finally, they remind us that grief and agony were as much a part of the wartime experience as were glory and triumph.

Images of Black

> It seemed the merriest of gatherings yet underneath the current of gaiety stalked always the grisly phantom of war; the blackgarb of a woman; the crepe band on a man's arm; the haunted look in a mother's eyes.
>
> – Eugenie Perry describing a common scene, 1918[11]

Photographic images are a rich source of information about clothing of the past and there are many such images in Canadian archives showing Victorian-era women dressed in mourning clothes. The weight of expectation to follow the rituals of mourning has always been heaviest on women, particularly on those of the middle and upper classes, whose mourning wear was used to display wealth and social status. Queen Victoria herself had promoted extravagant mourning practices during her reign; she wore black for forty years after her beloved husband, Prince Albert, died in 1861.[12] Photographic portraits of the deceased were common, as were portraits of women in mourning. Among Victoria's subjects however, mourning rituals had begun to relax towards the end of her reign. This trend, which later combined with the effects of the less sombre Edwardian era, helped to reduce the formality of mourning etiquette.[13] Given these changes one would expect, after Victoria's death, to see fewer photographs of women in mourning, and then an increase with the onslaught of the Great War. There were, after all, vast numbers of dead to be mourned. In fact, the women most inclined to wear mourning, those of the educated middle and upper classes, were from the same families as the officers who suffered proportionately greater casualties than other ranks.[14] Nevertheless, there is a paucity of wartime photographs of women in mourning.[15]

As we shall see, women were still wearing mourning dress, but technological and social change had come to the field of photography, and it became far less common for mourners and the dead to be photographed. Easy-to-use, inexpensive cameras were widely available by wartime, products of the Eastman Kodak Company. Photography became a popular leisure activity for ordinary people, while professionals, who had previously specialized in studio portraits, including those of women in mourning, saw their businesses decline. Amateur photographers were now deciding what subjects were worthy of preservation, and they largely chose not to take pictures of their families in grief.[16]

Nancy West argues in her book on Kodak's advertising campaigns that Kodak, more than any other company or individual, determined the use of snapshot photography and thus had an impact upon the shape of both memory and evidence. The company's advertising campaigns encouraged photographers to capture nostalgic images of domestic celebrations in their pictures.[17] Kodak determined that those most likely to take these snapshots would be independent young women who would take pictures of holidays, weddings, and new babies – not death. There were, of course, male amateur photographers, but, during the war, many of them were in the trenches. Some did take pictures – often prohibited – of the carnage surrounding them, but this was a radically different view of death from that of the Victorians. For the most part, death in the Great War was kept out of the picture frame. Photos of men going to or returning from war, or of families patiently waiting to hear news, were relatively safe images and thus were part of Kodak's advertising campaigns at the time.[18]

Prior to the war, pictures had been taken around the time of funerals, but, because First World War soldiers' bodies were not repatriated, families were denied the rituals of both funeral and burial. Memorial ceremonies were held for some of the dead soldiers on an individual basis, and municipalities organized general services for their many war-dead, but, with no body to see and mourn, death may have had an aura of unreality.[19] This would have been agonizingly augmented for the many families of soldiers reported missing in action. Even for relatives of those reported dead, hope may have lingered because of stories such as those of Lieutenant H.E. Lloyd Owen of Port Arthur and Montrealer Sergeant A.V. Hardwick.[20] Their families held memorials for them in May 1915 only to find out later that both were alive and being held prisoner in Germany.

Considering the upheavals in tradition taking place during the First World War, it is sadly fortunate that there are photographs of Trafford Jones' widow Madeline Jones, and his sister Gwen Alley, dressed in mourning black. The sisters-in-law, along with the Jones' three-year-old daughter Anne, had gone to England to be closer to their military husbands when the men were on leave. On a couple of occasions in the weeks after Trafford's death in May 1916, Madeline and Gwen took the rambunctious Anne to a park to play hide-and-go-seek. They did so with camera in hand and took turns capturing in Kodak fashion a few moments of Anne's childhood pleasure on film while unintentionally documenting each other's mourning clothes (see Figure 11).

The photos show the widow Madeline in two different outfits but both times wearing a black mushroom-style hat with a white under-rim and attached veil, a white collar, black blouse, jacket, skirt, and gloves. In one she has thick white cuffs at her wrists – weepers, designed to catch the tears. Trafford's sister, Gwen, is dressed in a black jacket and skirt and has a black hat but is not wearing a veil or black gloves. These last two pieces of mourning clothing were more formal. The veil in particular was a traditional and highly visible marker of grief, announcing the mourner's state and separating her from the world. Anyone seeing these young women in their twenties together in the park playing with little Anne might have guessed they were in mourning for a soldier.

The rules governing mourning attire for women were precise, according to Emily Holt's *Encyclopaedia of Etiquette*, first published in Toronto in 1901. Holt

FIGURE 11   A sombre Madeline Jones (with daughter Anne), attired in mourning clothes, 1916 – a literal embodiment of grief. [By permission of Suzanne Evans.]

advised that, for the first three weeks to a month, a widow's clothing should include a crepe-covered bonnet and long veil falling down her back and over her face. The inside rim of her hat should be covered with white pleats and she should wear white bands of fabric at the throat and wrists. Holt commented on many more details governing the lustre, weight, and texture of the dress fabric; the jewellery; the type of gloves worn; the material of the purse; and the black border around the handkerchief. Full mourning attire or sables were to be worn for one to one and a half years, followed by second mourning, when grey and lilac could be worn. A widow's social life was to be strictly circumscribed for the first six months of mourning, after which she was entitled to call on friends and attend the theatre – but only a matinee performance.[21]

The second edition of Holt's etiquette guide appeared in 1921. After Holt repeated her original instructions for dress and behaviour, she added a small paragraph:

> In general it may be said that the rules regulating the trappings of woe are being relaxed more and more. Many ladies of unquestionable taste and discretion now content themselves simply with wearing clothes that are black in color and have given up the rather ostentatiously funereal crêpe.[22]

The formality of mourning had been reduced, but the socially conservative etiquette book still dictated that, through the war years and beyond, it was appropriate to wear black.

Madeline Jones and Gwen Alley were in England at the time they took their candid mourning photographs. They may have bought their clothes in Britain, but Madeline's outfits are very similar in style to the mourning dresses Eaton's department store was advertising in Toronto's *Globe* newspaper in February and March of that year. It appears from the photographs that Madeline followed the rules of etiquette at least for the so-called "trappings of woe." However, even if she had been interested, it is unlikely that Madeline, a single mother in England with only a sister-in-law to help her, would have been able to seclude herself from society. The same would have been true for the many women involved in war-work both in England and Canada.

Two other photos of women in mourning, taken in Canada in the spring of 1915, show a similar adherence to the rules of etiquette from the perspective of two different generations. The snapshots are of Laura Dunsmuir, wife of the former lieutenant-governor of British Columbia, and one of her daughters.[23] They are in mourning for James, known as "Boy," son of Laura and James Dunsmuir Sr. Young James, intent on switching to the British Cavalry Regiment so he could see action, was sailing to England on the *Lusitania* when it was famously torpedoed by the Germans on 7 May 1915.

The sinking of the *Lusitania* had a galvanizing effect on Canadian public opinion. In Victoria, British Columbia, it ignited an outbreak of anti-German rioting resulting in property damage estimated at $20,000. Even Canadian suffragist Nellie McClung, not known for her eager support of the war, was shaken by this event. McClung later wrote, "It was the *Lusitania* that brought me to see the whole truth. Then I saw that we were waging war on the very Prince of Darkness ... I knew then that no man could die better than in defending civilization from this ghastly thing which threatened her."[24] The impact of the *Lusitania*'s sinking was even more personal and profound for those, such as the Dunsmuirs, who lost a loved one as a result. Laura Dunsmuir went into deep mourning for her son. The photo shows her in a long Victorian-style dress with black gloves and purse.[25] The picture of her daughter shows the young woman's black hat and shorter dress reflecting the fashions of the time.

That fashion should play a role in mourning clothes seems at odds with the message of utter sadness and seclusion they are meant to convey. Fashionable clothes are meant to stand out and be noticed, whereas a black veil hides the face with a colour that fades the individuality of the wearer into the shadows. At any time, this paradox invites different interpretations of mourning,[26] but during the war wearing black became politically controversial. It would be difficult to mourn with traditional pomp and expense those who had died of natural causes at home when so many young men were being killed in battle, nor could the vast number of violent deaths at the front be commemorated in the old ways. Not only were there no bodies to be buried, but these soldiers had died fighting for their country. Theirs was a communal death to be mourned by the nation but not with such sadness as to undermine the notion of their deaths' being an honourable and necessary sacrifice in the time of war.

Forego Gloomy Grief

> A newer heroism is abroad in this war ... and one of its reflections is a realization by women of the effect of mourning black on the spirit and energy of soldiers, their families and the public.[27]
>
> – *New York Times*, 7 July 1918

For those supportive of the war, black could be used simultaneously as an announcement of loss and as a demand for others to avenge the soldier's death that caused this mourning. However, there were others who, like the Kodak Company, were eager to push images of death out of view. Within many of the combatant nations there were individuals and groups who worried that the sight of mourners dressed in black would scare young men and dissuade them from enlisting. Readers of *The Times* of London discovered that the Germans were alert to the possible negative effects of mourning clothes. A report submitted to *The Times* by the subject of an unidentified neutral country referred to life in wartime Berlin:

> In the matter of mourning, it is agreed that the wearing of black can only tend to depress the spirits of those who have relatives at the front – so an association has been formed which proposes to substitute for all mourning a little scarfpin, with the inscription, "Stolz gabich ein teures Haupt furs Vaterland" (Proudly I gave a beloved one for the Father land).[28]

In May 1915, the day after the *Lusitania* was sunk, an editorial in the *Globe* made reference to an appeal by the National Council of Women of Canada, which suggested that, instead of wearing depressing black, women should "wear a band of royal purple on the arm, to signify that the soldier they mourn died gloriously for his King and Country."[29] The editorial also argued that mourning clothes were expensive and women would save money by not wearing them – money that could be donated to war charities.

The issue of mourning black was so potentially incendiary that President Woodrow Wilson became personally involved with it after the United States entered the war. According to the *New York Times*, he supported the Women's Committee of the Council of National Defense's suggestion that women put away their mourning clothes.[30] In fact, he authored the suggestion. In a behind-the-scenes effort to maintain public support for the war, and not wanting to advise American women himself on how to dress, Wilson wrote to suffragist Dr. Anna Howard Shaw, chair of the Council of National Defense's Women's Committee: "Your own committee might think it timely and wise to give some advice to the women of the country with regard to mourning."[31]

In the *New York Times* article, women in mourning were advised to wear only a black band on the left arm with a gold star for each member of the family killed in the war.[32] The Women's Committee explained: "The wearing of such insignia will ... express better than mourning the feeling of the American people that such losses are a matter of glory rather than of prostrating grief and depression."[33] An example of this view of glory was included in one of many letters sent to the committee from England, where, readers were told, with great determination many women avoided mourning. The article quoted from a letter by an unnamed English woman who had four sons in the war, one of whom had been killed. Wearing black, she came to believe, was a "selfish temptation to hide my pain behind a mourning that would hold off intrusion." She thought she should present herself as an inspiration, upholding her son's expectation "that [she] should regard his death as a happy promotion into higher service."[34]

Mrs. Gordon Southam, of Hamilton, Ontario, publicly packed up her mourning clothes for yet another reason. For her, mourning was a sign of inaction. Her brother had been killed in 1915 at St. Eloi, and her husband had been killed at the Battle of the Somme in 1916. In June 1918, she decided to trade in her mourning clothes for a YMCA uniform. Speaking to a reporter from the *New York Times* just before departing from New York for the front, she said: "The way for women to mourn in war time is to translate their grief into action against the enemy."[35] She believed her husband and brother "would have been ashamed to have [her] stay at home and waste time in selfish sorrow when there [was] so much work to be done for the soldiers."[36]

The strident calls to put away mourning in England, the United States, Germany, and Canada signalled that many women persisted in doing just the opposite. It is understandable that, in times of such intense grief, many would draw into themselves, seeking a place of security that traditional mourning could provide. James Gerard, American ambassador to Germany (1913-17), wrote in his memoirs of the war years in that country: "All the people you see have lost sons and brothers; mourning becomes visible over a wider area all the time."[37] In Canada, the number of advertisements for mourning clothes in newspapers and mail-order catalogues suggests that here, too, women were commonly donning black in their bereavement. Eaton's advertised mourning apparel and accessories in its catalogues and in the *Globe*, which, at the time, claimed a substantial circulation of eighty-five thousand per day. Eaton's mail-order catalogues were sent across the country to rural and urban homes, both wealthy and poor. They offered mourning veils, hats, and even black straight pins so that when a woman attached her veil to her hat there would be no glint of silver.[38]

As the National Council of Women argued, having to buy a new wardrobe of black clothes could be expensive.[39] Although Eaton's catalogue clothing was generally less costly than the items the company advertised in the newspaper, even these cheaper items could be out of reach for some Canadians. Many women depended on black dye as an inexpensive means of transforming ordinary outfits into suitable mourning clothes.[40]

Eaton's advertised its more expensive mourning wear in the *Globe*. On 27 October 1914, its advertisement addressed "Those Who Are Wearing Black," and it referred, in reverent tones, to the art of making mourning wear: "Material and design must be carefully considered. Not a shiny weave or exaggerated line can be permitted. Dull fabrics of best quality and dye, developed in some modish but conservative style – this is the ideal." All these details on the type and finish of fabrics plus descriptions of clothing appropriate for different stages of mourning indicate that the writers knew their subject and that their clients were following rules of etiquette. Eaton's advertised that it bought from fashion houses in New York specializing in mourning wear and imported black veils from Paris. The war had increased France's already strong tradition of mourning wear. Edna Woolman Chase, international editor of *Vogue*, commented that mourning "seeped like a dark tide through the towns and countryside as the casualty lists came back from the trenches."[41] Even though the suitability of wearing black was questioned, business remained steady for the fashion houses and for Courtaulds, the British company monopolizing black crepe production.[42] As for Eaton's Toronto store, on 1 March 1916, three departments were given over to a fashion show consisting solely of mourning garb.[43]

The Great War, and the resulting grief experienced by so many Canadians, visually changed the look of the country. Canadian poet and short story writer Eugenie Perry deftly described what a Canada in general mourning would have looked like in 1918. In an article published in the *Canadian Home Journal* she depicts a Home Products Fair at "one of Canada's Stores." It was a scene that, she implies, could be found across the country:

> It seemed the merriest of gatherings yet underneath the current of gaiety stalked always the grisly phantom of war; the blackgarb of a woman; the crepe band on a man's arm; the haunted look in a mother's eyes; the numerous men in khaki – all spoke of the grim conflict so far away, yet so near."[44]

Author Lucy Maud Montgomery gives us a glimpse of public opinion about mourning during the war in her novel *Rilla of Ingleside*, in which she consciously tries to provide an accurate depiction of the Canadian home front. This story of Canada at war follows the life of Rilla Blythe as her brothers and male friends go to war and her brother Walter is killed at the battle of Courcelette, in September 1916. The young gossiping character Irene is aghast at what she wrongly presumes is Rilla's indifference to Walter's death. Rilla wears white in deference to her brother's memory, but this is not enough for Irene, who reports to her friend Betty: "I asked Rilla right out why she didn't put on mourning for

Walter. She said her mother didn't wish it. But everyone is talking about it."[45] Although wearing mourning black was a matter of choice, its absence was noticed – and judged.

In more peaceful times it is difficult to imagine the tension felt by a country that had 600,000 soldiers engaged in a faraway war out of a total population of only 8,000,000. The battle was real yet displaced. The smell of rot, the sound of bombs, the sight of growing rows of graveyard crosses were not there to constantly remind Canadians of the price of war. The image of death came with the daily casualty lists and in bodily form, with the returning wounded and the blackgarbed women wandering the avenues of everyday life.

Medals of Sacrifice

> It was only logical that the nearest relatives of those so engaged should be remembered in some tangible manner to compensate in part for the desolation which invades and disrupts a home from which a dear and much beloved member has been taken.[46]
>
> – Clara Twidale on the creation of the Silver Cross

Mourning black was not the only physical memory of dead soldiers carried on a bereaved woman's body. As mentioned above, two medals were independently created for mothers: the bronze IOAMS medal and the Silver Cross medal. The reasons that the former lasted just a few years and the latter is still being made and awarded are to be found in the stories of their origins.

The IOAMS medal was created by the Associated Kin of the Canadian Expeditionary Forces, a group formed by Gordon Wright of London, Ontario. Wright was a prominent Londoner and temperance worker.[47] His wife Sarah (Rowell) Wright was also a temperance worker but with a much higher profile than her husband. As well as being in the leadership of the National Council of Women and the Social Services of Canada, she served as president of the Woman's Christian Temperance Union. This organization believed the family was the centre of a moral society and that the mother was the core of that centre.

The goals of the Associated Kin were to look after the interests of soldiers and their families and to secure new recruits for the war. The Canadian Patriotic Fund, discussed by Desmond Morton in his chapter on soldiers and their families in this volume, was also involved in these activities, with the exception of recruitment. By 1917 the Associated Kin, which had started in London, Ontario, and quickly spread across the province, had 109 centres in Canada.[48] It claimed to be modelled after an American group that started after the Civil War.[49] Although unnamed, most likely this was the powerful Grand Army of the Republic, an organization of Union Army veterans that demanded veterans' and widows' pensions and was later influential in the Republican Party. Like the Grand Army of the Republic, the Associated Kin was a group comprised of nationalist patriots. It was a strong supporter of conscription and demanded that conscientious objectors be permanently disenfranchised.[50] J.M. Skelton accused the Associated Kin of sending out letters to the families of soldiers on the casualty lists, calling on them to become, for a fee, members of the organization.[51] The group denied this, and while there is no remaining evidence of this tactic, it did aggressively solicit members through public meetings. For example, during the week of 17-23 September 1917, it held sixteen meetings in Toronto at Methodist and Presbyterian churches, a public school, and, clearly hoping for a large audience, the University of Toronto's Convocation Hall, which had a seating capacity of 1,730. The poster advertising these events asked "Have You Blood in the War?" Assuming an affirmative answer, it then demanded, "Be there because of your kin in the trenches. Be their Kin in the Churches."[52]

By the time these meetings were held, the Associated Kin already had a plan to honour bereaved mothers:

> Preparations are under way by the Society to present to every mother who has lost a son in the war some token commemorative of her sacrifice. It is proposed to name a trustee in each Province for this special undertaking to be carried out through the organization for the people of Canada. Also the Associated Kin are taking up this matter with other allied countries and hopes to form an international society to be known as the International Order of Allied Mothers in Sacrifice.[53]

The medal has a plaque at the top inscribed with the words "Associated Kin of C.E.F. The People of Canada." Below this hangs a bar with the soldier's name and at the bottom is a shield with a cross surrounded by maple leaves and the words, "International Order of Allied Mothers in Sacrifice." On the reverse of the shield is the mother's name in gold letters. A purple ribbon backs the medal. The awarding of the medals made news in April 1918 when mothers from Exeter,

Ontario, were decorated. In September of that year a much larger ceremony was held for the same purpose in Toronto at the Bond Street Congregational Church. More than one hundred mothers from Toronto, Hamilton, Dundas, Maddock, Shelbourne, and Paris, Ontario, were decorated with the medal. Three of the mothers each had two sons killed in the war. Their medals had two bars at the top inscribed with the names of their sons. One mother, no name given, had to wait until after the ceremony to receive her medal because it had to be specially made with four bars.[54]

With a nod to symbolism, the Associated Kin held its last awards ceremony on the recently devised celebration of Mother's Day, Sunday, 11 May 1919. They arranged for churches in London, Ontario, to hold decoration services and invited other organizations and churches across the country to do the same. The groups involved in the main London ceremony held at the Patricia Theatre were the local and national Associated Kin, the London and St. Thomas' chapters of the National Council of Women, and the mothers' clubs of London.

Today the Canadian War Museum holds two examples of the IOAMS medal, and the City of Toronto Archives has one photograph of a Canadian mother in mourning black, wearing the medal of sacrifice. In a gesture indicative of the IOAMS medal's failure to maintain a place in Canada's social memory of the Great War, someone has added a handwritten note at the bottom of the photograph that reads, "WW1 1916 Silver star mother?"[55] Both the date and the name of the medal are incorrect. There were no medals for bereaved mothers in Canada until 1918, and the suggested name is an anachronistic conflation of the Canadian Silver Cross and its American counterpart, the Gold Star. The mother in the photograph wears neither a star nor a cross but the bronze medal of the IOAMS.

Founder Gordon Wright declared that the Associated Kin was above politics, yet the group supported conscription and the removal of the right to vote for all fit men refusing to bear arms. These positions may have narrowed the appeal of the organization. But likely the Associated Kin, along with the IOAMS, faded into history because so much of the organization's work was dedicated to recruitment. When the war was over the Associated Kin lost a mainstay of its raison d'être. In contrast, the Silver Cross had the credibility of the national government behind it and it did not come with a stated recruitment agenda. As a cross it carries Christian symbolism in its name, and early references invoked that context. However, it takes the shape of a Maltese cross.[56] The only other symbolism carried by this medal to which the wearer would be showing affiliation is the crown and maple leaf: monarch and country.

FIGURE 12   Bereaved mother wearing IOAMS medal. [By permission of City of Toronto Archives, Fonds 1244, Item 654]

William Alexander Fraser, a popular Canadian author, first suggested the Silver Cross medal in a letter to the editor of Toronto's *Mail and Empire*, 22 September 1916. Fraser had already had a long publishing career in both fiction and non-fiction. His writing, often compared with that of British author Rudyard Kipling, was shaped by his experiences as an oil driller in disparate parts of the British Empire: Burma, India, Afghanistan, and Alberta. In addition to his books, Fraser published in well-known Canadian and American magazines and newspapers for an audience of men, women, and children.

Fraser's patriotism was at the root of his suggestion of a Silver Cross medal. He knew of no other cross like it in the world, and he wanted Canada to be the first country to create a medal of this kind. He hoped that it would be as cherished for its own purpose as was the Victoria Cross for military valour. His initial argument for the Silver Cross was made with the skill of a storyteller, providing a tangible context and packed with pathos, chivalry, and religious allusion:

Men might take off their hats when they met a woman with this medal on her breast; they could get up, even if tired, and give her a seat in a crowded car. Now, too often, this courtesy is extended to a fashionably attired girl, leaving the plain-looking woman to stand and perhaps that plain looking woman has made the sacrifice that Mary made when she gave her son for the good of man. Each of us knows some woman who is sitting at home eating her heart out in grief for the boy who will never put his arms around her neck again: we can give her the silver badge of her heroic sacrifice.[57]

Fraser knew he needed strong backers to bring his idea to fruition. He wrote to Prime Minister Robert Borden on 12 October, enclosing the newspaper clipping and asking for the prime minister's help in creating a "Silver Cross for Mothers." Borden responded seven days later with great interest. The prime minister was so impressed with what he later called "this wonderfully taking idea" that, in a follow-up memorandum, he said the crosses should not be conferred by a mere municipality but by the country at His Majesty's command. He thought it important they be made quickly and given to the mothers as soon as possible, when it would mean the most.[58]

From that time onward the idea for the Silver Cross quickly gained momentum, but support from high places and a strong literary advocate were not the only reasons for this. There was a widely held perception that this was not an ordinary war; rather, it was the greatest of all human catastrophes. This view compelled people to look beyond the symbols and means of memorializing they already had and to create new ones. The Associated Kin tried to reflect the enormous scale of the conflict by making its medal international, a laudable undertaking but difficult to attain and, as it turned out, impossible.

In the way it was depicted in the news, the Silver Cross symbolically reached out to a wider religious and historical community than did the IOAMS medal. Canadian mothers were compared with Mary, mother of Jesus, and the Spartan mother who counselled her son to return from battle either carrying his shield in victory or lying on it, having fought to the death.[59] By drawing on Christianity and the values of ancient Greece, archetypes upon which the image of the British Empire was based, the Silver Cross medal went beyond Canada's borders without anyone's having to negotiate with current international states. For Borden, the solely Canadian nature of the medal was likely very appealing. In the years between the initial suggestion of the medal and the time it was finally announced by the Privy Council in December 1919, he had been concerned with presenting Canada to the world not only as an essential contributor to the Allied war effort but also as a partner in the British Empire.

W.A. Fraser was remembered fondly for his suggestion of the Silver Cross when he died on 9 November 1933. "It was," the *Globe* obituary said, "Mr. Fraser's sympathetic imagination" that conceived of this honour for the "war's real heroines."[60] The criteria for the medal closely followed Fraser's original idea, except that it was called the Memorial Cross and was to be given to widows as well.[61]

Flying the Maple Leaves

> In thousands of homes in all parts of Canada will soon be seen these new service flags, proclaiming that men from these homes have gone forth to join Canada's army overseas.[62]
>
> – SATURDAY NIGHT, 1918

The third major mark of grief assumed by Canadian women during the First World War was the service flag, adopted late in the war and based upon an American precursor. The American serviceman Captain J.G. McIlroy of Cleveland, Ohio, designed the American service flag after the United States entered the war on 6 April 1917. It had a white centre, red border, and as many blue stripes as there were family members in the war. In the final design, stars replaced the stripes and blue changed to gold when a soldier was killed. Both homes and businesses flew the flags, with the paint company of Sherwin-Williams in Cleveland going so far as to fly three separate flags to honour its American, British, and Canadian employees who were fighting in the war. The service flag idea was quickly adopted in Canada, where maple leaves were used instead of stars.

In April 1918, *Saturday Night* magazine announced that homes across the country would be flying these new service flags. By July, the Canadian Service Flag Company of Toronto was advertising in the *Canadian Home Journal*, encouraging women to display the flag in their windows. The advertisement warned against substitutes, advising that "the correct design has a red border, white panel, blue maple leaves – Red leaves for those who have fallen."[63] Considering the flags only came into use during the last six or seven months of the war, they were quite popular. In the August issue of the magazine, pins, flags for the car, and stationery with the same design were also advertised. A government committee set up in 1919 to study the Canadian coat of arms observed that the maple leaf was a favourite Canadian emblem in part because of its use during the war on service flags, which "scores of thousands of Canadians displayed."[64] Although service flags have disappeared from use, the present Canadian flag is notably similar to the red-leafed service flag flown by bereaved Canadian families – perhaps even by the families of Trafford and Horace Jones.

Flowers were the memorial Horace wanted for his brother Trafford in the little cemetery where, he noted approvingly, "nearly all Canadians lay ... officers and men." Horace ended his last letter to his sister Netta by returning to the subject with which he had begun. Of the enclosed slips of clover he had picked from Trafford's grave he wrote: "Don't want to stir your grief Netta but thought you would like these." He asked that she show them to Madeline, who, by this time, was back in Canada. Not content with wild flowers, Horace made arrangements with a local Belgian farmer whose daughter was an expert with roses. She would plant a bush in the fall, and he would try to come and see it when he was on leave. He did not live to see the roses. The final news of Horace came from his captain in November 1916 on black-bordered mourning stationery. He was last seen wounded, walking towards an imperial dressing station. The state adopted responsibility for his commemoration as a soldier. Now Horace's name, along with 11,284 others without graves, is carved on the walls of that most famous of Canadian monuments, the Vimy Memorial in France.

Through his letters Horace acknowledged Netta's grief for Trafford, but any record of her feelings over Horace's death is as absent as are Horace's remains. Bereaved Canadian mother Anna Creery captured some of the very physical anguish Netta may have felt for her brother, whom she had raised like a son, in a seventeen-page pamphlet of poetry and prose, a few copies of which were printed near the end of the war. The title page reads:

Thoughts of Comfort for the Bereaved
By a Mother
Privileged to Give Five Sons to the Empire
Two of Whom Have Laid Down their Lives[65]

Creery's writings lean heavily on a Christian interpretation of sacrifice to answer her questions, and those of others, about the necessity of these war deaths. The answers come from biblical quotations, but the questions, like those in her poem "Missing," come from her heart. "Missing – Oh surely 'tis hardest of all to bear. / Where is he? Does he suffer? Perhaps needing my care?" Flags, medals, and mourning black were visible, but dim, reflections of that heartache and despair.

Charlotte Susan Wood was chosen as the official Silver Cross mother at the unveiling of the Vimy Memorial on 26 July 1936.[66] In the frequently reproduced black-and-white photograph of Wood on that summer day, she appears to be dressed in black except for a white collar, a colour combination marking the "second mourning" that older women often wore until they died. Greatly honoured to meet King Edward VIII but nonetheless forthright, she said to him: "Oh! Sir, I have just been looking at the trenches and I just can't figure out why our boys had to go through that."[67]

For Charlotte Susan Wood and others in the years after the war, wearing black may have come to represent a combination of the bleak, wrong-headedness of war as a strategy of diplomacy as well as a sign of sad remembrance. The medals, including the Silver Cross that cover Wood's breast, must have been worn with both pride and grief. It is difficult to imagine that mourning black, medals of sacrifice, and service flags could have only one meaning for the mother, widow, or sister of a dead soldier. These marks of grief tell a complicated story of the relationship between the heart and the nation in which women's clothing and adornments became a memory bank of the war.

Acknowledgments
This chapter is dedicated to Aileen (Alley Corkett) Howes (1919-2011), historian, storyteller, and recipient of the Memorial Cross.

Notes
1. Toronto Public Reference Library, S280, Horace Jones Papers, Baldwin Room.
2. John R. Gillis, "Memory and Identity: The History of a Relationship," in *Commemorations: The Politics of National Identity*, ed. John R. Gillis (Princeton: Princeton University Press, 1994), 10.
3. Melissa Zielke, "Forget-Me-Nots," *Material History Review* 58 (2003): 55.
4. Ibid.
5. Zielke, "Forget-Me-Nots," 53.
6. I use the term "medal" in the general sense of decoration or award; however, the Memorial Cross is technically a memento. The formal name for the Silver Cross is the Memorial Cross, but it did not get that name until it was officially struck in 1919. In all communications before then it was known as the Silver Cross and it is still better known by that name. I refer to it from now on as the Silver Cross.

7 Joy Damousi, *The Labour of Loss* (Cambridge: Cambridge University Press, 1999), 30. Two comprehensive works on the politicization of motherhood and sexual identity in wartime are Nicoletta F. Gullace, *"The Blood of Our Sons": Men, Women and the Renegotiation of British Citizenship during the Great War* (New York: Palgrave Macmillan, 2002); and Susan R. Grayzel, *Women's Identities at War: Gender, Motherhood, and Politics in Britain and France during the First World War* (Chapel Hill, NC: University of North Carolina Press, 1999).
8 Jonathan Vance, *Death So Noble: Memory, Meaning and the First World War* (Vancouver: UBC Press, 1997), 126.
9 Tanja Luckins, *The Gates of Memory: Australian People's Experiences and Memories of Loss and the Great War* (North Fremantle, W. Australia: Curtin University Books, 2004), 14.
10 Ibid.
11 Eugenie Perry, "Peace – The Stranger," *Canadian Home Journal* 14 (1918): 8.
12 Sonia A. Bedikian, "The Death of Mourning: From Victorian Crepe to the Little Black Dress," *Omega* 57, 1 (2008): 40.
13 Ibid., 44.
14 Pat Jalland, *Death in the Victorian Family* (Oxford: Oxford University Press, 1996), 373. For figures from Princess Patricia's Canadian Light Infantry, see Ralph Hodder-Williams, *Princess Patricia's Canadian Light Infantry*, vol. 2: *1914-19* (London: Hodder and Stoughton, 1923), 62.
15 According to Tanja Luckins, this lack of photographs is also true in Australia. In spite of many references to women in mourning, the only image she found of an individual woman in mourning black is the one on the cover of her book *The Gates of Memory* (personal communication, 23 May 2008). As for the United States, Sarah Greenough, Senior Curator of Photographs, National Gallery of Art, Washington, DC, and John Rohrbach, Senior Curator of Photographs, Amon Carter Museum, Fort Worth, Texas, were both unable to find First World War images of women in mourning black in their respective institutions' collections (personal communication, Nancy West, 14 August 2009).
16 Nancy West, *Kodak and the Lens of Nostalgia* (Charlottesville: University Press of Virginia, 2000), 139.
17 Ibid., xii, 140.
18 Ibid., 17, 199.
19 Jalland, *Death in the Victorian Family*, 374; and Luckins, *Gates of Memory*, 15.
20 "Mourned as dead; Is Alive," "Sergt. Hardwick Not Killed," *Globe* (Toronto), 19 May 1915, 3.
21 Emily Holt, *Encyclopaedia of Etiquette* (Toronto: Musson, 1921), 332, 327-30. Same pages for the 1901 edition.
22 Ibid., 330.
23 Royal BC Museum I-61611, I-61613.
24 Nellie McClung, *The Next of Kin* (Toronto: Thomas Allen, 1917), 15.

25 Given that Laura Dunsmuir is shown petting her dog and standing beside her granddaughter with another dog in a baby carriage, it is likely that the photographer was capturing a "Kodak moment" rather than the memory of mourning.
26 One aspect of this paradox is alluded to in A.L. Cochrane, "A Little Widow Is a Dangerous Thing," *International Journal of Psycho-Analysis* 17 (1936): 494-509. The author examines the interplay between repression and exaltation in a widow's sexuality – what he calls her "black magic." The idea and the title were already popular by 1936. A silent film by the same title came out in 1913.
27 "Insignia, Not Black Gowns," *New York Times*, 7 July 1918.
28 In Lou Taylor, *Mourning Dress: A Costume and Social History* (London: George Allen, 1983), 269-70.
29 "When Bowed Head Is Proudly Held," *Globe*, 8 May 1915, 10.
30 Set up in 1917, the committee's work included conservation drives and the implementation of child welfare programs. It also dealt with issues of home economy.
31 Woodrow Wilson to Dr. Anna Howard Shaw, 16 May 1918, in Arthur S. Link, ed., *The Papers of Woodrow Wilson* (Princeton: Princeton University Press, 1985), 48:28.
32 "President Approves War Mourning Bands," *New York Times*, 26 May 1918.
33 Ibid.
34 Ibid.
35 "Mrs. Southam in War Work: Widow of Major Says Women Should Work, Not Mourn," *New York Times*, 16 June 1918.
36 Ibid.
37 J.W. Gerard, *My Four Years in Germany* (New York: George H. Doran Co. 1917), 58.
38 Eaton's mail-order catalogue 1915-16, 1916, 1918-19, see http://www.collectionscanada.gc.ca/.
39 "When Bowed Head Is Proudly Held," *Globe*, 8 May 1915.
40 Indian logwood was commonly used as a black dye at least since the eighteenth century. See Taylor, *Mourning Dress*, 109.
41 Edna Woolman Chase and Ilka Chase, *Always in Vogue* (London: Gollanez, 1954), 100.
42 Taylor, *Mourning Dress*, 223.
43 A 1916 Parisian silk coat now held by the Canadian Museum of Civilization (D-101279) would have fit well in the Eaton's show.
44 Perry, "Peace," 8.
45 L.M. Montgomery, *Rilla of Ingleside* (Toronto: Seal Books, 1996 [1920]), 194.
46 Excerpt from speech by Clara Twidale on the origins of the Silver Cross medal given at the Ottawa Chapter meeting of the Remembrance Association of the Silver Cross Women of Canada (1956), Canadian War Museum, 1979-0335-001 58E6.
47 "Funeral of B.G.H. Wright," *Globe* 27 June 1927.
48 "Let Relations Get Together," *Globe*, 24 September 1917.
49 "Raise Soldier above Politics," *Globe*, 18 September 1917.
50 "New Demand Made by Associated Kin," *Globe*, 24 May 1917.
51 "Associated Kin Accept No Fees," *Globe*, 8 October 1917.

52 "In the Name of Kinship," *Globe*, 17 September 1917.
53 "A Mother's Sacrifice," *Globe*, 1 August 1917. Australia, New Zealand, and Italy were the foreign countries mentioned regarding discussions about the medal in a *Globe* article on 19 September 1917.
54 "Honor Mothers of the Fallen," *Globe*, 6 September 1918.
55 City of Toronto Archives, Fond 1244 item 654.
56 The Maltese is shaped like the Victoria Cross rather than the Latin crucifix and has bars of even lengths, with eight points symbolic of the eight points of courage.
57 "Heroine of the Trenches," *Mail and Empire* (Toronto), 22 September 1916.
58 LAC, MG 26 H, Robert L. Borden Papers, vol. 213.
59 Mary is referenced in the *Toronto Star*, 23 September 1916, and the Spartan mother is referenced in the *Globe*, 21 October 1916.
60 "Noted Novelist, W.A. Fraser Dies," *Globe*, 11 November 1933.
61 In May 2006 husbands became eligible to receive the medal. The first to receive the Silver Cross was Jason Beam, husband of the late Captain Nichola Goddard. As of January 2007, members of the Canadian Forces can choose up to three potential recipients for the award. The recipients do not have to be family members.
62 "Canada's New Flag," *Saturday Night*, 20 April 1918.
63 *Canadian Home Journal* 14 (1918): 49.
64 R. Matheson, *Canada's Flag* (Belleville, ON: Mica, 1986), 16.
65 Anna Creery, *Thoughts of Comfort* (Vancouver[?]: n.p., 1918[?]).
66 Each year the Legion chooses one Silver Cross recipient to represent all who have received the medal. The recipient participates in the national Remembrance Day ceremonies in Ottawa as well as other memorial functions throughout the year.
67 M.H. Halton, "His Majesty Voices Hope," *Winnipeg Free Press*, 28 July 1936.

PART 4:
CREATIVE RESPONSES

> Can we have lived through it all?
> Or was it some dream we dreamed?
> Gleaming memorial shafts
> Give us our answer.[1]
>
> – Phebe Florence Miller, 1924

The First World War is known for the explosion of poetry – both professional and amateur – that attended it, while fiction written by soldiers or written about the conflict continues to shape public memory and popular interpretations of the war. The best-known results of this literary flowering were British (including poetry by Siegfried Sassoon and Wilfred Owen, and memoirs by Robert Graves, and Vera Brittain) or European (Erich Maria Remarque's *All Quiet on the Western Front*), but writers throughout the combatant nations put pen to paper in an attempt to record the events and emotions they experienced during and after the war. Nor were they alone in turning to creative means to try to capture the experience for posterity. Men and women also turned to art, music, and other creative outlets in order to celebrate their nation in arms, grapple with grief, and otherwise draw meaning from the destruction. A growing number of international scholars, led by Margaret Higonnet, Sharon Ouditt, and (more recently) Jane Potter, look to women's writings of the war years in order to understand what women thought of the war and how they experienced it.[2] In Canada, L.M. Montgomery's Great War novel *Rilla of Ingleside* is the most-studied work of women's war fiction, fuelled in part by the recent growth of scholarly interest in the author as well as by the enduring popularity of the Anne of Green Gables series, of which it is part. For presenting a dramatically different perspective on the war, Francis Marion Beynon's portrayal of a Manitoba feminist pacifist in *Aleta Dey* deserves more attention than it has thus far received.[3] More broadly, Canadian fiction and poetry of the First World War, as well as the work of Canadian war artist Mary L. Riter, have received attention from scholars, but Newfoundlanders' creative responses to the Great War remain to be studied.[4]

Women produced creative responses to the war, but they were also the subjects of others' creative responses. In this section, Vicki Hallett examines the war poetry of poet and local postmistress Phebe Florence Miller in an attempt to determine Miller's role in reflecting, and helping to create, Newfoundland's cultural memory of the war. Lynn Kennedy similarly considers war poetry, this time written by both Canadian men and Canadian women, and reveals a reliance on metaphors of motherhood to express Canada's developing sense of nationhood. Amy Tector examines Canadian novels of the First World War, which feature disabled ex-soldiers, in order to determine the war's impact on gender roles for both men and women. Whether as creators or as subjects of others' creative acts, Canadian and Newfoundland girls and women are an integral part of the war story of Britain's two North American dominions.

Notes

1. Phebe Florence Miller, "The Silence," *Veteran* 4, 3 (1924): 40.
2. Sharon Ouditt, *Fighting Forces, Writing Women: Identity and Ideology in the First World War* (London: Routledge, 1994); Jane Potter, *Boys in Khaki, Girls in Print: Women's Literary Responses to the Great War, 1914-1918* (Oxford: Oxford University Press, 2005); Margaret R. Higonnet, ed. *Behind the Lines: Gender and the Two World Wars* (New Haven: Yale University Press, 1987).
3. Francis Marion Beynon, *Aleta Dey* (London: Virago Press, 1988 [1919]). On Beynon, see Brie McManus, "Francis Marion Beynon: The Forgotten Suffragist," *Manitoba History* 28 (1994): 22-30; and Barbara Roberts, "Women against War, 1914-1918: Frances Beynon and Laura Hughes," in *Up and Doing: Canadian Women and Peace*, ed. Janice Williamson and Deborah Gorham, 48-65 (Toronto: Women's Press, 1989).
4. Studies of *Rilla* include: Owen Dudley Edwards and Jennifer H. Litster, "The End of Canadian Innocence: L.M. Montgomery and the First World War," in *L.M. Montgomery and Canadian Culture*, ed. Irene Gammel and Elizabeth Epperley, 31-46 (Toronto: University of Toronto Press, 1999); Amy Tector, "A Righteous War? L.M. Montgomery's Depiction of the First World War in *Rilla of Ingleside*," *Canadian Literature* 179 (2003): 72-86; Alan R. Young, "L.M. Montgomery's *Rilla of Ingleside*: Romance and the Experience of War," in *Myth and Milieu: Atlantic Literature and Culture, 1918-1939*, ed. Gwendolyn Davies, 95-122 (Fredericton: Acadiensis, 1993). Beyond *Rilla*, see Donna Coates, "The Best Soldiers of All: Unsung Heroines in Canadian Women's Great War Fictions," *Canadian Literature* 151 (1996): 66-99. On Canadian women and art, see Susan Butlin, "Women Making Shells: Marking Women's Presence in Munitions Work, 1914-1918 – The

Art of Frances Loring, Florence Wyle, Mabel May, and Dorothy Stevens," *Canadian Military History* 5, 1 (1996): 41-48; Jim Burant, "No Man's Land: The Battlefield Painting of Mary Riter Hamilton," *Queen's Quarterly* 112, 1 (2005): 28-37; Karen Ann Reyburn, "Blurring the Boundaries: Images of Women in Canadian Propaganda of WWI" (MA thesis, University of Guelph, 1999).

Verses in the Darkness
A Newfoundland Poet Responds to the First World War

Vicki S. Hallett

> The winter twilight's gloomed apace,
> And deepened into winter night,
> Her son asleep, she sought the light
> And dashed the tear-drops from her face.[1]

These lines were written by Phebe Florence Miller in 1916. Miller was a poet and postmistress who lived in Topsail, Conception Bay, on the east coast of Newfoundland from 1889 to 1979. In the course of her long artistic life, she wrote many poems about Newfoundland and its people. Some of her most well known are those that tell stories about men and women's experiences of the First World War. In the Topsail post and telegraph office,[2] Miller sent people's letters and packages to the front lines and received news about the conflict, which she then relayed to the folk of her small community. On a practical level then, Miller helped maintain the tenuous links between Newfoundlanders and their loved ones who were fighting in the gloomy theatre of war. As a poet, Miller extended this role through writing, helping to preserve connections between Newfoundlanders and their humanity in an inhumane time. Such ephemeral bonds are imperative for the writer for, as Margaret Atwood maintains, "writing has to do with darkness, and a desire, or perhaps a compulsion to enter it, and, with luck, to illuminate it, and to bring something back out to the light."[3] Miller, in the darkness of the Great War and its aftermath, entered and spoke the

FIGURE 13   Phebe Florence Miller's prewar passport photo. [MUN Archives and Special Collections, P. Florence Miller Collection]

conflicting emotions felt by the Newfoundland people, illuminating their pride, grief, anger, and sorrow with her poetry.

Phebe Florence Miller's writing was her personal response to the horrific casualties suffered by Newfoundland in the First World War. Yet, it had broader political implications within the tiny Dominion. As is revealed by Lynn Kennedy and Amy Tector in this volume, Canadian literature about the war was intimately interconnected with dominant discourses of gender and nationalism. This chapter considers Phebe Florence Miller's unconventional life and her poems in the context of Newfoundland's first-wave feminist movement, the successes of which relied heavily on the importance of women's war work. Further, her war poetry, composed over the course of three decades, is examined as both constitutive of and constituted by Newfoundlanders' collective memory of the Great War.

Miller was a young woman just starting her literary career as the First World War broke out. Perhaps not the most likely of war poets, she was unmarried and childless and had no sweetheart or close relatives participating in the war overseas. She nevertheless felt a deep connection with Newfoundland soldiers and their families, particularly those from her small, closely knit outport home.[4] Topsail, at the time, was a community of only a few hundred people, connected to the capital, St. John's, by a short train journey. Miller, as its telegraph operator and a descendant of its pioneering settler families, would have known most of her neighbours personally and would have been related to many.[5] Her poems are thus imbued with an abiding sense of kinship with the soldiers and their loved ones.

Miss Miller, as she became known, published her first poem in the *Newfoundland Quarterly* in October 1916.[6] Yet it did not take long for her talent and sensitivity to be recognized. Her verses directly pertaining to the First World War were frequently featured in *The Veteran*,[7] a publication of the Great War Veteran's Association of Newfoundland, and *The Distaff*, a journal printed during the 1914-1918 conflict by the Women's Patriotic Association (WPA) of Newfoundland and devoted to showcasing the work of Newfoundland women in the war effort.[8] Contemporaries considered her to be closely attuned to the emotional and cultural nuances of Newfoundland. In 1922, the *Newfoundland Quarterly* claimed: "with the single exception of 'The Bard of Terra Nova'[9] himself, we know of no other local writer of dialect poems who has a deeper understanding of the hearts and minds of the people portrayed than Miss Miller."[10]

Miller's understanding of Newfoundlanders' thoughts and feelings about the First World War is reflected in her war poetry,[11] most of which focuses on the aftermath of the conflict and the collective memorialization of Newfoundland's fallen soldiers. One of her earliest war poems, however, features a woman who is waiting for her husband to return from the conflict. While she waits, this Newfoundland woman does what so many women of her generation did: she cares for her infant son and knits comforts for soldiers overseas. The poem is entitled "The Knitting Marianna," and it was featured in the 1916 issue of *The Distaff*.

Like the "Mariana" of Tennyson's original (the template of which Miller borrows, with apologies), Miller's Marianna is bereft in a dreary landscape after her loved one has abandoned her. But, unlike Tennyson's despairing woman, Miller's subject is determined to find purpose in work, work that is a practical and material way to help soldiers, like her husband, who are away at war. Miller's Marianna never contemplates the end of her own life, as does Tennyson's. Instead, she compares her own suffering to that of the soldiers in the trenches and, deeming it of lesser importance, steels herself for "the lonely years ahead."

THE KNITTING MARIANNA
(with apologies to Tennyson)

With blackest omen hung the clouds
The war clouds o'er a darkling world
Men mustered to the call in crowds.
The battle flags were all unfurled.
The homes they left were gloomed with care,
Where fields lay ripe before the door,
But all the homely tasks were o'er,
And Duty called them otherwhere.

She only said – "Oh heart so weary,
The lonely years ahead!
But living men are cold and dreary
And one must knit," she said.
...

And so at morn and noon and night,
Her needles joined the battle-song;
They clicked the glory of the right,
While comforts flourished, grey and long.[12]
Her idle tears away she flicked –
They only hindered needlecraft;
She smiled back when her baby laughed,
Grew wistful when he crowed and kicked.[13]

In Margot Duley's modern assessment of this poem, Miller "captures the courage, hard work and endurance of the many Newfoundland women who participated in the war effort," while also managing to represent "the mingled grief and pride in the war effort that was felt in many Newfoundland households."[14] And, while I agree with Duley that "The Knitting Marianna" gave voice to women whose hearts were breaking and whose lives were turned upside down as war raged in distant lands, it also reflects the frustration felt by women who had to stay at home while their men were away at battle. They, too, may have wanted to go and join the fight in some capacity. Indeed, many Newfoundland women did just that as nurses and volunteer ambulance drivers.[15] For the majority of Newfoundland women, however, their part in the war was a domestic one. This familial role of dedication to their hearths, coupled with their perceived duty to be providers of comforts for the war effort, was essential and valued as traditional women's labour. However, it was often a lonely and isolating experience, one that involved a great deal of both practical and emotional labour,[16] as Miller's poem evinces.

While the poem mentions women's knitting, it does not directly mention the WPA,[17] which was responsible for organizing the distaff work of hundreds of female volunteers and for getting the items delivered to the Newfoundland Regiment overseas.[18] As Margot Duley discusses (this volume), this organization and the work of its many volunteers was key to Newfoundland's war effort and gave women a new, and more respected, role in the public arena. It was a traditional role that simultaneously carried with it a novel dimension of public service. When the war was over, the record of this service lent women a public legitimacy in the realm of politics that they had not enjoyed previously.

Another striking feature of this particular poem is the trope of stoic motherhood that Miller invokes. Here is a mother raising her child in sadness while enduring hardship and sacrificing self as the wife of a soldier. Moreover, the woman symbolically represents a "mother of the nation,"[19] reproducing the next generation of soldiers while providing traditional support to current armies in the form of knitted clothing. Her distaff work is the work of all "good" Newfoundland women who can be considered as symbolic mothers of the nation, especially in a time of war. The mother's sacrifice parallels that of the soldier, yet, at the same time, is sublimated by the greater suffering of the men on the battlefield.[20]

Mothers in British colonies and former colonies like Newfoundland were also symbolic mothers and daughters of the Empire. Their work and sacrifices were considered necessary services to the King and the mother country of Great Britain. These were roles in which many women, including Phebe Florence Miller, took great pride. A letter to the women of the Empire sent by Queen Mary at the end of the Great War provides an excellent example of the discursive construction of women's key roles as imperial mothers and daughters. It had been forwarded to the president of the Daughters of the Empire (Newfoundland chapter), Mrs. Arch Macpherson, by the colonial secretary of Newfoundland on behalf of the governor. It was also sent to four prominent periodicals in Newfoundland at the time, the *Evening Telegram*, the *Daily News*, the *Mail and Advocate*, and the *Daily Star*.

In this missive, dated 5 December 1918, Her Majesty congratulates the women of the Empire on their performance during the war and encourages similar behaviour in the difficult time of rebuilding. It is a multi-layered message honouring the work of women during the war, while simultaneously encouraging them to remember the spirit of sacrifice that kept the home fires burning. She writes of the daughters of the Empire thus:

> During the war they have been given the high privilege of service, they have risen to the great opportunity and have proved their courage, steadfastness and ability ... I earnestly trust that though the thrill and glamour of war are over the spirit of selfsacrifice and helpfulness which it has kindled will not wane in the coming days ... Today more than ever the Empire needs her Daughters, for in the larger world of public and industrial work women are daily taking a more important place. As we have been united in all our work, whether of head or hands, in a real sisterhood of suffering and service during the war, let us go on working together with the same unity of purpose for the resettlement and reconstruction of our country. (sgd) Mary R.[21]

This letter encapsulates the spirit of Phebe Florence Miller's writing about the war years. In Miller's poetry about the war there is an acceptance of this hegemonic ideology of self-sacrifice and diligence for the mother country. Miller considered herself a daughter of the Empire, even though she does not explicitly identify as such. Evidence of this spirit can be seen in "The Knitting Marianna" and is further displayed in the other published poems I discuss below.

The trope of mother of the Empire would serve as a popular tool for maternalist feminist discourses that were often used during the successful women's suffrage campaign waged in Newfoundland in the decade following the First World War. The trope is particularly visible in the suffrage petition that was drawn up in 1920 by the Newfoundland Franchise League, which brought together members of the Women's Christian Temperance Union (WCTU) and the WPA, and was presented to the Newfoundland Dominion's House of Assembly. The petition was designed to call attention to the importance of women's acknowledged roles in Newfoundland society and to embarrass a government that lagged behind the rest of the Empire in terms of women's rights. It cited women's growing role in the work force and the unfairness of taxation of women without representation. The petition went on to mention women's war work alongside their traditional "business" of cooperatively running a household. It read, in part:

> We regard ourselves as Partners in the responsible business of homekeeping which is so vital to the best interest of the Dominion; and ... [T]he women of Newfoundland rose to every call made upon them during the Great War, and showed energy and executive ability in the organization of relief and other work, and that many of them served overseas as Nurses, VAD's and Ambulance Drivers.[22]

Even after this impassioned plea, Newfoundland women would not wrest franchise legislation from the Newfoundland government, under Walter S. Monroe, until 1925.[23]

Meanwhile, women (and men) of all political stripes would have become familiar with Phebe Florence Miller as she established herself as a prominent and serious poet by publishing numerous poems in local newspapers as well as *The Veteran* magazine and the *Newfoundland Quarterly*. While not a controversial figure, Miller was an artist who shared a concern with the wider public world, current events, and the state of the Newfoundland nation, much like the women of the WPA, the Ladies Reading Room,[24] and the WCTU. Such interest in public affairs was used as a second argument in favour of women's suffrage, in conjunction with discourses of maternal concern for the nation.

In contrast to "The Knitting Marianna," however, the majority of Miller's published poems about the war did not make explicit reference to women's work. These poems largely praised the male soldiers for their courage, endurance, and patriotism in a horrifying, though necessary, conflict.[25] Many of the poems featured women as grieving wives or sweethearts, mothers, and daughters, thus implicitly supporting their, and Miller's, roles as what Scates termed "mediators of loss and bereavement."[26] Witness Miller's poem, "The Little Silver Cross," published in the *Newfoundland Quarterly* in 1918:

THE LITTLE SILVER CROSS

My heart is aching with its sense of loss!
They hold to me a little silver cross –
The light smites it, athwart the white and blue
Of the brave ribbon that they pinned on you.
I only see a distant radiance shine
From out the years of glory that were mine ...
I feel, instead of silver, the dear thrill
Of your remembered touches; and my will,
That vowed so stoutly to refrain from tears,
Melts with the ache of unreturning years.[27]

In addition to reinforcing a gendered ideology of women's emotional labour, Miller's many poems functioned in various other ways to further the cause of nationalism, and to establish a certain cultural memory of the Great War, in Newfoundland. This idea of cultural memory is an important one, not only for the suffrage movement but also for the forces of nationalism that were felt in Newfoundland from the earliest agitations for self-governance in the 1830s until (and some would say beyond) Confederation with Canada in 1949. According to Maurice Halbwachs, one of the foundational thinkers on collective (or cultural) memory, it is only through social interaction that we acquire sustained memories about ourselves as groups. Such memory is a way for societies to understand past events through the lens of present concerns.[28]

In Newfoundland, cultural memory of the First World War has as its focus the devastating battle of Beaumont-Hamel on 1 July 1916, the anniversary of which became Memorial Day, a national day of remembrance. Of course, as contemporary concerns have shifted, so have interpretations of the battle.[29] However, in the early decades after the war, Newfoundlanders were largely led to believe that Beaumont-Hamel was a devastating, yet glorious crucible in which their nation was forged.[30] As Robert Harding asserts:

> By constructing a triumphant memory based upon selectivity, optimism, and conjured romanticism, local mythmakers hoped to offer grieving and bereaved Newfoundlanders an inspiring and noble message which rationalized their losses.[31]

Similarly, historian Sean Cadigan maintains that the most powerful authorities in Newfoundland at the time, those of British representatives and church leaders, joined forces after Beaumont-Hamel "in preaching duty to empire and glory, but the commemorations of the loss took on messianic overtones of sacrifice, resurrection and redemption."[32] The Newfoundland War Contingent Association, an elite group of men charged with the distribution of aid and comforts to Newfoundland soldiers and seamen overseas, issued the following statement after the battle's losses had been tallied: "Although we gloried in the noble sacrifices, our part was to care for the wounded, and comfort those whose men had died such glorious deaths, and the Casualty Lists that followed these glorious achievements in the field were sorrowful reading every morning."[33] In the face of such proselytizing discourse it would have been difficult to resist conversion to the cause of nationalism – even if temporarily.

Eric Caldicott and Anne Fuchs suggest that "cultural memory can be understood as a repertoire of symbolic forms and stories through which communities advance and edit competing identities."[34] Phebe Florence Miller's poem "The Silence," published in *The Veteran* in 1924, is an example of the cultural production of the time that served to perpetuate a particular memory of the Great War and the identities of those who were affected by it. The "messianic overtones," so prevalent in official messaging of the time, ring out in the poet's call for Newfoundlanders to "keep faith with the Silence" of fallen soldiers.

THE SILENCE

Today we keep the Silence –
The Silence that is yet so full of sound;
Of the call to arms;
Of silver bugle-notes;
Of droning drums;
Of brave mother-words spoken at the last moment;
Of lovers whispering in quiet places for the last time;
Of little kisses left on baby faces;
Of marching feet that vanish at the bend of the road –
Forever!

Then the wild fierce music of war
That fills us with glory even while it thrills us with pain!

The scream of falling shells;
The whine of bullets;
The tramp of the stretcher-bearers;
The throb of waiting hearts;
The wail –
Ah God, the wail of the mother, the maiden, the wife!
And then the Silence –
The intolerable echo of the Silence!
...

And hark!
Afar from the poppy-fields,
Where, "better than best,"
And with glory forever untarnished
Our brave ones sleep,
Comes, as a voice on the wind,
A message:

"For us it was no dream,
O Land that we died to shield!
We have left the music of life and its laughter;
Its wars, its problems, its honors.
Now it is yours to keep,
O keep, faith with the Silence!"[35]

This poem, along with a picture of the poet and an artistic border, appeared on a full page of the October 1924 edition of *The Veteran*. Published by the Great War Veteran's Association, the magazine enjoyed a good reputation and was widely read in the Dominion. The general tone of, and the advertising present in, *The Veteran* indicates that a male readership was assumed. Hence, many Newfoundlanders, mostly male, would have received Miller's plea for them to honour the memories of their glorious dead.

In slight contrast to "The Knitting Marianna," which appeared in *The Distaff* in 1916, the stalwart housewife whose "needles joined the battle-song" is nowhere present in this poem (also absent is the war nurse and the female ambulance driver). Women are given three roles, which are still defined by their relationship to men: mothers, maidens, and wives. They are present only as those who break the silence with brave words, whispered endearments, and piteous wailing.

As in "The Knitting Marianna," women are those left behind, those who maintain the maternal bonds of love through remembrance and grief, left to keep faith with the glorious war heroes and to honour their memory.

Their (male) memory would become Newfoundland's dominant cultural memory of the Great War, and while Miller does not specifically say that all of "our brave ones" are male soldiers, a reference that she uses in the poem implies that this is the case. "Better than Best" is a quotation from Field Marshal Haig, British commander in chief of the Newfoundland Regiment. Haig visited Newfoundland in July 1924 to help unveil the War Memorial at St. John's. A short chronicle of his visit, and a picture of him in full military regalia, feature in Miller's 1924 journal for the month of July.[36] According to Miller's entry, the Earl exclaimed, "while praising the 29th Division, to which the 1st Royal Nfld's were attached 'Newfoundlanders I salute you! You are better than the best!'" Miller felt this praise was well deserved and would "long make him beloved by Newfoundlanders everywhere."[37]

Beside the entry about her presence at the unveiling of the War Memorial in 1924 she pasted another of her poems about the war and its aftermath. "The Greater Remembrance" entreats Newfoundlanders to remember not only the war dead but also the war-wounded. It challenges Newfoundlanders to remember the heroes of the war in their hearts, not only in granite markers. Miller intimates that Newfoundlanders' memories of the war are fading and that their commitment to injured soldiers is lacking.

THE GREATER REMEMBRANCE

Keep them in remembrance!
For you they sacrificed the joy of life –
Paths, moonlight, starry nights and sunny days;
Home, idle hours, friendships, lovers' ways;
Chosen professions – flung them in the strife
To help the victory a Nation planned,
O Newfoundland!

...

Keep them in remembrance!
The Strong Man's Country – theirs they died to shield –
Shall strive to keep unspotted from the world
The honor of the banner they unfurled –

Verses in the Darkness

"Better than Best" – who rest in Flanders' Field!
Shall raise strong men to stand where they would stand,
O Newfoundland![38]

This poem, along with its accompanying journal entry, is once more assigning a particular meaning to the war – a meaning that resonates in Newfoundland's cultural memory of the conflict. According to Egyptologist Jan Assmann, cultural memory has distinctive temporal characteristics and methods of social transference:

> Distance from the everyday (transcendence) marks its temporal horizon. Cultural memory has its fixed points; its horizon does not change with the passing of time. These fixed points are fateful events of the past whose memory is maintained through cultural formation (texts, rites, monuments) and institutional communication (recitation, practice, observance). We call these "figures of memory."[39]

Miller's poem, her diary entry on the Marshal's visit, and her record of the unveiling of the War Memorial form a complex layering of cultural formations and institutional communication through which Newfoundland's cultural memory of the war was continually (re)created. The recitation of Marshal Haig's phrase "Better than Best" reinforces Newfoundland's connection to Empire even as the poem offers a Newfoundland-centric view of the conflict. Miller appeals to the Newfoundland national consciousness to remember the Great War and its fallen soldiers as a matter of national pride and dedication.

That Miller invokes these particular figures of memory in a journal submitted to a Canadian almanac contest is significant. For Miller, and many other Newfoundlanders, the First World War was a test of the Dominion of Newfoundland's mettle, a time when Newfoundland answered the call of the Empire and did so without reservation, thus proving its right to self-determination and statehood. Writing about Newfoundland in this manner, especially in a text meant for a Canadian readership, was a conscious effort to depict the island as a proud, independent nation, in every way an equal of Canada.

The first of July eventually became Canada Day and is celebrated as such in Newfoundland. However, it also remains Commemoration (Memorial) Day in the province. Today, in the midst of red-and-white flags and the celebration of Canada's imagined community,[40] the parades of veterans and soldiers file past the St. John's war memorial in the downtown core. Wreaths are laid and solemn speeches intoned as ceremonies are held commemorating the sacrifice of Newfoundlanders who have served in numerous conflicts overseas, and always the battle of Beaumont-Hamel remains the touchstone of Newfoundland's greatest loss.

As Liliane Weissberg posits: "Since the late eighteenth century, the political demands on memory have been particularly strong. The invention of nation-states called for a common past as well as a common future. Monuments urged the individual to remember, but to remember and define each individual as a member of a larger group."[41] National identities were created not only in monuments but also in poems about monuments, such as Miller's. Miller clearly wants to define Newfoundlanders as a people who share the common history of war, loss, and grief as well as a common future of remembrance.

Of course, cultural memory is not only enacted on a national scale but also on a more intimate, local scale as well. As Jay Winter, in his study of collective memory of the First World War, points out:

> The practice of naming on local war memorials is ... profoundly significant. It enabled ordinary people to locate this monumental moment in the history of the Empire within their own family narratives ... In a sense, touching the names, or just visiting the war memorials and placing on them a poppy, is a vital element in the preservation of the memory of empire.[42]

Local memorials to the Great War are certainly a key feature in Newfoundland's collective memory of the conflict. Phebe Florence Miller, ever a fervent supporter of Newfoundland, was also a dedicated citizen of Topsail, her life-long home. On the occasion of the unveiling of the Topsail War Memorial on 9 August 1922, Miller's poem, "Memory-Folded," was published in *The Veteran*.

MEMORY FOLDED

We hold you in lasting remembrance!

....

You, who on balmy nights of the Excursion, before the Black Cloud blotted out your world, were one with the gayness and the gladness that still goes by to the Railway Station;

....

Here, then, to You, whom we hold in lasting remembrance, in this Commemorative Corner, so redolent of your rich sweet youth, we set up our Memorial!
Here, in its polished granite your names are graven – deeply, deeply; here, for all time, they are written "golden forever, eagles, crying flames," that generations yet to be may learn of your glorious self-sacrifice!

Hills that you scaled in your strong young might, smile lovingly down upon them; meadows such as you tilled and reaped, slope gently down toward them; Constantly, under the wooden bridge, the brooklet whispers to them of well-remembered things;
And always, at night, when the sunset-glow has faded from their gold, your beloved, the Sea, sings in to them its murmurous requiem.

O in our hearts – the hearts that held you dear, those names are written in living letters, rainbow-edged with glory and with tears!
So, in this simple dignity of graven granite set amidst the landscape and the seascape that you loved; and in the loving hearts that held you dear –

We keep you in lasting remembrance![43]

Miller, in this poem, is defining the local setting as the place the young men of Topsail died to defend. She is bringing the conflict home through her evocation of the land and sea, the local spaces that she imagines were so beloved by the soldiers that they would give up their "rich sweet youth" to protect them. She connects the dead to the places they inhabited, places through which they now will be remembered. The people left behind are intimately linked to the place as well; the hearts of the people are the hearts of the land and sea.

Nowhere is Empire mentioned in this poem. Self-sacrifice is the glory of the dead, and it is implied that the sacrifice was for the localities they treasured, the land and sea upon which they farmed and fished, the bucolic pleasures of outport Newfoundland. It is these things, the poem implies, that they died for, not the glory and might of Empire or the far-flung ideals of democracy. Miller is personalizing the conflict at this moment of local memorial in Topsail, trying to find meaning in the deaths of so many resident sons on remote battlefields.

The names of these local sons are important, for they were often all that was left of those who died overseas. Many soldiers were buried in Europe near the battlegrounds on which they fell, and still others' remains were never recovered. Thus, names, etched in the very granite that makes up the rock that is Newfoundland, stand in for these missing bodies. The island itself might be the granite slab upon which the names are written, thus preserving the memory of the dead "in place," quite literally. The entire island was now, in Miller's evocation, a grave marker, a memorial to the fallen.

By 1926, Miller's poetry about the war had taken a different turn. The verse "Commemoration" was also published in *The Veteran* and provides yet another perspective on the conflict and its aftermath. In this verse Miller imagines a peaceful scene on the former battlefields of France. Fully eight years after the last shells tore through the earth and left people shattered in their wake, a new generation of children now play in blissful ignorance of such destruction.

Commemoration

O far away in sunny France –
So quiet now the guns are still!
The merry children sing and dance
Adown some sloping woodland hill.
....

They sit upon a grassy mound
To twine a wreath of roses rare;
They do not note the vivid ground,
Nor marvel that the flowers are fair.
....

For peace is over all the lands
Brooding with silent silver wings;
And children's little dimpled hands
Find beauty in the dust of things.

While here your favorite wood flowers blow
On slender vines that creep and cling;
I gather twin-flowers as I go –
Remembering, remembering.[44]

Memory is once again paramount, but now it is connected to living flowers, not granite monoliths. For Miller, there is no prescriptive need for the children to remember the conflict. Their vigil is unconscious and their ignorance of war a gift from those who lie beneath their playground: "Lest we forget" has not entered their consciousness. Miller does not have the heart to give them horrible memories. Memory is for those who cannot forget. Yet, here, memory is intertwined with renewal and growth, which is all around. Life is beginning again, despite all the death visited upon the soil. The dead are reborn in the flowers that bloom on the ground where they fell, and their memory is kept alive by those who enjoy their beauty.

These memories are more personal than national, though they too are part of the national consciousness. In this poem, Miller once again focuses on the trinity of memory – time past, present, and future. According to James Olney, "Memory, at least in part, is an adaptive function, with a self-adjusting and self-defining plasticity about it, turning back to the past so as to position itself and us for what is to be dealt with in the future."[45] When Miller wrote "Commemoration," eight years after the war, her thoughts had turned more fully towards the future. She had visions of a peaceful world where children would grow up not knowing the bloodshed that fertilized the flowers on French hillsides. Her vision is turned to a future time of peace in nations where war once reigned. For the poet, the Second World War is unimaginable at this moment. Indeed, in 1925, Newfoundland's new Memorial College was dedicated to the memory of fallen soldiers and seamen of the First World War.[46] On the occasion of the college's opening, the words of another local poet, Robert G. MacDonald, were read:

INSCRIPTION

Because they rest in grim Gallipoli;
Because they sleep on Beaumont Hamel's plain;
....

... in memory of them we,
Whose Land and theirs they saved, that not in vain
Their lives were given, have raised this fitting fane
....

To fertilize the mind of youth, to advance
And foster progress in a world at peace.[47]

Having come through "the war to end all wars," Miller and her contemporary MacDonald, like countless others, envisioned a lifetime of peace in which war was but a memory.

In a similar vein, with yet more distance between herself and the war, Miller composed another poem with recovery from the great world conflict on her mind. Penned in 1936 and entitled "From a Little Window," it envisions the poet as she gazes out her window at her young niece as she plays in the fields leading down towards Conception Bay and out to Bell Island. The island sits in the middle of the bay and was home to the world-famous iron ore mines that supplied so much raw material for both Allied and Axis armies.

From a Little Window

I look out from a little window
And I see things which are big:
A big blue bay with an island
That holds within its heart
An element which makes for mighty things –
Battleships to guard great nations;
Guns to deal death to the enemy;
Machinery to further the world's progress;
Railroads, that panting monsters may thunder by.
....
But now it is noontide.
And now I tap upon the little window,
And smile and wave my hand.
For now I see Elizabeth,
Three years old, and very, very sweet,
Scudding over the meadows,
Gathering simple buttercups –
Elizabeth,
With wind-curls in her hair,
And sunshine on her face!

And looking out of the little window
I forget all other mighty things;
For Elizabeth,
Three years old, and very, very sweet,
Holds the world, with all its mighty forces,
Between her small pink baby-hands.
And so Elizabeth is greater than them all![48]

This poem is certainly not of the same ilk as her flag-waving poems celebrating the courage of soldiers and long-suffering wives. In this poem, Miller epitomizes the antithesis of war in the tiny girl-child Elizabeth. For Miller, the female child who is cavorting in the meadow outside her window represents the combined forces of peace and renewal as she gathers flowers in her small hands. These forces, says the poet, are far greater than are those of mechanized progress and war as fuelled by the iron mines of Bell Island.

Miller, in this verse, seems to have grown tired of her patriotic poems of old. "From a Little Window" evinces a wearied acceptance of mechanized progress and a disillusioned familiarity with the conflicts of "great nations." One also gets the feeling, from the imagery of ostensibly masculine realms like war and industry juxtaposed with a small girl gathering wild flowers in a moment of innocence, that the poet was marking her own shift from darkness into light. Perhaps no longer content to be a nationalistic bard, justifying war and death, Miller wanted to cast her eye towards feminine signs of life and hope.

Perhaps indicative of a similar shift in the public mood after eighteen years of peace (but not prosperity), the poem was published, like so many of Miller's others, in *The Veteran*. This seems an unlikely venue, for such a sentiment did not fit terribly well with the hegemonic political discourses that Newfoundland's leaders clung to in the aftermath of the Great War. The war had to be justified and it had to be celebrated as an achievement by a struggling, and nearly bankrupt, Dominion in which national government had just been replaced by a non-democratic, British-appointed Commission of Government in 1934. Yet, as Cadigan points out, popular revolt was afoot: "Nationalism may have been fostered at Beaumont-Hamel, but it failed to thrive on war and railway debt, combined with neglect of the fisheries and cynicism about government's courting of international capital."[49] Transformation into nationhood was faltering.

In 1936, could the war, or at least the devastation at Beaumont-Hamel, be viewed absent its attendant shroud of nationalism without appearing to denigrate the memories of the thousands of dead and wounded soldiers, volunteers, and their families? Could it be seen as an event whose importance might be usurped by little girls with buttercups? Perhaps as partial answer, Miller's "From a Little Window" was featured in *The Veteran*, destined also to become part of Newfoundland's evolving cultural memory of the war.

As Jan Assmann notes, "Through its cultural heritage a society becomes visible to itself and to others. Which past becomes evident in that heritage and which values emerge in its identificatory appropriation tells us much about the constitution and tendencies of a society."[50] Thus, Phebe Florence Miller's contributions to Newfoundland's cultural memory of the First World War tell us a great deal about the general make-up of Newfoundland society in the early years of the war's aftermath.

It was a society that craved recognition as a nation, but one that also clung to its imperial connections. Proud of its defence of the Empire, and its unwavering answer to the call to war, Newfoundland created war memorials and other remembrances, such as the poetry of Phebe Florence Miller, which reflected the local landscape. It was a society fiercely proud of its sacrifice and of its war heroes. It was a society coping with the loss of a huge proportion of its young men, and not just in overseas battles. As Kevin Major describes Beaumont-Hamel: "It is the single greatest tragedy in the history of Newfoundland and Labrador. For a country of a quarter million, still reeling from the great seal hunt disasters of two springs before, it was a monstrous cruelty to bear."[51] Ultimately, it was a society, like so many others, that longed for a lasting peace.

Miller's artistic reactions to the realities of Beaumont-Hamel, and other bloody battles, acted as a diffuse light that shone on the pain and grief of a people struggling to find meaning in what must have seemed like irredeemable loss. It was light filtered through the longings of a quasi-nation attempting to assert itself on the global stage, yet still clinging to its imperial roots. Dominant ideologies of gender and nation were intricately negotiated within her bright art through poetic renderings of the many conflicting emotions felt by this foundering nation as it reeled from both human and economic devastation. As a result, Newfoundland's cultural memory of the Great War, which was both reflected in Miller's writing and created by it, must be contextualized by the impending collapse of the British Empire, the dynamics of Newfoundland nationalism, and the resurgence of feminist demands.

Miller's connections to, and influence upon, Newfoundland's suffrage movement are less clearly defined. Nonetheless, we can discern links, no matter how tenuous, between her writing life and that of the fledgling feminism of women in Newfoundland. Her publication of poems in *The Distaff* is but one connection,[52] yet it is an important one. It shows that she was in contact with the WPA and knew of its war work and that of its many female volunteers. Indeed, it demonstrates that she was sympathetic to their cause and inspired by their part in the war effort.

Further, the theme of stoic motherhood that runs through "The Knitting Marianna," while problematic for modern critics because of its nationalistic tendencies and imperial overtones, was powerful and resonated with Newfoundland men and women. This is why it became a key component of suffrage discourses in the successful postwar campaign for the franchise. Miller's life was also an unconventional example to other women who may have desired a life less ordinary. As an unmarried woman, a postmistress, and a poet, her roles in Newfoundland society may have been viewed with a mixture of complex emotions, ranging from pity to pride. Significantly, though, these roles were visible to many men and women throughout the Dominion. Miller was a literary figure when women in Newfoundland were not generally regarded as writers worth reading. As an exemplar of creativity and accomplished womanhood, Miller was a rare female role model.

Phebe Florence Miller was not a feminist caricature of the silenced woman of the past, nor was she a one-dimensional heroine who resisted all hegemonic gender ideologies. She was a poet and a woman of her times, one whose life and art are intricately intertwined with the cultural and societal norms of postwar Newfoundland. In its complexity, her poetry reveals an embedded and sometimes simultaneous mixing of acceptance and resistance to dominant ideologies of gender and national mythologies. Miller's art was both constituted by and constitutive of Newfoundland's shifting cultural memory of the war in the decades from 1914 to 1936.

Acknowledgments

Vicki Hallett would like to acknowledge the Institute for Social and Economic Research at Memorial University of Newfoundland for their support of her research. She would like to thank the editors of this collection for their hard work, dedication, and helpful editorial suggestions. As well, gratitude is extended to David Hopkins for everything.

Notes

1. Phebe Florence Miller, "The Knitting Marianna," *The Distaff* (1916): 10.
2. Miller would not be promoted to postmistress until 1928.
3. Margaret Atwood, *Negotiating with the Dead: A Writer on Writing* (Toronto: Anchor Books, 2003), xxiv.
4. An "outport" is a small coastal community in Newfoundland.
5. According to Bert Riggs' article "The Postmistress-Poet of Topsail," in *The Telegram* (St. John's), 8 July 2002: "The post office, which often housed the telegraph and wireless stations, was an important addition to many Newfoundland communities in the latter half of the nineteenth century. As the main centre for communications with the outside world, it was a gathering place where people learned of happenings both local and

international. It was vital that the person who operated these marvels of modern communications command the respect of the townspeople, as he or she was often privy to very personal and private information. Miller proved to be the soul of discretion, and during her long years of service to the community, she not only earned the respect of her fellow citizens, but became a true friend to all."

6 The Centre for Newfoundland Studies website describes *The Newfoundland Quarterly* thus: "The eminent *Newfoundland Quarterly* is Canada's longest running magazine, having started in 1901. It contains articles on all aspects of life and culture in Newfoundland and Labrador, written by the country's best authors." See http://collections.mun.ca/.

7 According to the Memorial University of Newfoundland Digital Archives Initiative (hereafter MUN DAI) website, "*The Veteran Magazine* is the organ of the Great War Veterans' Association of Newfoundland. It was published at St. John's, Newfoundland during the years 1920-1949." See http://collections.mun.ca/.

8 The Women's Patriotic Association, which published the magazine, was a crucial organization in the Franchise Movement after the war. The document description for *The Distaff*, on the MUN DAI website, explains: "A publication of the Women's Patriotic Association (WPA) during the First World War, *The Distaff*'s goal was 'obtaining funds to help the Red Cross branch of the Women's Patriotic Association. We are truly a woman's paper, devoting our space to an account of the work done in various spheres by energetic wives and daughters in Newfoundland.' (1916, p. 1) The success of the first issue in 1916 prompted a second one in 1917, and these are the only known issues." See http://collections.mun.ca/.

9 "The Bard of Terra Nova" is a reference to E.J. Pratt, still Newfoundland's most famous poet.

10 "Miss P. Florence Miller and her Cultivation of the Muse," *Newfoundland Quarterly* 22, 3 (1922): 25.

11 Joan Montgomery Byles, in her text *War, Women and Poetry, 1914-1945* (Newark: University of Delaware Press, 1995), 44, argues that "war poetry" should not be narrowly defined as poetry written from the front lines of war: poetry written by women outside the theatre of war, "the poetry of grief, mourning, and loss ... the poetry of protest, ... and the poetry of survival" must also be considered war poetry.

12 The "comforts flourished grey and long" is a reference to the famous wartime "Newfoundland Sock."

13 Miller, "Knitting Marianna," lines 1-12, 37-44.

14 Margot I. Duley, *Where Once Our Mothers Stood We Stand* (Charlottetown: Gynergy Books, 1993), 56-57.

15 Women's work as part of the Voluntary Aid Division in the First World War is well documented. For a first-person account, see Bert Riggs and William Rompkey, eds., *Your Daughter Fanny: The War Letters of Francis Cluett, VAD* (St. John's: Flanker Press, 2006). See also Terry Bishop Stirling and Linda Quiney's chapters in this volume.

16 The unpaid and unsung labour of Australian women during the First World War is the subject of Bruce Scates' article "The Unknown Sock Knitter: Voluntary Work, Emotional

Labour, Bereavement and the Great War," *Labour History* (Australia) 81 (2001): 29-49. Scates suggests that women's unpaid labour for the war effort included the knitting and distribution of comforts, and the unrecognized emotional labour entailed in these efforts, plus their negotiations of a nation's grief and sorrow.

17 Although there is no positive proof, it is highly likely that Miller knit for the WPA during the Great War, as she is known to have done during the Second World War. In a diary entry dated 11 March 1943, Miller records, "Knitted for WPA tonight." See Memorial University of Newfoundland (hereafter MUN), Archives and Manuscripts Division (hereafter AMD), P. Florence Miller Collection, 1943 diary, file 1.01.007, coll-016. The poem "The Knitting Marianna" shows that Miller was aware of the work of the WPA in the 1914-18 conflict and of that of women all over the island, who were creating warm garments for soldiers overseas. The poem reflects her deep respect for, and insight into, women's motivations for doing this work.

18 Distaff work is the traditional work of clothes making and knitting, usually done by women.

19 Such mothers, in predominantly white settler societies like Newfoundland, were implicitly reproducing the dominant white race and the hegemonic structures of patriarchal nationhood through not only physical reproduction of children but also through the symbolic production of cultural traditions. For analyses of women as racialized and gendered mothers of the nation, see Nira Yuval Davis and Floya Anthias, *Women-Nation-State* (London: Macmillan, 1995); Anne McClintock, *Imperial Leather: Race, Gender and Sexuality in the Colonial Conquest* (London: Routledge, 1995); Nira Yuval-Davis, *Gender and Nation* (London: Sage, 1997); and Enakshi Dua, "Beyond Diversity: Exploring the Ways in which the Discourse of Race Has Shaped the Institution of the Nuclear Family," in *Scratching the Surface: Canadian, Anti-Racist, Feminist Thought*, ed. Enakshi Dua and Angela Robertson, 237-59 (Toronto: Women's Press, 1999).

20 Lynn Kennedy (this volume) analyzes the symbolic roles of mothers in the war. For further discussion of mothers as symbolic bearers of the nation's grief, see Suzanne Evans' chapter in this volume.

21 Provincial Archives of Newfoundland and Labrador, GN 2.14.61, Women's Patriotic Association of Newfoundland. The importance of the WPA in war work as well as in gaining the franchise is examined in Duley, *Where Once Our Mothers*, as well as in her chapter in this collection and in Gale Warren's "Voluntarism and Patriotism: Newfoundland Women's War Work during the First World War" (MA thesis, Memorial University of Newfoundland, 2005).

22 Duley, *Where Once Our Mothers Stood*, 81-82.

23 And then the satisfaction was not full because women's voting age was twenty-five to men's twenty, and, in municipal elections, only female property holders got the franchise.

24 Largely upper-class St. John's women peopled the Ladies Reading Room, formed in St. John's in 1909. These were women with an interest in literature, politics, and debate. The Ladies Reading Room would prove to be a fertile breeding ground for feminist action. See Duley, *Where Once Our Mothers*, 42, for a full description.

25 Jane Potter, in her study of non-elite women's writing during the First World War, *Boys in Khaki, Girls in Print* (Oxford: University of Oxford Press, 2005), suggests that, while there was considerable protest of the war in the literature of the period, "most of what was published, particularly popular fiction and active service autobiography, was supportive of the war effort or, at the very least, accepted its necessity" (3). Similar sentiments can be found in the poetry of Newfoundland women and men, as presented in Elizabeth Russell Miller, ed., *Arms and the Newfoundlander: Poetry of the Great War* (St. John's: Harry Cuff Publications, 1994); in poems by British and German women as discussed by Byles in *War, Women and Poetry;* and in the work of American poet Martha Dickinson Bianchi, as analyzed by Marcy Tanten in "Martha Dickinson Bianchi: War Poet," *New England Quarterly* 80, 2 (2007): 317-21.

26 Scates, "Unknown Sock Knitter," 29.

27 Phebe Florence Miller, "The Little Silver Cross," lines 1-10, *Newfoundland Quarterly* 18, 2 (1918): 12, available at http://collections.mun.ca/.

28 Maurice Halbwachs, *On Collective Memory,* trans. Lewis A. Coser (Chicago: University of Chicago Press, 1992), 38.

29 For example, see Kevin Major's account of the battle in his history of the province, *As Near to Heaven by Sea: A History of Newfoundland and Labrador* (Toronto: Penguin, 2001). He describes the British decision to send the Newfoundland Regiment over the top as "a display of unfathomable stupidity," which treated the Newfoundland soldiers "like so much colonial excess" (330). Major does agree, though, that Newfoundlanders at the end of the war, and for decades after, wanted desperately to believe that the battle was justified. He also writes that Newfoundland nationalism was buoyed up by the war: "By the time peace came in 1918 Newfoundland had changed irrevocably. The war affirmed Newfoundland's view of itself as a separate nation, if but a minor one still under the considerable influence of Britain" (334). At Beaumont-Hamel the Newfoundland Regiment had lost 233 men, seen 386 wounded, and another 91 missing.

30 Joseph R. Smallwood and Robert D.W. Pitt, eds., *Encyclopedia of Newfoundland and Labrador,* vol. 1 (St. John's: Newfoundland Book Publishers, 1967), dedicates over four pages to the account of the Battle of Beaumont-Hamel. The piece describes the battle in detail and ends with a description of the large memorial site in France on property bought by the Newfoundland government. As for the effects of the battle felt in Newfoundland, the *Encyclopedia* says this: "The tragic losses incurred by the Newfoundland Regiment at Beaumont Hamel affected all areas of Newfoundland. The soldiers had come from all parts of the Colony and death has not discriminated between rich and poor, fisherman's son or merchant's son" (163) – a fine bit of unifying cultural memory in its own right.

31 Robert J. Harding, "Newfoundland's Cultural Memory of the Attack at Beaumont-Hamel, 1916-1925," *Newfoundland and Labrador Studies* 21, 1 (2006): 3.

32 Sean T. Cadigan, *Newfoundland and Labrador: A History* (Toronto: University of Toronto Press, 2009), 188.

33 Henry Reeves, *The Newfoundland War Contingent Association, 1915-1919, Final Report* (St. John's: The Newfoundland War Contingent Association, 1919), 17. The men who comprised the association were largely members of the elite class, who held various

leadership roles in Newfoundland and Great Britain or were destined to do so. As Sir E.P. Morris put it in a speech at the association's general meeting on 7 November 1917, "I hope I am not putting it too highly when I say that in future the open sesame to high office – civic as well as state office – will be through the Newfoundland War Contingent Association" (68).

34 Edric Caldicott and Anne Fuchs, eds., *Cultural Memory: Essays on European Literature and History* (Oxford: Peter Lang Press, 2003), 18.

35 P.F. Miller, "The Silence," lines 1-20, 26-38, *Veteran* 4, 3 (1924): 40, available at http://collections.mun.ca/.

36 This 1924 journal was a hand-crafted scrapbook-type manuscript that Miller sent to Dr. Chase's Great Almanac Contest, a Canadian diary-writing contest for which she won first prize. She also won first prize for her 1920 submission. The cover of the 1920 journal bears a picture of a Newfoundland caribou. In the introduction to the journal, Miller writes, "the caribou in birch-bark on the front cover is our war-symbol, splendidly worn by the Royal Newfoundland Regiment in the Great War." In these journals she writes about her daily life. She includes poems and details special events each month. In July 1924 she wrote a long entry about the unveiling of the St. John's War Memorial on 1 July. Here she recorded Earl Haig's comments about Newfoundland's soldiers. See MUN, AMD, Journal 1924, Florence Miller Collection, coll-016.

37 Interestingly, Kevin Major mentions the Earl's visit to unveil the War Memorial in his 2001 history. Major's depiction of the Earl and the welcome he received is decidedly less reverent than Miller's, referenced in note xxxvi: "And when the commander in chief himself, Douglas Haig, arrived in St. John's in 1924 to unveil the noble monument to the war that rises above the east end of Duckworth and Water Streets, he was welcomed with a display of pomp and pageantry termed 'the largest and most spectacular of its kind in the history of the country.' Royalty itself would hardly have been paid more homage" (331-32).

38 MUN, AMD, lines 1-7, 15-21, Journal 1924, Florence Miller Collection, coll-016.

39 Jan Assman, "Collective Memory and Cultural Identity," *New German Critique* 65 (1995): 129.

40 Benedict Anderson, *Imagined Communities: Reflections on the Origins and Spread of Nationalism,* London: Verso, 1983).

41 Liliane Weissberg, "Introduction," in *Cultural Memory and the Construction of Identity,* ed. Liliane Weissberg and Dan Ben-Amos, 1-15 (Detroit: Wayne State University Press, 1999), 12.

42 Jay Winter, *Remembering War: The Great War between Memory and History in the Twentieth Century* (New Haven, CT: Yale University Press, 2006), 178.

43 P.F. Miller, "Memory Folded," lines 1, 5-7, 12-26, *Veteran* 2, 3 (1922): 27.

44 P.F. Miller, "Commemoration," lines 1-4, 9-12, 17-24, *Veteran* 5, 4 (1926): 24.

45 James Olney, *Memory and Narrative: The Weave of Life Writing* (Chicago: University of Chicago Press, 1998), 343.

46 Memorial College would eventually grow to become Memorial University of Newfoundland.

47 Robert G. MacDonald, "Inscription," lines 1-2, 5-7, 13-14 in *Arms and the Newfoundlander: Poetry of the Great War,* ed. Elizabeth Russell Miller (St. John's: Harry Cuff Publications, 1994), 59. MacDonald wrote the poem specifically for the opening of the college.
48 P.F. Miller, "From a Little Window," lines 1-9, 14-30, *Veteran* 11, 2 (1936): 56.
49 Cadigan, *Newfoundland and Labrador*, 208.
50 Assman, "Collective Memory," 133.
51 Major, *As Near to Heaven*, 330.
52 Miller published a second poem in the 1917 issue of *The Distaff* entitled "The Way o' Things," but it was not directly related to the war and so I have not included it as part of this larger discussion.

"'Twas You, Mother, Made Me a Man"
The Motherhood Motif in the Poetry of the First World War

Lynn Kennedy

In the popular memory of Canadians, the First World War has become the moment at which their country came of age. Through its sacrifices on the battlefield and its efforts on the home front, it is believed, Canada threw off its identity as a dependent child of Mother England and claimed a place of respect for itself within the imperial family. In some ways, the poetry that Canadians wrote during this period reflected this growing sense of self. The changing symbolism in this poetry, particularly the use of motherhood metaphors, suggests an emerging emphasis on Canadian independence and self-reliance. Before the war, the poets of the young nation had evoked first Britain, and later, the Canadian landscape as the nurturers of a national identity. But increasingly during the war, poets focused their attention on the experiences and sacrifices of real women and mothers. Yet, ultimately, this transformation wrought by the war, both in poetic motifs and for the women to whom these motifs referred, remained incomplete. Tracing the poetic representations of Canadian motherhood in the poems of this era through these metaphors illuminates the nation's struggle to symbolically come of age.

Motherhood, throughout the nineteenth century, had been deemed the fundamental role of Canadian women. Of course women had fulfilled myriad other social and economic functions, but in the ideals of Victorian womanhood the conjoined identities of wife and mother dominated the lives of most women. Society rewarded women for fulfilling these roles with poems, prose, and other artistic expressions idealizing the motherhood role. "My Wife," written by

Lieutenant-Colonel J.R. Wilkinson, offers an example of this sentimentalization of being a wife and mother:

> I want her with the children
> To guard their tender feet;
> To soothe and ever bless them
> With her presence fair and sweet.
> 'Tis mother's subtle influence
> That makes or mars us all:
> By her early lessons given
> We either rise or fall.[1]

Such paeans suggested that this nurturing role contributed not only to the well-being of a woman's immediate family but also to the moral character of the nation. With the coming of the Great War, women's role in nurturing citizens and soldiers willing to defend their country would take on additional political import in the national discourse.

The use of motherhood in defining a patriotic purpose was not unique to Canada. Social theorist Martha Fineman notes that motherhood serves as a powerful political symbol because, "as a lived experience, Mother is virtually universally shared in our culture and, therefore, more intimately and intensely personalized than many other symbols."[2] For many years, the link between national identity and motherhood in Britain, and by extension the Empire, had been embodied in Queen Victoria. The mother of nine children, Victoria became the metaphorical mother of all Britain – the public matriarch. National motherhood, however, was not merely the duty of the sovereign. British society sanctified the patriotic role of mothers from all walks of life. The ideal suggested that British mothers raised proper citizens who would then spread British values throughout the Empire.[3] Poets and novelists summoned this imagery to garner support when the British war effort required such. British poet Margaret Peterson, for example, penned "A Mother's Dedication" during the First World War, ending with the lines "You are my all, I give you to the Nation, / God shall uphold you that you fight aright."[4] The poet thus extols the ultimate maternal sacrifice, the willing relinquishment of a son for the good of the nation.

The United States also created a link between motherhood and patriotic citizenship with the development of the ideal of "Republican Motherhood." The popular nineteenth-century American writer Lydia Sigourney directly linked motherhood to "the vital interests of our country," writing that "the degree of her [a mother's] diligence in preparing her children to be good subjects of a just government, will be the true measure of her patriotism."[5] Americans would also turn to maternal imagery when they became involved in the Great War. For example, the Four Minute Men, a group established to promote the American war effort, used a poem called "It's Duty Boy" in their presentations. In this verse a mother encourages her son to join the fight, stating "I'd rather you had died at birth or not been born at all, / Than know that I had raised a son who cannot hear the call."[6] Similarly, the popular song "America Here's My Boy" asserted that there were "a million mothers" willing to give their sons to the cause. The chorus begins:

> America, I raised a boy for you.
> America, You'll find him staunch and true,
> Place a gun upon his shoulder,
> He is ready to die or do.[7]

Clearly, supporters of the war in both the United States and Britain believed that maternal symbolism had great powers of moral suasion, able to convince both mothers and sons to give their all to the cause.

The popular narrative of the First World War in Canada, when it involves women at all, generally focuses on the increasing role that women took in the public sphere in the wake of this crisis. And indeed, as a number of the chapters in this volume demonstrate, an increasing number of women found employment, either paid or volunteer, to support the war effort. Ruth A. Frager and Carmela Patrias's study of women workers in Canada suggests that women employed in manufacturing increased from 70,700 in 1915 to approximately 113,000 in 1918. While women working in non-traditional fields challenged existing gender assumptions, and employment for young, single women became more accepted in the postwar years, the movement of women into jobs traditionally gendered male ended with the war.[8] The actual transformation in the lives of most women caused by the war, at least economically, remained somewhat limited. At the same time, motherhood remained an important role, both in the lived experience of most women and in the prominence it was given in the patriotic art and literature of this era. Authors and artists, as well as government officials, demanded of Canadian women a more activist maternal role, with representations of maternal sacrifice meant to inspire the sacrifice of others.

In these actions, the nation sought to attain a sense of self-reliance and shared national purpose, represented in the changing poetic and metaphorical uses of motherhood (if not in the lives of mothers themselves).

Poems have rarely been given the same respect as politics in defining the national identity, yet the metaphors and symbols used in these artistic expressions reveal much about how the nation understood itself and its position in the world. Literary scholars have emphasized the central importance of poetry to the Canadian reading public, particularly during the late nineteenth and early twentieth centuries. Donna Bennett, for example, notes that "poetry was the dominant form of 'literary' writing in Canada until the 1920s, and remained the most valued form long after."[9] Writing in the interwar years, Lionel Stevenson also celebrated poetry as the most important of literary forms that had been produced in Canada: "The poet draws his life from the latent forces of the country, and in his turn he gives form to that which must otherwise remain unrevealed to men."[10] Stevenson's words suggest not only the value placed on poetry but also its strong link to a sense of national identity.

Leon Surette suggests that "Canadian literary criticism has always been an enterprise in which the central purpose was the discovery of the Canadian-ness of the literature written in the country."[11] Nationalist poetry provides a direct insight into the shared symbolic language of the nation at any given point and, particularly, of Canada's maturing sense of itself as a nation. Such poetry presented a national sentiment distilled into the most essential ideas and metaphors. Don Gutteridge, writing about his own experiences as a poet of Canadian themes in the 1970s, argues that the poet's task is to locate myths and blueprints that "give our lives, separately or collectively, their unique *curve of meaning*. He asserts that, if the poet and audience share a similar background, then the meaning becomes profound: "If the poet belongs to the reader's own culture, or nation, the common elements of the symbol-patterns (the mythology of the poem) may be more numerous and recognizable than otherwise. Besides the universally human nature of the myths discovered, there will be a level of identification which can only be described as *nation-al*."[12] A similar sentiment was expressed by Lieutenant Colonel J.R. Wilkinson in 1899, who wrote in the introduction to a collection of his own poems:

> Rhythm and harmony may not always present that mysterious appeal to the soul that approves, and proves the worth of all. Yet, withal, I feel that some thoughts and emotions of patriotism, love of home, the song of nature,

the mystery of creation, and the impenetrable depths of infinitude, may be found and approved.[13]

The poet in this conception becomes an instrument in the creation of national identity, providing a useable set of symbols and metaphors.

Even before the crisis of the Great War created an urgent need to forge a cohesive sense of nationalism, poets, as well as politicians and social commentators, struggled with what an independent Canadian national identity might entail and how to instill this patriotic feeling into its citizens. In 1871, William A. Foster, a Toronto barrister and a leader in the Canada First Movement, lamented that, while "the citizen of the United States has a flag of his own, and a nationality of his own – the Canadian has ever had to look abroad for his."[14] In the following decades, Canadians continued to look to many sources to establish who they were as a nation. Britain and the Empire at first exerted the most powerful influence on this sense of self. Then the magnitude and grandeur of the Canadian geography began to provide a more independent sense of identity. Finally, a focus on individual citizens and the contributions that they made to their country emerged during the First World War era, marking a new sense of the nation's self-reliance.

In the years immediately following Confederation, literary references to Canada as an infant or child suggested a national identity that, while showing future promise, had not been fully formed. Poets and rhetoricians rushed to reaffirm the nascent nation's reliance on, and allegiance to, the "Mother Country." In a speech given before the Canadian Parliament, John A. Macdonald reassured his audience: "Some are apprehensive that the very fact of our forming this union shall hasten the time when we shall be severed from the Mother country. I have no apprehension of that kind. I believe it will have a contrary effect."[15] John George Bourinot, the clerk of the Canadian House of Commons, wrote: "The Confederation is only in its infancy, and yet it is proving its capacity for national expansion." But he then added that "the connection with the parent State does not depend on mere sentimentalism, but rests on the firm basis of sincere affection."[16] Confederation poet Charles G.D. Roberts reiterated the new nation's youth and promise in the last lines of his "An Ode to Canada":

O strong hearts of the North,
Let flame your loyalty forth,

And put the craven and base to an open shame,
Till earth shall know the Child of Nations by her name![17]

While the tone of this poem is laudatory, it suggests that the glory of the new nation lies in the future. For the present, most poets and politicians agreed, Canada needed to maintain its imperial roots; until Canada had a more fully formed self-identity, it would rely on Britain as its nurturer and guide – in other words, its "mother" country.

Into the early twentieth century, Canadian poets continued to celebrate Britain as their imperial parent. Wilfred Campbell's "England" hails that country as "the power of a world and the heart of a race." Canada is tied to this power as an imperial offspring:

And we of the newer and vaster West,
Where the great war-banners are furled,
And commerce hurries her teeming hosts,
And the cannon are silent along our coasts;
Saxon and Gaul, Canadians claim
A part of the glory and pride and aim
Of the Empire that girdles the world.[18]

Poet H.C. Cockin presents a similar theme in "This Fair Canadian Land":

O, Britain, dear Britain, ever glorious nation!
Whose strong arm in peace nigh engirdles the earth:
Canadians turn yet, aye, in proud exultation,
To the mother of nations that gave to them birth.[19]

In these poems the identity of the new nation remains firmly tied to Britain, much as a child's identity is tied to that of its mother.

In the late nineteenth century the land, and Canada's geographic assets, began to compete with the mothering role of Britain in shaping the national character and identity. Over forty years ago, Carl Berger identified the importance that the land has had in shaping a unique sense of national identity, writing of "the idea that Canada's unique character derived from her northern location, her severe winters and her heritage of 'northern races.'" In the same collection,

Frank Watt writes that "the one safe common denominator of all nationalistic Canadian writing is the land itself."[20] The essayist and poet Edward H. Dewart suggests a similar interpretation, arguing: "Countries of stern climate and unproductive soil have given some of the higher examples of unselfish patriotism. It is like a mother's love, instinctive and spontaneous."[21] Other late nineteenth-century poets and social commentators began to evoke the land as the "mother" of an emerging sense of independent nationalism, suggesting that Canada was on the "verge of national Manhood."[22]

Poets also linked a Canadian respect for freedom with the "nurturing" of the land. Thomas D'Arcy McGee begins his poem "Freedom's Journey" with the lines: "Freedom! A nursling of the North, / Rocked in the arms of stormy pines."[23] Similarly, Robert Kernighan's poem, "The Men of the Northern Zone," states: "Our hearts are as free as the rivers that flow / In the seas where the north star shines; / Our lives are as free as the breezes that blow / Thro' the crests of our native pines."[24] Kernighan clearly invests the land with mothering qualities, but he also invokes flesh-and-blood mothers to encourage a defence of the freedom that the land provides, asking:

> Shall the mothers that bore us bow the head
> And blush for degenerate sons?
> Are the patriot fires gone out and dead?
> Oh, brothers, stand to your guns![25]

Such poetic sentiments foreshadow the symbolic used of motherhood in the poetry of the First World War.

When this war began Canada was still a relatively young nation, still growing into a sense of national identity. War poetry, particularly popular verse, became a useful tool for encouraging a national sentiment, particularly given the growing centrality of Great War propaganda. Governments of the combatant nations turned to the developing field of advertising to sell the war. Pamphlets, posters, public speakers, and songs created a shared sense of national purpose. Canadian authors produced novels, essays, and poetry to garner support and to encourage personal sacrifice for the war effort.[26] Many of these artistic expressions found an immediate audience in newspapers and magazines; and even before the war's end, collections such as John Garvin's *Canadian Poems of the Great War* (1918) assured some of these poems a more permanent existence. In his foreword to this work, Garvin opines: "Great poets are the seers and prophets of a nation – of the world ... All writers of good verse cannot be great poets, and it is only the works of the latter that permanently endure; but those of minor qualities reflect and influence their own generation, and have an important mission in the evolution of national life."[27] War poetry's use as a marker of national identity thus becomes significant, and in the shifting symbolic uses of motherhood in this poetry we see the emergence of the idea of the First World War as Canada's coming of age.

Many of the symbolic motifs popular in the prewar era continued to have resonance during the First World War. The imagery of the imperial mother-child relationship had not disappeared. In fact, many Canadians continued to see their service in the war as part of their imperial duty. Britain, as a mother, was female, while the service offered by Canada focused on its male soldiers. For example, in Elspeth Honeyman's poem "Canada's Answer," she writes:

> Hear, O Mother of Nations, in the battle of Right and Wrong,
> The voice of your youngest nation, chanting her battle-song:
> Blood of your best you gave us, gave it that we might live
> Blood of our best we offer, the best of our youth we give.
> The price of a nation's manhood we offer to pay the debt –
> Did you dream, O Mother of Nations, that Canada could forget?[28]

The evocation of the "nation's manhood" suggests a recognition of Canada's growing maturity, but Britain continues to hold the dominant adult role in this poetic representation.

A similar formulation exists in Blanche E. Holt Murison's "The Mothering Heart." It is the relationship between imperial mother and Canadian soldier that forms the active relationship in the first stanza of the poem, which concludes: "The Mothering Heart of Empire / Is proud of its sons today." Ultimately, however, the poem shifts, giving the role of individual mothers equal importance to the role of imperial loyalties. The final stanza concludes:

> The Mothering Heart of Empire
> Is breaking with wild alarms.
> Dear God! Give peace, and bring them back,
> The sons to their mother's arms

> The glamour and glory of war! O men!
> The cost of it who can say?
> For only God and the mothers know
> The price that the mothers pay.[29]

The coexistence of this symbolism may suggest the tenuousness of Canada's growing independence. In this period of strife, the loyalty to Empire, nurtured over many years, drew Canada into the battle, but the nurturing influence of Canadian mothers provided the symbolic strength of the nation. Yet the sacrifices of real Canadian mothers began to supplant references to the imperial mother in much of the poetry of the First World War. Canadian mothers were not merely standing by in the war effort but taking an active role of their own.

The land also continued as a leading motif. During that war, Thomas Harkness Litster's "The Sons of 'Our Lady of Snows,'" celebrates the role that the Canadian landscape played in creating soldiers capable of defending their nation:

> They may come from the land of frost and snow,
> From the place where icicles grow,
> But they hold their own with the best of earth,
> Proud of the "Lady" who gave them birth
> Are the sons of "our Lady of Snows."[30]

The "Lady" in this poem is clearly the land, and the nurturing influences of both Empire and landscape remained salient symbols during the First World War. The portrayal of sacrificing, flesh-and-blood Canadian mothers, however, joined, and often superseded, these more metaphorical representations of motherhood. The evocation of the sacrifices of its citizenry provided a symbolic representation of Canada's "coming of age." And while Canadian soldiers took their place on the battlefield, the maternal sacrifice of women on the home front further shaped this new Canadian consciousness.

In 1911, *Saturday Night* published an essay suggesting the need to glorify mothers specifically because of their role in creating national sentiment:

> There is one class of women to whom no nation pays tribute in marble or bronze, but without whom no stable nation could long maintain the equal

fight with its neighbors. They are the noble, self-sacrificing mothers who toil and deny themselves to rear to manhood and womanhood the sons and daughters of the land. Only by the feeble words of the pen is tribute and honor paid them. Let us not be chary in our words of praise and commendation of our Canadian mothers, whose sons and daughters are so nobly guiding the helm of Destiny in this grand old Dominion towards the shores of success. Since their praises are not graven on tablets of stone, let them often be sung by tongue and pen.[31]

Such words represent a faith in the power of individual mothers to shape the citizenry of Canada. The Canadian branch of the Woman's Christian Temperance Union made similar references to the connection between motherhood and the strength of the nation. For this organization, motherhood was not merely a metaphor for nationalism, it was the actual force behind national identity. A 1912 editorial entitled "A God-Fearing Patriotism the Supreme Need" makes this position clear: "True patriotism is not merely a sentimental love for the maple leaf, or what not, but it is love prepared to sacrifice unto death for the best and highest interests of its country ... The vital question is not one of material resources, but rather in what moulds are the concepts and ideals of the coming citizenship going to be shaped."[32] The suggestion is that mothers would be responsible for shaping this patriotic citizenry.

A poem by Joaquin Miller for the WCTU's newsletter presents a similar theme. The first stanza reads:

> The bravest battle that ever was fought –
> Shall I tell you where and when?
> On the maps of the world you will find it not,
> 'Twas fought by the mothers of men.
> O, not with cannon and battle-shot,
> With sword or with noble pen.
> O, not with eloquent word or thought
> From the lips of wonderful men,
> But way down deep in a woman's heart –
> A woman who would not yield,
> Who bravely, silently did her part –
> There is that battle field.[33]

Such sentiments would become increasingly prevalent, and emotionally resonant, as Canada ventured into the First World War.

Many voices in Canadian culture urged a more activist role for women during the Great War, more so than during previous decades, reflecting their necessary contributions to the nation's war effort. Nellie McClung, a leading Canadian feminist, recognized the importance of women's participation on the home front and the sacrifices that they would be asked to make. McClung presented her 1917 work, *The Next of Kin*, as a record of the sentiments of Canadian women. To suggest women's general disdain for war she quotes a woman who queried: "What do the women of the world think of war? No woman ever wanted war, did she? No woman could bring a child into the world, suffering for it, caring for it, loving it, without learning the value of human life, could she?" In the midst of the crisis, however, McClung intimated that Canadian women would sacrifice if it was for a larger purpose: "I am willing to give my boy to die for others if I am sure that the others are going to be saved, but I am not willing that he should die in vain."[34] McClung touches on a similar theme in a poem included in this work entitled "At The Last!" Taking on the voice of a fallen soldier, she evokes the pain and despair of a mother who learns that her son has been lost. But she then offers words of reassurance:

> She's thinking of the thirst and pain;
> She's thinking of the saddest things;
> She does not know an angel came
> And led me to the water-springs,
> She does not know the quiet peace
> That fell upon my heart like rain,
> When something eased the scorching pain.
> She does not know, I gladly went
> And am with Death, content, content.[35]

This theme of ultimate sacrifice, shaping the experience not just of the soldiers but also of the mothers who let them go, appeared in many poems and novels written during this period.

A few poets also sought to render poetic the practical contributions of women on the home front. These verses extol the value of this labour and attempt to encourage others to do their part. Katherine Hale, for example, turns the traditional female task of knitting for the soldiers into a poetic celebration of women's contribution to the war effort:

> A tiny click of little wooden needles,
> Elfin amid the gianthood of war;
> Whispers of women, tireless and patient,
> Who weave the web afar.
>
> ....
>
> I like to think that soldiers, gaily dying
> For the white Christ on fields with shame sown deep,
> May hear the tender song of women's needles,
> As they fall fast asleep.[36]

While the final stanza seems to lack some of the moral certitude of the soldier's purpose as expressed in many war poems, the womanly contribution of knitting is clearly celebrated as worthy. Vicki Hallett's chapter in this volume examines the work of Newfoundland poet Phebe Florence Miller, including her poem "The Knitting Mariana," which also presents a vision of stoic motherhood – knitting while the men go off to war. The war turned such common tasks into symbolic activities, but it could also demand new contributions and labour patterns.

Nellie McClung suggests that taking up the work of the home front is a means of escaping some of the worry experienced by "Those Who Wait and Wonder":

> O work – thrice blessed of the gods –
> Abundant may you be!
> To hold us steady, when our hearts
> Grow cold and panicky!
>
> I cannot fret – and drive the plough, –
> Nor weep – and ply the spade;
> O blessed work – I need you now
> To keep me unafraid!
>
> No terrors can invade the place
> Where honest green things thrive;

Come blisters – backache – sunburnt face –
And save my soul alive![37]

McClung does not specify in this poem that women are her intended audience, but many women did find employment in the fields of Canada as part of the nation's effort to support the war. By suggesting the mutually beneficial possibilities of this labour, McClung undoubtedly hoped to inspire some women to take up their pitchforks as well as their knitting needles, expanding the contributions that women could make to the nation both during and presumably, given her feminist viewpoint, after the war. Yet, as Amy Tector suggests in this volume, even women who dealt with new challenges brought on by the war, such as caring for a disabled loved one, faced the expectation that they would conform to conventional gender norms in the postwar world. The fiction Tector explores reassures that, "despite these destabilizing changes, traditional sex roles would be retained" (this volume, 294). Women's nurturing work assured a continuity of their gendered role within society, even after the cataclysmic events of the First World War.

Canadian poets, both during and after the war, also made mothering itself a form of war work. The Canadian Red Cross Society, which provided invaluable labour from knitting socks to locating prisoners of war, often found its work equated with nurturing and maternalism.[38] Poets expounded on this theme, praising the nationalism that mothers exhibited, and, equally important, the nationalism that they instilled in their sons and in all young men. Unlike many previous poetic representations that used motherhood as a metaphor, the actions of women themselves became the central focus. In "The Young Veteran," noted jurist and former president of the Royal Society of Canada, William Douw Lighthall, celebrates both the feats achieved by a young soldier and the influence that the youth's mother had on his actions. Lighthall writes of "the boyheart of the soldier!" and uses the imagery of a knight on a crusade. Yet he also suggests that it is "His childlove of his mother / Illumining his strength!" that propels him to success.[39] Similarly, Thomas Harkness Litster's "His Mother's Letter" tells the story of how a mother's love inspires her son to do his duty. In the voice of the soldier, he writes:

Oh, mother, war's dangers are crowding,
I may never see you again;

> I feel your dear love me enshrouding,
> I would I might shield you from pain.

The poem concludes:

> Oh, mother o' mine, are you listening?
> I'm doing my bit best I can;
> Oh mother, the tear-drops are glistening,
> 'Twas you, mother, made me a man.[40]

In the poems of Lighthall and Litster, as in many representations of the war effort, the figure of the soldier takes the central and activist role. But these poets also acknowledge in their works the symbolic, and actual, value of motherhood in rousing the soldier's patriotism.

In her poem entitled "The Mother Gives," Isabel Eccleston Mackay writes of the sacrifice of a son from a mother's perspective:

> These hands whose weakness knew your baby weight,
> So heavy yet so dear, and held it fast
> Now loose the bond which love and service gave
> And let you go at last.

This sacrifice of the mother, however, comes with a higher purpose:

> Not for the lust of battle or its pride,
> Not for the dream of glory do I give,
> But that a dark and wicked thing may die,
> And Liberty may live![41]

These poetic sentiments represent the view that many Canadians took of the war. While it may have begun with a sense that it was an imperial lark that would come to a quick and glorious end, by 1917, most had come to understand the struggle as a battle between good and evil that would require great national sacrifice. This would be the testing ground thrusting Canada into a metaphorical adulthood, and in these poetic representations the role of women was fundamental to achieving the ultimate goal.

FIGURE 14 The soldier-mother relationship appeared in paintings like Harold H. Piffard's *His Constant Companion,* 1917, as well as in poetry. [From *Canada in Khaki,* No. 2, published for the Canadian War Records Office by The Pictorial Newspaper Co., London, 1917]

Published just after the war, Jean Blewett's poem, "The Woman Patriot," continues the theme of necessary sacrifice in defence of country. This is the female struggle, which runs parallel to the fight on the battlefield. Blewett's poem begins:

> Good-bye, dear lad, nay, never heed
> The tears I shed. Your country's need –
> Our country's need – comes first of all.
> Your ears have heard the clarion call,
> With patriot fire your soul's a-thrill;
> Dear heart! The best of blood must spill
> Ere peace is won. I love your zeal;

In this poem, the defence of the national ideals of "God, and Right, and Canada" necessitate the dangers that the son must face. Again, the sacrifice and sense of duty of the soldier would not be possible without the nurturing and citizenship training provided by his mother. Blewett makes this belief even more explicit in the conclusion of the poem:

> Since never soldier fought and died
> For country's honor, country's pride
> But owed his life, and courage strong
> To her who sang his cradle-song.
> Ah blazon on each flag unfurled,
> The patriot women of the world![42]

During the First World War the symbolic uses of motherhood had shifted from a metaphor applied to the Empire or the land to include a responsibility that sat on the shoulders of real women. Motherhood in these representations became the source and inculcator of the values that shaped the national identity.

Perhaps the ultimate sacrifice that a woman could make for her country was to have her child die in uniform. Suzanne Evans' chapter in this collection discusses the visible markers of grief, such as medals and service flags, that indicated an individual mother's or widow's sacrifice. The poetry of the war gave a literary voice to this loss and provided a shared symbol of suffering in the grieving mother. In the final stanza of her poem, "The Mother," Susan Frances

Harrison portrays a mother's relinquishment of her son, although difficult, as necessary for the protection of the nation and its values:

> Stiff in the trenches, and stark;
> Dead ere the battle was won:
> For that which is Right, for Love and Light,
> Freely I gave my son.
>
> After the bitter, the sweet;
> After the pain, the joy –
> I will not falter, nor flinch, nor faint;
> Proudly I give my boy.[43]

Katherine Hale evokes a similar pain in the "Hearts of Mothers," writing:

> They feel, the Givers of all Life,
> Great need to give again
> The utmost dower of womanhood,
> All mystery – all pain.[44]

The mothers who gave their sons for Canada's defence became the ultimate symbol of a nation that had found a degree of maturity in this struggle. While, perhaps ironically, these dead soldiers would never see full adulthood, the blood that they had spilled on the battlefield and the tears that their mothers shed on the home front together formed the seeds of a new sense of national independence and coming of age.

Historians and literary scholars alike have struggled to understand the meaning of the First World War for Canada's national identity. On the one hand, much of the poetry of the Great War has been either forgotten or ignored. Barry Callaghan, in his collection of poetry and prose from this war, suggests that the great horror of those who experienced these events led to a virtual forgetting.[45] Writing less than ten years after the armistice, Lionel Stevenson lauds John McCrae's "In Flanders Fields" for its poetical qualities but largely ignores the events that inspired its writing, noting only:

> Canada's share in the sacrifices and honours of the war and her rapid accession to a suffrage in international deliberations has confirmed, at least for the time, the note of mingled self-respect and filial affection in the country's relation with

the empire. It does not seem improbable that Canadian literature should soon begin to foreshadow the future trend of Canada's national consciousness.[46]

This is hardly an acknowledgment of the magnitude of the recent events or an overwhelming statement of any transformative changes that it may have wrought.

Yet in 1919, in contrast, looking back at the costs and benefits of the Great War, art and social commentator H.F. Gadsby concludes that, even if Canada did not receive a share of the war indemnities, it was worth the cost because: "Canada found her soul. Her soul means her nationhood." Gadsby discusses the growth and changes achieved by the war, claiming: "No longer are we daughters in our mother's house – we are sisters sitting around the table – married sisters if you like, with interests of our own, talking the affairs of the old homestead over."[47] More prosaically, in "Canada Growing Up," another author writes: "Canada has an entity – a separate heart and soul, is in other words a nation and not merely a colony of Mother England."[48] These authors write about what would become a popular and commonplace national observation – Canada had found its nationhood, its national identity, on the battlefields of Europe. Part of this process involved the recognition that Canada had the capacity to nurture its own citizenry. In other words, Canadian women, as mothers, more so than the Empire or the land, had shaped and nurtured the Canadian citizenry that had won this war.

Other scholars, however, emphasize a more dissonant transformation. Bruce Meyer writes the introduction to a collection that he contends will "allow the dead to tell their story in the authentic voice of their own experience," suggesting that such a story will "tell of a horrific transformation from Edwardian gentility to Modernist shock."[49] Lorrie Goldensohn, in a recent collection of American war poetry, makes a similar observation, noting that the horrors of the war, "along with the growing awareness of the misfit of old forms of unthinking patriotic loyalty, ... elicited a new, rebellious, and skeptical strain of thought and imagery."[50] In Britain, what one scholar characterizes as a movement away from the "public-school" sentiments and optimism of the war's beginning, is perhaps best characterized by Siegfried Sassoon. His poem "Glory of Women," far from being a sentimentalized celebration of sacrificing womanhood, sarcastically mocks: "You love us when we're heroes, home on leave, / Or wounded in a mentionable place."[51] In both the United States and Britain, the emphasis is generally on this move towards modernity and the increasing malaise expressed in the poetry of this era. However, in Canada, this literary explanation has had to be balanced with the more positive version of the coming-of-age story that lingers in the popular imagination.

The conflicting imagery and debate over the meaning of the war to Canadians may reflect what Leon Surette identifies as the "two contrary paradigms of our cultural destiny – continuity and breach – [that] operate simultaneously" in the Canadian literary canon.[52] Further, images of the horrors of war versus celebrations of the sentimentalism of sacrifice may suggest the contrast between high literature and what one scholar calls "commonplace magazine verse."[53] Scholarship based on Canadian war poems adjudged to have lasting literary merit tend to suggest the modernizing trends evinced in British and American poems of this era.[54] But Jonathan Vance argues that historians must look beyond the aesthetic qualities of this "good" poetry when considering literary representations of the war and its meaning to both its creators and the reading public. The amateur verse published in local newspapers and popular magazines generally eschews the ironic tones of modernity for what has been called "high diction." And, in this poetry, motherhood functions as a powerful symbol of sacrifice, loyalty, and devotion to country.[55] While perhaps not worthy as art or literature, such verse likely better suggests the popular sentiments of the era.

Another theme that emerges in the understanding of Canadian First World War poetry may be divisions based on gender. Carole Gerson suggests that the growth of academic influence over the study of literature that occurred in the 1920s meant that "the conferring of literary value shifted accordingly from the domain of a largely female reading audience to the control of an almost exclusively male professoriate and their influential friends, whose choices inevitably reflected their own class, gender, and racial orientations."[56] Occurring when it did, this shift undoubtedly shaped the value assigned to poetry produced during the war. A consideration of gender also raises the question of how the identity of the author shaped the use of motherhood imagery. This is not an easy question to answer. Common perceptions may suggest that male poets, especially those who were themselves soldiers, were more likely to focus on the experiences in the trenches, while leading female authors would be more likely to illuminate their own experiences and contributions to the war effort. But again, it should be considered whether this was a difference of gender perceptions or a contrast between poetry as literature and poetry as popular verse (particularly since most literary anthologies tend to privilege the soldier-poet's expression). Anthologies of war poetry in general tend to privilege the perspective of male poets, while the few anthologies of poetry by Canadian women tend not to highlight writings on the war.[57] Only an exhaustive investigation of locally published poems might suggest whether Canadian war poetry reflects clear gender divisions. This is certainly a question for future research.

Instilling a nationalist sentiment remained a source of concern for Canadian social commentators and politicians even as the First World War drew to a close. At a conference called in Winnipeg in 1919, attendees advocated a conformist citizenship and nationhood based on "service, obedience, obligation and fidelity to the state." At that conference, historian W.S. Wallace suggested a nationalism based "not on the factors of language and religion, but on those of a common fatherland, a common history, a common allegiance, common political ideals, and common hopes for the future." Poetry, and the metaphors and symbols of nationhood, continued to provide ammunition for instilling Canadian patriotism.[58] The desire to create a cultural expression that reflected a common Canadian identity suggested both the continued desirability of this goal and the fact that the experience of the First World War had not fully accomplished it for Canadians.

When Canadians think of First World War poetry, they may most commonly evoke John McCrae's "In Flanders Fields." This poem suggests the sacrifice of men on the battlefield who laid down their lives so that Canada might endure and develop into a fully mature nation. But many other poets, of varying degrees of skill, also put pen to paper during this period of national struggle in an attempt to engender patriotic sentiments in the people of Canada. Motherhood became an important symbol in many of these poems, encouraging women to contribute to the war effort and to sacrifice their sons to the cause. Motherhood also gave men in the trenches something for which to fight. The themes of motherhood and of nurturing a national identity had often appeared in Canadian poetry before, but in the late nineteenth century the imagery used evoked a metaphorical mother, either the imperial nurturing of the "Mother country" or the shaping influence of Canada's natural landscape. Jonathan Vance writes that, during the First World War, motherhood served a newly important role, becoming "at once the symbol of the past and the creator of the future."[59] The active and public role that Canadian mothers took during this war was increasingly celebrated in poetic representations. While the war may not have significantly transformed the lived experiences of many Canadian women, poetic odes to their role in nurturing the nation's citizenry, and to the sacrifices that they made for their country, did suggest a new symbolic understanding of the nation and its place in the world. Embedded in the shifting metaphors of motherhood found in Canadian poetry, albeit complex and incomplete, was a growing sense that the nation was beginning to come of age.

Notes

1. J. R. Wilkinson, "My Wife," in *Canadian Battlefields and Other Poems* (Toronto: William Briggs, 1899), 26-27.
2. Martha Albertson Fineman, "The Neutered Mother," in *Language, Symbolism, and Politics*, ed. Richard M. Merelman (Boulder: Westview Press, 1992), 169.
3. This maternal imagery is particularly apparent in portraiture of Victoria. See Susan P. Casteras, *Images of Victorian Womanhood in English Art* (London and Toronto: Associated University Presses, 1987), 23, 25; Frank Prochaska, "A Mother's Country: Mothers' Meetings and Family Welfare in Britain, 1850-1950," *History* 74 (1989): 381.
4. Margaret Peterson, "A Mother's Dedication," in *A Treasury of War Poetry: British and American Poems of the World War 1914-1917*, ed. George Herbert Clarke (Boston and New York: Houghton Mifflin Co., 1917), reprinted at http://beck.library.emory.edu/greatwar/poetry/.
5. Linda Kerber, "The Republican Mother: Female Political Imagination in the Early Republic," in *Women of the Republic: Intellect and Ideology in Revolutionary America*, ed. Linda Kerber, 265-88 (Chapel Hill: University of North Carolina Press, 1980); Lydia Howard Sigourney, *Letters to Mothers* (Hartford: Hudson and Skinner, 1838), 15-16.
6. Carol Oukrop, "The Four Minute Men Became National Network during World War I," *Journalism Quarterly* 52, 4 (1975): 632-37.
7. An original audio recording of this song is accessible at http://www.archive.org/ in the Collected Works of Peerless Quartet with Henry Burr.
8. Ruth A. Frager and Carmela Patrias, *Discounted Labour: Women Workers in Canada, 1870-1939* (Toronto: University of Toronto Press, 2005), 78-79.
9. Donna Bennett, "Conflicted Vision: A Consideration of Canon and Genre in English-Canadian Literature," in *Canadian Canons: Essays in Literary Value*, ed. Robert Lecker (Toronto: University of Toronto Press, 1991), 141.
10. Lionel Stevenson, *Appraisals of Canadian Literature* (Toronto: Macmillan of Canada, 1926 [reprint 1970]), 11.
11. Leon Surette, "Creating the Canadian Canon," in *Canadian Canons: Essays in Literary Value*, ed. Robert Lecker (Toronto: University of Toronto Press, 1991), 17.
12. Don Gutteridge, "Teaching the Canadian Mythology: A Poet's View," *Journal of Canadian Studies* 8, 1 (1973): 29-30.
13. Wilkinson, *Canadian Battlefields*, preface.
14. W.A. Foster, *Canada First; or, Our New Nationality: An Address* (Toronto: Adam, Stevenson and Co., 1871), 27. The Canada First Movement consisted of a group of young patriots who met together to discuss promoting nationalist sentiment.

15 John A. Macdonald, "Our Connection with Britain," reprinted in *Patriotic Recitations and Arbor Day Exercises*, ed. George W. Ross (Toronto: Warwick Bros. & Rutter, 1893), 136.
16 John George Bourinot, *Canada as a Home* (Toronto: J.S. Williams, Printer, 1882), 28, 30 (reprinted from *Westminster Review*, July 1882).
17 Charles G.D. Roberts, "An Ode to Canada," in *Patriotic Recitations and Arbor Day Exercises*, ed. George W. Ross (Toronto: Warwick Bros. & Rutter, 1893), 46.
18 Wilfred Campbell, stanza 5 of "England," in *The Poems of Wilfred Campbell* (Toronto: William Briggs, 1905), 298.
19 H.C. Cockin, stanza 2 of "This Fair Canadian Land," in *Raise the Flag and Other Patriotic Canadian Songs and Poems* (Toronto: Rose Publishing, 1891), 9.
20 Carl Berger, "The True North Strong and Free," in *Nationalism in Canada*, ed. Peter Russell (Toronto: McGraw Hill and Co., 1966), 4; and Frank Watt, "Nationalism in Canadian Literature," in Russell, *Nationalism*, 241.
21 E.H. Dewart, "The Claims of Our Country," in *Patriotic Recitations and Arbor Day Exercises*, ed. George W. Ross (Toronto: Warwick Bros. & Rutter, 1893), 149.
22 James Young, "Canadian Nationality: A Glance at the Present and Future," an address to the National Club of Toronto, 21 April 1891, 3-18, 33, CIHM/ICMH Microfiche series, no. 26111.
23 Thomas D'Arcy McGee, "Freedom's Journey," in *Patriotic Recitations and Arbor Day Exercises*, ed. George W. Ross (Toronto: Warwick Bros. & Rutter, 1893), 72.
24 Robert Kernighan, "The Men of the Northern Zone," in Ross, *Patriotic Recitations*, 64-65.
25 Ibid., 65.
26 Peter Buitenhuis, *The Great War of Words: British, American and Canadian Propaganda and Fiction, 1914-1933* (Vancouver: UBC Press, 1987).
27 John W. Garvin, "Editor's Foreword," in *Canadian Poems of the Great War*, ed. John W. Garvin (Toronto: McClelland and Stewart, 1918), 3.
28 Elspeth Honeyman, "Canada's Answer," in Garvin, *Canadian Poems*, 91.
29 Blanche E. Holt Murison, "The Mothering Heart," in Garvin, *Canadian Poems*, 163.
30 Thomas Harkness Litster, "The Sons of 'Our Lady of Snows,'" in T.H. Litster, *Songs in Your Heart and Mine* (Toronto: McClelland, Goodchild and Stewart, 1917), 101.
31 Edith Carew, "Monuments to Women in Canada," *Saturday Night*, 4 March 1911, 25.
32 "A God-Fearing Patriotism the Supreme Need," *Canadian White Ribbon Tidings*, 1 July 1912, 2236.
33 Joaquin Miller, "The Bravest Battle," *Canadian White Ribbon Tidings*, 1 April 1913, 91.
34 Nellie L. McClung, *The Next of Kin: Those who Wait and Wonder* (Boston: Houghton Mifflin Co., 1917), 9, 13.
35 McClung, *Next of Kin*, 208-9.
36 Katherine Hale, "Grey Knitting," in Garvin, *Canadian Poems*, 73. Katherine Hale was the penname of Amelia Garvin.
37 McClung, *Next of Kin*, 58.

38 Sarah Glassford, "'The Greatest Mother in the World': Carework and the Discourse of Mothering in the Canadian Red Cross Society during the First World War," *Journal of the Association for Research on Mothering* 10, 1 (2008): 219-32.
39 William Douw Lighthall, "The Young Veteran," in Garvin, *Canadian Poems*, 105.
40 Litster, "His Mother's Letter," in Litster, *Songs in Your Heart*, 117-18.
41 Isabel Ecclestone Mackay, "The Mother Gives," in Garvin, *Canadian Poems*, 134.
42 Duncan Campbell Scott's "To the Canadian Mother 1914-1918" also recognized the sacrifice that Canadian women made in sending their sons to war. Found in Duncan Campbell Scott, *Selected Poems of Duncan Campbell Scott* (Toronto: Ryerson Press, 1951), 170-72.
43 S. Frances Harrison, "The Mother," in Garvin, *Canadian Poems*, 80.
44 Katherine Hale, "The Hearts of Mothers," in Garvin, *Canadian Poems*, 73-74.
45 Barry Callaghan, "Foreword," in *We Wasn't Pals: Canadian Poetry and Prose of the First World War*, ed. Barry Callaghan and Bruce Meyer (Toronto: Exile Editions Ltd., 2001), xvi.
46 Stevenson, *Appraisals*, 65-67, 225.
47 H.F. Gadsby, "Canada Finds Her Soul," *Saturday Night*, 10 May 1919, 4.
48 "Canada Growing Up," *Saturday Night*, 17 May 1919, 18.
49 Bruce Meyer, "Introduction," in Callaghan and Meyer, *We Wasn't Pals*, xix.
50 Lorrie Golfensohn, ed., *American War Poetry: An Anthology* (New York: Columbia University Press, 2006), 153.
51 Jon Stallworthy, ed., *The Oxford Book of War Poetry* (Oxford: Oxford University Press, 1984), xxvi, 178.
52 Surette, "Creating the Canadian Canon," 18.
53 Henry W. Wells, "The Awakening in Canadian Poetry," *New England Quarterly* 18, 1 (1945): 10.
54 Joel Baetz, "Battle Lines: English-Canadian Poetry of the First World War" (PhD diss., York University, 2005), 8.
55 Jonathan F. Vance, *Death So Noble: Memory, Meaning, and the First World War* (Vancouver: UBC Press, 1997), 5, 89-90.
56 Carole Gerson, "The Canon between the Wars: Field-Notes of a Feminist Literary Archaeologist," in *Canadian Canons: Essays in Literary Value*, ed. Robert Lecker (Toronto: University of Toronto Press, 1991), 47.
57 Jo Gill, *Women's Poetry* (Edinburgh: Edinburgh University Press, 2007), 154, cites Catherine Reilly's observation that "women's poetry has been 'under-represented' in most selections of war poetry." For examples of anthologies of Canadian women poets, see Wanda Campbell, ed., *Hidden Rooms: Early Canadian Women Poets* (London, ON: Canadian Poetry Press, 2000); and Rosemary Sullivan, ed., *Poetry by Canadian Women* (Toronto: Oxford University Press, 1989).
58 Quoted in Tom Mitchell, "'The Manufacture of Souls of Good Quality': Winnipeg's 1919 National Conference on Canadian Citizenship, English-Canadian Nationalism, and the New Order after the Great War," *Journal of Canadian Studies* 31, 4 (1996-97): 5, 8.
59 Vance, *Death So Noble*, 150.

12

"Mother, Lover, Nurse"
The Reassertion of Conventional Gender Norms in Representations of Disability in Canadian Novels of the First World War

Amy Tector

Basil Norman, the protagonist of Arthur Beverley Baxter's 1920 short story "The Blower of Bubbles," is a noble soldier who is paralyzed after being wounded in the Great War. His wife, Lilias, talks about tending to her wheelchair-bound husband. She must nurse him constantly but does not view her work as a burden. Quite the opposite, as she explains: "To live day by day ... near a soul like Basil's, to commune with a brain like his ... is a happiness few women can experience."[1] Up to this point in the story, Lilias' sentiments conform to prewar Edwardian ideals of female self-sacrifice, yet her very next sentence complicates this vision. As she confesses, "If it were not too cruel, I could feel thankful for his wound that has given him so completely to me."[2] In Baxter's depiction, Lilias is Basil's benign jailor. Although she obfuscates her feelings with the expression "if it were not too cruel," she cannot conceal the fact that she is pleased about her husband's paralysis. His disability has weakened and "unmanned" him, and Lilias is eager to step in to fill the power vacuum in their relationship. Baxter's uneasiness with women's increased power in the face of masculine disability reflects society's wider concerns about the war's perceived disruption of gender norms. His worries are echoed again and again in interwar fiction of the period as Canadian authors struggled to reconcile the perceived transformation of male and female roles in the face of masculine disability.

While some scholars in this volume, like Linda J. Quiney and Terry Bishop Stirling, highlight women's wartime role as Voluntary Aid Detachment nurses in the conflict, there is also a need to investigate how civilian women were affected by the duties of caring for disabled soldiers. The popular fiction of the interwar years offers valuable insight into cultural attitudes towards disability and gender. The 130,000 Canadians who were wounded or who became ill during their service with the Canadian Expeditionary Force came home with government promises of pensions and rehabilitation ringing in their ears. Despite these political commitments, the burden of soldiers' care often fell to women. Many mothers, wives, and sisters spent the postwar years tending injured or ill loved ones, or working outside the home to support their families. Wounded soldiers needed women's care but often resented their own dependence. While disabled men fought to reassert their masculinity, women tried to reconcile their new responsibilities with the pressures to meet the ideals of womanhood. Canadian fiction of the period tended to reassure its readership that, despite these destabilizing changes, traditional sex roles would be retained. Novels featuring disabled soldiers were especially useful in this project because they often argued that even disabled men who were "less" masculine could reclaim their positions of patriarchal dominance. The feared transformation of conventional gender roles was averted and, instead, men and women's traditional positions were reasserted.

Canadian war novels featuring disabled protagonists were usually written by men who tended to flatten the representation of women, consigning them to one of three stereotypical roles: mothers, lovers, or nurses. As both Lynn Kennedy and Vicki S. Hallett indicate elsewhere in this volume, women writers often documented the female experience of war. While poets like Phoebe Florence Miller and Katherine Hale, and novelists like L.M. Montgomery, Nelly McClung, and Francis Marion Beynon, offered a female perspective on the conflict, they did not explore disability issues in much depth. Most of the plots of the Canadian novels that feature disabled soldiers follow a similar pattern, tracking the recruit from enlistment, through his battle experiences, his injury, and his readjustment to civilian life. The majority of the novels then focus on the soldiers' sweethearts or wives, who nurse them back to health.

The women depicted in these novels were not professional nurses on the battlefield but, rather, ordinary Canadians who were coping with the unexpected needs of men they had been taught by society to believe would take care of them. The Victorian era had idealized a passive femininity. Coventry Patmore's 1885 poem, "The Angel in the House," celebrates feminine selflessness and domesticity, and, in many households, the sweet docility it praised became a model for which to strive.[3] Such a viewpoint was not without its challengers, and, as early as 1891, feminist writer Charlotte Perkins Gilman penned a short story entitled "An Extinct Angel," satirizing the very concept. Nonetheless, as the interwar novels demonstrate, it continued to hold sway in conservative Canada. The ideal woman was self-sacrificing, submissive, sexually pure, docile, and maternal. The return of wounded soldiers presented a problem, however. Despite women's supposed natural tendency to nurture, caring for a disabled man's needs required more emotional and physical strength than was expected of a gentle "Angel in the House." After all, if the family breadwinner was unable to work, the burden fell to his wife, who additionally would have to nurse her husband and care for any children. To "take on" a sweetheart or husband who had been severely wounded required a woman to be "brave."[4] There were thus two contradictory messages for women who cared for disabled soldiers: they were expected to be tender and submissive and, at the same time, to shoulder household and financial responsibilities.

Using disability studies to analyze the relationships between these women and the men for whom they cared is particularly fruitful. This relatively new critical field in the humanities argues for disability's inclusion as a foundational category of social experience, along with ethnicity, gender, class, and sexuality.[5] Contrary to our modern impression of disability as a fixed and tragic condition, value judgments about bodily difference have fluctuated over the ages. In certain cultures or eras, people who hallucinate have been revered as seers, while those experiencing seizures have been considered powerful.[6] The introduction of standardized medical treatment at the end of the nineteenth century reduced the acceptance of bodily difference, replacing it with a scientific approach that pathologized deviant bodies.[7]

The First World War refined this medical approach. With thousands of men injured by combat, science took a pragmatic turn and rehabilitation came to the fore. The desire was to return disabled soldiers to the wholeness that they had lost in the war, making them "normal" once again. The drive to rehabilitate was powered by ideological considerations: if the soldiers who fought in the war could be returned to health, the combatant nations could also be rebuilt. Much of Europe had been "crippled" by massive economic, infrastructure, and population losses, but these injuries could be "fixed" just as surely as a man who had lost a leg could walk again, thanks to a prosthesis. There was also a pressing economic factor behind the trend towards rehabilitation: the postwar economy needed every man to contribute and could not sustain a non-working veteran population.[8] By integrating the disabled into the able-bodied population, the medical community and political leaders wished to elide differences. Such an approach had serious consequences in that society came to treat disabilities as shameful secrets rather than the natural bodily variations to be expected in a multifaceted world.

It was not until the 1970s that critics challenged many of the assumptions surrounding the denial-of-difference strategy. Their arguments would eventually be placed under the rubric of "disability studies." British activists began looking at disability not as a medical problem to be cured by science but as an issue to be addressed through identity politics. They argued that disability was a social construction rather than a biological fact. They distinguished between "impairment," which was the bodily defect or deficit, and "disability," which was the disadvantage imposed by society upon the impairment. Thus, a double-leg amputee's impairment was the absence of limbs, and his disabilities were the barriers that abound in a wheelchair-inaccessible world. If the amputee could easily move from home to work and social gatherings, he would have continued to be impaired but would no longer have been disabled. The amputee's disability was the world's unwillingness to accommodate his needs. By contrast, the social model of disability put the onus for change on society, celebrating rather than concealing the differences inherent in the disabled body. It moved disability from something that had to be compensated for to something that had to be accommodated. Present-day disability studies challenge how disability is represented and expose how society excludes those deemed physically or mentally "abnormal." Normality itself is considered just as fluid a concept as disability. Indeed, it is worth remembering that, from Aristotle to Freud, the female body has often been considered inherently defective, an irregular or "lesser" version of the male.[9]

Society's preconceptions about disability strongly influenced how the authors of First World War fiction portrayed gender. Injured or ill soldiers were often depicted as having been emasculated by their wounds. This concern in fiction was also a real-world anxiety. Historian Deborah Cohen's analysis of the plight of British war veterans, many of whom were unmarried when the conflict ended, illustrates disabled soldiers' deep concerns about their ability to form relationships: "nurses in military hospitals reported that many wounded soldiers dreaded the once-longed for reunions with sweethearts. They did not know how their loved ones would respond to their injuries."[10] War wounds raised a great many anxieties about sexuality because emotional and physical injuries on the battlefield could render men impotent. One of the most famous depictions

FIGURE 15   The wounded ex-soldier in this 1916 Colman's Mustard advertisement needs a woman to spread mustard on his dinner. Contemporary fiction suggested he was not doomed to suffer such emasculation indefinitely. From *Canada in Khaki*, published for the Canadian War Records Office, ca. 1916. [Reproduced by permission of Unilever plc]

"Mother, Lover, Nurse"

of this was the British author D.H. Lawrence's portrayal of the paralyzed and impotent First World War veteran, Clifford Chatterley, in *Lady Chatterley's Lover*. Not only was Clifford unable to walk, but he was also incapable of sexually satisfying his wife, driving her into the passionate arms of his gamekeeper, Mellors. While no Canadian author explored the implications of impotence as thoroughly (or explicitly) as Lawrence, novelists illustrated the existence of such concerns in their sexualized depictions of nursing care.

J. Murray Gibbon's 1920 novel *The Conquering Hero* is a melodramatic romance whose wounded protagonist offers a comforting wish fulfilment for injured soldiers: not only is Donald McDonald sexually unharmed by his war injuries but he actually exploits the illicit sexuality inherent in the closeness of nursing. Donald is gassed and "filled with shrapnel" during battle. His time in hospital gives him a taste for the nursing staff: "fair-haired, rosy-cheeked Old Country maidens at whose sight his heart went pit-a-pat."[11] Providing nursing care was one of the few socially sanctioned physical intimacies allowed between unmarried men and women at that time, and it was a woman's only legitimate reason for touching a man in his own bed. In the novel, the hospital is thus a site of pain but also a place of sexual awakening and pleasure for the virginal Donald. The nurses become Donald's sexual ideal, and he is determined to find and marry a woman just like one of those who cared for him.

After Donald's discharge from hospital, he returns to Canada to work as a wilderness guide in the forests of New Brunswick. Gibbon's commitment to melodramatic romance explains the unexpected plot twist that sees the phlegmatic Donald bump into an exiled Polish princess in the woods. The fact that this princess is also a silent movie "vamp" only accentuates Gibbon's strange view of what the typical New Brunswick camping trip entails. Needless to say, Donald is enthralled by the glamorous princess. He soon conflates her in his mind with the "Old Country" maidens who looked after him in France. After meeting her, Donald is plagued by a sexually charged dream of seduction in which his mother transforms into one of the women who nursed him in the hospital, finally becoming Stephanie, the Princess. Gibbon's language clearly reflects Donald's desires:

> She enticed him into an inner chamber, although he knew that she was a witch luring him to destruction. With a tremendous effort he turned to escape, but to his ears there came the voice calling – rich, low, musical. He turned again and flung himself passionately into the outstretched arms.[12]

Donald vilifies Stephanie, calling her a "witch," but he is also obviously excited about visiting her "inner chamber" as he passionately flings himself into it. The fact that the image changes from Donald's early feminine ideal (embodied by his mother) to his burgeoning desires (represented by his English nurses) and culminates in his lust for the Princess indicates the connection between the three female stereotypes: mother, nurse, and lover. Here Gibbon is playing with a popular turn-of-the-century trope that combines "lustful vampires" with "potent mother" figures to embody a femme fatale.[13] The sexually loose woman united with the power of the maternal created an almost irresistibly attractive force. Literary and cultural historians have located this figure in everything from Pre-Raphaelite paintings to the work of George Bernard Shaw.[14] In Gibbon's novel, the convergence of the femme fatale with the image of the nurse proves immensely alluring to Donald. By illustrating Donald's healthy sex drive in response to the Princess's overwhelming appeal, Gibbon assures the reader that, though he may have been injured in the war, he is still a sexually healthy man.

Displaying masculine self-control, Donald never acts upon his longings for the Princess, and, by the end of the novel, he is engaged to his young Scottish neighbour, Kate. Significantly, she is described as "the girl of his dreams," but she bears no resemblance to the erotic and exotic Princess. Instead, Kate has "fair hair, blue eyes, rosy cheeks, natural healthy waist, low heeled shoes,"[15] and her appearance recalls the nurses who had first excited Donald. Far from writing about a man rendered impotent by his time in battle, Gibbon reassures his readers that the disabled soldier will be able to easily reintegrate into peacetime society. After resisting the temptations of the provocative Princess, Donald is rewarded with a socially sanctioned romantic relationship with his ideal woman: a nurse substitute in sensible shoes.

Gibbon was not the only author anxious about relations between men and women, and it is evident that Canadian novelists like Ralph Connor and Robert Stead looked beyond sexual issues to expose how the war and disability problematized gender norms. One particular area of concern for these authors involved the challenges that women faced in caring for injured men.

Ralph Connor explores the worries of nursing a wounded partner in his 1925 novel *Treading the Winepress*. In this tale, Diana marries the war-invalided Merrick when she believes that her fiancé Tony has been killed. The marriage is not a success because Merrick's disability has made him weak, neurotic, and unmanly. As Di's friend Patty says, "You know how he depends so terribly on

Di, absurd I call it and terribly selfish." Merrick's demands on Di are oppressive, and Patty judges his treatment of her to be "shameful."[16] The difficulties in Di and Merrick's marriage have a basis in fact. Historian Jessica Meyer looked at British pension records and uncovered numerous examples of how wives of neurasthenic soldiers suffered under their husbands' irritability, anger, and frustration.[17] Her findings are upheld in the fiction of the time. In *Treading*, Connor depicts Di as terribly put upon by her demanding, invalid husband, but she recognizes that, as a woman, her obligation is to sacrifice her own needs and desires in order to care for him. She is the ideal Angel in the House, nobly forfeiting her peace of mind for the good of her husband. Forgoing happiness is not enough, however. Merrick is an unreasonable and almost monstrous invalid. The pain of his war wounds has perverted his formerly sunny disposition, and in one of his querulous fits, he grabs the steering wheel from the chauffeur, causing the accident that takes Di's life. Connor portrays the nursing of a disabled husband as so difficult that it literally kills the wife. Di and Merrick's story, although secondary to the larger romantic plot in the novel, is nonetheless a tragic example of the perceived difficulties inherent in taking care of an injured soldier.

Robert Stead's *Grain* (1926) also explores the demands that a disabled man places on a marriage. Jo Claus' husband Dick has developed tuberculosis in the trenches and is invalided home. Back on the farm he is not fussy or unmanly like Merrick; rather, he is stoical and brave in the face of his illness, never uttering a word of complaint, except to bemoan his inability to help out more. Jo respects the fact that Dick has enlisted and served the state. As she says to her former sweetheart, Gander, "He has done so much. He has made such a sacrifice. For you, for me, for all of us."[18] Jo admires Dick's fulfilment of his patriotic duty, but his physical weakness places huge strains on their relationship.

Jo must contend with the practical difficulties of a husband who cannot contribute to the household income. Stead's depiction of her struggles is rooted in historical reality. For, as Meyer discovered in her research, masculine disability brought about financial and physical hardships that posed substantial problems for postwar marriages.[19] In *Grain*, Dick's inability to perform physical labour is a major liability, and Jo and Dick are in financial trouble because of his weakness. When Gander arrives at their farm, he sees "many spots where a man's muscle and management were needed."[20] A "man's muscle," his physical strength, is key to success on a wheat farm. Dick's disability prevents him from performing typical masculine functions, and so he is feminized and infantilized for his perceived bodily failings. Jo refers to him as a "boy" and she broods over him like a mother.[21] He is weak and feeble in contrast to Gander, who is strong and confident.

Dick's injury even affects how his wife's body is perceived. His hands are "slender and soft," while hers become rough and hard as a result of the work she must do in his place.[22] It is not only Jo's hands that have changed:

> Her dress was rough and drab, with a button missing at the neck; her hair was none too tidy; her whole attire suggested haste and overwork ... This was the real Jo – Jo Claus, at home, at work, with the responsibilities of her sick man and her profitless farm dragging down upon her.[23]

This description encapsulates the contradictory messages that women who cared for disabled soldiers received. On the one hand, Jo is courageous for looking after her sick husband. This new incarnation is the "real" Jo, indicating that the trials of tending the farm and Dick's illness have brought out unlooked-for heroic characteristics. On the other hand, the responsibilities that she takes on diminish her femininity and attractiveness. Unlike the writers Isabel Ecclestone Mackay or Katherine Hale, whom Kennedy (this volume) cites, Jo is not completing traditionally female duties and, this being the case, is not liberated by her work. Instead, her work exhausts and bewilders her, and she does not relish her new responsibilities. She tells Gander that if she were not tied to Dick she might consider "flitting away." Her sense of duty forbids that, however, and she comments, "You've no idea how much he needs me!"[24] Working like a man, she struggles to meet the requirements of ideal womanhood. In both *Treading the Winepress* and *Grain* the female heroines, like the wives of disabled British soldier studied by Meyer, are "forced into unwanted emancipation from traditional gender roles."[25] These women long for able-bodied husbands because they never wanted to assume the traditional male responsibilities that were thrust upon them by their spouses' war wounds and illnesses.

While her husband's disability is disastrous for Jo, in some novels the wife enjoys the power that the unexpected role-reversal affords her. Historian David Gerber notes this trend across a broad spectrum of cultural representations throughout history:

> While the disabled veteran's goal is to reclaim his masculinity from the forces that feminize him, a woman's is more ambiguous, for she must help him

succeed at his project, thus subverting her own claims to the newfound equality she gained in wartime in his absence.[26]

Novelists expressed the above ambiguity in their writing, often fearing that women became too strong because of men's wounds. In the epilogue to Basil King's 1917 novel *The High Heart*, the female protagonist Alix cares for her newborn baby and her war-wounded husband, who has been lamed and has lost an arm in battle. Both her baby and husband Larry are sleeping, and Alix, in her role as nurse, waits for her charges to waken so that she can begin her duties. Larry is slowly recovering from his wounds, but Alix thinks, "in the meantime he is my other baby."[27] Her statement is startling because, up to this point in the novel, Larry has been a strong, forceful presence. He is the only character to consistently stand up to the rich autocratic Brokenshire family who tries to crush Alix's spirits; he supports the American entrance into the war when few others do; and he is a hero, having sustained his injuries in an act of battlefield bravery. Yet, once hurt and placed under the maternal nursing care of his wife, Larry is reduced to Alix's "other baby." King indicates something dark in this dynamic, as Alix continues: "and in a way, I love to have it so. I can be more to him. In proportion as he needs me the bond is closer."[28] Their relationship is unhealthy because their intimacy is premised upon Larry's weakness and dependency. As Gerber points out, women were not always willing to subvert their claims to equality. Alix's sentiment indicates King's unease with women's power as her contentment is in direct proportion to her husband's suffering.

As Hallett (this volume) discusses in her chapter on the poetry of Phebe Florence Miller, the trope of "stoic motherhood" is common in First World War literature. Often women's power in fiction comes from their maternal associations. Jo and Alix are depicted as motherly figures in their wounded husbands' lives, and this depiction is a recurring dynamic. Such a representation has two consequences: first, it infantilizes the disabled man, who is "lessened" by his war injury; second, it raises the status of his wife because motherhood is a source of authority. Mariana Valverde argues that first-wave feminists exploited the notion that women were the "Mothers of the race" in order to demand greater parity with men: "Women did not merely have just enough babies or too much sex: through their childbearing they either helped or hindered the forward march of (Anglo-Saxon) civilisation."[29] Women's maternal role was thus of primary importance. While men fought in the war to defend civilization against barbaric Germany, women propagated that civilization by producing more children. Motherhood was not a private decision but, rather, a sacrosanct responsibility that served the greater good.

Indeed, maternal imagery was so powerful that war propagandists appropriated it for their use. Not only were young men exhorted to go to battle to save their own mothers, but, to make enlistment more compelling, recruiters often portrayed England as a mother figure. Such personification was typical of the time. Jonathan Vance explains the pervasiveness of the mother image:

> If Christ became the spiritual symbol of the ideals for which Canadian soldiers fought, an allegorical maternal figure became one of the most potent secular symbols. In countless recruiting posters, patriotic cartoons and sheet-music covers, she was a lioness or bear whose call for aid brought her cubs running from the corners of the globe.[30]

Figured as a fierce, protective animal, like a lion or a bear, the mother was a force to be reckoned with. Motherhood was a source of pride and power for women. Women who looked after infantilized disabled soldiers in the fiction of the period were elevated to positions of importance because they were "mothering" the wounded. As Kennedy (this volume) argues, the power of the mother was exploited throughout Canadian First World War literary discourse to indicate Canada's growth as a nation.[31]

Novels like *The High Heart* depict changes in traditional gender power relationships, with motherly women being ascendant over childish, weakened husbands or sweethearts. This fiction encapsulates fears that women were becoming dangerously authoritative. These concerns, whether or not they were grounded in reality, were at the centre of the disquiet that novelists expressed about women's nursing role. As Sandra Gilbert notes, the female nurse's "evolution into active, autonomous, transcendent subject is associated with [the patient's] devolution into passive, dependent, immanent medical object."[32] Although King depicts Alix as noble for looking after her invalid husband, beneath the surface is a deep-seated unease with this destabilized relationship.

While there were certainly fears that women were exploiting their newfound power, Canadian novelists rarely demonized them, instead using the disabled man's triumphant reassertion of traditional gender roles as proof of the naturalness of male domination. If a feminized, infantilized disabled soldier is able to reclaim his position as head of the household, the subtext read, then able-bodied returned servicemen should have no problem asserting themselves.

Another of King's novels, *The City of Comrades* (1919), supports this statement. It opens with its protagonist, Frank Melbury, exiled in New York where he is a homeless alcoholic. His rigid and disciplinarian father, Edward, has disinherited Frank (whose Montreal family is wealthy and connected) because he had been too rebellious in his younger years. As an adult, Frank realizes that had he instead been subject to the "gentler handling" advocated by his mother, he might not have turned to alcohol.[33] Frank's anti-social behaviour is a direct result of his being over-fathered and under-mothered. King thus rejects the idea, popular in the late nineteenth and early twentieth centuries, that the growth of cities and enforced school attendance, along with the father's absence from home due to work, created a powerfully negative female influence over boys.[34] Instead, he illustrates that Edward Melbury's aggressive paternalism is damaging and that mother-love is all-important.

Frank's relationship with the feminine is entirely defined by his quest for maternal affection. This need is crystallized after he enlists in the Canadian Expeditionary Force and is injured in battle, losing an eye and the use of one of his legs. The full extent of his vulnerability is made clear while he is boarding the hospital ship that is to take him home. He is bewildered, crashing into people, until rescued by his love interest, Regina. He is grateful for her assistance. As Frank reflects, "It is one of the results of the war that men, who are often reduced to the mere shreds of human nature, grow accustomed to being taken care of by women, who remain the able-bodied ones."[35] Frank has lost the basic ability to care for himself and been "reduced" to relying upon women. What's more, he becomes habituated to this reversal of typical gender roles.

Frank and Regina quickly slip into the mother-son relationship typical of so many novels featuring disabled men. When bringing Frank a life-jacket, Regina is described as a mother fussing over her child.[36] Rather than resenting her attitude, Frank actually plays up Regina's maternal instincts when he exaggerates his helplessness. While Regina encourages his independence, he insists that he needs her help and speaks "in the tones of a boy feigning an indisposition to stay away from school."[37] Frank thus exploits Regina's impulse to infantilize him. He uses the common perception of the disabled as enfeebled in order to become more intimate with her. Frank does not rail against his lost independence or reliance on women. Part of his equanimity can be traced to his battles with his father's unyielding power. Frank values a masculinity that allows for feminine weakness because he has seen how damaging unchecked patriarchy can be. His notions of gender roles are not rigid. As he thinks, "Men are used to the eternal-feminine streak in themselves and one another."[38] Frank is thus able to embrace the help that Regina provides and to feel calm at the infantilizing effects of his wounds.

The larger reason for Frank's acceptance of Regina's actions lies in his own conception of his injuries. Unlike our modern understanding of the First World War, Frank sees his time at the front as positive because it has cured him of his alcoholism and sense of shame: "I had gone away one man and I was coming back another. My old self had not only been melted down in the crucible, but it had been stamped with a new image and superscription. I was of a new value and a new currency."[39] The war has actually healed Frank of a greater wound, that of addiction, than the ones with which he was sent home.

Frank's motivation is now to encourage the United States to enter the war, and he knows his wounds are huge propaganda tools for the Entente powers. He thus considers his disabilities an asset and is resigned to his loss of physical strength because he believes so passionately in his duty to encourage enlistment. His perceived diminishment as a man is merely an unavoidable side effect of his larger purpose. Frank only fights against his enfeeblement when he fears that it will hinder his plans to propagandize the war. He realizes what would happen if he were to become engaged to Regina:

> I should be seized in the soft, tender, irresistible embrace of the feminine in American life, the element that is more powerful than any other, and I should have no more fight than a new born infant against a nurse. There would be a whole array of mothers and potential mothers to see that I had not.[40]

Frank worries about an "array of mothers" squared against his holy mission to promote the United States' entrance into the war. His language is confrontational and antagonistic as he talks about the "powerful" force that he will have to overcome. Frank fears being weakened, and having "no more fight than a new born infant," because his recruiting mission has been threatened. If Frank cannot spread war propaganda, then his life will have no meaning. Faced with that danger, Frank suddenly fights against the "irresistible embrace of the feminine." Maternal power is a force for good in this novel, as long as the wounded soldier does not forget his duty by yielding to it completely. Ultimately, Frank must reassert his masculine dominance and reject the effeminizing force of womanhood.

Concerns about the emasculating and infantilizing effects of war injuries were most prominent in fictional representations of shell shock. This was a wide-ranging diagnosis covering a variety of mental disorders brought about by both the trauma and the boredom of trench warfare. Symptoms could include memory loss, mutism, blindness, deafness, and/or paralysis. The closest equivalent in modern understanding is post-traumatic stress disorder. Although there was a great deal of doubt and confusion surrounding the diagnosis in the early stages of the war, the medical community eventually came to accept shell shock as a legitimate wound. Despite this acceptance, the military was more ambivalent, and a shell shock diagnosis carried the taint of malingering or even cowardice. Sir Andrew Macphail, the official historian of the Canadian Army Medical Corps, believed that shell shock was simply an unmanly manifestation of childishness and femininity, which exposed an absence of courage.[41] While servicemen would have preferred to have their symptoms considered a wound, or even an illness, they were instead often viewed as signs of cowardice or, worse yet, insanity. These attitudes carried on after the war. Although thousands of Canadian veterans were in receipt of pensions for "shell shock and neurasthenia" by 1927, their attending physicians still harboured doubts about the reality of their symptoms.[42]

The ambivalent status of shell shock as a real injury affected how its sufferers were regarded. Although some doctors, such as W.H.R. Rivers, who treated famed British war poet Siegfried Sassoon, viewed shell shock sympathetically, George Mosse argues that the perception at the time was that a "true" man was someone who controlled his emotions and passions, and since shellshock sufferers could not do so, they were lessened.[43] This attitude comes through very clearly in Connor's *Treading the Winepress*. Indeed, when the novel's main character, Tony Mackinroy, suffers from shell shock, he and his love interest Miriam must realign their gendered identities, which have been knocked askew by the war, before they can achieve their happy ending.

True to Connor's position as propagandist for the Canadian government, at the outset of the novel Tony is a fearless soldier who believes fervently in the righteousness of the conflict. Things unravel for Tony, however, after he returns from war. The trauma of his experiences overseas, which include several near brushes with death in high-seas naval battles and a protracted period of amnesia, not to mention the violent demise of most of his crew as well as his first fiancée, Di, renders him shell shocked. Once back in Canada, Tony rejects all of his friends: "for a full week he lay in a state approaching coma, eating nothing to speak of, opening his lips to no one, except to emit now and then a heart-breaking moan."[44] Given all that he has been through, Tony's difficulty in integrating his traumas and adjusting to civilian life is understandable.

Connor does not portray Tony's struggles sympathetically; rather, he describes him as a "nervous, egotistic, self-centered, bad-tempered recluse."[45] Connor's depiction is in keeping with the military understanding of shell shock. Tony's despair is perceived as unmanly, selfish, and shameful. As kindly Reverend Steele tells Miriam: "Egotism is a pathological symptom. In an extreme case it becomes a mania."[46] Steele's words carry the weight of moral condemnation. Tony is insensitive and self-involved rather than legitimately affected by the war.

Connor's inability to see those suffering from the psychological effects of war in a heroic light is not surprising. In portraying Tony as merely self-indulgent rather than as justifiably traumatized by what he has seen, Connor does not need to probe either how the war was waged or whether the conflict was meaningless. Tony was a heroic soldier who did his duty. The fact that he forgets his obligations during peace is not an indictment of the conflict but, rather, shows a want of manliness on Tony's part. His illness is thus not a result of the meaningless of the war, nor of the brutality of how it was waged, but is attributable to his own failure to be manly.

Tony is not the only one who fails in his gender role. For a time after the war, Miriam becomes radically "un-womanly," embodying many of society's fears about changing female positions. She adopts a "New Woman" manner, an attitude first articulated in the feminist fiction of novelist Sarah Grand in the latter half of the nineteenth century. New Women novels idealized educated, financially independent, politically active women who were free to choose whether or not to marry or have children. The New Woman was portrayed either as a figure of admiration by advocates of women's rights or as a lesson in the self-destructiveness of female power by those suspicious of the feminist cause.[47] Connor fell into the latter camp. Miriam's friend Patty is extremely apprehensive of her new attitudes and worries that she is self-destructive. Patty fretfully describes Miriam as "hard, bitter, reckless ... She's awfully sure of herself."[48] While this description of a strong-willed, intelligent, independent woman is attractive to the twenty-first century reader, to the early twentieth-century reader it portrayed a radical break with the Victorian and Edwardian idealizations of feminine domesticity and passivity.

Tony's shell shock actually "rescues" Miriam from her rejection of her traditional role. Her love for him forces her to give up her old lifestyle and to tap into what Connor portrays as her innate feminine desire to nurture. Luckily, Miriam's work as an ambulance driver during the war has made her familiar with shell shock, or the "more deadly wounds of the spirit."[49] She restores Tony's sense of masculine duty and self-control by forcing him to recognize the weakness of his response to his trauma. She gets him to care about people less fortunate than himself and fosters his outside interests, which include advocating for war widows, acting as a role model for wayward boys, and stopping a rum-smuggling outfit.[50] Tony's actions in these deeds are decisive and manly. As he acknowledges in a letter to her: "You helped me back to ... a regaining of my manhood."[51] Miriam's nurturing thus restores him to his traditional masculine role. Miriam's cure of Tony is vital because his shell shock threatened the social order. It made him seem effeminate, which, according to Mosse, caused great anxiety at the time because it "endangered the clear distinction between genders which was generally regarded as an essential cement of society."[52] Connor's novel thus threatens and then restores the gender balance.

Miriam's intelligent nurturing saves Tony from his failure to be manly, counteracting the feminizing effects of war trauma. At the same time, Miriam's work for Tony's recovery returns her to her "natural" position as a passive Angel in the House as opposed to the over-bearing and out-of-control New Woman that Patty feared she was becoming. By regaining their conventional gender roles, Miriam and Tony can be rewarded with a traditional happy ending. At the close of the novel, conservative values are reasserted when Miriam gives up her "wonderful opportunity" at a career as a public speaker and activist in England in order to become Tony's wife.[53] The novel ends with Tony's asserting his masculine prerogative and telling Miriam he is about to kiss her. Miriam, the tough-minded, cigarette-smoking woman who drove an ambulance through war-torn Flanders, turns into a fluttery female and responds, "Oh Tony! Do ... If you don't I think I shall die."[54] Thanks to Miriam's able and intelligent nursing, Tony is once again a man, and she can gratefully give up the independence she has achieved to assume a traditional position as Tony's helper.

While most novels of the period offer a comforting vision of disabled men who successfully reassert their manhood and affirm themselves as the heads of households, *Janet of Kootenay*, written by Evah McKowan and published in 1919, proposes an alternative to traditional gender relations. Janet creates a partnership with the disabled Captain Fenton, in which not only are her competency and expertise recognized and appreciated but Fenton is not infantilized because of his injuries. Janet does not glory in her wounded male partner's weaknesses, as does Alix in *The High Heart*, nor does she give up her own values and desires to conform to traditional expectations of wifely duty, as does Miriam in *Treading the Winepress*. This delicate negotiation of masculine-feminine roles is particularly interesting because Janet is the only avowed feminist in any of the war novels that feature disabled protagonists. McKowan thus proposes a surprisingly progressive view of gender relations, especially when considering that her 1919 novel is one of the earlier ones to be set during the conflict.

Lamed and unable to do many tasks, Fenton cannot climb trees, scrub floors, swim across rivers, or drive a car. Living in a farming community like Dick Claus, these restrictions should affect Fenton's quality of life. Although she acknowledges the unaccommodating world of the farm, McKowan is uninterested in examining the lived experience of disability and glosses over any potential difficulties Fenton might face as an injured farmer. His property is still prosperous and he is one of the most respected men in the community. Thus, although seriously wounded in the war, Fenton, unlike most of the other disabled characters, is not portrayed as a weak victim.

Similarly, in contrast to Jo Claus or Diana, Janet does not consider her romantic partner less of a man because of his disability. While Fenton refers to himself as "useless" and "a cripple,"[55] Janet refuses to essentialize him because of his wound. Indeed, it is only at the end of their first meeting that Janet notices that he uses a cane and walks with a limp. Throughout their relationship, Janet pragmatically looks at the socially constructed ways that her love interest's wounds affect him, and this approach effectively removes the pity and horror with which disability was so often regarded. She notes that, though he could not climb up her pine tree to cut off its top, he is not to be pitied as he was able to use his wits and shoot the top off.[56]

Janet never thinks of Fenton as victimized by his wounds, which means that she does not infantilize him. In fact, she gets annoyed with him when she feels he unnecessarily dwells on his disabilities. When he tells her he could not drive her new car, she responds with irritation: "Why is it that you keep reminding me of something that I would otherwise never think of?"[57] When Fenton claims that living with him would be too great a sacrifice on her part, Janet merely laughs. She is a woman blessed with infinite common sense, and she finds his romantic desire to protect her ridiculous. She handily deflects his arguments against marriage and thinks of all contingencies, including the procurement of the marriage licence, the arrangement of their honeymoon, and even where they will pick up their wedding rings. The capable Janet will easily manage Fenton's injuries. Unlike the wives in King's story, Janet is a confident woman and has no need to have her husband weakened in order for her to feel empowered. Fenton's wound is secondary to Janet and rarely affects how she thinks of him.

Although independent and an accomplished farmer, Janet nonetheless recognizes her own yearning for a husband. She surprises herself by relishing the possibility of entering into a traditional relationship with Fenton, one in which his strong masculinity will take precedence over her passive femininity:

> And I – Janet Kirk – have come to be of the opinion that it must be wonderful to have some one to order one's goings and comings ... The right start is in selecting a man who could, and would, be the head of the house, who might consult one deliciously over small trifles, but who would decide big matters for himself, relieving one of unnecessary responsibility.[58]

Though Janet claims to be looking forward to being "deliciously" relieved of decision making, Fenton's injuries mean that she will always bear more responsibility in the household than is allowed for by the conventional husband-wife dynamic. Fenton's disabilities guarantee that their relationship is more of a partnership than what is typically found under patriarchy. While Janet does not take pleasure in Fenton's wounds, she is pleased that he sensibly acknowledges when she is better suited to a task than he. As she writes to her friend Nan, "It fills me with joy that Captain Fenton – I mean Claymore – has never objected that I am to furnish and drive the car for our honeymoon. That should augur well for our future together."[59] The reader is left with no doubt that Fenton will be well cared for with Janet in the (literal) driver's seat.

An examination of the gender dynamics in fiction that features disabled protagonists offers a revealing window through which to scrutinize cultural attitudes during the First World War. Rather than depicting the war as a transformative moment in Canadian gender relations, novels featuring disabled soldiers reinstate heterosexual norms and the "natural" dominance of men. Canadian novelists attempted to reconcile the "Angel in the House" ideal of feminine docility, purity, and selflessness with the realities of nursing men weakened by combat. Some novelists portrayed the wives of disabled soldiers as tragic victims, unable to attain the feminine ideal because of the duties imposed by their husbands' wounds. Others wrote anxiously of women who gloried in their new-found power over men. Most novelists created a space wherein their heroines returned to a passive feminine role, and the heroes reasserted their dominant position. The exploration of disability and its impact on daily life was thus secondary to the need to enforce traditional gender norms. Only *Janet of Kootenay*, whose protagonist is an avowed feminist and "New Woman," imagines a space in which men and women could form a partnership. *Janet*, rather than marking a new point of departure for Canadian society's understanding of gender issues, is, instead, the exception to the rule: the conservative view of male-female relations continued to hold sway in Canadian culture, despite the upheavals of war and its aftermath of male disability.

Notes

1. Arthur Beverley Baxter, *The Blower of Bubbles* (Toronto: McClelland and Stewart, 1920), 88.
2. Ibid.
3. Sandra M. Gilbert and Susan Gubar, *The Norton Anthology of Literature by Women: The Tradition in English* (New York: W.W. Norton Co., 1985), 956.
4. Deborah Cohen, *The War Come Home: Disabled Veterans in Britain and Germany, 1914-1939* (Berkeley: University of California Press, 2001), 106.
5. See Henri-Jacques Stiker, *A History of Disability*, trans. William Sayers (Ann Arbor: University of Michigan Press, 1997); Michael Davidson and Tobin Siebers, "Introduction," *Publications of the Modern Language Association of America* 120 (2005): 2518-22; Simi Linton, "What Is Disability Studies," *Publications of the Modern Language Association of America* 120, 2 (2005): 518-22.
6. Joseph A. Flaherty, "Normal," in *The Encyclopaedia of Disability*, ed. Gary L. Albrecht (Thousand Oaks, CA: Sage, 2005), 1153.
7. Rosemarie Garland Thomson, *Extraordinary Bodies: Figuring Physical Disability in American Culture and Literature* (New York: Columbia University Press, 1997), 78.
8. David D. Yuan, "Disfigurement and Reconstruction in Oliver Wendell Holmes's, "The Human Wheel, Its Spokes and Felloes," in *The Body and Physical Difference: Discourses of Physical Disability*, ed. David T. Mitchell and Sharon L. Snyder, 71-88 (Ann Arbor: University of Michigan Press, 1997).
9. Helen Deutsch and Felicity Nussbaum, *Defects: Engendering the Modern Body* (Ann Arbour: University of Michigan Press, 2000), 10.
10. Cohen, *War Come Home*, 106.
11. John Murray Gibbon, *The Conquering Hero* (Toronto: S.B. Gundy, 1920), 91.
12. Ibid., 92.
13. Gilbert and Gubar, *Literature by Women*, 958.
14. Ibid.

15 Gibbon, *Conquering Hero*, 165-66.
16 Ralph Connor, *Treading the Winepress* (New York: George Doran, 1925), 300-1.
17 Jessica Meyer, "'Not Septimus Now': Wives of Disabled Veterans and Cultural Memory of the First World War in Britain," *Women's History Review* 13, 1 (2004): 124-28.
18 Robert Stead, *Grain* (Toronto: McClelland and Stewart, 1993), 195.
19 Meyer, "Not Septimus," 120-24.
20 Ibid., 191.
21 Stead, *Grain*, 181-93.
22 Ibid., 183-91.
23 Ibid., 190.
24 Ibid., 182.
25 Meyer, "Not Septimus," 120.
26 David Gerber, "Introduction: Finding Disabled Veterans in History," in *Disabled Veterans in History* (Ann Arbor: University of Michigan Press, 2000) 1-54. See also David Gerber, ed., *Corporealties: Discourses of Disability* (Ann Arbor: University of Michigan Press, 2000), 10.
27 Basil King, *The Thread of the Flame* (New York: Harper and Brothers, 1920), 416.
28 King, *Thread*, 416.
29 Mariana Valverde, "When the Mother of the Race Is Free: Race, Reproduction and Sexuality in First Wave Feminism," in *Gender Conflicts: New Essays in Women's History*, ed. Franca Iacovetta and Mariana Valverde (Toronto: University of Toronto Press, 1992), 4.
30 Jonathan Vance, *Death So Noble: Memory, Meaning, and the First World War* (Vancouver: UBC Press, 1997), 150.
31 See also Sarah Glassford, "'The Greatest Mother in the World'": Carework and the Discourse of Mothering in the Canadian Red Cross Society during the First World War," *Journal of the Association for Research and Mothering* 10, 1 (2008): 219-32.
32 Sandra Gilbert, "Soldier's Heart: Literary Men, Literary Women and the Great War," in *Behind the Lines: Gender and the Two World Wars*, ed. Margaret Higonnet, Jane Jenson, Sonya Michel, and Margaret Collins Weitz (New Haven: Yale University Press, 1987), 211.
33 Basil King, *The City of Comrades* (New York: Harper and Brothers, 1919), 170.
34 Jeffrey A. Keshen, *Propaganda and Censorship during Canada's Great War* (Edmonton: University of Alberta Press, 1996), 128.
35 King, *City of Comrades*, 217.
36 Ibid., 240.
37 Ibid., 259.
38 Ibid., 100.
39 Ibid., 216.
40 Ibid., 269.
41 Tom Brown, "Shell Shock in the Canadian Expeditionary Force, 1914-1918," in *Canadian Health Care and the State: A Century of Evolution*, ed. C. David Naylor (Toronto: Hannah Institute for the History of Medicine, 1983), 315.

42 Terry Copp, "From Neurasthenia to Post-Traumatic Stress Disorder: Canadian Veterans and the Problem of Persistent Emotional Difficulties," in *The Veterans' Charter and Post World War II Canada*, ed. Peter Neary and J.L. Granatstein (Montreal and Kingston: McGill-Queen's University Press, 1999), 150-51.
43 George Mosse, "Shell Shock as a Social Disease," *Journal of Contemporary History* 35, 1 (2000): 101.
44 Connor, *Treading*, 332.
45 Ibid., 380.
46 Mosse, "Shell Shock," 368.
47 Gilbert and Gubar, *Literature by Women*, 959.
48 Connor, *Treading*, 304.
49 Ibid., 332.
50 Ibid., 338-69.
51 Ibid., 379.
52 Mosse, "Shell-Shock," 102-3.
53 Connor, *Treading*, 381.
54 Ibid., 394.
55 Evah McKowan, *Janet of Kootenay: Life, Love and Laughter in an Arcady of the West* (Toronto: McClelland and Stewart, 1919), 72.
56 Ibid., 105.
57 Ibid., 259.
58 Ibid., 328.
59 Ibid., 277.

Conclusion
A "Sisterhood of Suffering and Service"

SARAH GLASSFORD AND AMY SHAW

In early December 1918, Queen Mary issued a message to the women of the British Empire that was telegrammed to the governors and governors general of the dominions and passed on to the headquarters of a variety of newspapers and leading women's organizations. Surveying the four long years of war that had just come to a close and the part played by women therein, the Queen commented: "we have been united in all our work, whether of head or hands, in a real sisterhood of suffering and service during the war." Throughout the war, she asserted, women across the British Empire had "been given the high privilege of service, they ha[d] risen to the great opportunity and ha[d] proved their courage, steadfastness and ability."[1]

As studies of the Canadian women's suffrage movement attest, "sisterhood" in Canada took a hit during the First World War, with women divided in supporting or opposing both the Wartime Elections Act and the war itself, among other things.[2] Similarly, we should question Queen Mary's assumption that women's experiences across the incredibly diverse British Empire *were*, in fact, the same, since there were many who did not suffer and did not (or could not) offer their service. Yet the fact remains that women and girls in Britain's two North American dominions did not sit idly by while the Great War took place around and without them. Service and suffering may not have been universal, but they seem to have been potent elements of the majority of Canadian and Newfoundland women's and girls' experiences of the Great War. Even those who opposed the war or particular elements of it often undertook some form of service – for example, the humanitarian work of the Red Cross for the sick and wounded attracted many women who could not in good conscience support other war work – while feminist pacifists like Gertrude Richardson or Francis Marion Beynon certainly suffered for their beliefs in their stridently prowar communities. Together, the themes of suffering and service weave their way throughout this volume and unite an assortment of individual studies into a fascinating portrait of the female populations of two countries at war.

There are, of course, striking absences from this portrait of female wartime experience in Newfoundland and Canada. This volume is an important first step, not an end point. It represents an attempt to draw together new and recent work and to foster a sense that there *is* an existing body of literature and knowledge on this topic; it is not a definitive statement of what it meant to be a woman or a girl in these places in those times. We hope this volume will encourage other scholars to take up the challenge; that they will use it as a starting point and move on to study the many aspects of women's Great War experiences that remain at best partially examined and at worst completely ignored. Perhaps most fervently, we hope to see someone investigate the most glaring gap that currently exists: the absence of research specifically into the experiences and activities of women and girls in Quebec. During the past decade, two articles by Geneviève Allard and Mélanie Morin-Pelletier have illuminated the experience of Nursing Sisters – some of them *québecoises* – overseas, but the story of Quebec women and girls at home remains untold.[3] Some of our authors touch on Quebec women's involvement in a wider Canadian context; however, given the contrast between French Canada's and English Canada's attitudes towards the war and key issues (such as conscription), we desperately need to investigate the distinctive elements of Quebec women's wartime experiences as well as the ways in which they mirrored those of other Canadians and Newfoundlanders.

Across Canada and Newfoundland, class, race, ethnicity, age, religion, and region offer a wealth of areas to address in terms of women's experiences, as do the differences between women in urban areas versus women in rural areas and, in the case of Newfoundland, St. John's versus the outports. A woman deemed to be an enemy alien, for example, might be reasonably supposed to have experienced a very different war from many of the women profiled in this volume. At the same time, while a local focus on individual experiences is highly valuable, the field would also benefit from attention to the international networks in which many women's groups operated – the international women's suffrage movement is only one example. The wartime activities and attitudes of a wealth of women's voluntary organizations wait to be studied (be they war charities, church groups, reform organizations, or suffrage associations), while our understanding of women whose responses to the war were more ambivalent or outrightly oppositional would benefit from further study. To borrow a page from the literature on women in the Second World War and the postwar era, the impact of the First World War on the interwar period could also bear greater scrutiny: how did women's wartime experiences affect their lives thereafter? Clearly, there is much work to be done.

As we await the fuller picture we will have as a result of future research, what can be said about the ways in which Newfoundland and Canadian women and girls experienced the First World War? Perhaps, at the most basic level, we must conclude that each woman's experience of the war was unique. Gender alone did not produce a single, universal wartime experience. Moreover, some impacts of the war were quite mundane, such as is shown in author L.M. Montgomery's December 1914 journal observation: "this war is at least extending my knowledge of geography."[4]

On a grander scale, and in spite of the many differences between them, many Canadian and Newfoundland women seem to have shared a sense of being important contributors to the dominions' war efforts. The First World War is generally accepted as being the first "total war," in which all the resources of the state were directed towards its prosecution. In such a context, the activities of women could not but be seen as key to the success of the war effort. The coining of the term "home front" to describe the role of non-combatants in such a war reveals the belief that broad, unified participation was necessary to win the war. Today we recognize women's formal, paid work as being clearly bent towards such an end, but their voluntary, unpaid labour through hundreds of war charities and voluntary organizations also constituted an integral part of the wartime economy.

Aside from its economic value, women's wartime work also served as an emotional resource. Their support for the war helped create the impression of unity in sacrifice that was critical to how ordinary people tried to make sense of the war. The First World War was widely understood both as a crusade and as an individual and national test of strength. In 1916, Newfoundland's Lady Davidson observed: "there is nothing that tests a people like a real national trial," adding, "we shall learn more in the present time of stress than in centuries of the old self-satisfied days of peace and profit."[5] Like a fire, the sufferings and sacrifices of the war would purify both combatants and the wider society.

Furthermore, in countries as internally divided (in their different ways) as Newfoundland and Canada, the cleansing fire of the Great War, it was hoped, might serve as a unifying event, bringing together populations more often divided along religious, linguistic, ethnic, and/or class lines.[6] Women's suffering and service constituted an integral part of this community-in-sacrifice. The stoic support of the women at home also stood alongside the bravery of Canadian and Newfoundland soldiers (so triumphantly displayed at Vimy Ridge and so tragically at Beaumont-Hamel) in indicating to Britain, the Empire, and, indeed, the world, the maturity of the two dominions. Contemporaries believed that the war was transforming these two dominions and, in the process, their citizens.

As various authors in this volume show, women and girls found themselves playing significant roles in the rhetoric that suffused the First World War, often being presented (both literally and figuratively) as exactly what the country was fighting for. Most notably, the public was urged to defend Newfoundland and Canadian women and children from the depredations that the German "Hun," had allegedly visited upon the women and children of Belgium. More Victory Bonds purchased, more soldiers enlisted, and more bandages rolled meant a more fearsome Allied force battling Germany in the trenches of Western Europe and keeping women and children safe at home in North America. In a more abstract way, women and girls also represented the values of the society for which Canadian and Newfoundland men were avowedly fighting: values such as honour, justice, liberty, duty, and virtue. They also served as an appreciative audience for men's heroism. The latter role gave rise to the so-called "white feather" campaigns, in which some women bestowed white feathers, as an emblem of cowardice, upon any apparently able-bodied man not in uniform. The frequent appearance in contemporary poetry and fiction of the desire to keep a son, brother, or husband at home, battling in a woman's heart with the duty to encourage him to enlist, further attests to women's consciousness of the moral power they possessed in wartime.[7] The war exalted women and girls as symbols and bestowed upon them additional moral power, but this power rested firmly upon traditional beliefs about gender. It is difficult to avoid concluding that the Great War did not usher in a sweeping transformation of prevailing gender norms.

The personal responses of women and girls to the experience of war are as important as are their tangible and symbolic contributions to the war effort. As Canadian and Newfoundland women helped to shape their respective dominions' responses to the war, they were, in turn, shaped by the war. They worried

FIGURE 16   Harald H. Piffard's, "The Fatal Message," ca. 1916, eloquently conveys the suffering and loss experienced by millions of women and girls during wartime. [From *Canada in Khaki*, published for the Canadian War Records Office, ca. 1916]

Conclusion

about their absent loved ones. They grieved for those who were killed and, less personally, for the suffering that the war was causing women and children overseas. They welcomed home the men who survived, nursed and cared for those who returned from the fighting broken in body or mind, and raised their children in an altered postwar society. Recognizing and understanding women's emotional responses to the war are crucial steps towards understanding how the war shaped the societies of Newfoundland and Canada both during and after the conflict. On a personal level, the transformative power of the Great War was everywhere evident.

Historically, there has been a certain silence around women's participation in the Great War, and this can be seen in the way the war has been memorialized in stone and bronze. The First World War memorials peppered across Canada arose from a postwar impulse to visibly commemorate wartime losses. For their creators these monuments served as spaces for the ceremonial expression of public grief and remembrance, while the language and imagery they employed influenced the way the war would be imagined and remembered – a role they continue to fill today.[8] The spectacular Vimy Ridge Memorial in France features, at the front of the monument, the cloaked figure of a sorrowful woman, representing Canada as a young nation mourning its dead. Newfoundland's National War Memorial in St. John's includes sculpted figures of soldiers, sailors, and lumbermen around its base, while a draped female figure, representing Newfoundland's willingness to serve and the spirit of loyalty to the Empire, stands atop the cenotaph. Canada's National War Memorial in Ottawa is similarly surmounted by two draped female figures, in this case representing peace and freedom, respectively. That the large group of figures in the main part of the monument below was carefully constructed to include all branches of the service (including Nursing Sisters) in accurately portrayed uniforms makes the symbolic, impersonal presence of the female figures above more notable. Thousands of smaller provincial or local monuments uphold this trend. Despite their very tangible presence in the war, in its public commemoration women remain largely ephemeral, passive, and silent – ideals, or idealized mourners, rather than flesh-and-blood workers for the nation at war. The nearly universal absence of women and girls from these war memorials, save as allegorical figures, both represents and has contributed to the popular memory of the war as a male endeavour. Of course there are no civil servants, captains of industry, or farmers on these memorials either; however, the privileging of the (male) soldier not only glorifies a particular type of wartime participation – fighting – but also works to largely exclude an entire gender from the story of how Canada and Newfoundland experienced the Great War. It is past time to transform our collective memory of the Great War into one that recognizes the different parts played by both men and women of all ages.

When Canada and Newfoundland went to war in 1914, for better or for worse their entire populations went to war with them. The girls and women at home did not remain frozen in place for the duration of the conflict and come back to life after the 1918 Armistice returned society to a peacetime "normality." Instead, they comprised – along with men and boys too old, too young, or otherwise disinclined to fight – home-front societies that were changed by the experience of war. That the war as experienced by those who stayed at home did not include trenches, barbed wire, or poison gas did not make it less of a formative experience. That the women at home were excluded from the councils of war and state that made crucial political and economic decisions between 1914 and 1918 did not keep them from playing a vital role in the wartime economy and the wartime body politic. In mixed-gender and women-only organizations; as individuals and members of families; in their homes, workplaces, churches, and communities, the women and girls of Newfoundland and Canada by and large rallied to the cause and threw themselves into the war effort. For four long years they worked, wept, and waited, served, suffered, and sacrificed. If we wish to understand this period in the histories of Britain's two North American dominions, we cannot overlook the toils and tears of women and girls. They are integral parts of the story of Canada and Newfoundland during the Great War, and, with this volume, we attempt to write them back in.

Notes

1 "Message from HER MAJESTY THE QUEEN to the WOMEN OF THE EMPIRE," 5 December 1918, Provincial Archives of Newfoundland and Labrador, GN 2.14.61, file 61, box 8.
2 See, for example, Barbara Roberts, *A Reconstructed World: A Feminist Biography of Gertrude Richardson* (Montreal and Kingston: McGill-Queen's University Press, 1996), chap. 4 (entitled "Sisterhood Divided" and set during the First World War). See also Tarah Brookfield, "Divided by the Ballot Box: The Montreal Council of Women and the 1917 Election," *Canadian Historical Review* 89, 4 (2008): 473-501.
3 Geneviève Allard, "Des anges blancs sur le front: L'expérience de guerre des infirmières militaires canadiennes pendant la Première Guerre mondiale," *Bulletin d'histoire politique*

8, 2-3 (2000): 119-33; Mélanie Morin-Pelletier, "Des oiseaux bleus chez les Poilus: Les infirmières des hôpitaux militaires canadiens-français postés en France, 1915-1919," *Bulletin d'histoire politique* 17, 2 (2009): 57-74.

4 L.M. Montgomery, *The Selected Journals of L.M. Montgomery*, vol. 21, *1910-1921*, ed. Mary Rubio and Elizabeth Waterston (Toronto: Oxford University Press, 1987), 157.
5 Lady Davidson, "Comradeship," *The Distaff* (1916): 2.
6 Jonathan Vance, *Death So Noble: Memory, Meaning, and the First World War* (Vancouver: UBC Press, 1997), 227.
7 See, for example, L.M. Montgomery, *Rilla of Ingleside* (Toronto: Seal Books, 1996); Katherine Hale, "The Hearts of Mothers," *Canadian Magazine* 48, 2 (1916): 140; Isabel Ecclestone Mackay, "The Recruit," *Canadian Magazine* 48, 3 (1916): 231.
8 Vance, *Death So Noble,* chaps 2 and 7; Alan R. Young, "'We Throw the Torch': Canadian Memorials of the Great War and the Mythology of Heroic Sacrifice," *Journal of Canadian Studies* 24, 4 (1989/90): 5-28.

Selected Bibliography

The following list of secondary sources pertaining to women and girls of Newfoundland and Canada during the First World War is far from definitive, but it may serve as a useful starting point for scholars who are researching this field.

Newfoundland

Doran, Barbara. "Women's War Efforts: First and Second World Wars in the Women's Patriotic Association of Newfoundland." Paper for History 3813, Memorial University of Newfoundland, 1982.

Duley, Margot I. "'The Radius of Her Influence for Good': The Rise and Triumph of the Women's Suffrage Movement in Newfoundland, 1909-1925." In *Pursuing Equality: Historical Perspectives on Women in Newfoundland and Labrador,* ed. Linda Kealey, 14-65. St. John's: Institute of Social and Economic Research, 1993.

–. *Where Once Our Mothers Stood We Stand: Women's Suffrage in Newfoundland.* Charlottetown, PEI: Gynergy Books, 1993.

Macfarlane, David. *The Danger Tree: Memory, War, and the Search for a Family's Past.* New York: Walker and Co., 1991.

Nevitt, Joyce. *White Caps and Black Bands: Nursing In Newfoundland to 1934.* St. John's: Jesperson Press, 1978.

Rompkey, Bill, and Bert Riggs, eds. *Your Daughter Fanny: The War Letters of Frances Cluett, VAD.* St. John's: Flanker Press, 2006.

Warren, Gale Denise. "The Patriotic Association of the Women of Newfoundland: 1914-18." *Newfoundland Quarterly* 92, 1 (1998): 23-32.

–. "Voluntarism and Patriotism: Newfoundland Women's War Work during the First World War." MA thesis, Memorial University of Newfoundland, 2005.

Canada

Allard, Geneviève. "Des anges blanc sur le front: L'expérience de guerre des infirmières militaires canadiennes pendant la Première Guerre Mondiale." *Bulletin d'Histoire Politique* 8, 2-3 (2000): 119-33.

And We Knew How to Dance: Women in WWI. Produced by Silva Basmajian. National Film Board of Canada. 1993.

Baker, Marilyn. "To Honor and Remember: Remembrances of the Great War, The Next-of-Kin Monument in Winnipeg." *Manitoba History* 2 (1981): 8-11.

Barron Norris, Marjorie. *Sister Heroines: The Roseate Glow of Wartime Nursing, 1914-1918*. Calgary: Bunker to Bunker, 2002.

Beck, Boyde, and Adele Townshend. "'The Island's Florence Nightingale.'" *Island Magazine* 34 (1993): 1-6.

Bongard, Ella Mae. *Nobody Ever Wins a War: The World War I Diaries of Ella Mae Bongard, R.N.* Ottawa: Janeric Enterprises, 1997.

Boutilier, Beverly Lynn. "Educating for Peace and Co-operation: the Women's International League for Peace and Freedom in Canada, 1919-1929." MA thesis, Carleton University, 1988.

Brookfield, Tarah. "Divided by the Ballot Box: The Montreal Council of Women and the 1917 Election." *Canadian Historical Review* 89, 4 (2008): 473-501.

Burant, Jim. "No Man's Land: The Battlefield Painting of Mary Riter Hamilton." *Queen's Quarterly* 112, 1 (2005): 28-37.

Butlin, Susan. "Women Making Shells: Marking Women's Presence in Munitions Work, 1914-1918: The Art of Frances Loring, Florence Wyle, Mabel May, and Dorothy Stevens." *Canadian Military History* 5, 1 (1996): 41-48.

Cleverdon, Catherine. *The Women's Suffrage Movement in Canada*. Toronto: University of Toronto Press, 1974.

Coates, Donna. "The Best Soldiers of All: Unsung Heroines in Canadian Women's Great War Fictions." *Canadian Literature* 151 (1996): 66-99.

–. "Myrmidons and Insubordinates: Australian and Canadian Women's Fictional Responses to the Great War." PhD diss., University of Calgary, 1993.

Cook, Tim. "Wet Canteens and Worrying Mothers: Alcohol, Soldiers and Temperance Groups in the Great War." *Histoire sociale/Social History* 35, 70 (2002): 311-30.

Cook, Tim, and Natascha Morrison. "Longing and Loss from Canada's Great War." *Canadian Military History* 16, 1 (2007): 53-60.

Davis, Angela. "Mary Riter Hamilton: An Artist in No-Man's Land." *The Beaver* 69, 5 (1989): 6-16.

DeZoete, Jennifer A. "From Spring to Summer: Mary Lorraine Shortt's Reactions to the Great War, 1914-1918." Paper submitted for History 601B, University of Waterloo, 2003.

Dirk, Marcel M.C. "Imperial Order Daughters of the Empire and the First World War." MA thesis, Carleton University, 1987.

Doll, Maurice F.V. *The Poster War: Allied Propaganda Art of the First World War*. Edmonton: Alberta Community Development, 1993.

Edwards, Owen Dudley, and Jennifer H. Litster. "The End of Canadian Innocence: L.M. Montgomery and the First World War." In *L.M. Montgomery and Canadian Culture*, ed. Irene Gammel and Elizabeth Epperley, 31-46. Toronto: University of Toronto Press, 1999.

Evans, Suzanne. *Mothers of Heroes, Mothers of Martyrs: World War I and the Politics of Grief*. Montreal and Kingston: McGill-Queen's University Press, 2007.

Fahrni, Magda, and Yves Frenette. "'Don't I Long for Montreal': L'identité hybride d'une jeune migrante franco-américaine pendant la Première Guerre mondiale." *Histoire sociale/Social History* 41, 81 (2008): 75-98.

Fallis, Donna. "World War I Knitting." *Alberta Museums Review* (Fall 1984): 8-10.

Fingard, Judith. "University Women of the Great War Generation." *Collections of the Royal Nova Scotia Historical Society* 43 (1991): 1-19.

Fowler, T. Robert. "The Canadian Nursing Service and the British War Office: The Debate over Awarding the Military Cross, 1918." *Canadian Military History* 14, 4 (2005): 31-42.

Galloway, Orpha E., ed. *Women of the War Years: Stories of Determination and Indomitable Courage*. Gladstone, MB: Orpha E. Galloway, 2000.

Geller, Gloria. "The War-Time Elections Act of 1917 and the Canadian Women's Movement." *Atlantis* 2, 1 (1976): 88-106.

Giffen, Phillip. "Annie's War." *Manitoba History* 55 (2007): 40-50.

Glassford, Larry A. "'The Presence of So Many Ladies': A Case Study of the Conservative Party's Response to Female Suffrage in Canada, 1918-1939." *Atlantis* 22, 1 (1997): 19-30.

Glassford, Sarah Carlene. "'The Greatest Mother in the World': Carework and the Discourse of Mothering in the Canadian Red Cross Society during the First World War." *Journal of the Association for Research on Mothering* 10, 1 (2008): 219-32.

–. "'Marching as to War': The Canadian Red Cross Society, 1885-1939." PhD diss., York University, 2007.

Gwyn, Sandra. *Tapestry of War: A Private View of Canadians in the Great War*. Toronto: Harper Collins, 1992.

Heap, Ruby. "Canadian Physiotherapy and Dietetics during the Great War: The Carving of New Professional Spaces for Women." In *Canadian and American Women: Moving from Private to Public Experiences in the Atlantic World*, ed. Valeria Gennara Lerda and Roberto Maccarini, 275-95. Milano: Selene Edizioni, 2001.

–. "Training Women for a New 'Woman's Profession': Physiotherapy Education at the University of Toronto, 1917-40." *History of Education Quarterly* 35, 2 (1995): 135-58.

Huneault, Kristina. "Heroes of a Different Sort: Representations of Women at Work in Canadian Art of the First World War." MA thesis, Concordia University, 1994.

Jameson, Sheilagh S. "Give Your Other Vote to the Sister." *Alberta Historical Review* 15, 4 (1967): 10-16.

Jones, Esyllt W. *Influenza 1918: Disease, Death and Struggle in Winnipeg*. Toronto: University of Toronto Press, 2007.

–. "Searching for the Springs of Health: Women and Working Families in Winnipeg's 1918-1919 Influenza Epidemic." PhD diss., University of Manitoba, 2003.

Kalmakoff, Elizabeth. "Naturally Divided: Women in Saskatchewan Politics, 1916-1919." *Saskatchewan History* 46, 2 (1994): 3-18.

Kearney, Kathryn. "Canadian Women and the First World War." *Women's Studies/Cahiers de la femme* 3, 1 (1981): 95-96.

Lewis, Norah. "'Isn't This a Terrible War'? The Attitudes of Children to Two World Wars." *Historical Studies in Education* 7, 2 (1995): 193-215.

–. *"I Want to Join Your Club": Letters from Rural Children, 1900-1920*. Waterloo: Wilfrid Laurier University Press, 1996.

MacDonald, Sharon. "Hidden Costs, Hidden Labours: Women in Nova Scotia during Two World Wars." MA thesis, St. Mary's University, 1999.

Mann, Susan. *Margaret Macdonald, Imperial Daughter*. Montreal and Kingston: McGill-Queen's University Press, 2005.

–. *The War Diary of Clare Gass, 1915-1918*. Montreal and Kingston: McGill-Queen's University Press, 2000.

–. "Where Have All the Bluebirds Gone? On the Trail of Canada's Military Nurses, 1914-1918." *Atlantis* 26, 1 (2001): 35-43.

Marshall, Debbie. *Give Your Other Vote to the Sister: A Woman's Journey into the Great War*. Calgary: University of Calgary Press, 2007.

McIntosh, Terresa. "Other Images of War: Canadian Women War Artists of the First and Second World Wars." MA thesis, Carleton University, 1990.

McKenzie, Andrea. "Women at War: L.M. Montgomery, the Great War, and Canadian Cultural Memory." In *Storm and Dissonance: L.M. Montgomery and Conflict,* ed. Jean Mitchell, 83-105. Newcastle: Cambridge Scholars, 2008.

McManus, Brie. "Francis Marion Beynon: The Forgotten Suffragist." *Manitoba History* 28 (1994): 22-30.

McPherson, Kathryn. "Carving Out a Past: The Canadian Nurses' Association War Memorial." *Histoire sociale/Social History* 29, 58 (1996): 417-29.

Millar, Nancy. "Maude Riley: Never a Trailer." *Alberta History* 54, 3 (2006): 11-16.

Miller, Ian Hugh Maclean. *Our Glory and Our Grief: Torontonians and the Great War*. Toronto: University of Toronto Press, 2002. (Especially Chapter 4, "Women and War: Public and Private Spheres.")

Moody, Barry M. "Acadia and the Great War." *Youth, University and Canadian Society*. ed. Paul Axelrod and John G. Reid, 143-60. Montreal and Kingston: McGill-Queen's University Press, 1989.

Morin, Mélanie. "Lire entre les Lignes: Témoignages d'Infirmières Militaires Canadiennes en Service Outre-Mer Pendant la Première Guerre Mondiale." MA thesis, Université de Moncton, 2005.

Morin-Pelletier, Mélanie. "Des oiseaux bleus chez les Poilus: Les infirmières des hôpitaux militaires canadiens-français postés en France, 1915-1919." *Bulletin d'histoire politique* 17, 2 (2009): 57-74.

Morris Craig, Grace. *But This Is Our War*. Toronto: University of Toronto Press, 1981.

Morton, Desmond. "Entente Cordiale? La Séction Montréalaise du Fonds Patriotique Canadien, 1914-1923: Le Benevolat de Guerre à Montréal." *Revue d'histoire de L'Amérique française* 53, 2 (1999): 29-36.
–. *Fight or Pay: Soldiers' Families in the Great War*. Vancouver: UBC Press, 2004.
–. "Supporting Soldiers' Families: Separation Allowance, Assigned Pay, and the Unexpected." In *Canada and the First World War: Essays in Honour of Robert Craig Brown*, ed. David Mackenzie, 194-229. Toronto: University of Toronto Press, 2005.
Nicholson, G.W.L. *Canada's Nursing Sisters*. Toronto: Hakkert, 1975.
Paquin, Yvette. "Les Soeurs Grises en Tenue de Service: L'influenza de 1918." *Cahiers Nicoletains* 8, 2 (1986): 101-21.
Pickles, Katie. *Female Imperialism and National Identity: Imperial Order Daughters of the Empire*. Manchester: Manchester University Press, 2002.
Pieroth, Doris H. "Homestead on Hold: Edna Tompkins's Peace River Letters, 1916." *Pacific Northwest Quarterly* 80, 4 (1989): 147-53.
Quiney, Linda J. "'Assistant Angels': Canadian Women as Voluntary Aid Detachment Nurses during and after the Great War, 1914-1930." PhD diss., University of Ottawa, 2002.
–. "Assistant Angels: Canadian Voluntary Aid Detachment Nurses in the Great War." *Canadian Bulletin of Medical History* 15, 1 (1998): 189-206.
–. "Borrowed Halos: Canadian Teachers as Voluntary Aid Detachment Nurses during the Great War." *Historical Studies in Education* 15 (2003): 79-99.
–. "Bravely and Loyally They Answered the Call." *History of Intellectual Culture* 5, 1 (2005): 1-19. http://www.ucalgary.ca/hic/.
–. "'Filling the Gaps': Canadian Voluntary Nurses, the 1917 Halifax Explosion, and the Influenza Epidemic of 1918." *Canadian Bulletin of Medical History* 19 (2002): 351-74.
–. "'Sharing the Halo': Social and Professional Tensions in the Work of World War One Canadian Volunteer Nurses." *Journal of the Canadian Historical Association* 9, 1 (1998): 105-24.
–. "'We Must Not Neglect Our Duty': Enlisting Women Undergraduates for the Red Cross during the Great War." In *Cultures, Communities, and Conflict: Histories of Canadian Universities and War*, ed. Paul Stortz and Lisa Panayotidis. Toronto: University of Toronto Press, in press.
Ramkhalawansingh, Ceta. "Women during the Great War." In *Women at Work, Ontario, 1850-1930*, ed. Janice Acton, Penny Goldsmith, and Bonnie Shepard, 261-307. Toronto: Women's Press, 1974.
Reyburn, Karen Ann. "Blurring the Boundaries: Images of Women in Canadian Propaganda of WWI." MA thesis, University of Guelph, 1999.
Riegler, Natalie. "Sphagnum Moss in World War I: The Making of Surgical Dressings by Volunteers in Toronto, Canada, 1917-1918." *Canadian Bulletin of Medical History* 6 (1989): 27-43.
Roberts, Barbara. *A Reconstructed World: A Feminist Biography of Gertrude Richardson*. Montreal and Kingston: McGill-Queen's University Press, 1996

–. "Why Do Women Do Nothing to End the War?" Canadian Feminist Pacifists and the Great War. Ottawa: CRIAW, 1985.
–. "Women against War, 1914-1918: Frances Beynon and Laura Hughes." In *Up and Doing: Canadian Women and Peace*, ed. Janice Williamson and Deborah Gorham, 48-65. Toronto: Women's Press, 1989.
Rutherdale, Robert. *Hometown Horizons: Local Responses to Canada's Great War.* Vancouver: UBC Press, 2004. (Especially Chapter 6, "Gendered Fields.")
Sangster, Joan. "Mobilizing Women for War." In *The First World War in Canada: Essays in Honour of Robert Craig Brown,* ed. David Mackenzie, 157-93. Toronto: University of Toronto Press, 2005.
Sheehan, Nancy. "The IODE, the Schools and World War I." *History of Education Review* 13 (1984): 29-44.
Staton, Pat. *It Was Their War Too: Canadian Women and World War I.* Toronto: Green Dragon Press, 2006.
Street, Kori. "Bankers and Bomb Makers: Gender Ideology and Women's Paid Work in Banking and Munitions during the First World War in Canada." PhD diss., University of Victoria, 2001.
–. "'Toronto's Amazons': Militarised Femininity and Gender Construction in the Great War." MA thesis, University of Toronto, 1991.
Stuart, Meryn. "Social Sisters: A Feminist Analysis of the Discourses of Canadian Military Nurse Helen Fowlds, 1915-18." In *Place and Practice in Canadian Nursing History*, ed. Jayne Elliott, Meryn Stuart, and Cynthia Toman, 25-39. Vancouver: UBC Press, 2008.
–. "War and Peace: Professional Identities and Nurses' Training, 1914-1930." In *Challenging Professions: Historical and Contemporary Perspectives on Women's Professional Work,* ed. Elizabeth Smyth, Sandra Acker, Paula Bourne, and Alison Prentice, 171-93. Toronto: University of Toronto Press, 1999.
Szychter, Gwen. "The War Work of Women in Rural British Columbia: 1914-1919." *British Columbia Historical News* 27 (1994): 5-9.
Tector, Amy. "A Righteous War? L.M. Montgomery's Depiction of the First World War in *Rilla of Ingleside*." *Canadian Literature* 179 (2003): 72-86.
Tennyson, Brian. "Premier Hearst, the War and Votes for Women." *Ontario History* 57, 3 (1965): 115-21.
Tingley, Mary Ellen. "The Impact of War: Wolfville Women, 1914-1918." MA thesis, Acadia University, 1983.
Toman, Cynthia. "'A Loyal Body of Empire Citizens': Military Nurses and Identity at Lemnos and Salonika, 1915-17." In *Place and Practice in Canadian Nursing History*, ed. Jayne Elliott, Meryn Stuart, and Cynthia Toman, 8-24. Vancouver: UBC Press, 2008.
Vance, Jonathan F. *Death So Noble: Memory, Meaning, and the First World War.* Vancouver: UBC Press, 1997.
Wicks, Terri L. Monture, ed. *Charlotte Edith Anderson Monture: Diary of a War Nurse.* Ohsweken, ON: privately printed, 1996.
Wilson, Barbara M., ed. *Ontario and the First World War, 1914-1918: A Collection of Documents.* Toronto: University of Toronto Press, 1977.

Wilson-Simmie, Katherine. *Lights Out: The Memoir of Nursing Sister Kate Wilson, Canadian Army Medical Corps 1915-1917.* Ottawa: CEF Books, 2004.
Woodard Bean, Mary Jean. *Julia Grace Wales: Canada's Hidden Heroine and the Quest for Peace.* Ottawa: Borealis Press, 2005.
Young, Alan R. "L.M. Montgomery's *Rilla of Ingleside*: Romance and the Experience of War." In *Myth and Milieu: Atlantic Literature and Culture, 1918-1939,* ed. Gwendolyn Davies, 95-122. Fredericton: Acadiensis, 1993.
–. "'We Throw the Torch': Canadian Memorials of the Great War and the Mythology of Heroic Sacrifice." *Journal of Canadian Studies* 24, 4 (1989/90): 5-28.

Contributors

Kristine Alexander holds a PhD in history from York University. Her dissertation looked at empire, internationalism, and the Girl Guide movement in interwar England, Canada, and India. In the fall of 2010, she began a SSHRC postdoctoral fellowship at the University of Western Ontario.

Terry Bishop Stirling is a graduate of Memorial University and Queen's University and teaches history at Memorial University of Newfoundland. She specializes in Newfoundland and Labrador history with a particular interest in the history of women, voluntarism, and public health and welfare. She is also an active public historian with several voluntary and government heritage organizations.

Margot I. Duley, Dean Emerita of the College of Liberal Arts and Sciences at the University of Illinois at Springfield, is co-editor of *The Cross Cultural Study of Women* (Feminist Press, 1986) and author of *Where Once Our Mothers Stood We Stand* (Gynergy, 1993). With a PhD in history from the School of Oriental and African Studies, University of London, she focuses her research on women's movements globally, including those in Newfoundland, where she was born.

Suzanne Evans is currently a research fellow at the Canadian War Museum. She has a PhD in religious studies from the University of Ottawa and is the author of *Mothers of Heroes, Mothers of Martyrs: World War I and the Politics of Grief* (McGill-Queen's University Press, 2007).

Sarah Glassford holds a PhD in history from York University. An article from her SSHRC-supported doctoral and postdoctoral research on the history of the Canadian Red Cross Society was awarded the 2009 Hilda Neatby Prize for women's history. She teaches at the University of Ottawa and Carleton University.

Vicki S. Hallett holds a PhD in women's studies from York University. She is currently a postdoctoral research fellow with the Institute for Social and Economic Research at Memorial University of Newfoundland, where she teaches in the women's studies department.

Lynn Kennedy is an associate professor at the University of Lethbridge, specializing in American history. She is the author of *Born Southern: Childbirth, Motherhood, and Social Networks in the Old South* (Johns Hopkins University Press, 2010).

Desmond Morton is Hiram Mills Professor of History Emeritus at McGill University in Montreal and the author of over forty books on Canada's military, political, and industrial relations history. He is a fellow of the Royal Society of Canada, an officer of the Order of Canada, and holds the Canadian Forces Decoration. He was principal of the University of Toronto's Mississauga campus and founding director of the McGill Institute for the Study of Canada. He is married to the Montreal artist Gael Eakin.

Alison Norman completed her PhD dissertation, entitled "Race, Gender, and Colonialism: Public Life among the Six Nations of Grand River, 1899-1939," at the University of Toronto in 2010. Her current project looks at British women's activism on behalf of First Nations peoples in Canada in the early twentieth century.

Linda J. Quiney's doctoral dissertation on Canadian volunteer nurses in First World War military hospitals at home and overseas was followed by Hannah Postdoctoral Fellowship research into women's role in the transformation of the Canadian Red Cross from wartime work into peacetime public health efforts. She teaches history at the University of British Columbia.

Amy Shaw is an associate professor at the University of Lethbridge and is author of *Crisis of Conscience: Conscientious Objection in Canada during the First World War* (UBC Press, 2009). She is currently researching concepts and expressions of masculinity among Canadian soldiers of the South African war.

Kori Street is an associate professor at Mount Royal University, where she is chair of Entrepreneurship, Nonprofit Studies, International Business and Aviation. She is currently working on research involving the testimonies of Holocaust survivors.

Amy Tector holds a PhD in Canadian Literature from the Centre d'études nord américaines at the Université Libre de Bruxelles. Her dissertation focuses on the representation of disability in Canadian novels of the First World War. She is a photo archivist at Library and Archives Canada.

Terry Wilde is a graduate of the University of Toronto and York University. He specializes in Canadian medical and labour history.

Index

Abbott, Maude, 109
activism, gendered, 51, 66-70
Aikins, James, 185-86
Alexandra Workers, 55, 65
Allard, Geneviève, 316
Allen, Lois, 1-2, 13
Alley, Gwen, 223, 225
Ames, Herbert, 199, 201, 202, 210, 211, 214
And We Knew How to Dance, 5-6
Assmann, Jan, 256, 262-63
Associated Kin of the Canadian Expeditionary Forces, 220, 230-32, 234
Atwood, Margaret, 245
Ayres, Ruby, 129f

Baird, Helen, 69
Bank of Nova Scotia (BNS), 158-60
Barbour, Alice, 67
battles: Beaumont-Hamel, 2-3, 64, 127, 252-53, 262-63, 267nn29-30; Gallipoli, 62-63
Baxter, Arthur Beverley: "The Blower of Bubbles," 293
Beam, Jason, 240n61
Belgium, 11, 38-39

Bennett, Donna, 273
Bennett, R.B., 153, 154
Berlin, 227
Beynon, Francis Marion, 316; *Aleta Dey,* 241
black crepe, 221, 224, 225, 229
black magic. *See* sexuality, of femme fatale
Booth-Clibborn, Kate, 84
Borden, J.W., 209
Borden, Robert, 15-16, 84, 89, 197, 234; government, 199-200
Bouller, Etta, 198
Bourinot, John George, 274
Bowring, Edgar, 65
Boyer, Aurelien, 158
Brant, Cameron Dee, 33
Brantford, 35-36
Brantford Expositor, 38-39
Britain: collapse of empire, 263; mothering role of, 274-76, 277-78; pay scales of military, 203-4; reception of volunteers, 128; Royal Victoria Hospital Corps, 128-29; VAD headquarters, 109, 113; VAD nurses, 107-8, 121n8
British Columbia, 213
British Journal of Nursing, 139, 145n25

British Red Cross. *See* Red Cross, British
Brittain, Vera, 145n11
Brock Rangers, 34, 40, 41f
Brock Rangers Benefit Society (BRBS), 40-41, 43
Broder, Bride, 154-55
Brown, Margaret, 29, 36-37, 38, 42
Browning, Adeline, 63, 65, 69
Burke, Margaret, 69
Butler, Norine, 88
Byles, Joan Montgomery, 265n11

Cadigan, Sean, 253, 262
Caldicott, Eric, 253
Callaghan, Barry, 286
Campbell, Alexander, 182-83
Campbell, Dora, 182-83
Campbell, Wilfred: "England," 275
Canada: cost of living, 215n7; home front, 229-30; imperial connections, 11-12, 270, 275-78, 289; military history, 4, 6; as a nation, 274-76; national mythology, 151; population, 196
Canada First Movement, 290n14
Canadian Army Medical Corps: enlistment, 35
Canadian Army Medical Corps (CAMC), 82, 99; military nurses, 103, 105, 121n2, 128-29; and VADs, 109, 111-12
Canadian Expeditionary Force (CEF), 196, 294; pay scales, 197-98, 215n8; paymasters, 202, 203, 204, 215n3; Separation Allowance, 202-3
Canadian Girl Guides. *See* Girl Guides, Canadian
Canadian Home Journal, 235-36
Canadian Magazine, 11
Canadian Patriotic Fund (CPF): beneficiaries, 196, 201-2, 205-10; benefits scale, 203; compulsory savings plan, 211; and deserted wives, 205-6; and domestic service, 207; and government responsibility, 202-3; and hostility, 179, 213-14; ladies auxiliaries, 54, 212; motivation, 200f, 201; precursors, 39, 56, 61, 198; responsibilities, 198-99, 210-12; Third Responsibility, 210-12, 218n52, 218n59
Canadian Red Cross. *See* Red Cross, Canadian
Canadian War Museum (CWM), 173, 232
Cantlie, James, 110-11
Carey, Joseph (Mrs.), 208
Carnegie, David, 165
Carson, John Wallace, 206-7
Cashin, Gertrude, 58
casualties, 215n3; Canadian, 52, 118, 184-85, 236; and nationalism, 253; Newfoundland, 127, 128, 219, 267nn29-30; officers, 222; questions about, 236-37
Cavell, Edith, 108, 122n26
censorship: of letters, 62, 180, 182, 195; of news stories, 162
Chambers, Ernest J., 162
Chase, Edna Woolman, 229
children, 174; French-Canadian, 175; German, 175, 179; Ukrainian, 175, 179. *See also* girls
citizenship: and conscription, 33-34; demands of, 79; gender and, 2, 3; Iroquois, 33-34; patriotism and, 279; war effort and, 16-17, 51, 70
Cluett, Frances (Fanny), 127-28, 132, 135-38, 140-44, 146n34, 147n59
Coaker, William, 63
Cockin, H.C.: "This Fair Canadian Land," 275
Cody, Henry John, 84, 96n39
Cohen, Deborah, 296
comfort production: Newfoundland, 59-60, 61-64, 73n51, 265n16; Six Nations, 37-38, 41-42; U of T, 82
commemoration: of Beaumont-Hamel losses, 253, 255; of bereaved mothers, 231, 237; of Canadian soldiers, 236; of Six Nations soldiers, 36

334   *Index*

Commemoration Day. *See* Memorial Day
Condell, Diana, 117
Connor, Ralph: *Treading the Winepress,* 299-300, 306-7
conscientious objectors, 16, 231
conscription, 16, 96n41, 162, 175, 231-32, 316; debates, 65-66; of First Nations people, 33
Cook, Tim, 183
Cooke, O.A., 4
Cooper, Gwendolyn, 69-70
Copp, Charles, 110
correspondence, 179-84, 195; pen pal clubs, 179-80, 184, 190; postcards, 177-79, 182-83
Corrigan, Beatrice, 89, 97n63
Coultas, Jeanette, 126, 128, 133, 135-36, 140, 142, 144, 146n34
Cowan Mission, 55
Creery, Anna, 236-37
Crowdy, Elsie, 127-30
Crowther, T.W., 153
cultural memory. *See* memory, cultural

Daily Mail, 56
Daily News, 65, 250
Daily Star, 250
Damousi, Joy, 220
Davidson, Lillian, 180
Davidson, Margaret, 55, 56-57, 317
Davidson, Walter, 55, 56, 57, 184
Davis, Evelyn, 36-37, 42
Davis, Walter, 38
death, 222-23, 226, 230; views of, 227-28, 256-58
Department of Indian Affairs (DIA), 36, 38, 39
Department of Militia, 202-3, 204, 205-6; bureaucracy, 208-9
Dewart, Edward H., 276
Dickinson, Ethel, 130, 142, 145n15
disability, 52, 184, 189, 215n3; and gender norms, 299-300; and gender roles, 20, 293-95; medical approach to, 295-96; and rehabilitation, 295-96; socially constructed, 296, 309; studies, 296
discrimination: classist, 109-10; racist, 34-35, 36, 41-43, 48n41; sexist, 76-81, 84-85, 91-93
disease/illness: shell shock, 306-7, 308; smallpox, 41-42; Spanish flu, 142; trench foot, 37-38, 62; tuberculosis, 65, 300
distaff, 101n2; work (*see* women's work)
Distaff, The, 54, 58, 247, 254, 263-64, 265n8
Donnelley, Madeline, 130
Donner, Henriette, 135, 136
Doull, Marion, 117
Duke of Connaught, 198, 199
Duley, Margaret, 73n50
Duley, Margot I., 4, 16-17, 248
Duley, Tryphena: *A Pair of Grey Socks,* 64
Dunsmuir, James, 225
Dunsmuir, Laura, 225, 226, 239n25
Durham, Mabel, 11

Eastman Kodak Company. *See* Kodak
Eaton's, 225, 228-29
Elliot, G.W., 210-11
Ellis, Mrs. Hodgson, 84
Emerson, Jean, 130
Empire Manufacturing Company, 156-57
enfranchisement: conditional, 89; and disenfranchisement, 16, 231; of Native veterans, 34; Newfoundland, 65; racism and, 48n41; war service and, 23n29, 58; of women, 3, 15-16, 17, 36, 69-70, 189; of women vs. men, 266n23
enlistment: in Canadian Army Medical Corps, 35; Canadians, 96n40, 120n1; in CEF, 15, 196; CPF and, 200f, 201, 202; First Nations people, 32, 33-34; Newfoundlanders, 51-53, 64, 122n30, 127; *vs.* population, 196, 230; from U of T, 81
Evans, Suzanne, 22n24, 171

Evening Telegram, 250
Ewart, T.W., 217n44

Falconer, Robert, 81, 86, 91
Falconer, Sophie, 81, 82-83, 83-84
Family Herald and Weekly Star, 179, 180
femininity: boundaries of, 164-65; class-based conceptions of, 159; conventional values of, 177; New Woman and, 307, 311; passive, 5, 11, 157, 294-95; upper-class, 76-77, 78-81, 88; Victorian, 114, 124n60; wars and, 150
feminist fiction: "An Extinct Angel," 295; *Janet of Kootenay,* 308-11
Ferrier, Dorothy Josephine, 97n63
Ferry, Howard, 204
Fineman, Martha, 271
First World War: anticipated, 107; Armistice, 188-89; and cultural memory, 2-3, 252-53, 318; duration, 196; liberating effects, 131, 132, 148-51, 174-75; and modernity, 287-88
Flavelle, Joseph, 88-89, 153, 162-63, 164, 168n22, 213
Foringer, Alonzo Earl: "The Greatest Mother in the World," 116
Forsey, Bertha, 128, 131, 134, 137, 139, 144, 145n10
Foster, William A., 274
Fowlds, Helen, 1, 2
Frager, Ruth A., 272
Fraser, Helen, 100, 101n4
Fraser, William Alexander, 233-35
Free Press Prairie Farmer, 179
Freed, Alma, 206, 217n33
Fuchs, Anne, 253
fundraising: for medical causes, 65, 83-84, 198; for Red Cross, 186-87; Six Nations women, 40-41; U of T, 82, 83; WPA, 61
Furse, Katherine, 113, 114
Fussell, Paul, 182, 190

Gallishaw, Henrietta, 135

Garlow, Amelia, 37, 38, 42, 43
Garvin, John, 276-77
Gass, Clare, 147n55
Geisel, Carolyn, 67
gender: balance, 306-11; boundaries, 160, 288-89; ideology, 149, 151, 152, 157-58, 160-61, 163-66, 263; roles, 296-98
gender norms: disability and, 20; interwar fiction and, 293-95, 298-310; in Iroquois society, 31-32; and parameters of war work, 15, 26, 44-45, 148-49; traditional, 11, 95n13, 282, 293-95, 298-310; transformation of, 17, 19-20, 131-32, 148-51, 174-75
Gerard, James, 228
Gerber, David, 301-2
Gerson, Carole, 288
Gery, Doreen, 119, 125n67
Gibbon, J. Murray: *The Conquering Hero,* 298-99
Gilbert, Sandra, 303
Gilkison, Augusta, 29, 36-37, 45n1
Gillis, John, 219
Gilman, Charlotte Perkins: "An Extinct Angel," 295
Girl Guides, 185; Canadian, 185-88, 193n57
girls: correspondence clubs, 179-80; Great War and, 190; in history, 4, 22n14; in propaganda materials, 174-75; relationships with fathers, 176-77, 179-85; as symbols of home, 176; war work of, 185-88, 187, 193n57; women viewed as, 88
Glassford, Sarah, 26, 90
Globe (Toronto), 148, 154-55, 165, 225, 227, 228-29, 235, 240n53
Globe and Mail, 39, 173
Goddard, Nichola, 240n61
Goldensohn, Lorrie, 287
Goodridge, May Kennedy, 69
Goodwin, Alice, 1
Gosling, Armine, 54, 58, 69, 128, 132-33, 146n27

Graham, Jean, 159
Granatstein, J.L., 3, 175
Grand River Reserve. *See* Six Nations, Grand River Reserve
Grant, John, 209
Grant, Peter, 26
Grayzel, Susan, 144n4
Great Depression, 214
Great War. *See* First World War
Greenough, Sarah, 238n15
Gunn, Jean, 121n2
Gutteridge, Don, 273
Gwyn, Sandra, 120n1, 150, 151

Haig, Douglas, 255, 256, 268nn36-37
Halbwachs, Maurice, 252
Haldimand County Patriotic Society (HCPS), 44
Haldimand Tract, 30, 33
Hale, Katherine, 280, 291n36, 301; "The Hearts of Mothers," 286
Halifax Explosion, 89-90
Hall, Bessie, 112-13, 113-14
Hall, Jeannie, 209
Hamilton, 213, 218n59
Hanna, Martha, 180
Harding, John, 183
Harding, Robert, 252
Hardwick, A.V., 223
Harrison, Susan Frances: "The Mother," 285-86
Henderson, Viola, 109
Higonnet, Margaret, 241
Hill, Helen, 37, 39
Hill, Henrietta Porter, 40
Hill, Josiah Chief, 37, 48n50
historical film: *And We Knew How to Dance*, 5-6
historical forgetfulness, 6
historiography: of Canada and the Great War, 174; of children, 8, 21n13, 22n14; of the Great War, 26, 30, 99-100, 150; neglect factors, 8-11; of women and war, 4-7, 9-10, 99-100, 150-51
Holden, Elizabeth, 134-35
Holt, Emily, 223-24, 225
Horwood, Julia, 13, 58
hospitals. *See* military hospitals
Howes, Aileen, 219, 237
Hughes, Sam, 197, 198, 204, 207
Huss, Marie-Monique, 177, 182

ideological accommodation, 164-65
ideology. *See* gender, ideology
Imperial Munitions Board (IMB), 151, 153, 161-62, 162-63
Imperial Order Daughters of the Empire (IODE), 12-13, 55
imperialism: in Canada, 11-12, 270, 275-78, 289; of Girl Guides, 185-87; of IODE, 12-13, 36, 55, 57; and mothers/daughters, 249-50, 275, 277-78; in Newfoundland, 57, 65-66, 70, 126-27, 263-64; social, 107
infantalization: of disabled men, 300-302, 304-5, 306
inflation, 212, 213
Ingalls, C.M., 208, 209
Inglis, 151, 162
Innes, Stephanie, 173
International Order of Allied Mothers in Sacrifice (IOAMS), 220, 231, 240n53. *See also* IOAMS medal
interwar fiction: *Aleta Dey*, 241; "The Blower of Bubbles," 293; *The City of Comrades*, 304; *Grain*, 299-301; *The High Heart*, 302, 303; *Lady Chatterley's Lover*, 298; *Rilla of Ingleside*, 7, 175, 229-30; *Treading the Winepress*, 299-300. *See also* feminist fiction
IOAMS medal, 220, 221, 230, 231-32, 233f, 234, 237, 240n53
IODE. *See* Imperial Order Daughters of the Empire (IODE)
Irish, Mark, 153, 154, 161-62, 163, 168n22, 170n57

Iroquois: children, 32; citizenship, 33-34; loyalty to Britain, 29-31; women's roles and status, 31-32. *See also* Six Nations

Jamieson, Keith, 30
Jarvis, F.S., 211
Jensen, Philip, 65
Johnson, Jill, 128, 135, 136, 139, 140, 141, 146n27
Johnson, Sybil, 110, 113, 128, 130-32, 135-43, 146n27
Jones, Horace, 219, 236
Jones, Madeline, 223, 224f, 225
Jones, Netta, 219, 236
Jones, Trafford, 219, 223, 236

Kealey, Linda, 4, 5, 151
Kernighan, Robert: "The Men of the Northern Zone," 276
Keshen, Jeffrey, 10, 13, 176
Khaki League, 122n29
King, Basil: *The City of Comrades,* 304; *The High Heart,* 302, 303
knitting, 25-26, 29-30, 37-43, 82, 86, 100, 265n16, 280-82; Newfoundland socks, 60-64, 265n12
Kodak, 222-23, 226, 239n25

Labour Gazette, 201, 215n7
Lawrence, D.H.: *Lady Chatterley's Lover,* 298
LeMessurier, Mabel W., 101n2
Liddiard, Jean, 117
Lighthall, William Douw: "The Young Veteran," 282
Lind, Frank "Mayo," 62-64
Litster, Thomas Harkness: "His Mother's Letter," 282-83; "The Sons of 'Our Lady of Snows,'" 278
London (Ontario), 230, 231
loss, 319f; coming to terms with, 70, 263; financial, 52-53, 295; and mourning, 19, 220-21, 224-25, 226-27 (*see also* mourning clothes); as sacrifice, 220-21, 320; women and, 19-20, 251-52, 285-86. *See also* casualties; sacrifice
Lowe, Graham, 150, 159
Lower, Arthur, 3, 21n3
Loyal and Patriotic Society, 198
Luckins, Tanja, 221, 238n15
Lusitania, 225-26

MacAdams, Roberta, 8-9, 99
Macdonald, John A., 274
Macdonald, Lyn, 110
Macdonald, Margaret, 8, 9
MacDonald, Robert G.: "Inscription," 260, 269n47
Machin, H.A.C., 207
Mackay, Isabel Eccleston, 301; "The Mother Gives," 283
Maclean's Magazine, 151
MacMurchy, Marjory, 157, 166
Macphail, Andrew, 306
MacPhail, Dorothy, 110
Macpherson, Arch (Mrs.), 250
Macpherson, Eleanora, 58
MacPherson, Grace, 117-18, 132-33, 146n27
Maheux, Angeline, 195, 201-2
Maheux, Frank, 195, 197, 201-2
Mail and Advocate, 63, 250
Mail and Empire, 233
Mairs, E.M., 185
Major, Kevin, 3, 263, 267n29, 268n37
male dominance: of ambulance corps, 19-20; of cultural memory, 19-20; in industry, 14; as natural, 116, 303-6, 310-11; patriarchal, 166, 294
Maltese cross, 232, 240n56
Manley, Morris, 177
Mann, Susan, 8, 9, 146n46
Maple Leaf Club, 180, 184, 190
maple leaves. *See* service flags, Canadian
Margeson, J.W., 208
marriage: and Assigned Pay, 196, 201-3, 209; compulsory, 203; families of

home *vs.* overseas troops, 216n25; in CEF, 215n4; and CPF benefits, 205-7; disabled husbands and, 296, 298, 299-301; as partnership, 309-11; in PF, 197; and Separation allowance, 206-7
Marshall, Debbie, 8-9
Marten, James, 183
Martin, John Clovis, 204
Martin, Oliver M., 43-44
masculine dominance, 304-5
maternal feminism, 18, 51, 66, 70, 79, 104-5, 112, 250-51, 263-64
maternalism: patriotic, 66-67, 118-19, 271
McAvity's, 162
McClung, Nellie, 2, 25, 93, 225-26, 280; "At the Last!", 280; *The Next of Kin,* 280; "Those Who Wait and Wonder," 281-82
McCoy, M.H., 89
McCrae, John: "In Flanders Fields," 286-87, 289
McGee, Thomas D'Arcy: "Freedom's Journey," 276
McIlroy, J.G., 235
McKillop, A.B., 77
McKinney, Louise, 92-93
McKowan, Evah: *Janet of Kootenay,* 308-11
McNeil, Fannie, 69
McPherson, Kathryn, 114, 123n44
medals: memento as, 237n6; for women, 230-35 (*see also* IOAMS medal; Silver Cross)
memorial ceremonies, 223, 255
Memorial College, 260, 268n46
Memorial Cross. *See* Silver Cross
Memorial Day, 252-53, 256-57
memory: Australian, 221; collective, 10, 13, 36; cultural, 20, 26-27, 36, 241-42, 252-53, 255-58, 262-63, 267n30; figures of, 256; national, 2-4, 21n3; and national consciousness, 259-60; political demands on, 257; women and, 219-20
Meyer, Bruce, 287
Meyer, Jessica, 183, 300, 301

military convalescent homes, 108-9, 122n29, 140
military hospitals: in Belgium, 136; bombed, 147n59; Canadian, 84, 95n35, 138-40, 146n46; convalescent, 109; in Dardanelles, 136; in England, 129f, 133-35, 136; in France, 135, 136; in Salonika, 134-35
Military Hospitals Commission, 65
military nurses. *See* Nursing Sisters
Military Voters Act, 15
Miller, Ian Hugh Maclean, 4
Miller, Janet, 128
Miller, Joaquin, 279
Miller, Phebe Florence, 19-20, 241, 246f; "Commemoration," 259-60; community connections, 247; female role model, 264; "From a Little Window," 261-62; "The Greater Remembrance," 255-56; journal entries, 255, 256, 268n36; "The Knitting Marianna," 245, 247-49, 254-55, 266n17; "The Little Silver Cross," 252; "Memory Folded," 256-58; as postmistress, 264n2, 264n5; "The Silence," 253-55; and suffrage movement, 263; "The Way o' Things," 269n52
modernity, 287-89; war and, 190, 196
Mohawk Institute, 32, 40
Monroe, Walter S., 251
Montgomery, Lucy Maud, 7, 171, 175, 229-30, 241; journal entry, 317; *Rilla of Ingleside,* 7, 175, 229-30
Montreal, 109, 110, 122n29, 212, 218n59
Montreal Star, 165
Monture, Edith Anderson, 34-35
Moody, Barry, 77
Moore, Mary Macleod, 119
morality: and child welfare, 212-13; of mothers, 79, 160, 212, 230, 271; of nurses, 114; of soldiers, 206, 212, 281; women's employment and, 6, 9, 148-49, 160-62, 163, 165-66

Morey, Frances, 129
Morin-Pelletier, Mélanie, 316
Morris, E.P., 267n33
Morris, Isabella, 58
Morris, Philip, 208, 210, 212
Morton, Desmond, 3, 171, 175, 184, 189
Moses, James D., 43-44, 49n76
Moss, Mark, 33
Mosse, George, 306
motherhood, 249; landscape and, 275-76; as metaphor, 270-71; and national identity, 278-79, 289-90; as nurturing, 303-5; as political symbol, 271-72; in propaganda, 271-72; as sacred responsibility, 302-3; theme of, 263-64
mourning black. *See* mourning clothes
mourning clothes, 238n15, 239n43; effect of, 226-27; etiquette of, 223-24, 225; making, 228-29, 239n40; meaning of, 220, 222, 227-28, 228-29
Murison, Blanche E. Holt: "The Mothering Heart," 277-78
Murray, Howard, 162-63, 170n57
music, 176-77
Myers, Tamara, 187

National Council of Women of Canada (NCWC), 106, 227, 228, 232
national identity, 270; Canada *vs.* US, 274; Great War and, 286-87; landscape and, 275-76; motherhood and, 278-79, 285-86; poetry and, 272-74, 276-77
National Service Commission Board (NSCB), 153
National War Memorial (St. John's), 255
nationalism: foundations of, 289-90; Great War and, 274; of mothers, 282-83; myths and, 2-3, 21n3; Newfoundland, 246, 252-53, 256, 262-63, 267n29; in poetry, 273-76; unifying, 3
nationalist poems: "An Ode to Canada," 274-75; "England," 275; "Freedom's Journey," 276; "This Fair Canadian Land," 275
Naylor, James, 151
New Woman, 307, 311
New York Times, 226, 227, 228
Newfoundland: allegiance to Britain, 52; Beaumont-Hamel Memorial Park, 3; Commission of Government, 262; contributions, 64; cultural memory, 242, 252-53, 255, 267n30; effects of war effort, 52-53, 70; health education movement, 65, 66-67, 68-69; imperial connections, 57, 65-66, 70, 126-27, 263-64; Ladies Reading Room, 54, 266n24; military history, 3, 4; nurses, 128-29, 130, 133; outports, 245, 247, 264n4; pre- and postwar status, 69-70; society of, 263; socks, 60, 61-62, 63-64, 265n12; suffragists, 53-54, 65, 143-44, 250-51, 263-64; VADs, 53, 122n30, 126-30, 132-33, 145n16; war costs, 56; women in Britain and US, 100, 101n4; women's movement in, 16-17, 246
Newfoundland Quarterly, 247, 265n6
Newfoundland Regiment. *See* Royal Newfoundland Regiment
Newfoundland War Contingent Association, 253, 267n33
Newfoundland Women's Franchise League, 58, 65, 68-70, 250-51
Newfoundland Women's Patriotic Association, 12, 18
Nightingale, Florence, 108, 112, 122n26, 123n42
Nursing Sisters, 15; casualties, 118; demand for, 133; experience with wounds, 137-40; from Newfoundland, 53; Six Nations, 34-36; *vs.* VADs, 100, 103, 106, 108, 111-14, 118-19, 123n44, 139-40, 145n25; war work, 84, 131; warrior-nurse, 119

Ogilvie, G., 158
Oliver, Frank, 213
Olney, James, 260
114th Battalion. *See* Brock Rangers
oral histories, 5-6, 17-18, 155
orderlies, 138-39, 146n46
Ormsby, George, 181
Ormsby, Margaret, 181, 189
Ottawa Journal, 185
Ouditt, Sharon, 112, 114, 241
Owen, H.E. Lloyd, 223

pacifism, 6, 16, 231
Pankhurst, Sylvia, 152
Pankhurstism, 79
Parr, Joy, 4
Parsons, Maysie, 128-29, 133, 136, 137
Parsons, W.H., 128
paternalism, 14, 20, 77, 116, 166, 213, 277, 294, 303-5, 310
Patmore, Coventry: "The Angel in the House," 294
Patrias, Carmela, 272
Patriotic Association. *See* Canadian Patriotic Fund (CPF), precursors
patriotic fantasy, 177-79
Patriotic Fund. *See* Canadian Patriotic Fund (CPF), precursors
patriotism: and citizenship, 279; and CPF, 213; gendered, 85-86, 87, 103-6, 108-9, 111-12, 118-19, 119-20; imperialist, 68, 126-27, 185-86, 249-50; motherhood as, 66-67, 118-19, 271; poetry and, 59-60, 64, 86, 289-90; rhetoric of, 11, 25-26, 64, 67, 116-17; sentimental, 131, 176, 233-34; of Six Nations, 29, 33-34, 35, 36, 39, 40-41, 42-43, 44-45; and suffrage, 18, 106; and war work, 155; and women's work, 163-65
Payne, J.L., 159-60
Pellatt, Henry, 186, 188
Pellatt, Mary, 186

Pension Board, 208
pensions, 196, 215n3, 306
Permanent Force (PF), 197; pay scales, 197, 216n25
Perry, Eugenie, 221
Peters, Wesley, 204
Peterson, Margaret: "A Mother's Dedication," 271
photographs, 116-18; popular subjects of, 222-23, 239n25; propagandist, 178f; of women in mourning clothes, 221-22, 224f, 232, 233f, 237, 238n15
Pierson, Ruth Roach, 10
Piffard, Harald H.: "The Fatal Message," 319f
Pike, Edith, 117
Plumptre, Adelaide, 89, 96n61
poison gas, 138
politics: of Associated Kin, 232-33; of class and gender, 76; of enfranchisement, 16; of identity, 221, 296; *vs.* poetry, 273; women and, 70, 77, 93, 249, 266n24
politics of identity, 220-21
Potter, Jane, 241, 267n25
Poutanen, Mary Anne, 187
power: mothering and, 300-303; of role reversal, 293, 301-2
Powless, Olive, 180, 189
Powless, William F., 43-44, 180
Pratt, E.J., 265n9
Prentice, Alison, 5
Price, Evelyn, 184
prohibition, 66-67
propaganda: atrocity, 175; buttons, 179; fiction as, 305-7; girls in, 174-75; maternal imagery in, 220, 284f, 303; official, 176; patriotic, 25, 276-77; political, 57; postcards, 177-79, 182-83; recruiting, 13, 14f, 22n24, 90-91, 170n58, 175-76; visual, 116-18, 124n57
propagandist illustrations: "The Greatest Mother in the World," 116, 124n57

Index   341

Queen Alexandra's Imperial Military Nursing Service (QAIMNS), 130, 131, 133-35
Queen Mary, 249-50, 315
Queen Mary's Needlework Guild (QMNG), 55, 59-60
Queen Victoria, 222, 271, 290n3
Quiney, Linda, 26, 88, 132, 139

racism. *See* discrimination, racist
Read, Daphne, 17-18, 155
recruiting: academic incentives, 84-85, 95n24, 96nn41-42; on campus, 95n24, 95n26; munitions workers, 162-63; nurses and VADs, 129-30, 145n25; peer pressure and, 81; in poorest regions, 201; priorities of, 197; US, 304-5; VADs, 116-17, 131-32, 136, 145n16; women's roles in, 13, 14f, 22n24, 65-66; YWCA, 13-14. *See also* propaganda, recruiting
red cross (symbol), 115-16
Red Cross, American, 116, 134
Red Cross, British, 122n20; Brigade Nursing Divisions, 107-8
Red Cross, Canadian, 13, 58, 61-62, 82-83, 86, 88, 214, 282
Reid, Helen, 212, 214
Reilly, Catherine, 292n57
Reville, F.D., 31
Richardson, Gertrude, 316
Riegler, Natalie, 26
Riggs, Bert, 264n5
Rinehart, Mary Roberts, 88
Ritchie-England, Grace, 16
Riter, Mary L., 242
Rivers, W.H.R., 306
Roberts, Barbara, 6
Roberts, Charles G.D.: "An Ode to Canada," 274-75
Rogers, Aileen, 173, 174, 180, 181, 183-84, 189
Rogers, Lawrence, 173, 180-81, 182, 183-84, 185
Rogers, May, 173

Rohrbach, John, 238n15
Rosie the Riveter, 10
Royal Newfoundland Regiment, 2-3, 51-52, 62-63, 63-64, 127, 267nn29-30, 268n36; next-of-kin designations, 73n59; and WPA, 66
Ruell, Eunice Holbrook, 59-60
Russell Motor Car Company, 151, 156-57, 162
Rutherdale, Robert, 4, 26, 39, 153-54, 170n58

sacrifice: Australian, 62, 220; Christian interpretations of, 235, 236; and coming of age, 278-79; heroic, 121n4, 128, 186, 220, 249-50; heroic *vs.* supreme, 106, 121n13; for home localities, 258; ideology of, 250; maternal, 271-72, 280, 283-86; national, 283, 285; of VADs, 108
Sangster, Joan, 6
Saskatchewan, 211
Sassoon, Siegfried, 306; "Glory of Women," 287
Saturday Night, 186, 235, 278-79
Scates, Bruce, 26, 265n16
Scott, Duncan Campbell, 34, 37, 40, 42, 43, 292n42
Scott, Madeline, 117
Sears, Jean, 120, 125n73
Second World War, 10-11, 213-14
Seeley, Alex S. (Mrs.), 217n33
Separation Allowance, 196, 201, 202-3, 204-5, 206-10, 216n20, 217n33
Separation Allowance Review Board, 208
service flags: American, 235; Canadian, 220, 221, 235-36
sexism. *See* discrimination, sexist
sexuality, 114, 119, 166, 295, 296-98, 310; of femme fatale, 239n26, 299
Sharpe, W.H., 206, 217n33
Shaw, Anna Howard, 227
shell shock, 306-7, 308
Sigourney, Lydia, 271-72

Silver Cross, 220, 221, 230, 232-35, 237, 237n6, 239n46, 240n67; eligibility, 240n61
Simcoe Packet, 201
sisterhood, 17-18, 250, 315-16; of suffering and service, 55, 85
Six Nations, 180; acculturation, 18, 30, 36; enlisted men, 33; Grand River Reserve, 29-33; Longhouse faith, 32, 33, 37. *See also* Iroquois
Six Nations Council, 30, 31, 38, 42-43; hereditary *vs.* elected, 32-33, 43-44, 49n76
Six Nations Women's Patriotic League (SNWPL), 29, 36-40, 41-45
Skelton, J.M., 231
smallpox, 41-42
Smith, C., 43-44
Smith, Henry, 203, 204
Smith, John (Mrs.), 198
Snow, Joseph, 64
social control, 210-13, 214, 217n33, 218n52
Soldier Settlement scheme, 189
Southam, Gordon (Mrs.), 228
Southcott, Mary, 69, 131
St. John Ambulance Association (SJAA), 18; home-nursing classes, 107, 110-11; iconography, 116; makeup, 106-7; VAD program, 99, 103-5, 110, 111-12; and VAD status, 119-20; Voluntary Medical Aid Plan, 108, 121n5
St. John Ambulance Brigade: gendered roles, 107
St. John's, 53, 55, 67, 122n20
Stacey, C.P., 3
Starr, Mrs. F.N.G., 84
Stead, Robert, 299; *Grain,* 299-301
Stevens, James, 209-10
Stevenson, Lionel, 273, 286-87
Street, Kori, 5
Strong-Boag, Veronica, 92, 189
Styres, Mary Sophia Smith, 40
suffrage, female, 3, 15-16, 17, 65, 69-70, 76, 89, 189, 266n23

Suffrage War Auxiliary, 105
suffragists: Newfoundland, 65, 143-44, 250-51, 263-64; petition campaign, 69-70; *vs.* Wartime Elections Act, 16; Newfoundland, 53-54
Summerfield, Penny, 166
Summers, Anne, 105, 117, 120, 121n8
Surette, Leon, 273

Taschereau, Marie, 120
Tector, Amy, 282
temperance movement, 66-67
Tennyson, Alfred, 247-48
Thompson, Flossie, 184
Thompson, Gordon V., 176-77, 178f
Thompson, John Herd, 175
Times, The (London), 226-27
Toman, Cynthia, 10-11
Topsail (NL), 245, 247
Toronto Daily Star, 187, 188
Toronto Star, 79
transformation: of Canada, 151; family policies and, 196; of gender norms, 17, 19-20, 303; of gender roles, 85-86, 87-91, 91-93, 294-95, 301, 304-5; horrific, 287; limits of, 20, 51, 160, 166, 272; progress and, 3; thesis, 11; of varsity women, 76; of views of ethnic backgrounds, 11, 16; of voluntary organizations, 12-13, 17; of women's self-image, 10-11
trench foot, 37-38, 62
tuberculosis, 65
Twidale, Clara, 230, 239n46
Tyrell, George, 181, 185
Tyrell, Jessie, 181

Undergraduate Women's Association (U of T), 86-87
United States, 231, 235, 271-72, 305-6
University of Toronto (U of T), 94nn3-4, 95n14; after WWI, 91-93; enrolment, 84, 87; gendering, 77-81; before WWI, 76-81; during WWI, 75, 81-91

Index 343

Valcartier, 196
Valverde, Mariana, 4-5, 302
Vance, Jonathan, 4, 151, 171, 220, 288, 289, 303
Varsity, The, 75, 77-79, 80f, 82, 85-86, 88-91, 93, 95n13
Veteran, The, 253-54, 257-58, 259, 262, 265n7
veterans, 189
Victory Bonds, 176, 187, 211; Victory Loan campaign, 91, 176
Vimy Ridge Memorial, 236, 237, 320
Vogue, 229
Voluntary Aid Detachment workers (VADs), 135; ambulance drivers, 88, 117-18, 128, 130, 132-33; Australians, 135; casualties, 118; class, 119-20, 136; experience with wounds, 137-40; female soldiers, 104, 118-20; General Service, 147n53; graduate nurses *vs.*, 100, 103, 106, 111, 112-14, 118-19, 123n44, 139-40, 145n25; nurse/patient relationship, 124n59; nurses, 53, 88, 96n56, 103-4, 108-9, 110, 116-18, 127-28 (*see also* Newfoundland, VADs); social parameters, 127-30; training, 99, 104-5, 109-10, 111-12, 123n32, 131-32; uniform, 112-15
voluntary organizations, 12-13, 40-41, 44-45; mixed *vs.* all-female, 112; Six Nations, 32, 40-41; U of T, 83, 84; women's leadership, 68. *See also specific organizations*

Walker, James, 34
Wallace, W.S., 289
war: antithesis of, 262; costs, 198; financing, 199-200; gendered language of, 118-19; as imperial lark, 283; modern, 190, 196; total, 75, 174, 179, 317; and women's status, 220-21; wrong-headedness of, 237
War Measures Act, 204

war memorials: 114th Battalion flag, 41f; and cultural memory, 256-58; National War Memorial (St. John's), 69, 268nn36-37; Newfoundland as, 259; Soldiers' Tower (U of T), 91; Veterans Park (Ohsweken), 41; Vimy Ridge, 236, 237, 320; women's place in, 320
war novels: gender roles in, 296-98; *A Pair of Grey Socks*, 64. *See also* interwar fiction
war poems: "Charge of the Knitting Brigade," 86
war poems by men: "In Flanders Fields," 286-87; "Glory of Women," 287; "His Mother's Letter," 282-83; "Inscription," 260; "The Men of the Northern Zone," 276; "My Wife," 270-71; "The Sons of 'Our Lady of Snows,'" 278; "The Young Veteran," 282
war poems by women: "At the Last!", 280; "Commemoration," 259-60; "From a Little Window," 261-62; "The Greater Remembrance," 255-56; "The Hearts of Mothers," 286; "The Knitting Marianna," 245, 247-49, 254-55, 266n17; "The Little Silver Cross," 252; "Memory Folded," 256-58; "The Mother," 285-86; "The Mother Gives," 283; "The Mothering Heart," 277-78; "A Mother's Dedication," 271; "The Silence," 253-55; "Those Who Wait and Wonder," 281-82; "The Way o' Things," 269n52
war poetry: and cultural memory, 241-42, 245; defined, 265n11; gender divisions in, 288-89; literary value, 288-89; maternal imagery in, 270-72, 277-78; and national identity, 276-77; women's, 247-49, 251-52, 267n25, 292n57; women's work in, 280-85. *See also* war poems by men; war poems by women; *specific war poets*
war work. *See* women's work

344   Index

Ward, W.R., 203-4
Wartime Elections Act, 15-16, 89
Watson, Janet, 118-19
Watt, Frank, 276
Weissberg, Liliane, 257
West, Nancy, 222
Western Front, 12, 62-63, 63-64
Western Military Hospital, 128
Wharton, Gerald, 203
Whitworth, Sandra, 75
wife: defined, 205-6, 208
Wilkinson, J.R., 273-74; "My Wife," 270-71
Willys-Overland, 156-57
Wilson, Daniel, 76, 94n4
Wilson, Violet, 113
Wilson, Woodrow, 227
women: absence of, 320-21; activist role, 280; contradictory roles, 301-2; emotional labour of, 252, 265n16; enrolled at U of T, 78; gendered roles of, 107, 163-65, 282; as historians, 219-20; knitting, as icon, 12; literary representations of, 19-20; male-defined roles of, 254-55; as mothers, 166, 231-32, 249-50, 266n19; as mothers of the race, 302-3; as mourners, 220, 221-22; of Newfoundland, 250-51; of Quebec, 316; rights of, 92-93; stereotypical roles, 294-95, 299; traditional roles, 270; upper-class, 266n24
Women Warriors, 87-88
Women's Christian Temperance Union (WCTU), 54, 67, 230, 250, 279
Women's Committee of the Council of National Defense, 227, 239n30
women's employment: Australia, 144n4; in banking, 151-52, 158-60, 164; context of, 13-14, 88-89, 105, 149-54; and gender roles, 99; in manufacturing, 272; marriage and, 157-58, 160-61; in munitions production, 17-18, 19, 53, 87, 100, 127, 153-56, 161-63; public support for, 151-52; on street railway systems, 152, 156-57; and strikes, 156; in supervisory positions, 157-60
Women's Home Guard, 15
women's movement, 104, 105, 120; pre- and postwar, 54-55
Women's Patriotic Association (WPA), 51-52, 56-59, 61-66, 250, 251, 265n8; leadership, 54-55
Women's War Conference, 16
women's work, 12, 266n18; agricultural, 87-88, 187-88; Australia, 265n16; and charity fatigue, 90-91; class-based attitudes towards, 154-57; class-based participation, 105, 107-8, 127-31, 149; France and Belgium, 182, 183; and gender identity, 151-52, 249; gendered roles, 75, 81-83, 148-49; of girls, 185-88; historical value of, 9; imperial honours for, 64, 66; of Native women, 29-30, 37-45; Newfoundland, 53, 100, 101n4; parameters of, 18-19; peer pressure and, 86, 282-83; and public roles, 249; Red Cross work, 95n31; regional needs, 153-54; Six Nations, 29-30, 37-43, 41f; value of, 53-54, 68. *See also* fundraising; knitting; women's employment
Wood, Charlotte Susan, 237
Wright, Gordon, 230, 232
Wright, Sarah Rowell, 230
Wrong, Mrs. G.M., 84

YWCA, 1, 13-14, 87-88, 161-62

Zielke, Melissa, 219-20

Index 345

Printed and bound in Canada by Friesens

Set in Trajan and Minion by Artegraphica Design Co. Ltd.

Copy editor: Joanne Richardson

Proofreader and indexer: Dianne Tiefensee